«Literate Programming»

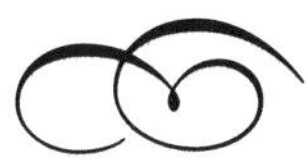

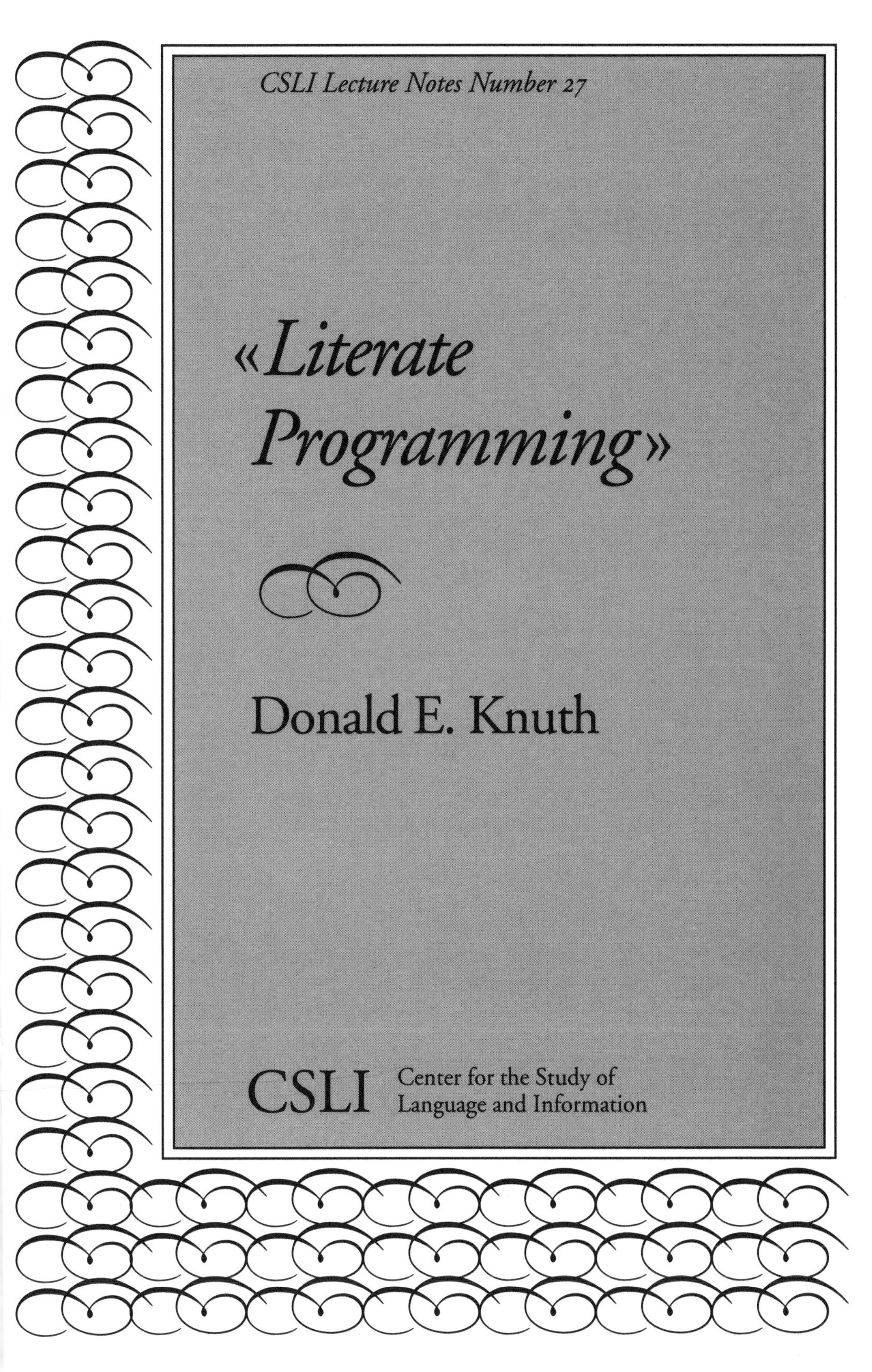
CSLI Lecture Notes Number 27
«Literate Programming»
Donald E. Knuth
CSLI Center for the Study of Language and Information

Printed in the United States
98 5 4

Library of Congress Cataloging-in-Publication Data

Knuth, Donald Ervin, 1938-
Literate programming / Donald E. Knuth
xvi,368 p. 23 cm. -- (CSLI lecture notes ; no. 27)
Includes bibliographical references and index.
ISBN 0-937073-80-6 (paper) -- ISBN 0-937073-81-4 (cloth)
1. Electronic digital computers--Programming. I. Title.
II. Series.
QA76.6.K644 1991
005.1'1--dc20 91-39510
CIP

Acknowledgments

"Computer programming as an art" originally appeared in *ACM Turing Award Lectures: The First Twenty Years*, pp. 33–46. Copyright ©1987 by ACM Press, A Division of the Association for Computing Machinery, Inc. (ACM). Reprinted by permission.

"Structured programming with **go to** statements" originally appeared in *Computing Surveys* **6** (December 1974), pp. 261–301. Copyright ©1974 by Association for Computing Machinery, Inc. Reprinted by permission.

"A structured program to generate all topological sorting arrangements" originally appeared in *Information Processing Letters* **2** (1974), pp. 153–157. Copyright ©1974 by Elsevier Science Publishers B.V. Reprinted by permission.

"Literate programming" originally appeared in *The Computer Journal* **27** (1984), pp. 97–111. Copyright ©1984 by The British Computer Society. Reprinted by permission.

Chapter 5 originally appeared as "Programming Pearls: Literate Programming" by Jon Bentley and D. E. Knuth, in *Communications of the ACM* **29** (May 1986), pp. 364–369. Copyright ©1986 by ACM Press. Copyrights and Permissions courtesy Association for Computing Machinery, Inc.

Chapter 6 originally appeared as "Programming Pearls: A Literate Program" by Jon Bentley, D. E. Knuth, and M. D. McIlroy, in *Communications of the ACM* **29** (June 1986), pp. 471–483. Copyright ©1986 by ACM Press. Copyrights and Permissions courtesy Association for Computing Machinery, Inc.

"How to read a `WEB`" originally appeared in *Computers & Typesetting*, Volume B, pp. viii–xiii. Copyright ©1986 by Addison-Wesley Publishing Co. Reprinted by permission of Addison-Wesley Publishing Co., Inc., Reading, MA.

The first part of Chapter 8 consists of excerpts from *METAFONT: The Program* (*Computers & Typesetting*, Volume D), modules 95–101, 120–128, 303, and 391–392. Copyright ©1986 by Addison-Wesley Publishing Co. Reprinted by permission of Addison-Wesley Publishing Co., Inc., Reading, MA.

The second part of Chapter 8 consists of excerpts from *TeX: The Program* (*Computers & Typesetting*, Volume B), modules 110, 113, and parts 42 and 43. Copyright ©1986 by Addison-Wesley Publishing Co. Reprinted by permission of Addison-Wesley Publishing Co., Inc., Reading, MA.

Chapter 9 consists of excerpts from sections 10–12 of *Mathematical Writing* (MAA Notes number 14, pp. 20–28). Copyright ©1989 by the Mathematical Association of America.

"The Errors of TeX" and "The Error Log of TeX" originally appeared in *Software—Practice & Experience* **19** (1989), pp. 607–685. Copyright ©1989 by John Wiley & Sons Ltd. Reprinted by permission of John Wiley & Sons, Ltd.

to Phyllis Winkler

who first typed and typeset most of these words

from the days of Snopake to the days of electronic glue

Preface

Computer programs are fun to write, and well-written computer programs are fun to read. One of life's greatest pleasures can be the composition of a computer program that you know will be a pleasure for other people to read, and for yourself to read.

Computer programs can also do useful work. One of life's greatest sources of satisfaction is the knowledge that something you have created is contributing to the progress or welfare of society.

Some people even get paid for writing computer programs! Programming can therefore be triply rewarding—on aesthetic, humanitarian, and economic grounds.

Of course I don't mean to imply that programming is easy. Easy things are often amusing and relaxing, but their value soon fades. Greater pleasure, deeper satisfaction, and higher wages are associated with genuine accomplishments, with the successful fulfillment of a challenging task.

I have spent a good deal of my life trying to help make computer programming as rewarding as possible, in all three senses. At first, I thought programming was primarily analogous to musical composition—to the creation of intricate patterns, which are meant to be performed. But lately I have come to realize that a far better analogy is available: Programming is best regarded as the process of creating *works of literature*, which are meant to be read.

Literature of the program genre is performable by machines, but that is not its main purpose. The computer programs that are truly beautiful, useful, and profitable must be readable by people. So we ought to address them to people, not to machines. All of the major problems associated with computer programming—issues of reliability, portability, learnability, maintainability, and efficiency—are ameliorated when programs and their dialogs with users become more literate.

I was therefore delighted when John Hobby and Dikran Karagueuzian proposed recently that a collection of some of my essays about programming be published in book form. I'm hoping that this book will enhance the pleasures of programming for many readers, and that it will help to improve the quality and utility of their programs, as well as the sizes of their well-earned paychecks.

John Hobby has made an excellent choice of material—please excuse my blatant humility here—and he has asked me to write a brief introduction to the book as a whole as well as an introduction to each of its parts. The first part, Chapter 1, explains my conviction that computer programming is an art form; this is the philosophy that guides all of the ensuing material. Then Chapter 2 is my best attempt to capture the essence of *structured programming*, the systematic use of abstraction that allows us to build large programs from small components.

Each chapter in this book is associated with its date of publication, because an understanding of historical trends gives important insights into the progress that has been made as the art of programming has developed. Chapter 2 is filled with dozens of small examples to illustrate topics in structured programming, a subject that was widely debated at the time that chapter was written; Chapter 3, dated the same year (1974), presents a more substantial example, which illustrates how the ideas of structured programming "scale up" to slightly larger applications. The derivation of the program in Chapter 3 is reasonably simple and elegant, but the program's final appearance leaves much to be desired. Thus we can conclude from Chapters 2 and 3 that another basic idea was still lacking in 1974; structured programming by itself did not make programs sufficiently readable.

Additional experience accumulated by thousands of programmers during the 70s made it possible to identify a vital missing ingredient, and the advent of computer typography in the 80s made it possible for programmers to create documents that look as attractive as the contents of the finest technical books and journals. Therefore by 1984 it was possible for me to publish the paper that appears in Chapter 4, the paper that gave "literate programming" its name.

I originally published Chapter 4 in the British *Computer Journal*, because my experience as an editor of technical journals and as a teacher of international graduate students had given me a strong impression that British scientists and engineers are far more interested in a literary approach than are their American counterparts. However, I secretly wanted this work to become accepted in my own native land; so I was overjoyed to learn that some of the American programmers I respect most highly had been stimulated by it. Jon Bentley was even motivated to introduce literate programming to readers of his popular *Programming Pearls* in *Communications of the ACM*; the two columns he devoted to this topic are reprinted in Chapters 5 and 6. Jon also inaugurated what I hope will become a long-lasting tradition, by asking M. D. McIlroy to be the world's first literary critic of a computer program. (Like all authors, I wish some parts of the criticism had not been so harsh, but that's part of the literary game too; McIlroy set excellent standards for future critics to follow. Indeed, the tradition was continued in a series of columns moderated by Chris Van Wyk in subsequent volumes of the *Communications*.) The more we pursue the idea of programs as literature, the better our programs become.

Chapter 7 can be read independently. It is a reader's manual, a brief introduction to the style in which I chose to present Pascal programs as "webs" when I wrote the fairly large-scale systems known as TEX and METAFONT. The main reason for my early enthusiasm about literate programming was the fact that the discipline it provided made those programs significantly better than they would otherwise have been. Textbook examples such as those in Chapters 2 and 3 can be quite instructive, but a successful methodology of programming must also work on large examples. The notion of scale can be appreciated only by looking at fairly sizable systems, and many people have told me that they enjoyed reading the full programs for TEX and/or METAFONT during a "vacation." Chapter 8 attempts to give a taste of such an experience, by presenting a few excerpts that can be understood pretty much in isolation. Simple routines for arithmetic and string manipulation come first; some highly intricate yet highly instructive algorithms used by TEX to hyphenate words come last; but the main lesson to be learned from Chapter 8 is the way in which literate programming can improve the readability of large, industrial-strength programs.

I introduced a small group of undergraduate students to the notion of literate programming in 1987, and I looked closely at the programs they wrote. In 8 cases out of 10, the results were quite successful, and in the other 2 cases the results were at least no worse than ordinary. Then I taught a special course at Stanford about Mathematical Writing, and two hours of that class were devoted to an analysis of what was good and what was not so good about the students' first literate programs. A summary of those class discussions, transcribed by Paul Roberts, appears in Chapter 9.

Chapter 10 goes more deeply into my own mistakes and what I think I've learned from them. The entire history of the development of TEX, and how it changed as I shifted to a more literate programming style, is summarized in that chapter by focusing on the errors that were corrected throughout TeX's evolution. Chapter 11, which is sort of an appendix to Chapter 10, presents the complete log of changes made to TeX—more than 1000 entries covering a period of more than 14 years. (This chapter includes about 300 items recently discovered in the Stanford Archives, which document every bug that I excised as I brought my first big literate program to life; I had previously thought that those records were irretrievably lost.) I know of no better way to gain an understanding of the problems involved in a medium-size software project than to scan through a complete list like this one.

All of the programs in this book, with one exception, are expressed in the Pascal language or in some closely related dialect of ALGOL 60. The exception is the short program in Chapter 12, which illustrates literate programming in C. I wrote TeX, METAFONT, and dozens of auxiliary programs by using a system called WEB, which is described in Chapter 4; WEB produces Pascal programs as output. Chapter 4 also points out, however, that the notion of literate programming is by no means tied to any particular programming language. And indeed, it has turned out that all of my own programming during the 1990s has been done in CWEB, a variant of WEB that was created by Silvio Levy (and to which I contributed a few small refinements).

My wife will tell you that I frequently emerge from my office shouting "CWEB programming is great fun!" I cannot sufficiently express the joy it gives me. I like CWEB even better than WEB, because it works well in conjunction with the compiler's diagnostic messages and with the standard debugging tools available on my machine. Chapter 12 gives the flavor of CWEB by presenting a program for one of UNIX's simple utility programs, the word-counting routine called 'wc'. My fondest hope is that readers who look at Chapter 12 will realize how wonderful it would be if the entire UNIX system and its successors were written in the style of Chapter 12 or something similar.

Literate programming is still a fairly new concept, still in its infancy, still undergoing much-needed experimentation. Many people have contributed important ideas and independent approaches to the creation of systems that improve on WEB in various ways. In this book I describe the techniques that have worked best for me, but I have never imagined that any of my ideas would be the "last word" in any sense. I am sure that people with differing tastes will prefer a system that differs from my own initial attempts.

The time is now ripe for second-generation systems that integrate literate programming into complete programming environments. In order to help researchers who may want to be part of that important next step,

I have compiled a bibliography of all the relevant papers currently known to me. This bibliography, entitled Further Reading, follows Chapter 12.

Each chapter has its own bibliography, taken from the relevant original publication. In a few cases I have added references to work that came out after the chapter was written, so that the technical details are still reasonably up-to-date throughout, although the outlook reflected in each chapter is a product of its own time. For example, Chapter 2 contains an anachronistic reference to research results of DeMillo, Eisenstadt, and Lipton that were obtained after my paper was originally published, because those results provide quantitative confirmation of qualitative arguments that were put forward in 1974. I have also taken this opportunity to spruce up the style of my original writing, especially by changing 'which' to 'that' in dozens of places where I should have known better. In general, I've tried to edit these chapters so that they now stand as I wish them to be remembered, while retaining their historical context.

The ideas presented in this book are largely due to the computing community as a whole. I have tried to provide a useful synthesis and to be an adequate spokesperson for all who have contributed to the art of programming, and I have tried to acknowledge special contributions by giving appropriate credit in each chapter. I am grateful for generous research support received from the National Science Foundation, the Office of Naval Research, and the System Development Foundation, without which TEX and WEB and their relatives could not have been born. And I owe a special debt of gratitude to Beth Bryson, who made the present book possible by gathering together a wide variety of difficult technical material from many different sources and putting it all together in a uniform typographic framework. Never before have I had such skillful and perceptive assistance when preparing a book for publication.

Donald E. Knuth
Stanford, California
October 1991

Contents

Chapter 1

Computer Programming as an Art (1974)

[The A. M. Turing Award is presented annually by the Association for Computing Machinery (ACM) to an individual selected for contributions of a technical nature to the computing community. In particular, these contributions should have had significant influence on a major segment of the computer field. The recipient is traditionally asked to present a public lecture at the ACM Annual Conference. In 1974, the conference opened in San Diego on November 11; Bernard A. Galler, chair of the 1974 Turing Award Committee, began the ceremony by reading the formal award citation.]

Introduction by B. A. Galler

"The 1974 A. M. Turing Award is presented to Professor Donald E. Knuth of Stanford University for a number of major contributions to the analysis of algorithms and the design of programming languages, and in particular for his most significant contributions to the 'art of computer programming' through his series of well-known books. The collections of techniques, algorithms, and relevant theory in these books have served as a focal point for developing curricula and as an organizing influence on computer science."

Such a formal statement cannot put into proper perspective the role which Don Knuth has been playing in computer science, and in the computer industry as a whole. It has been my experience with respect to the first recipient of the Turing Award, Professor Alan J. Perlis, that at every meeting in which he participates he manages to provide the insight into the problems being discussed that becomes the focal point of discussion for the rest of the meeting. In a very similar way, the vocabulary, the examples, the algorithms and the insight that Don Knuth has provided in his excellent collection of books and papers have begun to find their way into a great many discussions in almost every area of the field. This does not happen easily. As every author knows, even a single volume requires a great deal of careful organization and hard work. All the more must we appreciate the clear view and the patience and energy which Knuth must have had to plan seven volumes and to set about implementing his plan so carefully and thoroughly.

It is significant that this award and the others that he has been receiving are being given to him after three volumes of his work have been published. We are clearly ready to signal to everyone our appreciation of Don Knuth for his dedication and his contributions to our discipline. I am very pleased to have chaired the Committee that has chosen Don Knuth to receive the 1974 A. M. Turing Award of the ACM.

Computer Programming as an Art, by D. E. Knuth

When *Communications of the ACM* began publication in 1959, the members of ACM's Editorial Board made the following remark as they described the purposes of ACM's periodicals [2]: "If computer programming is to become an important part of computer research and development, a transition of programming from an art to a disciplined science must be effected." Such a goal has been a continually recurring theme during the ensuing years; for example, we read in 1970 of the "first steps toward transforming the art of programming into a science" [26]. Meanwhile we have actually succeeded in making our discipline a science, and in a remarkably simple way, merely by deciding to call it "computer science."

Implicit in these remarks is the notion that there is something undesirable about an area of human activity that is classified as an "art"; it has to be a Science before it has any real stature. On the other hand, I have been working for more than 12 years on a series of books called "The *Art* of Computer Programming." People frequently ask me why I picked such a title; and in fact some people apparently don't believe that I really did so, since I've seen at least one bibliographic reference to some books called "The *Act* of Computer Programming."

In this talk I shall try to explain why I think "Art" is the appropriate word. I will discuss what it means for something to be an art, in contrast to being a science; I will try to examine whether arts are good things or bad things; and I will try to show that a proper viewpoint of the subject will help us all to improve the quality of what we are now doing.

One of the first times I was ever asked about the title of my books was in 1966, during the last previous ACM national meeting held in Southern California. This was before any of the books were published, and I recall having lunch with a friend at the convention hotel. He knew how conceited I was, already at that time, so he asked if I was going to call my books "An Introduction to Don Knuth." I replied that, on the contrary, I was naming the books after *him*. His name: Art Evans. (The Art of Computer Programming, in person.)

From this story we can conclude that the word "art" has more than one meaning. In fact, one of the nicest things about the word is that it is used in many different senses, each of which is quite appropriate in connection with computer programming. While preparing this talk, I went to the library to find out what people have written about the word "art" through the years; and after spending several fascinating days in the stacks, I came to the conclusion that "art" must be one of the most interesting words in the English language.

The Arts of Old

If we go back to Latin roots, we find *ars, artis* meaning "skill." It is perhaps significant that the corresponding Greek word was τέχνη, the root of both "technology" and "technique."

Nowadays when someone speaks of "art" you probably think first of "fine arts" such as painting and sculpture, but before the twentieth century the word was generally used with quite a different significance. Since this older meaning of "art" still survives in many idioms, especially when we are contrasting art with science, I would like to spend the next few minutes talking about art in its classical sense.

In medieval times, the first universities were established to teach the seven so-called "liberal arts," namely grammar, rhetoric, logic, arithmetic, geometry, music, and astronomy. Note that this is quite different from the curriculum of today's liberal arts colleges, and that at least three of the original seven liberal arts are important components of computer science. At that time, an "art" meant something devised by man's intellect, as opposed to activities derived from nature or instinct; "liberal" arts were liberated or free, in contrast to manual arts such as plowing (cf. [6]). During the middle ages the word "art" by itself usually meant logic [4], which usually meant the study of syllogisms.

Science vs. Art

The word "science" seems to have been used for many years in about the same sense as "art"; for example, people spoke also of the seven liberal sciences, which were the same as the seven liberal arts [1]. Duns Scotus in the thirteenth century called logic "the Science of Sciences, and the Art of Arts" (cf. [12, p. 34f]). As civilization and learning developed, the words took on more and more independent meanings,

Science and Art

Our discussion indicates that computer programming is by now *both* a science and an art, and that the two aspects nicely complement each other. Apparently most authors who examine such a question come to this same conclusion, that their subject is both a science and an art, whatever their subject is (cf. [25]). I found a book about elementary photography, written in 1893, which stated that "the development of the photographic image is both an art and a science" [13]. In fact, when I first picked up a dictionary in order to study the words "art" and "science," I happened to glance at the editor's preface, which began by saying, "The making of a dictionary is both a science and an art." The editor of Funk & Wagnall's dictionary [27] observed that the painstaking accumulation and classification of data about words has a scientific character, while a well-chosen phrasing of definitions demands the ability to write with economy and precision: "The science without the art is likely to be ineffective; the art without the science is certain to be inaccurate."

When preparing this talk I looked through the card catalog at Stanford library to see how other people have been using the words "art" and "science" in the titles of their books. This turned out to be quite interesting.

For example, I found two books entitled *The Art of Playing the Piano* [5, 15], and others called *The Science of Pianoforte Technique* [10], *The Science of Pianoforte Practice* [30]. There is also a book called *The Art of Piano Playing: A Scientific Approach* [22].

Then I found a nice little book entitled *The Gentle Art of Mathematics* [31], which made me somewhat sad that I can't honestly describe computer programming as a "gentle art."

I had known for several years about a book called *The Art of Computation*, published in San Francisco, 1879, by a man named C. Frusher Howard [14]. This was a book on practical business arithmetic that had sold over 400,000 copies in various editions by 1890. I was amused to read the preface, since it shows that Howard's philosophy and the intent of his title were quite different from mine; he wrote: "A knowledge of the Science of Number is of minor importance; skill in the Art of Reckoning is absolutely indispensable."

Several books mention both science and art in their titles, notably *The Science of Being and Art of Living* by Maharishi Mahesh Yogi [24]. There is also a book called *The Art of Scientific Discovery* [11], which analyzes how some of the great discoveries of science were made.

So much for the word "art" in its classical meaning. Actually when I chose the title of my books, I wasn't thinking primarily of art in this sense, I was thinking more of its current connotations. Probably the most interesting book that turned up in my search was a fairly recent work by Robert E. Mueller called *The Science of Art* [29]. Of all the books I've mentioned, Mueller's comes closest to expressing what I want to make the central theme of my talk today, in terms of real artistry as we now understand the term. He observes: "It was once thought that the imaginative outlook of the artist was death for the scientist. And the logic of science seemed to spell doom to all possible artistic flights of fancy." He goes on to explore the advantages which actually do result from a synthesis of science and art.

A scientific approach is generally characterized by the words logical, systematic, impersonal, calm, rational, while an artistic approach is characterized by the words aesthetic, creative, humanitarian, anxious, irrational. It seems to me that both of these apparently contradictory approaches have great value with respect to computer programming.

Emma Lehmer wrote in 1956 that she had found coding to be "an exacting science as well as an intriguing art" [23]. H. S. M. Coxeter remarked in 1957 that he sometimes felt "more like an artist than a scientist" [7]. This was at the time C. P. Snow was beginning to voice his alarm at the growing polarization between "two cultures" of educated people [34, 35]. Snow pointed out that we need to combine scientific and artistic values if we are to make real progress.

Works of Art

When I'm sitting in an audience listening to a long lecture, my attention usually starts to wane at about this point in the hour. So I wonder, are you getting a little tired of my harangue about "science" and "art"? I really hope that you'll be able to listen carefully to the rest of this, anyway, because now comes the part about which I feel most deeply.

When I speak about computer programming as an art, I am thinking primarily of it as an art *form*, in an aesthetic sense. The chief goal of my work as educator and author is to help people learn how to write *beautiful programs*. It is for this reason I was especially pleased to learn recently [33] that my books actually appear in the Fine Arts Library at Cornell University. (However, the three volumes apparently sit there neatly on the shelf, without being used, so I'm afraid the librarians may have made a mistake by interpreting my title literally.)

My feeling is that when we prepare a program, the experience can be just like composing poetry or music; as Andrei Ershov has said [9], programming can give us both intellectual and emotional satisfaction, because it is a real achievement to master complexity and to establish a system of consistent rules.

Furthermore, when we read other people's programs, we can recognize some of them as genuine works of art. I can still remember the great thrill it was for me to read the listing of Stan Poley's `SOAP II` assembly program in 1958; you probably think I'm crazy, and styles have certainly changed greatly since then, but at the time it meant a great deal to me to see how elegant a system program could be, especially by comparison with the heavy-handed coding found in other listings I had been studying at the same time. The possibility of writing beautiful programs, even in assembly language, is what got me hooked on programming in the first place.

Some programs are elegant, some are exquisite, some are sparkling. My claim is that it is possible to write *grand* programs, *noble* programs, truly *magnificent* ones!

I discussed this recently with Michael Fischer, who suggested that computer programmers should begin to sell their original programs, as works of art, to collectors. The ACM could set up a panel to certify the authenticity of each genuinely new piece of code; then discriminating dealers and a new class of professionals called program critics would establish appropriate market values. This might be a nice way to raise our salaries if we could get it started.

Taste and Style

In a more serious vein, I'm glad that the idea of *style* in programming is now coming to the forefront at last, and I hope that most of you have seen the excellent little book on *Elements of Programming Style* by Kernighan and Plauger [16]. In this connection it is most important for us all to remember that there is no one "best" style; everybody has their own preferences, and it is a mistake to try to force people into an unnatural mold. We often hear the saying, "I don't know anything about art, but I know what I like." The important thing is that you really *like* the style you are using; it should be the best way you prefer to express yourself.

Edsger Dijkstra stressed this point in the preface to his *Short Introduction to the Art of Programming* [8]:

> It is my purpose to transmit the importance of good taste and style in programming, [but] the specific elements of style presented serve only to illustrate what benefits can be derived from "style" in general. In this respect I feel akin to the teacher of composition

> at a conservatory: He does not teach his pupils how to compose a particular symphony, he must help his pupils to find their own style and must explain to them what is implied by this. (It has been this analogy that made me talk about "The Art of Programming.")

Now we must ask ourselves, What is good style, and what is bad style? We should not be too rigid when judging other people's work. The early nineteenth-century philosopher Jeremy Bentham put it this way [3, Bk. 3, Ch. 1]:

> Judges of elegance and taste consider themselves as benefactors to the human race, whilst they are really only the interrupters of their pleasure. ... There is no taste which deserves the epithet *good*, unless it be the taste for such employments which, to the pleasure actually produced by them, conjoin some contingent or future utility: there is no taste which deserves to be characterized as bad, unless it be a taste for some occupation which has a mischievous tendency.

When we apply our own prejudices to "reform" other people's taste, we may be unconsciously denying them some entirely legitimate pleasure. That's why I don't condemn a lot of things programmers do, even though I would never enjoy doing them myself. The important thing is that they are creating something *they* feel is beautiful.

In the passage I just quoted, Bentham does give us some advice about certain principles of aesthetics that are better than others, namely the "utility" of the result. We have some freedom in setting up our personal standards of beauty, but the ideal situation occurs when the things we regard as beautiful are also regarded by other people as useful. I must confess that I really enjoy writing computer programs; and I especially enjoy writing programs which do the greatest good, in some sense.

There are many senses in which a program can be "good," of course. In the first place, a program is especially good when it works correctly. Secondly, a program is often good if it is easy to change, when the time for adaptation arises. Both of these goals are achieved when the program is easily readable and understandable to a person who knows the appropriate language.

Another important way for a production program to be good is for it to interact gracefully with its users, especially when recovering from human errors in the input data. It's a real art to compose meaningful error messages or to design flexible input formats that are not error-prone.

Another important aspect of program quality is the efficiency with which the computer's resources are actually being used. I am sorry to say that many people nowadays are condemning program efficiency, telling us that it is in bad taste. The reason for this is that we are now experiencing a reaction from the time when efficiency was the only reputable criterion of goodness; programmers in the past have tended to be so preoccupied with efficiency that they have produced needlessly complicated code. The result of this unnecessary complexity has been that net efficiency has gone down, due to the difficulties of debugging and maintenance.

The real problem is that programmers have spent far too much time worrying about efficiency in the wrong places and at the wrong times. Premature optimization is the root of all evil (or at least most of it) in programming.

We shouldn't be penny wise and pound foolish, nor should we always think of efficiency in terms of so many percent gained or lost in total running time or space. When we buy a car, many of us are almost oblivious to a difference of $50 or $100 in its price, while we might make a special trip to a particular store in order to buy a 50¢ item for only 25¢. My point is that there is a time and place for efficiency; I have discussed its proper role in my paper on structured programming, which appears in the current issue of *Computing Surveys* [21] [Chapter 2 of this volume].

Less Facilities: More Enjoyment

One rather curious thing I've noticed about aesthetic satisfaction is that our pleasure is significantly enhanced when we accomplish something with limited tools. For example, the program of which I personally am most pleased and proud is a compiler I once wrote for a primitive minicomputer that had only 4096 words of memory, 16 bits per word. It makes a person feel like a real virtuoso to achieve something under such severe restrictions.

A similar phenomenon occurs in many other contexts. For example, people often seem to fall in love with their Volkswagens but rarely with their Lincoln Continentals (which presumably run much better). When I learned programming, it was a popular pastime to do as much as possible with programs that fit on only a single punched card. I suppose it's this same phenomenon that makes APL enthusiasts relish their "one-liners." When we teach programming nowadays, it is a curious fact that we rarely capture the heart of a student for computer science until he or she has taken a course that allows "hands on" experience with a minicomputer.

The use of our large-scale machines with their fancy operating systems and languages doesn't really seem to engender any love for programming, at least not at first.

It's not obvious how to apply this principle to increase programmers' enjoyment of their work. Surely programmers would groan if their manager suddenly announced that the new machine will have only half as much memory as the old. And I don't think anybody, even the most dedicated "programming artists," can be expected to welcome such a prospect, since nobody likes to lose facilities unnecessarily. Another example may help to clarify the situation: Film-makers strongly resisted the introduction of talking pictures in the 1920s because they were justly proud of the way they could convey words without sound. Similarly, a true programming artist might well resent the introduction of more powerful equipment; today's mass storage devices tend to spoil much of the beauty of our old tape sorting methods. But today's filmmakers don't want to go back to silent films, not because they're lazy but because they know it is quite possible to make beautiful movies using the improved technology. The form of their art has changed, but there is still plenty of room for artistry.

How did they develop their skill? The best film-makers through the years usually seem to have learned their art in comparatively primitive circumstances, often in other countries with a limited movie industry. And in recent years the most important things we have been learning about programming seem to have originated with people who did not have access to very large computers. The moral of this story, it seems to me, is that we should make use of the idea of limited resources in our own education. We can all benefit by doing occasional "toy" programs, when artificial restrictions are set up, so that we are forced to push our abilities to the limit. We shouldn't live in the lap of luxury all the time, since that tends to make us lethargic. The art of tackling miniproblems with all our energy will sharpen our talents for the real problems, and the experience will help us to get more pleasure from our accomplishments later on less restricted equipment.

In a similar vein, we shouldn't shy away from "art for art's sake"; we shouldn't feel guilty about programs that are just for fun. I once got a great kick out of writing a one-statement ALGOL program that invoked an innerproduct procedure in such an unusual way that it calculated the mth prime number, instead of an innerproduct [19]. Some years ago the students at Stanford were excited about finding the shortest FORTRAN program that prints itself out, in the sense that the program's output is identical to its own source text. The same problem was considered for many other languages. I don't think it was a waste of time for people to work on this; nor would Jeremy Bentham, whom I quoted earlier, deny the "utility" of such pastimes [3, Bk. 3, Ch. 1]. "On the contrary," he wrote, "there is nothing, the utility of which is more incontestable. To what shall the character of utility be ascribed, if not to that which is a source of pleasure?"

Providing Beautiful Tools

Another characteristic of modern art is its emphasis on creativity. It seems that many artists these days couldn't care less about creating beautiful things; only the novelty of an idea is important. I'm not recommending that computer programming should be like modern art in this sense, but it does lead me to an observation that I think is important. Sometimes we are assigned to a programming task that is almost hopelessly dull, giving us no outlet whatsoever for any creativity; and at such times a person might well come to me and say, "So programming is beautiful? It's all very well for you to declaim that I should take pleasure in creating elegant and charming algorithms, but how am I supposed to make this mess into a work of art?"

Well, it's true, not all programming tasks are going to be fun. Consider the "trapped housewife," who has to clean off the same table every day: there's not room for creativity or artistry in every situation. But even in such cases, there is a way to make a big improvement: It is still a pleasure to do routine jobs if we have beautiful things to work with. For example, a person will really enjoy wiping off the dining room table, day after day, if it is a beautifully designed table made from some fine quality hardwood.

Sometimes we're called upon to *perform* a symphony, instead of to compose one; and it's a pleasure to perform a really fine piece of music, although we are suppressing our freedom to the dictates of the composer. Sometimes a programmer is called upon to be more a craftsman than an artist; and a craftman's work is quite enjoyable when good tools and materials are present.

Therefore I want to address my closing remarks to the system programmers and the machine designers who produce the systems that the rest of us must work with. *Please*, give us tools that are a pleasure to use, especially for our routine assignments, instead of providing something we have to fight against. Please, give us tools that encourage us to write better programs, by enhancing our pleasure when we do so.

It's very hard for me to convince college freshmen that programming is beautiful, when the first thing I have to tell them is how to punch "slash slash `JOB` equals so-and-so." Even job control languages can be designed so that they are a pleasure to use, instead of being strictly functional.

Computer hardware designers can make their machines much more pleasant to use, for example, by providing floating-point arithmetic that satisfies simple mathematical laws. The facilities presently available on most machines make the job of rigorous error analysis hopelessly difficult, but properly designed operations would encourage numerical analysts to provide better subroutines that have certified accuracy (cf. [20, p. 204]).

Let's consider also what software designers can do. One of the best ways to keep up the spirits of system users is to provide routines that they can interact with. We shouldn't make systems too automatic, so that the action always goes on behind the scenes; we ought to give the programmer-users a chance to direct their creativity into useful channels. One thing all programmers have in common is that they enjoy working with machines; so let's keep them in the loop. Some tasks are best done by machine, while others are best done by human insight; and a properly designed system will find the right balance. (I have been trying to avoid misdirected automation for many years, cf. [18].)

Program measurement tools make a good case in point. For years programmers have been unaware of how the real costs of computing are distributed in their programs. Experience indicates that nearly everybody has the wrong idea about the real bottlenecks in their programs; it is no wonder that attempts at efficiency go awry so often, when programmers are never given a breakdown of costs according to the lines of code they have written. Their job is something like that of a newly married couple who try to plan a balanced budget without knowing how much the individual items like food, shelter, and clothing will cost. All that we have been giving programmers is an optimizing compiler, which mysteriously does something to the programs it translates but which never explains what it does. Fortunately we are now seeing, at last, the appearance of systems that give the user credit for some intelligence; they automatically provide instrumentation of programs and appropriate feedback about the real costs. These experimental systems have been a huge success, because they produce measurable improvements, and especially because they are fun to use. So I am confident that it is only a matter of time before the use of such systems is standard operating procedure. My paper in *Computing Surveys* [21] [Chapter 2 of this volume] discusses such things further, and presents some ideas for other ways in which an appropriate interactive routine can enhance the satisfaction of user programmers.

Language designers also have an obligation to provide languages that encourage good style, since we all know that style is strongly influenced by the language in which it is expressed. The present surge of interest in structured programming has revealed that none of our existing languages is really ideal for dealing with program structure and data structure, nor is it clear what an ideal language should be. Therefore I look forward to many careful experiments in language design during the next few years.

Summary

To summarize: We have seen that computer programming is an art, because it applies accumulated knowledge to the world, because it requires skill and ingenuity, and especially because it produces objects of beauty. Programmers who subconsciously view themselves as artists will enjoy what they do and will do it better. Therefore we can be glad that people who lecture at computer conferences speak about the *state of the Art.*

References

[1] Nathan Bailey, *The Universal Etymological English Dictionary* (London: T. Cos, 1727). See "Art," "Liberal," and "Science."

[2] Walter F. Bauer, Mario L. Juncosa, and Alan J. Perlis, "ACM publication policies and plans," *J. ACM* **6** (Apr. 1959), 121–122.

[3] Jeremy Bentham, *The Rationale of Reward*, translated from *Théorie des peines et des récompenses*, 1811, by Richard Smith (London: J. & H. L. Hunt, 1825).

[4] *The Century Dictionary and Cyclopedia* **1** (New York: The Century Co., 1889).

[5] Muzio Clementi, *The Art of Playing the Piano*, translated from *L'art de jouer le pianoforte* by Max Vogrich (New York: Schirmer, 1898).

[6] Sidney Colvin, "Art," *Encyclopædia Britannica*, editions 9, 11, 12, 13 (1875–1926).

[7] H. S. M. Coxeter, "Convocation address," *Proceedings of the 4th Canadian Mathematical Congress* (1957), 8–10.

[8] Edsger W. Dijkstra, *EWD316: A Short Introduction to the Art of Programming*, Technical University Eindhoven, Eindhoven, The Netherlands (August 1971), 97 pp.

[9] Andrei P. Ershov, "Aesthetics and the human factor in programming." *Communications of the ACM* **15**,7 (July 1972), 501–505.

[10] Thomas Fielden, *The Science of Pianoforte Technique* (London: Macmillan, 1927).

[11] George Gore, *The Art of Scientific Discovery* (London: Longmans, Green, 1878).

[12] William Hamilton, *Lectures on Logic* **1** (Edinburgh: Wm. Blackwood, 1874).

[13] John A. Hodges, Elementary Photography: *The "Amateur Photographer" Library* **7** (London, 1893). Sixth edition, revised and enlarged (1907), 58.

[14] C. Frusher Howard, Howard's *Art of Computation* and golden rule for equation of payments for schools, business colleges and self-culture ... (San Francisco: C. F. Howard, 1879).

[15] J. N. Hummel, *The Art of Playing the Piano Forte* (London: Boosey, 1827).

[16] B. W. Kernighan and P. J. Plauger, *The Elements of Programming Style* (New York: McGraw-Hill, 1974).

[17] Richard Kirwan, *Elements of Mineralogy* (London: Elmsly, 1784).

[18] Donald E. Knuth, "Minimizing drum latency time," *Journal of the ACM* **8** (April 1961), 119-150.

[19] Donald E. Knuth and J. N. Merner, "ALGOL 60 confidential," *Communications of the ACM* **4**,6 (June 1961), 268–272.

[20] Donald E. Knuth, Seminumerical Algorithms: *The Art of Computer Programming* **2** (Reading, Massachusetts: Addison-Wesley, 1969).

[21] Donald E. Knuth, "Structured programming with **go to** statements," *Computing Surveys* **6**,4 (December 1974), 261–301. [Reprinted with minor changes in *Current Trends in Programming Methodology*, Raymond T. Yeh [Ed.], **1** (Englewood Cliffs, New Jersey: Prentice-Hall, 1977), 140–194; *Classics in Software Engineering*, Edward Nash Yourdon [Ed.] (New York: Yourdon Press, 1979), 259–321.]

[22] George Kochevitsky, *The Art of Piano Playing: A Scientific Approach* (Evanston, Illinois: Summy-Birchard, 1967).

[23] Emma Lehmer, "Number theory on the SWAC," *Proceedings of Symposia on Applied Mathematics* **6** (American Mathematical Society, 1956), 103–108.

[24] Maharishi Mahesh Yogi, *The Science of Being and Art of Living* (London: Allen & Unwin, 1963).

[25] Moses L. Malevinsky, *The Science of Playwriting* (New York: Brentano's, 1925).

[26] Zohar Manna and Amir Pnueli, "Formalization of properties of functional programs," *Journal of the ACM* **17**,3 (July 1970), 555–569.

[27] Albert H. Marckwardt, Preface to *Funk and Wagnall's Standard College Dictionary* (New York: Harcourt, Brace & World, 1963), vii.

[28] John Stuart Mill, *A System of Logic, Ratiocinative and Inductive* (London, 1843). The quotations are from the introduction, §2, and from Book 6, Chapter 11 (12 in later editions), §5.

[29] Robert E. Mueller, *The Science of Art* (New York: John Day, 1967).

[30] Albert Ross Parsons, *The Science of Pianoforte Practice* (New York: Schirmer, 1886).

[31] Daniel Pedoe, *The Gentle Art of Mathematics* (London: English U. Press, 1953).

[32] John Ruskin, *The Stones of Venice* **3** (London, 1853).

[33] Gerard A. Salton, Personal communication, 21 June 1974.

[34] C. P. Snow, "The two cultures," *The New Statesman and Nation* **52** (6 October 1956), 413–414.

[35] C. P. Snow, *The Two Cultures: and a Second Look* (Cambridge: Cambridge University Press, 1964).

Chapter 2

Structured Programming with **go to** Statements (1974)

You may go when you will go,
And I will stay behind.
—Edna St. Vincent Millay [66]

Most likely you go your way and I'll go mine.
—Song title by Bob Dylan [31]

Do you suffer from painful elimination?
—Advertisement, J. B. Williams Co.

Abstract

A consideration of several different examples sheds new light on the problem of creating reliable, well-structured programs that behave efficiently. This study focuses largely on two issues: (a) improved syntax for iterations and error exits, making it possible to write a larger class of programs clearly and efficiently without **go to** statements; and (b) a methodology of program design, beginning with readable and correct, but possibly inefficient, programs that are systematically transformed if necessary into efficient and correct but possibly less readable code. The discussion brings out opposing points of view about whether or not **go to** statements should be abolished; some merit is found on both sides of this question. Finally, an attempt is made to define the true nature of structured programming and to recommend fruitful directions for further study.

[Originally published in Computing Surveys, Volume 6, December 1974, as part of a special issue on Programming.]

0. Introduction

A revolution is taking place in the way we write programs and teach programming, because we are beginning to understand the associated mental processes more deeply. It is impossible to read the recent book *Structured Programming* [16; 53] without having it change your life. The reasons for this revolution and its future prospects have been aptly described by E. W. Dijkstra in his 1972 Turing Award Lecture, "The Humble Programmer" [25].

As we experience this revolution, each of us naturally is developing strong feelings one way or the other, as we agree or disagree with the revolutionary leaders. I must admit to being a nonhumble programmer, egotistical enough to believe that my own opinions of the current trends are not a waste of the reader's time. Therefore I want to discuss several of the things that struck me most forcefully as I have been thinking about structured programming during the last year; several of my blind spots were removed as I was learning these things, and I hope I can convey some of my excitement to the reader. Hardly any of the ideas I will mention are my own; they are nearly all the work of others, but perhaps I may be presenting them in a new light. I write this essay in the first person to emphasize the fact that what I'm saying is just one man's opinion; I don't expect to persuade everyone that my present views are correct.

Before beginning a more technical discussion, I should confess that my title was chosen primarily to generate attention. There are doubtless some readers who are convinced that abolition of **go to** statements is merely a fad, and they may see this title and think, "Aha! Knuth is rehabilitating the **go to** statement, and we can go back to our old ways of programming again." Another class of readers will see the heretical title and think, "When are diehards like Knuth going to get with it?" I hope that both classes of people will read on and discover that what I am really doing is striving for a reasonably well balanced viewpoint about the proper role of **go to** statements. I argue for the elimination of **go to**'s in certain cases, and for their introduction in others.

I believe that by presenting such a view I am not in fact disagreeing sharply with Dijkstra's ideas, since he recently wrote the following: "Please don't fall into the trap of believing that I am terribly dogmatical about [the **go to** statement]. I have the uncomfortable feeling that others are making a religion out of it, as if the conceptual problems of programming could be solved by a single trick, by a simple form of coding discipline!" [27]. In other words, it seems that fanatical advocates of the New Programming are going overboard in their strict enforcement of morality and purity in programs. Sooner or later people are going to find that their beautifully structured programs are running at only half the speed—or worse—of the dirty old programs they used to write; and they will mistakenly blame the structure instead of recognizing what is probably the real culprit—the system overhead caused by typical compiler implementation of Boolean variables and procedure calls. Then we'll have an unfortunate counterrevolution, something like the current rejection of the "New Mathematics" in reaction to its over-zealous reforms.

It may be helpful to consider a further analogy with mathematics. In 1904, Bertrand Russell published his famous paradox about the set of all sets that aren't members of themselves. This antinomy shook the foundations of classical mathematical reasoning, since it apparently brought very simple and ordinary deductive methods into question. The ensuing crisis led to the rise of "intuitionist logic," a school of thought championed especially by the Dutch mathematician, L. E. J. Brouwer; intuitionism abandoned all deductions that were based on questionable nonconstructive ideas. For a while it appeared that intuitionist logic would cause a revolution in mathematics. But the new approach angered David Hilbert, who was perhaps the leading mathematician of the time. Hilbert said, "Forbidding a mathematician to make use of the principle of the excluded middle is like forbidding an astronomer his telescope or a boxer the use of his fists." He characterized the intuitionist approach as seeking "to save mathematics by throwing overboard all that is troublesome. ... They would chop up and mangle the science. If we would follow such a reform as they suggest, we could run the risk of losing a great part of our most valuable treasures" [80, pp. 98–99, 148–150, 154–157, 184–185, 268–270].

Something a little like this is happening in computer science. In the late 1960s we witnessed a "software crisis," which many people thought was paradoxical because programming was supposed to be so easy. As a result of the crisis, people are now beginning to renounce every feature of programming that can be considered guilty by virtue of its association with difficulties. Not only **go to** statements are being questioned; we also hear complaints about floating-point calculations, global variables, semaphores, pointer variables, and even assignment statements. Soon we might be restricted to only a dozen or so programs that are sufficiently simple to be allowable; then we will be almost certain that these programs cannot lead us into any trouble, but of course we won't be able to solve many problems.

In the mathematical case, we know what happened: The intuitionists taught the other mathematicians a great deal about deductive methods, while the other mathematicians cleaned up the classical methods and eventually "won" the battle. And a revolution did, in fact, take place. In the computer science case, I imagine that a similar thing will eventually happen. Purists will point the way to clean constructions, and others will find ways to purify their use of floating-point arithmetic, pointer variables, assignments, etc., so that the classical tools can be used with comparative safety.

Of course all analogies break down, including this one, especially since I'm not yet conceited enough to compare myself to David Hilbert. But I think it's an amusing coincidence that the present programming revolution is being led by another Dutchman (although without extremist views corresponding to Brouwer's); and I do consider assignment statements and pointer variables to be among computer science's "most valuable treasures."

At the present time I think we are on the verge of discovering at last what programming languages should really be like. I look forward to seeing many responsible experiments with language design during the next few years; and my dream is that by 1984 we will see a consensus developing for a really good programming language (or, more likely, a coherent family of languages). Furthermore, I'm guessing that people will become so disenchanted with the languages they are now using—even COBOL and FORTRAN—that this new language, UTOPIA 84, will have a chance to take over. At present we are far from that goal, yet there are indications that such a language is very slowly taking shape.

Will UTOPIA 84, or perhaps we should call it NEWSPEAK, contain **go to** statements? At the moment, unfortunately, there isn't even a consensus about this apparently trivial issue, and we had better not be hung up on the question too much longer since there are fewer than ten years left.

I will try in what follows to give a reasonably comprehensive survey of the **go to** controversy, arguing both pro and con, without taking a strong stand one way or the other until the discussion is nearly complete. In order to illustrate different uses of **go to** statements, I will discuss many example programs, some of which tend to negate the conclusions we might draw from the others. There are two reasons why I have chosen to present the material in this apparently vacillating manner. First, since I have the opportunity to choose all the examples, I don't think it's fair to load the dice by selecting only program fragments that favor one side of the argument. Second, and perhaps most important, I tried this approach when I lectured on the subject at UCLA in February 1974, and it worked beautifully: Nearly everybody in the audience had the illusion that I was largely supporting his or her views, regardless of what those views were!

1. Elimination of go to Statements

Historical Background

At the IFIP Congress in 1971 I had the pleasure of meeting Dr. Eiichi Goto of Japan, who cheerfully complained that he was always being eliminated. Here is the history of the subject, as far as I have been able to trace it.

The first programmer who systematically began to avoid all labels and **go to** statements was perhaps D. V. Schorre, then of UCLA. He has written the following account of his early experiences [85]:

> Since the summer of 1960, I have been writing programs in outline form, using conventions of indentation to indicate the flow of control. I have never found it necessary to take exception to these conventions by using **go to** statements. I used to keep these outlines as original documentation of a program, instead of using flow charts ... Then I would code the program in assembly language from the outline. Everyone liked these outlines better than the flow charts I had drawn before, which were not very neat—my flow charts had been nick-named "balloon-o-grams."

He reported that this method made programs easier to plan, to modify and to check out.

When I met Schorre in 1963, he told me of his radical ideas, and I didn't believe they would work. In fact, I suspected that they were really his rationalization for not finding an easy way to put labels and **go to** statements into his META-II subset of ALGOL [84], a language that I liked very much except for this omission. In 1964 I challenged him to write a program for the eight-queens problem without using **go to** statements, and he responded with a program using recursive procedures and Boolean variables, very much like the program later published independently by Wirth [97].

I was still not convinced that all **go to** statements could or should be done away with, although I fully subscribed to Peter Naur's observations that had appeared about the same time [73]. Since Naur's comments were the first published remarks about harmful **go to**'s, it is instructive to quote some of them here:

> If you look carefully you will find that surprisingly often a **go to** statement which looks back really is a concealed **for** statement. And you will be pleased to find how the clarity of the algorithm improves

> when you insert the **for** clause where it belongs ... If the purpose [of a programming course] is to teach ALGOL programming, the use of flow diagrams will do more harm than good, in my opinion.

The next year we find George Forsythe also purging **go to** statements from algorithms submitted to *Communications of the ACM* (cf. [51]). Incidentally, the second example program at the end of the original ALGOL 60 report [72] contains four **go to** statements, to labels named AA, BB, CC, and DD, so it is clear that the advantages of ALGOL's control structures weren't fully perceived in 1960.

In 1965, Edsger Dijkstra published the following instructive remarks [19]:

> Two programming department managers from different countries and different backgrounds—the one mainly scientific, the other mainly commercial—have communicated to me, independently of each other and on their own initiative, their observation that the quality of their programmers was inversely proportional to the density of goto statements in their programs. ... I have done various programming experiments ... in modified versions of ALGOL 60 in which the goto statement was abolished ... The latter versions were more difficult to make: we are so familiar with the jump order that it requires some effort to forget it! In all cases tried, however, the program without the goto statement turned out to be shorter and more lucid.

A few months later, at the ACM Programming Languages and Pragmatics Conference, Peter Landin put it this way [57]:

> There is a game sometimes played with ALGOL 60 programs—rewriting them so as to avoid using **go to** statements. It is part of a more embracing game—reducing the extent to which the program conveys its information by explicit sequencing ... The game's significance lies in that it frequently produces a more "transparent" program—easier to understand, debug, modify, and incorporate into a larger program.

Peter Naur reinforced this opinion at the same meeting [74, p. 179].

The next chapter in the story is what many people regard as the first, because it made the most waves. Dijkstra submitted a short article to *Communications of the ACM* devoted entirely to a discussion of **go to** statements. In order to speed publication, the editor decided to publish Dijkstra's article as a letter, and to supply a new title, "Go to statement considered harmful." This note [21] rapidly became well-known; it expressed Dijkstra's conviction that **go to**'s "should be abolished from all 'higher level' programming languages (i.e., everything except, perhaps, plain machine code). ... The **go to** statement as it stands is just too primitive; it is too much an invitation to make a mess of one's program." He encouraged looking for alternative constructions that may be necessary to satisfy all needs. Dijkstra also recalled that Heinz Zemanek had expressed doubts about **go to** statements as early as 1959; and that Peter Landin, Christopher Strachey, C. A. R. Hoare and others had been of some influence on his thinking.

By 1967, the entire XPL compiler had been written by McKeeman, Horning, and Wortman, using **go to** only once ([65], pp. 365–458; the **go to** is on page 385). In 1971, Christopher Strachey [87] reported that, "It is my aim to write programs with no labels. I am doing quite well. I have got the operating system down to 5 labels and I am planning to write a compiler with no labels at all." In 1972, an entire session of the ACM National Conference was devoted to the subject [42; 58; 101]. The December, 1973, issue of *Datamation* featured five articles about structured programming and elimination of **go to**'s [2; 12; 30; 64; 67]. Thus, it is clear that sentiments against **go to** statements have been building up. In fact, the discussion has apparently caused some people to feel threatened; Dijkstra once told me that he actually received "a torrent of abusive letters" after publication of his article.

The tide of opinion first hit me personally in 1969, when I was teaching an introductory programming course for the first time. I remember feeling frustrated on several occasions at not seeing how to write programs in the new style; I would run to Bob Floyd's office asking for help, and he usually showed me what to do. This was the genesis of our article [50] in which we presented two types of programs that did not submit gracefully to the new prohibition. We found that there was no way to implement certain simple constructions with **while** and conditional statements substituted for **go to**'s, unless extra computation was specified.

During the last few years several languages have appeared in which the designers proudly announced that they have abolished the **go to** statement. Perhaps the most prominent of these is BLISS [99], which originally replaced **go to**'s by eight so-called "escape" statements. And the eight weren't even enough; the authors wrote, "Our mistake was in assuming that there is no need for a label once the **go to** is removed," and they later [100, 101] added a new statement "**leave** ⟨ label ⟩ **with** ⟨ expression ⟩" which goes to the place *after* the statement identified by the ⟨ label ⟩. Other **go to**-less languages for systems programming have similarly introduced other statements which provide "equally powerful" alternative ways to jump.

In other words, it seems that there is widespread agreement that **go to** statements are harmful, yet programmers and language designers still feel the need for some euphemism that "goes to" without saying **go to**.

A Searching Example

What are the reasons for this? In [50], Floyd and I gave the following example of a typical program for which the ordinary capabilities of **while** and **if** statements are inadequate. Let's suppose that we want to search a table $A[1] \ldots A[m]$ of distinct values, in order to find where a given value x appears; if x is not present in the table, we want to insert it as an additional entry. Let's suppose further that there is another array B, where $B[i]$ equals the number of times we have searched for the value $A[i]$. We might solve such a problem as follows:

Example 1

```
for i := 1 step 1 until m do
  if A[i] = x then go to found fi;
not found: i := m + 1; m := i;
  A[i] := x; B[i] := 0;
found: B[i] := B[i] + 1;
```

(In the present discussion I shall use an ad hoc programming language that is very similar to ALGOL 60, with one exception: The symbol **fi** is required as a closing bracket for all **if** statements, so that **begin** and **end** aren't needed between **then** and **else**. I don't really like the looks of **fi** at the moment; but it is short, performs a useful function, and connotes finality, so I'm confidently hoping that I'll get used to it. Alan Perlis has remarked that **fi** is a perfect example of a cryptic notation that can make programming unnecessarily complicated for beginners; yet I'm more comfortable with **fi** every time I write it. I still balk at spelling *other* basic symbols backwards, and so do most of the people I know; a student's paper containing the code fragment "**esac; comment** bletch **tnemmoc**;" is a typical reaction to this trend!)

There are ways to express Example 1 without **go to** statements, but they require more computation and aren't really more perspicuous. Therefore, this example has been widely quoted in defense of the **go to** statement, and it is appropriate to scrutinize the problem carefully.

Let's suppose that we've been forbidden to use **go to** statements, and that we want to do *precisely* the computation specified in Example 1 (using the obvious expansion of such a **for** statement into assignments and a **while** iteration). If this means not only that we want the same results, but also that we want to do the same operations in the same order, the mission is impossible. But if we are allowed to weaken the conditions just slightly, so that a relation can be tested twice in succession (assuming that it will yield the same result each time, i.e., that it has no side effects), we can solve the problem as follows:

Example 1a

$i := 1$;
while $i \le m$ **and** $A[i] \ne x$ **do** $i := i + 1$;
if $i > m$ **then** $m := i$; $A[i] := x$; $B[i] := 0$ **fi**;
$B[i] := B[i] + 1$;

The **and** operation used here stands for McCarthy's sequential conjunction operator [62, p. 185]; i.e., "p **and** q" means "**if** p **then** q **else false fi**", so that q is not evaluated when p is false. Example 1a will do exactly the same sequence of computations as Example 1, except for one extra comparison of i with m (and occasionally one less computation of $m + 1$). If the iteration in this **while** loop is performed a large number of times, the extra comparison has a negligible effect on the running time.

Thus, we can live without the **go to** in Example 1. But Example 1a is slightly less readable, in my opinion, as well as slightly slower; so it isn't clear what we have gained. Furthermore, if we had made Example 1 more complicated, the trick of transforming it to Example 1a would no longer work. For example, suppose we had inserted another statement into the **for** loop, just before the **if** clause; then the relations $i \le m$ and $A[i] = x$ wouldn't have been tested consecutively, and we couldn't in general have combined them with **and**.

John Cocke told me an instructive story relating to Example 1 and to the design of languages. Some PL/I programmers were asked to do the stated search problem without using jumps, and they came up with essentially the following two solutions:

(a)
```
DO I = 1 TO M WHILE(A(I)¬ = X);
END;
IF I > M THEN
  DO; M = I; A(I) = X; B(I) = 0; END;
B(I) = B(I) + 1;
```

(b)
```
FOUND = 0;
DO I = 1 TO M WHILE(FOUND = 0);
  IF A(I) = X THEN FOUND = 1;
END;
IF FOUND = 0 THEN
  DO; M = I; A(I) = X; B(I) = 0; END;
B(I) = B(I) + 1;
```

Solution (a) is best, but since it involves a null iteration (with no explicit statements being iterated) most people came up with Solution (b). The instructive point is that Solution (b) doesn't work; there is a serious bug, which caused great puzzlement before the reason was found. Can the reader spot the difficulty? (The answer appears on page 81.)

As I've said, Example 1 has often been used to defend the **go to** statement. Unfortunately, however, the example is totally unconvincing in spite of the arguments I've stated so far, because the method in Example 1 is almost *never* a good way to search an array for x! The following modification to the data structure makes the algorithm much better:

Example 2

$A[m+1] := x;\ i := 1;$
while $A[i] \neq x$ do $i := i + 1;$
if $i > m$ **then** $m := i;\ B[i] := 1;$
else $B[i] := B[i] + 1$ **fi**;

Example 2 beats Example 1 because it makes the inner loop considerably faster. If we assume that the programs have been handcoded in assembly language, so that the values of i, m, and x are kept in registers, and if we let n be the final value of i at the end of the program, Example 1 will make $6n+10$ ($+3$ if not found) references to memory for data and instructions on a typical computer, while the second program will make only $4n + 14$ ($+6$ if not found). If, on the other hand, we assume that these programs are translated by a typical "90% efficient compiler" with bounds-checking suppressed, the corresponding run-time figures are respectively about $14n + 5$ and $11n + 21$. (The appendix on p. 80 explains the ground rules for these calculations.) Under the first assumption we save about 33% of the run-time, and under the second assumption we save about 21%, so in both cases the elimination of the **go to** has also eliminated some of the running time.

Efficiency

The ratio of running times (about 6 to 4 in the first case when n is large) is rather surprising to people who haven't studied program behavior carefully. Example 2 doesn't look *that* much more efficient, but it is. Experience has shown (see [44, 49]) that most of the running time in non-IO-bound programs is concentrated in about 3% of the source text. We often see a short inner loop whose speed governs the overall program speed to a remarkable degree; speeding up the inner loop by 10% speeds up everything by almost 10%. And if the inner loop has 10 instructions, a moment's thought will usually cut it to 9 or fewer.

My own programming style has of course changed during the last decade, according to the trends of the times (e.g., I'm not quite so tricky anymore, and I use fewer **go to**'s), but the major change in my style has been due to this inner loop phenomenon. I now look with an extremely jaundiced eye at every operation in a critical inner loop, seeking to modify my program and data structure as in the change from Example 1 to Example 2, so that some of the operations can be eliminated. The reasons for this approach are that (a) it doesn't take long, since the inner loop is short; (b) the payoff is real; and (c) I can then afford to be less efficient in the other parts of my programs, which therefore are more readable and more easily written and debugged. Tools are being developed to make this critical-loop identification job easy (see, for example, [44] and [82]).

Thus, if I hadn't seen how to remove one of the operations from the loop in Example 1 by changing to Example 2, I would probably (at least) have made the **for** loop run from m to 1 instead of from 1 to m, since it's usually easier to test for zero than to compare with m. And if Example 2 were really critical, I would improve on it still more by "doubling it up" so that the machine code would be essentially as follows.

Example 2a

```
A[m + 1] := x; i := 1; go to test;
loop:  i := i + 2;
test:  if A[i] = x then go to found fi;
       if A[i + 1] ≠ x then go to loop fi;
       i := i + 1;
found: if i > m then m := i; B[i] := 1;
       else B[i] := B[i] + 1 fi;
```

Here the loop variable i increases by 2 on each iteration, so we need to do that operation only half as often as before; the rest of the code in the loop has essentially been duplicated to make this work. The running time has now been reduced to about $3.5n+14.5$ or $8.5n+23.5$ under our respective assumptions—again this is a noticeable saving in the overall running speed, if, say, the average value of n is about 20, and if this search routine is performed a million or so times in the overall program. Such loop-optimizations are not difficult to learn and, as I have said, they are appropriate in just a small part of a program, yet they very often yield substantial savings. (Of course if we want to improve on Example 2a still more, especially for large m, we'll use a more sophisticated search technique; but let's ignore that issue at the moment, since I want to illustrate loop optimization in general, not searching in particular.)

The improvement in speed from Example 2 to Example 2a is only about 12%, and many people would pronounce that insignificant. The conventional wisdom shared by many of today's software engineers calls for ignoring efficiency in the small; but I believe this is simply an overreaction to the abuses they see being practiced by penny-wise-and-pound-foolish programmers, who can't debug or maintain their "optimized" programs. In established engineering disciplines a 12% improvement, easily obtained, is never considered marginal; and I believe the same viewpoint should prevail in software engineering. Of course I wouldn't bother making such optimizations on a one-shot job, but when it's a question of preparing quality programs, I don't want to restrict myself to tools that deny me such efficiencies.

There is no doubt that the "grail" of efficiency leads to abuse. Programmers waste enormous amounts of time thinking about, or worrying about, the speed of noncritical parts of their programs, and such attempts at efficiency actually have a strong negative impact when debugging and maintenance are considered. We *should* forget about small efficiencies, about 97% of the time. Premature optimization is the root of all evil.

Yet we should not pass up our opportunities in that critical 3%. Good programmers will not be lulled into complacency by such reasoning, they will be wise to look carefully at the critical code; but only *after* the critical code has been identified. It is often a mistake to make a priori judgments about what parts of a program are really critical, since the universal experience of programmers who have been using measurement tools has been that their intuitive guesses fail. After working with such tools for seven years, I've become convinced that all compilers written from now on should be designed to provide all programmers with feedback indicating what parts of their programs are costing the most; indeed, this feedback should be supplied automatically unless it has been specifically turned off.

After a programmer knows which parts of which routines are really important, a transformation like doubling up of loops will be worthwhile. Note that this transformation introduces **go to** statements—and so do several other loop optimizations; I will return to this point later. Meanwhile I have to admit that the presence of **go to** statements in Example 2a has a negative as well as a positive effect on efficiency; a nonoptimizing compiler will tend to produce awkward code, since the contents of registers can't be assumed known when a label is passed. When I computed the running times cited above by looking at a typical compiler's output for this example, I found that the improvement in performance was not quite as much as I had expected.

Error Exits

For simplicity I have avoided a very important issue in the previous examples, but it must now be faced. All of the programs we have considered exhibit bad programming practice, since they fail to make the necessary check that m has not gone out of range. In each case before we perform "$m := i$" we should precede that operation by a test such as

if $m = max$ **then go to** *memory overflow*;

here max is an appropriate threshold value. I left this statement out of the examples since it would have been distracting, but we need to look at it now since it is another important class of **go to** statements: an *error exit*. Such checks on the validity of data are very important, especially in software, and it seems to be the one class of **go to**'s that still is considered ugly but necessary by today's leading reformers. (I wonder how Val Schorre has managed to avoid such **go to**'s during all these years.)

Sometimes it is necessary to exit from several levels of control, cutting across code that may even have been written by other programmers; and the most graceful way to do this is a direct approach with a **go to** or its equivalent. Then the intermediate levels of the program can be written under the assumption that nothing will go wrong.

I will return to the subject of error exits later.

Subscript Checking

In the particular examples given above we can, of course, avoid comparing m with max if we have dynamic range-checking on all subscripts of A. But this usually aborts the program, giving us little or no control over the error recovery; so we probably want to test m anyway. And ouch, what subscript checking does to the inner loop execution times!

In Example 2, I will certainly want to suppress range-checking in the **while** clause since its subscript can't be out of range unless $A[m+1]$ was already invalid in the previous line. Similarly, in Example 1 there can be no range error in the **for** loop unless a range error occurred earlier. It seems senseless to have expensive range checks in those parts of my programs that I *know* are clean.

In this respect I should mention Hoare's almost persuasive arguments to the contrary [38, p. 18]. He points out quite correctly that the current practice of compiling subscript range checks into the machine code while a program is being tested, then suppressing the checks during production runs, is like a sailor who wears his life preserver while training on land but leaves it behind when he sails! On the other hand, that sailor isn't so foolish if life vests are extremely expensive, and if he is such an excellent swimmer that the chance of needing one is quite small compared with the other risks he is taking. In the foregoing examples we typically are much more certain that the subscripts will be in range than that other aspects of our overall program will work correctly. John Cocke observes that time-consuming range checks can be avoided by a smart compiler, which first compiles the checks into the program and then moves them out of the loop. Wirth [95] and Hoare [37] have pointed out that a well-designed **for** statement can permit even a rather simple-minded compiler to avoid most range checks within loops.

I believe that range checking should be used far more often than it currently is, but not everywhere. On the other hand I am really assuming infallible hardware when I say this; surely I wouldn't want to remove the parity check mechanism from the hardware, even under a hypothetical assumption that it was slowing down the computation. Additional memory protection is necessary to prevent my program from harming someone else's, and theirs from clobbering mine. My arguments are directed toward compiled-in tests, not towards hardware mechanisms that are really needed to ensure reliability.

Hash Coding

Now let's move on to another example, based on a standard hashing technique but otherwise designed for the same application as above. Here $h(x)$ is a hash function that takes on values between 1 and m; and $x \neq 0$. In this case m is somewhat larger than the number of items in the table, and "empty" positions are represented by 0.

Example 3

$i := h(x)$;
while $A[i] \neq 0$ **do**

```
    begin if A[i] = x then go to found fi;
       i := i − 1; if i = 0 then i := m fi;
    end;
not found: A[i] := x; B[i] := 0;
found: B[i] := B[i] + 1;
```

If we analyze this as we did Example 1, we see that the trick leading to Example 2 doesn't work any more. Yet if we want to eliminate the **go to** we can apply the idea of Example 1a by writing

while $A[i] \neq 0$ **and** $A[i] \neq x$ **do** ...

and by testing afterwards which condition caused termination. This version is perhaps a little bit easier to read; unfortunately it makes a redundant test, which we would like to avoid if we were in a critical part of the program.

Why should I worry about the redundant test in this case? After all, the extra test whether $A[i]$ was 0 or x is being made outside of the **while** loop, and I said before that we should generally confine our optimizations to inner loops. Here, the reason is that this **while** loop *won't* usually be a loop at all; with a proper choice of h and m, the operation $i := i - 1$ will tend to be executed very infrequently, often less than once per search on the average [52, Section 6.4]. Thus, the entire program of Example 3, except perhaps for the line labeled *not found*, must be considered as part of the inner loop, if this search process is a dominant part of the overall program (as it often is). The redundant test will therefore be significant in this case.

Despite this concern with efficiency, I should actually have written the first draft of Example 3 without that **go to** statement; my first draft should in fact have probably used a **while** clause written in an extended language, such as

while $A[i] \notin \{0, x\}$ **do** ...

since this formulation abstracts the *real* meaning of what is happening. Someday there may be hardware capable of testing membership in small sets more efficiently than if we program the tests sequentially, so that such a program would lead to better code than Example 3. And there is a much more important reason for preferring this form of the **while** clause: It reflects a symmetry between 0 and x that is not present in Example 3. For example, in most software applications it turns out that the condition $A[i] = x$ terminates the loop far more frequently than $A[i] = 0$; with this knowledge, my second draft of the program would be the following.

Example 3a

```
i := h(x);
while A[i] ≠ x do
  begin if A[i] = 0
    then A[i] := x; B[i] := 0;
      go to found;
    fi;
    i := i − 1; if i = 0 then i := m fi;
  end;
found: B[i] := B[i] + 1;
```

This program is easy to derive from the **go to**-less form, but not from Example 3; and it is better than Example 3. So again we see the advantage of delaying optimizations until we have obtained more knowledge of a program's behavior.

It is instructive to consider Example 3a further, assuming now that the **while** loop is performed many times per search. Although this should not happen in most applications of hashing, there are other programs in which a loop of the above form is present, so it is worth examining what we should do in such circumstances. If the **while** loop becomes an inner loop affecting the overall program speed, the whole picture changes; that redundant test outside the loop becomes utterly negligible, but the test "**if** $i = 0$" suddenly looms large. We generally want to avoid testing conditions that are almost always false, inside a critical loop. Therefore, under these new assumptions I would change the data structure by adding a new element $A[0] = 0$ to the array and eliminating the test for $i = 0$ as follows.

Example 3b

```
i := h(x);
while A[i] ≠ x do
  if A[i] ≠ 0
  then i := i − 1
  else if i = 0
    then i := m;
    else A[i] := x; B[i] := 0;
      go to found;
    fi;
  fi;
found: B[i] := B[i] + 1;
```

The loop now is noticeably faster. Again, I would be unhappy with slow subscript range checks if this loop were critical. Incidentally, Example 3b was derived from Example 3a, and a rather different program would have emerged if the same idea had been applied to Example 3; then a test "**if** $i = 0$" would have been inserted *outside* the loop, at label "not found," and another **go to** would have been introduced by the optimization process.

As in the first examples, the program in Example 3 is flawed in failing to test for memory overflow. I should have done this, for example, by keeping a count, n, of how many items are nonzero. The "not found" routine would then begin with something like "$n := n + 1$; **if** $n = m$ **then go to** *memory overflow*."

Text Scanning

The first time I consciously applied the top-down structured programming methodology to a reasonably complex job was in the late summer of 1972, when I wrote a program to prepare the index to my book *Sorting and Searching* [52]. I was quite pleased with the way that program turned out (there was only one serious bug), but I did use one **go to** statement. In this case the reason was somewhat different, having nothing to do with exiting from loops; I was exiting, in fact, from an **if-then-else** construction.

The following example is a simplified version of the situation I encountered. Suppose we are processing a stream of text, and that we want to read and print the next character from the input; however, if that character is a slash ("/") we want to "tabulate" instead (i.e., to advance in the output to the next tab-stop position on the current line); however, two consecutive slashes means a "carriage return" (i.e., to advance in the output to the beginning of the next line). After printing a period (".") we also want to insert an additional space in the output. The following code clearly does the trick.

Example 4

```
   x := read char;
   if x = slash
   then x := read char;
      if x = slash
      then return the carriage; go to char processed;
      else tabulate;
      fi;
   fi;
   write char (x);
   if x = period then write char (space) fi;
char processed:
```

An abstract program with similar characteristics has been studied by Peterson et al. [77, Fig. 1(a)]. In practice we occasionally run into situations where a sequence of decisions is made via nested **if-then-else**'s, and then two or more of the branches merge into one. We can manage such decision-table tasks without **go to**'s by copying the common code into each place, or by defining it as a procedure, but this does not seem conceptually simpler than to make such cases **go to** a common part of the program. Thus, in Example 4, I could avoid the **go to** by copying "*write char* (x); **if** x = *period* **then** *write char* (*space*) **fi**" into the program after "*tabulate*;" and by making corresponding changes. But this would be a pointless waste of energy just to eliminate a perfectly understandable **go to** statement. The resulting program would actually be harder to maintain than the former, since the action of printing a character now appears in two different places. The alternative of declaring procedures avoids the latter problem, but it is not especially attractive, either. Still another alternative is:

Example 4a

```
x := read char;
double slash := false;
if x = slash
then x := read char;
   if x = slash
   then double slash := true;
   else tabulate;
   fi;
fi;
if double slash
then return the carriage;
else write char (x);
   if x = period
   then write char (space);
   fi;
fi;
```

I claim that this is conceptually no simpler than Example 4; indeed, one can argue that it is actually more difficult, because it makes the *entire* routine aware of the "double slash" exception to the rules, instead of dealing with it in one exceptional place.

A Confession

Before we go on to another example, I must admit what many readers already suspect, namely, that I'm subject to substantial bias because I actually have a vested interest in **go to** statements! The style for the series of books I'm writing was set in the early 1960s, and it would be too difficult for me to change it now; I present algorithms in my books using informal English language descriptions, and **go to** or its equivalent is almost the only control structure I have. Well, I rationalize this apparent anachronism by arguing that (a) an informal English description seems advantageous because many readers tell me they automatically read English, but skip over formal code; (b) when **go to** statements are used judiciously together with comments stating nonobvious loop invariants, they are semantically equivalent to **while** statements, except that indentation is missing to indicate the structure; (c) the algorithms are nearly always short, so that accompanying flowcharts are able to illustrate the structure; (d) I try to present algorithms in a form that is most efficient for implementation, and high-level structures often don't do this; (e) many readers will get pleasure from converting my semiformal algorithms into beautifully structured programs in a formal programming language; and (f) we are still learning much about control structures, and I can't afford to wait for the final consensus.

In spite of these rationalizations, I'm uncomfortable about the situation, because I find others occasionally publishing examples of algorithms in "my" style but without the important parenthesized comments and/or with unrestrained use of **go to** statements. In addition, I also know of places where I have myself used a complicated structure with excessively unrestrained **go to** statements, especially the notorious Algorithm 2.3.3A for multivariate polynomial addition [48]. The original program had at least three bugs; exercise 2.3.3–14, "Give a formal proof (or disproof) of the validity of Algorithm A," was therefore unexpectedly easy. Now, in the second edition, I believe that the revised algorithm is correct, but I still don't know any good way to prove it; I've had to raise the difficulty rating of exercise 2.3.3–14, and I hope someday to see the algorithm cleaned up without loss of its efficiency.

My books emphasize efficiency because they deal with algorithms that are used repeatedly as building blocks in a large variety of applications. It is important to keep efficiency in its place, as mentioned above, but when efficiency counts we should also know how to achieve it.

In order to make it possible to derive quantitative assessments of efficiency, my books show how to analyze machine language programs; and those programs are expressed in `MIXAL`, a symbolic assembly language that explicitly corresponds one-for-one to machine language. This approach has its uses, but there is a danger of placing too much stress on assembly code. Programs in MIXAL are like programs in machine language, devoid of structure; or, more precisely, the structure of such programs is difficult for our eyes to perceive. Comments are provided to explain the program and to relate it to the global structure illustrated in flowcharts, but they don't really give the reader a simple way to understand what is going on; and it is easy to make mistakes, partly because we rely so much on comments that might possibly be inaccurate descriptions of what the program really does. It is clearly better to write programs in a language that reveals the control structure, even if we are intimately conscious of the hardware at each step; therefore I will be discussing a structured assembly language called PL/MIX in the fifth volume of *The Art of Computer Programming*. Such a language (analogous to Wirth's PL360 [96] should really be supported by each manufacturer for each machine in place of the old-fashioned structureless assemblers that still proliferate.

On the other hand I'm not really unhappy that MIXAL programs appear in my books, because I believe that MIXAL is a good example of a "quick and dirty assembler," a genre of software which will always be useful in its proper role. Such an assembler is characterized by language restrictions that make simple one-pass assembly possible, and it has several noteworthy advantages when we are first preparing programs for a new machine: (a) it is a great improvement over numeric machine code; (b) its rules are easy to state; and (c) it can be implemented in an afternoon or so, thus getting an efficient assembler working quickly on what may be very primitive equipment. So far I have implemented six such assemblers, at different times in my life, for machines or interpretive systems or microprocessors that had no existing software of comparable utility; and in each case other constraints made it impractical for me to take the extra time necessary to develop a good, structured assembler. Thus I am sure that the concept of a quick-and-dirty-assembler is useful, and I'm glad to let MIXAL illustrate what one is like. However, I also believe strongly that such languages should never be improved to the point where they are too easy or too pleasant to use; one must restrict their use to primitive facilities that are easy to implement efficiently. I would never switch to a two-pass process, or add complex pseudo-operations, macrofacilities, or even fancy error diagnostics to such a language, nor would I maintain or distribute such a language as a standard programming tool for a real machine. All such ameliorations and refinements should appear in a structured assembler. Now that the technology is available, we can condone unstructured languages only as a bootstrap-like means to a limited end, when there are strong economic reasons for not implementing a better system.

Tree Searching

But I'm digressing from my subject of **go to** elimination in higher level languages. A few weeks ago I decided to choose an algorithm at random from my books, to study its use of **go to** statements. The very first example I encountered [52, Algorithm 6.2.3C] turned out to be another case where existing programming languages have no good substitute for **go to**'s. In simplified form, the loop where the trouble arises can be written as follows.

Example 5

```
compare:
  if A[i] < x
  then if L[i] ≠ 0
    then i := L[i]; go to compare;
    else L[i] := j; go to insert fi;
  else if R[i] ≠ 0
    then i := R[i]; go to compare;
    else R[i] := j; go to insert fi;
  fi;
insert: A[j] := x;
  L[j] := 0; R[j] := 0; j := j + 1;
```

This is part of the well-known "tree search and insertion" scheme, where a binary search tree is being represented by three arrays: $A[i]$ denotes the information stored at node number i, and $L[i]$, $R[i]$ are the respective node numbers for the roots of that node's left and right subtrees; empty subtrees are represented by zero. The program searches down the tree until finding an empty subtree where x can be inserted. Variable j points to an appropriate place to do the insertion. For convenience, I have assumed in this example that x is not already present in the search tree.

Example 5 has four **go to** statements, but the control structure is saved from obscurity because the program is so beautifully symmetric between L and R. I know that these **go to** statements can be eliminated by introducing a Boolean variable, which becomes true when $L[i]$ or $R[i]$ is found to be zero. But I don't want to test this variable in the inner loop of my program.

Systematic Elimination

A good deal of theoretical work has been addressed to the question of **go to** elimination, and I shall now try to summarize the findings and to discuss their relevance.

S. C. Kleene proved a famous theorem in 1956 [46] which says, in essence, that the set of all paths through any flowchart can be represented as a "regular expression" R built up from the following operations:

s	the single arc s of the flowchart
$R_1; R_2$	concatenation (all paths consisting of a path of R_1 followed by a path of R_2)
$R_1 \cup R_2$	union (all paths of either R_1 or R_2)
R^+	iteration (all paths of the form $p_1; p_2; \ldots; p_n$ for some $n \geq 1$, where each p_i is a path of R)

These regular expressions correspond loosely to programs consisting of statements in a programming language related by three operations: sequential compositions, conditionals (**if-then-else**), and iterations (**while** loops). Thus, we might expect that these three program control structures would be sufficient for all programs. However, closer analysis shows that Kleene's theorem does not relate directly to control structures; the problem is only superficially similar. His result is suggestive but not really applicable in this case.

The analogous result for control structures was first proved by G. Jacopini in 1966, in a paper written jointly with C. Böhm [7]. Jacopini showed, in effect, that any program given, say, in flowchart form can be transformed systematically into another program, which computes the same results and which is built up from statements in the original program using only the three basic operations of composition, conditional, and iteration, plus possible assignment statements and tests on auxiliary variables. Thus, **go to** statements can always be removed in principle. A detailed exposition of Jacopini's construction has been given by H. D. Mills [69].

Recent interest in structured programming has caused many authors to cite Jacopini's result as a significant breakthrough and as a cornerstone of modern programming technique. Unfortunately, these authors are unaware of the comments made by Cooper in 1967 [15] and later by Bruno and Steiglitz [9], namely, that from a practical standpoint the theorem is meaningless. Indeed, any program can obviously be put into the "beautifully structured" form

```
p := 1;
while p > 0 do
  begin if p = 1 then perform step 1;
      p := successor of step 1 fi;
    if p = 2 then perform step 2;
      p := successor of step 2 fi;
    ...
    if p = n then perform step n;
      p := successor of step n fi;
  end.
```

Here the auxiliary variable p serves as a program counter representing which box of the flowchart we're in, and the program stops when p is set to zero. We have eliminated all **go to**'s, but we've actually lost all the structure.

Jacopini conjectured in his paper that auxiliary variables are necessary in general, and that the **go to**'s in a program of the form

```
L1: if B1 then go to L2 fi;
    S1;
    if B2 then go to L2 fi;
    S2;
    go to L1;
L2: S3;
```

cannot always be removed unless additional computation is done. Floyd and I proved this conjecture with John Hopcroft's help [50]. Sharper results were later obtained by Ashcroft and Manna [1], Bruno and Steiglitz [9], Peterson, Kasami, and Tokura [77], Kosaraju [55], and Lipton, Eisenstadt, and DeMillo [59]. The theorem of Lipton, Eisenstadt, and DeMillo is especially noteworthy. They proved that, for all large integers n, there exists an n-statement program using **go to** statements that cannot be converted to any "structured" program of less than $(1.3)^{\sqrt{n}}$ statements, unless that program runs at least $\frac{1}{2}\log_2 n$ times slower than the original because of the extra bookkeeping necessary. This holds even if the "structured" program has **go to** statements that jump out of (but not into) loops.

Jacopini's original construction was not merely the trivial flowchart emulation scheme indicated above; he was able to salvage much of the given flowchart structure if it was reasonably well behaved. A more general technique of **go to** elimination, devised by Ashcroft and Manna [1], made it possible to capture still more of a given program's natural flow; for example, their technique applied to Example 5 yields

Example 5a

$t :=$ **true**;
while t **do**
  begin if $A[i] < x$
    then if $L[i] \neq 0$ **then** $i := L[i]$;
      else $L[i] := j$; $t :=$ **false fi**;
    else if $R[i] \neq 0$ **then** $i := R[i]$;
      else $R[i] := j$; $t :=$ **false fi**;
    fi;
  end;
$A[j] := x$;

But, in general, their technique may cause a program to grow exponentially in size; and when error exits or other recalcitrant **go to**'s are present, the resulting programs will indeed look rather like the flowchart emulator sketched above.

If such automatic **go to** elimination procedures are applied to badly structured programs, we can expect the resulting programs to be at least as badly structured. Dijkstra pointed this out already in 1968 [21], saying:

> The exercise to translate an arbitrary flow diagram more or less mechanically into a jumpless one, however, is not to be recommended. Then the resulting flow diagram cannot be expected to be more transparent than the original one.

In other words, we shouldn't merely remove **go to** statements because it's the fashionable thing to do; the presence or absence of **go to** statements is not really the issue. The underlying structure of the program is what counts, and we want only to avoid usages that somehow clutter up the program. Good structure can be expressed in FORTRAN or COBOL, or even in assembly language, although less clearly and with much more trouble. The real goal is to formulate our programs in such a way that they are easily understood.

Program structure refers to the way in which a complex algorithm is built up from successively simpler processes. In most situations this structure can be described very nicely in terms of sequential compositions, conditionals, and simple iterations, together with **case** statements for multiway branches. Undisciplined **go to** statements make program structure harder to perceive, and they are often symptoms of a poor conceptual formulation. But there has been far too much emphasis on **go to** elimination instead of on the really important issues; people have a natural tendency to set up an easily understood quantitative goal like the abolition of jumps, instead of working directly for a qualitative goal like good program structure. In a similar way, many people have set up "zero population growth" as a goal to be achieved, when they really desire living conditions that are much harder to quantify.

Probably the worst mistake any one can make with respect to the subject of **go to** statements is to assume that "structured programming" is achieved by writing programs as we always have and then eliminating the **go to**'s. Most **go to**'s shouldn't be there in the first place! What we really want is to conceive of our program in such a way that we rarely even *think* about **go to** statements, because the real need for them hardly ever arises. The language in which we express our ideas has a strong influence on our thought processes. Therefore, Dijkstra [21] asks for more new language features—structures that encourage clear thinking—in order to avoid the **go to**'s temptations toward complications.

Situation Indicators

The best such language feature I know has recently been proposed by C. T. Zahn [103]. Since his suggestion is still in the experimental stage, I will take the liberty of modifying his "syntactic sugar" slightly, without changing the basic idea. The essential novelty in his approach is to introduce a new quantity into programming languages, called a *situation indicator*. My current preference is to write his situation-driven construct in the following two general forms.

```
(a)   loop until ⟨situation⟩_1 or ··· or ⟨situation⟩_n:
               ⟨statement list⟩_0;
      repeat;
      then ⟨situation⟩_1 ⟹ ⟨statement list⟩_1;
               ⋮
               ⟨situation⟩_n ⟹ ⟨statement list⟩_n;
      fi;

(b)   begin until ⟨situation⟩_1 or ... or ⟨situation⟩_n:
               ⟨statement list⟩_0;
      end;
      then ⟨situation⟩_1 ⟹ ⟨statement list⟩_1;
               ⋮
               ⟨situation⟩_n ⟹ ⟨statement list⟩_n;
      fi;
```

There is also a new statement, "⟨situation⟩," which means that the designated situation has occurred: Such a statement is allowed only within $\langle$statement list$\rangle_0$ of an **until** construct which declares that situation.

In form (a), ⟨statement list⟩$_0$ is executed repeatedly until control leaves the construct entirely or until one of the named situations occurs; in the latter case, the statement list corresponding to that situation is executed. The behavior in form (b) is similar, except that no iteration is implied; one of the named situations must have occurred before the **end** is reached. The **then** ... **fi** part may be omitted when there is only one situation name.

The above rules should become clear after looking at what happens when Example 5 above is recoded in terms of this new feature:

Example 5b

```
loop until left leaf hit or
           right leaf hit:
  if A[i] < x
  then if L[i] ≠ 0 then i := L[i];
    else left leaf hit fi;
  else if R[i] ≠ 0 then i := R[i];
    else right leaf hit fi;
  fi;
  repeat;
  then left leaf hit  ⟹  L[i] := j;
       right leaf hit  ⟹  R[i] := j;
  fi;
  A[j] := x; L[j] := 0; R[j] := 0; j := j + 1;
```

Alternatively, using a single situation name,

Example 5c

```
loop until leaf replaced:
  if A[i] < x
  then if L[i] ≠ 0 then i := L[i]
    else L[i] := j; leaf replaced fi;
  else if R[i] ≠ 0 then i := R[i]
    else R[i] := j; leaf replaced fi;
  fi;
repeat;
A[j] := x; L[j] := 0; R[j] := 0; j := j + 1;
```

For reasons to be discussed later, Example 5b is preferable to 5c.

It is important to emphasize that the first line of the construct merely declares the situation indicator names, and that situation indicators are *not* conditions that are being tested continually; ⟨situation⟩ statements are simply transfers of control having a form that the compiler can treat very efficiently. Thus, in Example 5c the statement *leaf replaced* is essentially a **go to** that jumps out of the loop.

This use of situations is, in fact, semantically equivalent to a restricted form of **go to** statement, which Peter Landin discussed already in 1965 [56] before most of us were ready to listen. Landin's device has been reformulated by Clint and Hoare [13] in the following way: Labels are declared at the beginning of each block, just as procedures normally are, and each label also has a ⟨ label body ⟩ just as a procedure has a ⟨ procedure body ⟩. Within the block whose heading contains such a declaration of label L, the statement **go to** L according to this scheme means "execute the body of L, then leave the block." It is easy to see that this is exactly the form of control provided by Zahn's situation mechanism, with each ⟨ label body ⟩ replaced by the corresponding ⟨ statement list ⟩ in the **then** ... **fi** postlude and with ⟨ situation ⟩ statements corresponding to Landin's **go to**. Thus, Clint and Hoare would have written Example 5b as follows:

```
while true do
  begin label left leaf hit; L[i] := j;
    label right leaf hit; R[i] := j;
    if A[i] < x
    then if L[i] ≠ 0 then i := L[i];
      else goto left leaf hit fi;
    else if R[i] ≠ 0 then i := R[i];
      else goto right leaf hit fi;
    fi;
  end;
A[j] := x; L[j] := 0; R[j] := 0; j := j + 1;
```

I believe the program reads much better in Zahn's form, with each ⟨ label body ⟩ set in the code between that which logically precedes and follows.

Landin also allowed his "labels" to have parameters like any other procedures; this is a valuable extension to Zahn's proposal, so I shall use situations with value parameters in several of the examples below.

As Zahn [103] has shown, situation-driven statements blend well with the ideas of structured programming by stepwise refinement. Thus, Examples 1 to 3 can all be cast into the following more abstract form, using a situation *found* with an integer parameter:

```
begin until found:
  search the table for x and insert it if not present;
end;
then found (integer j) ⟹ B[j] := B[j] + 1;
fi;
```

This much of the program can be written before we have decided how to maintain the table. At the next level of abstraction, we might decide to represent the table as a sequential list, as in Example 1, so that the program segment "search the table ..." would expand into

```
for i := 1 step 1 until m do if A[i] = x then found(i) fi;
m := m + 1; A[m] := x; found(m);
```

Note that this **for** loop is more disciplined than the one in our original Example 1, because the iteration variable is not used outside the loop; it now conforms to the rules of ALGOL W and ALGOL 68. Such **for** loops provide convenient documentation and avoid common errors associated with global variables; their advantages have been discussed by Hoare [37].

Similarly, if we want to use the idea of Example 2 we might write the following code as the refinement of "search the table ...":

```
begin integer i;
  A[m + 1] := x; i := 1;
  while A[i] ≠ x do i := i + 1;
  if i > m then m := i; B[m] := 0 fi;
  found(i);
end;
```

And finally, if we decide to use hashing, we obtain the equivalent of Example 3, which might be written as follows.

```
begin integer i;
  i := h(x);
  loop until present or absent:
    if A[i] = x then present fi;
    if A[i] = 0 then absent fi;
    i := i − 1;
    if i= 0 then i := m fi;
  repeat;
  then present  ⟹ found(i);
       absent   ⟹ A[i] := x; found(i);
  fi;
end;
```

The **begin until** ⟨ situation ⟩ construct also provides a natural way to deal with decision-table constructions such as the text-scanning application we have discussed.

Example 4b

```
begin until normal character input or double slash:
```

```
    char x;
    x := read char;
    if x = slash
    then x := read char;
      if x = slash
      then double slash;
      else tabulate;
        normal character input (x);
      fi;
    else normal character input (x);
    fi;
  end;
  then normal character input (char x) ⟹ write char (x);
    if x = period then write char (space) fi;
    double slash ⟹ return the carriage;
  fi;
```

This program states the desired actions a bit more clearly than any of our previous attempts were able to do.

Situation indicators handle error exits too. For example, we might write a program as follows:

```
  begin until error or normal end:
    ...
    if m = max then error ('symbol table full') fi;
    ...
    normal end;
  end;
  then error (string S) ⟹ print ('unrecoverable error', S);
    normal end ⟹ print ('computation complete');
  fi;
```

Comparison of Features

Of course, situation indicators are not the only decent alternatives to **go to** statements that have been proposed. Many authors have suggested language features that provide roughly equivalent facilities, but expressed in terms of exit, jumpout, break, or leave statements. Kosaraju [55] has proved that such statements are sufficient to express all programs without **go to**'s and without any extra computation, but only if an exit from arbitrarily many levels of control is permitted. Furthermore, Kosaraju's construction may require exponential growth in the program size (see the theorem of Lipton, Eisenstadt, and DeMillo cited earlier).

The earliest language features of this kind, besides Landin's proposal, provided essentially only one exit from a loop; this means that the code appearing in the **then** ... **fi** postlude of our examples would be inserted into the body itself before branching. (See Example 5c.) The separation of such code as in Zahn's proposal is better, mainly because the body of the construct corresponds to code that is written under different "invariant assumptions," which are inoperative after a particular situation has occurred. Thus, each situation corresponds to a particular set of assertions about the state of the program. The code following that situation takes cognizance of those assertions, which are rather different from the assertions in the main body of the construct. For this reason I prefer Example 5b to Example 5c.

Language features allowing multiple exits have been proposed by G. V. Bochmann [6], and independently by Shigo et al. [86]. These are semantically equivalent to Zahn's proposals, with minor variations; but they express such semantics in terms of statements that say "**exit to** ⟨label⟩." I believe Zahn's idea of situation indicators is an improvement on the previous schemes, because the specification of situations instead of labels encourages a better *conception* of the program. The identifier given to a label is often an imperative verb like *insert* or *compare*, saying what action is to be done next, while the appropriate identifier for a situation is more likely to be an adjective like *found*. The names of situations are very much like the names of Boolean variables, and I believe this accounts for the popularity of Boolean variables as documentation aids, in spite of their inefficiency.

Putting this another way, it is much better from a psychological standpoint to write

loop until *found* ... ; *found*; ... **repeat**

than to write

search: **while true do**
  begin ... ; **leave** *search*; ... **end**.

The **leave** or **exit** statement is operationally the same, but intuitively different, since it talks more about the program than about the problem.

The PL/I language allows programmer-defined ON-conditions, which are similar in spirit to situation indicators. A programmer first *executes* a statement "ON CONDITION (identifier) block," which specifies a block of code that is to be executed when the identified situation occurs. Then an occurrence of that situation is indicated by writing SIGNAL CONDITION (identifier). However, the analogy is not very close, since control returns to the statement following the SIGNAL statement after execution of the specified block of code, and the block may be dynamically respecified.

Some people have suggested to me that situations should be called "conditions" instead, by analogy with Boolean expressions. However, that terminology would tend to imply a relation that is continually being monitored, instead of a happening. By writing "**loop until** *yprime* is near *y*: ..." we seem to be saying that the machine should keep track of whether or not *y* and *yprime* are nearly equal; a better choice of words would be a situation name like "**loop until** *convergence established*: ..." so that we can write "**if** $abs(yprime - y) < epsilon \times y$ **then** *convergence established*." A situation arrives when the program has *discovered* that the state of computation has changed.

Simple Iterations

So far I haven't mentioned what I believe is really the most common scenario in which **go to** statements are needed by an ALGOL or PL/I programmer, namely a simple iterative loop with one entrance and one exit. The iteration statements most often proposed as alternatives to **go to** statements have been "**while** *B* **do** S" and "**repeat** *S* **until** B." However, in practice, the iterations I encounter very often have the form

```
A: S;
   if B then go to Z fi;
   T; go to A;
Z:
```

where *S* and *T* *both* represent reasonably long sequences of code. If S is empty, we have a **while** loop, and if *T* is empty we have a repeat loop, but in the general case it is a nuisance to avoid the **go to** statements.

A typical example of such an iteration occurs when *S* is the code to acquire or generate a new piece of data, *B* is the test for end of data, and *T* is the processing of that data. Another example is when the code preceding the loop sets initial conditions for some iterative process; then *S* is a computation of quantities involved in the test for convergence, *B* is the test for convergence, and *T* is the adjustment of variables for the next iteration.

Dijkstra [27] aptly named this a loop that is performed "*n* and a half times." The usual practice for avoiding **go to**'s in such loops is either to duplicate the code for *S*, writing

$$S;\ \textbf{while}\ \overline{B}\ \textbf{do begin}\ T;\ S\ \textbf{end};$$

where $\overline{B}$ is the negation of relation B; or to figure out some sort of "inverse" for T so that "T^{-1}; T" is equivalent to a null statement, and writing

$$T^{-1};\ \mathbf{repeat}\ T;\ S\ \mathbf{until}\ B;$$

or to duplicate the code for B and to make a redundant test, writing

$$\mathbf{repeat}\ S;\ \mathbf{if}\ \overline{B}\ \mathbf{then}\ T\ \mathbf{fi};\ \mathbf{until}\ B;$$

or its equivalent. The reader who studies **go to**-less programs as they appear in the literature will find that all three of these rather unsatisfactory constructions are used frequently.

I discussed this weakness of ALGOL in a letter to Niklaus Wirth in 1967, and he proposed two solutions to the problem, together with many other instructive ideas in an unpublished report on basic concepts of programming languages [95]. His first suggestion was to write

$$\mathbf{repeat\ begin}\ S;\ \mathbf{when}\ B\ \mathbf{exit};\ T;\ \mathbf{end};$$

and readers who remember 1967 will also appreciate his second suggestion,

$$\mathbf{turn\ on\ begin}\ S;\ \mathbf{when}\ B\ \mathbf{drop\ out};\ T;\ \mathbf{end}.$$

Neither set of delimiters was felt to be quite right, but a modification of the first proposal (allowing one or more single-level **exit** statements within **repeat begin** ... **end**) was later incorporated into an experimental version of the ALGOL W language. Other languages such as BCPL and BLISS incorporated and extended the **exit** idea, as mentioned above. Zahn's construction now allows us to write, for example,

loop until *all data exhausted*:
  S;
  if B **then** *all data exhausted* **fi**;
  T;
repeat;

and this is a better syntax for the $n + \frac{1}{2}$ problem than we have had previously.

On the other hand, it would be nicest if our language would provide a single feature that covered all simple iterations without going to a rather "big" construct like the situation-driven scheme. A programmer who uses the simpler feature is thereby announcing plainly that a simple iteration is being performed, having exactly one condition, which is being tested exactly once each time around the loop. Furthermore, by providing special syntax for this common case we make it easier for a compiler to produce more efficient code, since the compiler can rearrange the machine instructions so that the test appears physically at the end of loop. (Many hours of computer time are now wasted each day executing unconditional jumps to the beginning of loops.)

Ole-Johan Dahl has recently proposed a syntax that I think is the first real solution to the $n + \frac{1}{2}$ problem. He suggests writing the general simple iteration defined above as

$$\textbf{loop}\text{: } S\text{; } \textbf{while } \overline{B}\text{: } T\text{; } \textbf{repeat}\text{;}$$

where, as before, S and T denote sequences of one or more statements separated by semicolons. Note that as in two of our original **go to**-free examples, the syntax refers to condition $\overline{B}$ which represents staying *in* the iteration, instead of to condition B which represents exiting. This may be the secret of its success.

Dahl's syntax may not seem appropriate at first, but actually it reads well in every example I have tried, and I hope the reader will reserve judgment until seeing the examples in the rest of this chapter. One of the nice properties of his syntax is that the word **repeat** occurs naturally at the end of a loop rather than at its beginning, since we read actions of the program sequentially. As we reach the end, we are instructed to repeat the loop, instead of being informed that the *text* of the loop (not its execution) has ended. Furthermore, the above syntax avoids ALGOL's use of the word **do** (and also the more recent unnatural delimiter **od**); the word **do** as used in ALGOL has never sounded quite right to native speakers of English, it has always been rather quaint for us to say "**do** *read* $(A[i])$" or "**do begin**"! Another feature of Dahl's proposal is that it is easily axiomatized along the lines proposed by Hoare [35, 39]:

$$\frac{\{P\}S\{Q\} \qquad \{Q \wedge \overline{B}\}T\{P\}}{\{P\}\ \textbf{loop}\text{: } S\text{; } \textbf{while } \overline{B}\text{: } T\text{; } \textbf{repeat}\text{; } \{Q \wedge \neg\overline{B}\}}$$

(Here I am using braces around the assertions, as in Wirth's Pascal language [98], instead of following Hoare's original notation "$P\{S\}Q$", since assertions are, by nature, parenthetical remarks.)

The nicest thing about Dahl's proposal is that it works also when S or T is empty, so that we have a uniform syntax for all three cases; the **while** and **repeat** statements found in ALGOL-like languages of the late 1960s are no longer needed. When S or T is empty, it is appropriate to delete the preceding colon. Thus

loop while $\overline{B}$:
  T;
repeat;

takes the place of "**while** $\overline{B}$ **do begin** T **end**;" and

loop:
  S;
while $\overline{B}$ **repeat**:

takes the place of "**repeat** S **until** B;". At first glance these may seem strange, but probably less strange than the **while** and **repeat** statements did when we first learned them.

If I were designing a programming language today, my current preference would be to use Dahl's mechanism for simple iteration, plus Zahn's more general construct, plus a **for** statement whose syntax would be perhaps

loop for $1 \leq i \leq n$:
  S;
repeat;

with appropriate extensions. These control structures, together with **if** ... **then** ... **else** ... **fi**, will comfortably handle all the examples discussed so far in this chapter, without any **go to** statements or loss of efficiency or clarity. Furthermore, none of these language features seem to encourage overly complicated program structure.

2. Introduction of go to Statements

Now that I have discussed how to remove **go to** statements, I will turn around and show why there are occasions when I actually wish to *insert* them into a **go to**-less program. The reason is that I like well-documented programs very much, but I dislike inefficient ones; and there are some cases where I simply seem to need **go to** statements, despite the examples stated above.

Recursion Elimination

Such cases come to light primarily when I'm trying to optimize a program (originally well structured), often involving the removal of implicit or explicit recursion. For example, consider the following recursive procedure that prints the contents of a binary tree in symmetric order. The tree is represented by L, A, and R arrays as in Example 5, and the recursive procedure is essentially the definition of symmetric order.

Example 6

```
procedure treeprint(t); integer t; value t;
  if t ≠ 0
  then treeprint(L[t]);
    print(A[t]);
    treeprint(R[t]);
  fi;
```

This procedure may be regarded as a model for a great many algorithms that have the same structure, since tree traversal occurs in so many applications. We shall assume for now that printing is our goal, with the understanding that this is only one instance of a general family of algorithms.

It is often useful to remove recursion from an algorithm because of important economies of space or time, even though this tends to cause some loss of the program's basic clarity. (And, of course, we might also have to state our algorithm in a language like FORTRAN or in a machine language that doesn't allow recursion.) Even when we use ALGOL or PL/I, every compiler I know imposes considerable overhead on procedure calls; this is to a certain extent inevitable because of the generality of the parameter mechanisms, especially call by name and the maintenance of proper dynamic environments. When procedure calls occur in an inner loop the overhead can slow a program down by a factor of two or more. But if we hand-tailor our own implementation of recursion instead of relying on a general mechanism we can usually find worthwhile simplifications, and in the process we occasionally get a deeper insight into the original algorithm.

A good deal has been published about recursion elimination, especially in the work of Barron [3], Cooper [14], Manna and Waldinger [60], McCarthy [62], and Strong [88; 91]; but I'm amazed that very little of this is about "down-to-earth" problems. I have always felt that the transformation from recursion to iteration is one of the most fundamental concepts of computer science, and that students should learn it at about the time they are learning data structures. This topic is the subject of Chapter 8 in my multivolume work; but it's only by accident that the recursion chapter wasn't Chapter 3, since it belongs conceptually near the very beginning. The material just wouldn't fit comfortably into any of the earlier volumes, although there are many algorithms in Chapters 1–7 that are recursions in disguise. Therefore it surprises me that the literature on recursion removal is primarily concerned with "baby" examples like computing factorials or reversing lists, instead of with a sturdy toddler like Example 6.

Now let's **go to** work on the Example 6. I assume, of course, that the reader knows the standard way of implementing recursion with a stack [18], but I want to make simplifications beyond this. Rule number one for simplifying procedure calls is:

> If the last action of procedure p before it returns is to call procedure q, simply **go to** the beginning of procedure q instead.

(We must forget for the time being that we don't like **go to** statements.) It is easy to confirm the validity of this rule, if, for simplicity, we assume parameterless procedures. For the operation of calling q is to put a return address on the stack, then to execute q, then to resume p at the return address specified, then to resume the caller of p. The simplification above makes q resume the caller of p. When $q = p$ the argument is perhaps a bit subtle, but it's all right. (I'm not sure who originated this principle; I recall learning it from Gill's paper [32, p. 183], and then seeing many instances of it in connection with top-down compiler organization. Under certain conditions the BLISS/11 compiler [102] is capable of discovering this simplification. Incidentally, the converse of the above principle is also true (see [50]): **go to** statements can always be eliminated by declaring suitable procedures, each of which calls another as its last action. This analysis shows that procedure calls include **go to** statements as a special case; it cannot be argued that procedures are conceptually simpler than **go to**'s, although some people have made such a claim.)

As a result of applying the above simplification and adapting it in the obvious way to the case of a procedure with one parameter, Example 6 becomes

Example 6a

```
procedure treeprint(t); integer t; value t;
L: if t ≠ 0
     then treeprint(L[t]);
       print(A[t]);
       t := R[t]; go to L;
     fi;
```

But we don't really want that **go to**, so we might prefer to write the code as follows, using Dahl's syntax for iterations as explained above.

Example 6b

```
procedure treeprint(t); integer t; value t;
  loop while t ≠ 0:
    treeprint(L[t]);
```

```
    print(A[t]);
    t := R[t];
  repeat;
```

If our goal is to impress somebody, we might tell them that we thought of Example 6b first, instead of revealing that we got it by straightforward simplification of the obvious program in Example 6.

There is still a recursive call in Example 6b; and this time it's embedded in the procedure, so it looks as though we have to **go to** the general stack implementation. However, the recursive call now occurs in only one place, so we need not put a return address on the stack; only the local variable t needs to be saved on each call. (This is another simplification that occurs frequently.) The program now takes the following nonrecursive form.

Example 6c

```
procedure treeprint(t); integer t; value t;
  begin integer stack S; S := empty;
L1: loop while t ≠ 0:
      S <= t; t := L[t]; go to L1;
L2:   t <= S;
      print(A[t]);
      t := R[t];
    repeat;
    if nonempty(S) then go to L2 fi;
  end.
```

Here for simplicity I have extended ALGOL to allow a "stack" data type, where $S <= t$ means "push t onto S" and $t <= S$ means "pop the top of S to t, assuming that S is nonempty."

It is easy to see that Example 6c is equivalent to Example 6b. The statement "**go to** *L1*" initiates the procedure, and control returns to the following statement (labeled *L2*) when the procedure is finished. Although Example 6c involves **go to** statements, their purpose is easy to understand, given the knowledge that we have produced Example 6c by a mechanical, completely reliable method for removing recursion. Hopkins [42] has given other examples where **go to** at a low level supports high-level constructions.

But if you look at the above program again, you'll probably be just as shocked as I was when I first realized what has happened. I had always thought that the use of **go to** statements was a bit sinful, say a "venial sin"; but there was one kind of **go to** that I certainly had been taught to regard as a mortal sin, perhaps even unforgivable, namely one that goes into the middle of an iteration! Example 6c breaks the cardinal rule, yet it is perfectly easy to understand Example 6c by comparing it with Example 6b.

In this particular case we can remove the **go to**'s without difficulty; but in general, when a recursive call is embedded in several complex levels of control, there is no equally simple way to remove the recursion without resorting to something like Example 6c. As I say, it was a shock when I first ran across such an example. Later, Jim Horning confessed to me that he also was guilty, in the syntax-table-building program for the XPL system [65, p. 500], because XPL doesn't allow recursion; see also [54] [Chapter 3 of this volume]. Clearly a new doctrine about sinful **go to**'s is needed—some sort of "situation ethics."

The new morality that I propose may perhaps be stated thus: "Certain **go to** statements that arise in connection with well-understood transformations are acceptable, provided that the program documentation explains what the transformation was." The use of four-letter words like **goto** can occasionally be justified even in the best of company.

This situation is very similar to what people have commonly encountered when proving a program correct. To demonstrate the validity of a typical program Q, it is usually simplest and best to prove that some rather simple but less efficient program P is correct and then to prove that P can be transformed into Q by a sequence of valid optimizations. I'm saying that a similar thing should be considered standard practice for all but the simplest software programs. Programmers should create a program P that is readily understood and well-documented, and then should optimize it into a program Q that is very efficient. Program Q may contain **go to** statements and other low-level features, but the transformation from P to Q should be accomplished by completely reliable and well-documented "mechanical" operations.

At this point many readers will say, "But programmers should only write P, and an optimizing compiler will produce Q." To this I say, "No, the optimizing compiler would have to be so complicated (much more so than anything we have now) that it will in fact be *un*reliable." I have another alternative to propose, a new class of software that will be far better.

Program Manipulation Systems

For 15 years or so I have been trying to think of how to write a compiler that really produces top quality code. For example, most of the `MIX` programs in my books are considerably more efficient than any of today's most visionary compiling schemes would be able to produce. I've tried to study the various techniques that a hand-coder like myself uses, and to fit them into some systematic and automatic system. A few years ago, several students and I looked at a typical sample of FORTRAN programs [49], and we all tried hard to see how a machine could produce code that would compete with our best hand-optimized object programs. We found ourselves always running up against the same problem: The compiler needs to be in a dialog with the programmer. It needs to know properties of the data, and whether certain cases can arise, etc. And we couldn't think of a good language in which to have such a dialog.

For some reason we all (especially me) had a mental block about optimization, namely that we always regarded it as a behind-the-scenes activity, to be done in the machine language, which the programmer isn't supposed to know. This veil was first lifted from my eyes in the fall of 1973, when I ran across a remark by Hoare [40] that, ideally, a language should be designed so that an optimizing compiler can describe its optimizations in the *source* language. Of course! Why hadn't I ever thought of it?

Once we have a suitable language, we will be able to have what seems to be emerging as the programming system of the future: an interactive *program manipulation system*, analogous to the many symbol-manipulation systems that are presently undergoing extensive development and experimentation. We are gradually learning about program transformations, which are more complicated than formula manipulations but really not very different. A program manipulation system is obviously what we've been leading up to, and I wonder why I never thought of it before. Of course, the idea isn't original with me; when I told Hoare, he said, "Exactly!" and referred me to recent work by Darlington and Burstall [17], which describes a system that removes some recursions from a LISP-like language (curiously, without introducing any **go to**'s). The system proposed by Darlington and Burstall also does some conversion of data structures (from sets to lists or bit strings) and some restructuring of a program by combining similar loops. I discovered later that program manipulation is just part of a much more ambitious project undertaken by Cheatham and Wegbreit [11]; another publication about source-code optimizations has also appeared recently (Schneck and Angel [83]). Since LISP programs are easily manipulated as LISP data objects, there has also been a rather extensive development of similar ideas in this domain, notably by Warren Teitelman (see [89, 90]). The time is clearly ripe for program manipulation systems, and a great deal of further work suggests itself.

A programmer using such a system writes a beautifully-structured, but possibly inefficient, program P, then interactively specifies transformations to make it efficient. Such a system will be much more powerful and reliable than a completely automatic one. We can also imagine the system manipulating measurement statistics concerning how much of the total running time is spent in each statement, since the programmer will want to know which parts of the program deserve to be optimized, and how much effect an optimization will really have. The original program P should be retained along with the transformation specifications, so that it can be properly understood and maintained as time passes. As I say, this idea certainly isn't my own; it is so exciting I hope that *everyone* soon becomes aware of its possibilities.

A "calculus" of program transformations is gradually emerging, a set of operations that can be applied to programs without rethinking the specific problem each time. I have already mentioned several of these transformations: doubling up of loops (Example 2a), changing final calls to **go to**'s (Example 6a), using a stack for recursions (Example 6c), and combining disjoint loops over the same range [17]. The idea of macro-expansions in general seems to find its most appropriate realization as part of a program manipulation system.

Another well-known example is the removal of invariant subexpressions from loops. We are all familiar with the fact that such subexpressions make a program more readable than the corresponding program would be with invariant subexpressions moved out of their loops; yet we consciously remove them when the running time of the program is important.

Still another type of transformation occurs when we go from high-level "abstract" data structures to low-level "concrete" ones (see Hoare's chapter in [16] for numerous examples). In the case of Example 6c, we can replace the stack by an array and a pointer, arriving at

Example 6d

```
procedure treeprint(t); integer t; value t;
  begin integer array S[1 : n]; integer k; k := 0;
L1: loop while t ≠ 0:
        k := k + 1; S[k] := t;
        t := L[t]; go to L1;
L2:     t := S[k]; k := k − 1;
        print(A[t]); t := R[t];
    repeat;
    if k ≠ 0 then go to L2 fi;
  end.
```

Here the programmer must specify a safe value for the maximum stack size n, in order to make the transformation legitimate. Alternatively, we may wish to implement the stack by a linked list. This choice can usually be made without difficulty, and it illustrates another area in which interaction is preferable to completely automatic transformations.

Recursion vs. Iteration

Before leaving the *treeprint* example, I would like to pursue the question of **go to** elimination from Example 6c, since this leads to some interesting issues. It is clear that the first **go to** is just a simple iteration, and a little further study shows that Example 6c is just one simple iteration inside another, namely (in Dahl's syntax)

Example 6e

```
procedure treeprint(t); integer t; value t;
  begin integer stack S; S := empty;
    loop:
      loop while t ≠ 0:
        S <= t;
        t := L[t];
      repeat;
    while nonempty(S):
      t <= S;
      print(A[t]);
      t := R[t];
    repeat;
  end.
```

Furthermore, there is a rather simple way to understand this program, by providing suitable "loop invariants." At the beginning of the first (outer) loop, suppose the stack contents from top to bottom are $t_n, \ldots, t_1$ for some $n > 0$; then the procedure's remaining duty is to accomplish the effect of

treeprint(t);
print$(A[t_n])$; *treeprint*$(R[t_n])$;
. . . ;
print$(A[t_1])$; *treeprint*$(R[t_1])$; (∗)

In other words, the purpose of the stack is to record postponed obligations to print the A's and right subtrees of certain nodes. Once this concept is grasped, the meaning of the program is clear and we can even see how we might have written it without ever thinking of a recursive formulation or a **go to** statement: The innermost loop ensures $t = 0$, and afterwards the program reduces the stack, maintaining (∗) as the condition to be fulfilled, at key points in the outer loop.

A careful programmer might notice a source of inefficiency in this program: When $L[t] = 0$, we put t on the stack, then take it off again. If there are n nodes in a binary tree, about $n/2$ on the average, will have $L[t] = 0$, so we might wish to avoid this extra computation. It isn't easy to do that to Example 6e without major surgery on the structure; but it *is* easy to modify Example 6c (or 6d), by simply bracketing the source of inefficiency, including the **go to** and the label and all.

Example 6f

```
procedure treeprint(t); value t; integer t;
  begin integer stack S; S := empty;
L1: loop while t ≠ 0:
L3:   if L[t] ≠ 0
      then S <= t; t := L[t]; go to L1;
L2:     t <= S;
      fi;
      print(A[t]);
      t := R[t];
    repeat;
    if nonempty(S) then go to L2 fi;
  end.
```

Here we notice that a further simplification is possible: The statement **go to** *L1* can become **go to** *L3* because t is known to be nonzero.

An equivalent **go to**-free program analogous to Example 6e is

Example 6g

```
procedure treeprint(t); value t; integer t;
  begin integer stack S; S := empty;
    loop until finished:
      if t ≠ 0
      then
        loop while L[t] ≠ 0:
          S <= t;  t := L[t];
        repeat;
      else
        if nonempty(S)
        then t <= S;
        else finished;
        fi;
      fi;
```

```
      print(A[t]);
      t := R[t];
   repeat;
end.
```

I derived this program by thinking of the loop invariant (∗) in Example 6e and acting accordingly, *not* by trying to eliminate the **go to**'s from Example 6f. So I know this program is well structured, and I therefore haven't succeeded in finding an example of recursion removal where **go to**'s are strictly necessary. It is interesting, in fact, that our transformations originally intended for efficiency led us to new insights and to programs that still possess decent structure. However, I still feel that Example 6f is easier to understand than 6g, given that the reader is told the recursive program it comes from and the transformations that were used. The recursive program is trivially correct, and the transformations require only routine verification; by contrast, a mental leap is needed to invent (∗).

Does recursion elimination help? Clearly there won't be much gain in this example if the *print* routine itself is the bottleneck. But let's replace *print*$(A[t])$ by

$$i := i + 1; \quad B[i] := A[t];$$

i.e., instead of printing the tree, let's assume that we merely want to transfer its contents to some other array B. Then we can expect to see an improvement.

After making this change, I tried the recursive Example 6 vs. the iterative Example 6d on the two main ALGOL compilers available to me. Normalizing the results so that Example 6d takes 1.0 units of time per node of the tree, with subscript checking suppressed, I found that the corresponding recursive version took about 2.1 units of time per node using our ALGOL W compiler for the 360/67; and the ratio was 1.16 using the SAIL compiler for the PDP-10. (Incidentally, the relative run-times for Example 6f were 0.8 with ALGOL W, and 0.7 with SAIL. When subscript ranges were dynamically checked, ALGOL W took 1.8 units of time per node for the nonrecursive version, and 2.8 with the recursive version; SAIL's figures were 1.28 and 1.34.)

Boolean Variable Elimination

Another important program transformation, somewhat less commonly known, is the removal of Boolean variables by code duplication. The following example is taken from Dijkstra's treatment [24, pp. 91–93] of

Hoare's "Quicksort" algorithm. The idea is to rearrange a sequence of array elements $A[m] \dots A[n]$ so that they are partitioned into two parts: The left part $A[m] \dots A[j-1]$, for some appropriate j, will contain all the elements less than some given value v; the right part $A[j+1] \dots A[n]$ will contain all the elements greater than v; and the element $A[j]$ lying between these parts will be equal to v. Partitioning is done by scanning from the left until finding an element greater than v, then scanning from the right until finding an element less than v, then scanning from the left again, and so on, moving the offending elements to the opposite side, until the two scans come together; a Boolean variable *up* is used to distinguish the left scan from the right.

Example 7

```
i := m; j := n; v := A[j];
up := true;
loop:
   if up then if A[i] > v then A[j] := A[i]; up := false fi;
   else if v > A[j] then A[i] := A[j]; up := true fi;
   fi;
   if up then i := i + 1 else j := j − 1 fi;
while i < j repeat;
A[j] := v;
```

The manipulation and testing of *up* is rather time-consuming here. We can, in general, eliminate a Boolean variable by storing its current value in the program counter—by duplicating the program, letting one part of the text represent **true** and the other part **false**, with jumps between the two parts in appropriate places. Example 7 therefore becomes

Example 7a

```
        i := m; j := n; v := A[j];
        loop: if A[i] > v then A[j] := A[i]; go to upf fi;
upt: i := i + 1;
        while i < j repeat; go to common;
        loop: if v > A[j] then A[i] := A[j]; go to upt fi;
upf: j := j − 1;
        while i < j repeat;
common: A[j] := v;
```

Again we have come up with a program that has jumps into the middle of iterations, yet we can understand it since we know that it came from a previously understood program, by way of an understandable transformation.

Of course this program is messier than the first, and we must ask again if the gain in speed is worth the cost. If we are writing a sort procedure that will be used many times, we will be interested in the speed. The average running time of Quicksort was analyzed by Hoare in his 1962 paper on the subject [34], and it turns out that the body of the loop in Example 7 is performed about $2N \ln N$ times while the statement *up* := **false** is performed about $(N \ln N)/3$ times, if we are sorting N elements. All other parts of the overall sorting program (not shown here) have a running time of order N or less, so when N is reasonably large the speed of the inner loop governs the speed of the entire sorting process. (Incidentally, a recursive version of Quicksort will run just about as fast, since the recursion overhead is not part of the inner loop. But in this case the removal of recursion is of great value for another reason, because it cuts the auxiliary stack space requirement from order N to order $\log N$.)

Using these facts about inner loop times, we can make a quantitative comparison of Examples 7 and 7a. As with Example 1, it seems best to make two comparisons, one with the assembly code that a decent programmer would write for the examples, and the other with the object code produced by a typical compiler that does only local optimizations. The assembly-language programmer will keep i, j, v, and *up* in registers, while a typical compiler will not keep variables in registers from one statement to another unless they happen to be there by coincidence. Under these assumptions, the asymptotic running time for an entire Quicksort program based on these routines will be

	Assembled	*Compiled*
Example 7	$20\frac{2}{3}N \ln N$	$55\frac{1}{3}N \ln N$
Example 7a	$15\frac{1}{3}N \ln N$	$40N \ln N$

expressed in memory references to data and instructions. So Example 7a saves more than 25% of the sorting time.

I showed this example to Dijkstra, cautioning him that the **go to** leading into an iteration might be a terrible shock. I was extremely pleased to receive his reply [29]:

> Your technique of storing the value of *up* in the order counter is, of course, absolutely safe. I did not faint! I am in no sense "afraid" of a program constructed that way, but I cannot consider it beautiful: it is really the same repetition with the same terminating condition, that "changes color" as the computation proceeds.

He went on to say that he looks forward to the day when machines are so fast that we won't be under pressure to optimize our programs; yet

> For the time being I could not agree more with your closing remarks: if the economies matter, apply "disciplined optimalization" to a nice program, the correctness of which has been established beyond reasonable doubt. Your massaging of the program text is then no longer trickery ad hoc, it is perfectly safe and sound.

It is hard for me to express the joy that this letter gave me; it was like having all my sins forgiven, since I need no longer feel guilty about my optimized programs.

Coroutines

Several of the people who read the first draft of this study observed that Example 7a can perhaps be understood more easily as the result of eliminating *coroutine* linkage instead of Boolean variables. Consider the following program:

Example 7b

```
coroutine move i;
  loop: if A[i] > v
    then A[j] := A[i]; resume move j;
    fi;
    i := i + 1;
  while i < j repeat;
coroutine move j;
  loop: if v > A[j]
    then A[i] := A[j]; resume move i;
    fi;
    j := j − 1;
  while i < j repeat;
i := m; j := n; v := A[j];
call move i;
A[j] := v;
```

When a coroutine is "resumed," let's assume that it begins after its own **resume** statement; and when a coroutine terminates, let's assume that the most recent **call** statement is thereby completed. (Actual coroutine linkage is slightly more involved, see Chapter 3 of [16], but this description will suffice for our purposes.) Under these conventions, Example 7b is precisely equivalent to Example 7a. At the beginning of *move i* we know that $A[k] \le v$ for all $k < i$, and that $i < j$, and that $\{A[m], \ldots, A[j-1], A[j+1], \ldots, A[n]\} \cup \{v\}$ is a permutation of the original contents of $\{A[m], \ldots, A[n]\}$; a similar statement holds at the beginning of *move j*. This separation into two coroutines can be said to make Example 7b conceptually simpler than Example 7; but on the other hand, the idea of coroutines admittedly takes some getting used to.

Christopher Strachey once told me about the example that first convinced him of the importance of coroutines as control structures. Consider two binary trees represented as in Examples 5 and 6, with their A array information in increasing order as we traverse the trees in symmetric order of their nodes. The problem is to *merge* these two array sequences into one ordered sequence. This requires traversing both trees more or less asynchronously, in symmetric order, so we need two versions of Example 6 running cooperatively. A conceptually simple solution to this problem can be written with coroutines, or by forming an equivalent program that expresses the coroutine linkage in terms of **go to** statements; it appears to be cumbersome (though not impossible) to do the job without using either feature.

Quicksort: A Digression

Dijkstra also sent another instructive example in his letter [28]. He decided to create the program of Example 7 from scratch, as if Hoare's algorithm had never been invented, starting instead with modern ideas of semi-automatic program construction based on the following *invariant* relation:

$$\begin{aligned} &v = A[n] \\ &\wedge \forall k(m \le k < i \Longrightarrow A[k] \le v) \\ &\wedge \forall k(j < k \le n \Longrightarrow A[k] \ge v). \end{aligned}$$

The resulting program is unusual, yet perhaps cleaner than Example 7:

```
i := m; j := n − 1; v := A[n];
loop while i ≤ j:
   if A[j] ≥ v then j := j − 1;
   else A[i] :=: A[j]; i := i + 1;
   fi;
repeat;
if j ≤ m then A[m] :=: A[n]; j := m fi;
```

Here ":=:" denotes the interchange (i.e., swap) operation. At the conclusion of this program, the A array will be different than before, but we will have the array partitioned as desired for sorting (i.e., the elements $A[m] \ldots A[j]$ are $\leq v$ and the elements $A[j+1] \ldots A[n]$ are $\geq v$).

Unfortunately, however, this "pure" program is less efficient than Example 7, and Dijkstra noted that he didn't like it very much himself. In fact, Quicksort is really quick in practice because there is a method that is even better than Example 7a: A good Quicksort routine will have a faster inner loop, which avoids most of the "$i < j$" tests. Dijkstra recently [29] sent me another approach to the problem, which leads to a much better solution. First we can abstract the situation by considering any notions "small" and "large" so that: (a) an element $A[i]$ is never both small and large simultaneously; (b) some elements might be neither small nor large; (c) we wish to rearrange an array so that all small elements precede all large ones; and (d) there is at least one element that is not small, and at least one that is not large. Then we can write the following program in terms of this abstraction.

Example 8

```
i := m; j := n;
loop:
   loop while A[i] is small:
      i := i + 1; repeat;
   loop while A[j] is large:
      j := j − 1; repeat;
while i < j:
   A[i] :=: A[j];
   i := i + 1; j := j − 1;
repeat;
```

At the beginning of the first (outer) loop we know that $A[k]$ is not large for $m \leq k < i$, and that $A[k]$ is not small for $j < k \leq n$; also that there exists a k such that $i \leq k \leq n$ and $A[k]$ is not small, and a k such that $m \leq k \leq j$ and $A[k]$ is not large. The operations in the loop are easily seen to preserve these "invariant" conditions. Note that the inner loops are now extremely fast, and that they are guaranteed to terminate; therefore the proof of correctness is simple. At the conclusion of the outer loop we know that $A[m] \ldots A[i-1]$ and $A[j]$ are not large, that $A[i]$ and $A[j+1] \ldots A[n]$ are not small, and that $m \leq j \leq i \leq n$.

Applying this to Quicksort, we can set $v := A[n]$ and write

"$A[i] < v$" in place of "$A[i]$ is small"

"$A[j] > v$" in place of "$A[j]$ is large"

in the above program. This gives a very pretty algorithm, which is essentially equivalent to the method published by Hoare [36] in his first major application of the idea of invariants, and discussed in his original paper on Quicksort [34]. Note that since $v = A[n]$, we know that the first execution of "**loop while** $A[j] > v$" will be trivial; we could move this loop to the end of the outer loop just before the final **repeat**. This would be slightly faster, but it would make the program harder to understand, so I would hesitate to do it.

The Quicksort partitioning algorithm actually given in my book [52] is better than Example 7a, but somewhat different from the program we have just derived. My version can be expressed as follows (assuming that $A[m-1]$ is defined and $\leq A[n]$):

```
i := m − 1; j := n; v := A[n];
loop until pointers have met:
   loop: i := i + 1;
   while A[i] < v repeat;
   if i ≥ j then pointers have met; fi;
   A[j] := A[i];
   loop: j := j − 1;
   while A[j] > v repeat;
   if i ≥ j then j := i; pointers have met; fi;
   A[i] := A[j];
repeat;
A[j] := v;
```

At the conclusion of this routine, the contents of $A[m] \ldots A[n]$ have been permuted so that $A[m] \ldots A[j-1]$ are $\leq v$ and $A[j+1] \ldots A[n]$ are $\geq v$ and $A[j] = v$ and $m \leq j \leq n$. The assembled version will make about $11N \ln N$ references to memory on the average, so this program saves 28% of the running time of Example 7a.

When I first saw Example 8 I was chagrined to note that it was easier to prove than my program, it was shorter, and (the crushing blow) it also seemed about 3% faster, because it tested "$i < j$" only half as often. My first mathematical analysis of the average behavior of Example 8 indicated that the asymptotic number of comparisons and exchanges would be the same, even though the partitioned subfiles included all N elements instead of $N - 1$ as in the classical Quicksort routine. But suddenly it occurred to me that my new analysis was incorrect because one of its fundamental assumptions breaks down: The elements of the two subfiles after partitioning by Example 8 are not in random order! This was a surprise, because randomness *is* preserved by the usual Quicksort routine. When the N keys are distinct, v will be the largest element in the left subfile, and the mechanism of Example 8 shows that v will tend to be near the left of that subfile. When that subfile is later partitioned, it is highly likely that v will move to the extreme right of the resulting right sub-subfile. So that right sub-subfile will be subject to a trivial partitioning by its largest element; we have a subtle loss of efficiency on the third level of recursion. I still haven't been able to analyze Example 8, but empirical tests have borne out my prediction that it is in fact about 15% slower than the book algorithm.

Therefore, there is no reason for anybody to use Example 8 in a sorting routine. Although it is slightly cleaner looking than the method in my book, it is noticeably slower, and we have nothing to fear by using a slightly more complicated method once it has been proved correct. Beautiful algorithms are, unfortunately, not always the most useful.

This is not the end of the Quicksort story (although I almost wish it was, since I think the preceding paragraph makes an important point). After I had shown Example 8 to my student, Robert Sedgewick, he found a way to modify it, preserving the randomness of the subfiles, thereby achieving both elegance and efficiency at the same time. Here is his revised program.

Example 8a

```
i := m − 1; j := n; v := A[n];
loop:
   loop: i := i + 1;
   while A[i] < v repeat;
   loop: j := j − 1;
   while A[j] > v repeat;
while i < j:
   A[i] :=: A[j];
repeat;
A[i] :=: A[n];
```

(As in the previous example, we assume that $A[m-1]$ is defined and $\le A[n]$, since the j pointer might run off the left end.) At the beginning of the outer loop the invariant conditions are now

$$m-1 \le i < j \le n;$$
$$A[k] \le v \text{ for } m-1 \le k \le i;$$
$$A[k] \ge v \text{ for } j \le k \le n;$$
$$A[n] = v.$$

It follows that Example 8a ends with

$$A[m]\dots A[i-1] \le v = A[i] \le A[i+1]\dots A[n]$$

and $m \le i \le n$; hence a valid partition has been achieved.

Sedgewick also found a way to improve the inner loop of the algorithm from my book, namely:

```
i := m − 1;  j := n;  v := A[n];
loop:
   loop: i := i + 1;  while A[i] < v repeat;
   A[j] := A[i];
   loop: j := j − 1;  while A[j] > v repeat;
while i < j;
   A[i] := A[j];
repeat;
if i ≠ j then j := j + 1;
A[j] := v;
```

Each of these programs leads to a Quicksort routine that makes about $10\frac{2}{3}N \ln N$ memory references on the average; the former is preferable (except on machines for which exchanges are clumsy), since it is easier to understand. Thus I learned again that I should always keep looking for improvements, even when I have a satisfactory program.

Axiomatics of Jumps

We have now discussed many different transformations on programs; and there are more that could have been mentioned (e.g., the removal of trivial assignments as in [48, exercise 1.1–3], or [52, exercise 5.2.1–33]). This should be enough to establish that a program manipulation system will have plenty to do.

Some of these transformations introduce **go to** statements that cannot be handled very nicely by situation indicators, and in general we might expect to find a few programs in which **go to** statements survive. Is it really a formidable job to understand such programs? Recent work has shown, fortunately, that the answer is no.

The **go to** statement has traditionally been troublesome in connection with correctness proofs and language semantics; for example, Hoare and Wirth presented an axiomatic definition of Pascal [39] in which everything but real arithmetic and the **go to** was defined formally. Clint and Hoare showed how to extend this to situation-indicator **go to**'s (i.e., those that don't lead into iterations or conditionals), but they stressed that the general case appears to be fraught with complications. Just recently, however, Hoare has discovered that there is, in fact, a rather simple way to give an axiomatic definition of **go to** statements; indeed, he now wishes quite frankly that it hadn't been quite so simple. For each label L in a program, the programmer should state a logical assertion $\alpha(L)$ that is to be true whenever we reach L. Then the axioms

$$\{\alpha(L)\}\ \textbf{go to}\ L\ \{\textbf{false}\}$$

plus the rules of inference

$$\{\alpha(L)\}S\{P\}\ \vdash\ \{\alpha(L)\}L: S\{P\}$$

are allowed in program proofs, and all properties of labels and **go to**'s will follow if the assertions $\alpha(L)$ are selected intelligently. One must, of course, carry out the entire proof using the same assertion $\alpha(L)$ for each appearance of the label L, and some choices of assertions will lead to more powerful results than others.

Informally, $\alpha(L)$ represents the desired state of affairs at label L; this definition says essentially that a program is correct if $\alpha(L)$ holds at L and before all "**go to** L" statements, and that control never "falls through" a **go to** statement to the following text. Stating the assertions $\alpha(L)$ is precisely analogous to formulating loop invariants. Thus, it is not difficult to deal formally with tortuous program structure if it turns out to be necessary; all we need to know is the "meaning" of each label.

Reduction of Complication

There is one remaining use of **go to** for which I have never seen a good replacement, and in fact it's a situation where I still think **go to** is the right idea. This situation typically occurs after a program has made a multiway branch to a rather large number of different but related cases. A little computation often suffices to reduce one case to another; and when we've reduced one problem to a simpler one, the most natural thing is for our program to **go to** the routine that solves the simpler problem.

For example, consider writing an interpretive routine (e.g., a microprogrammed emulator), or a simulator of another computer. After decoding the address and fetching the operand from memory, we do a multiway branch based on the operation code. Let's say the operations include no-op, add, subtract, jump on overflow, and unconditional jump. Then the subtract routine might be

subtract: *operand* := −*operand*; **go to** *add*;

the add routine might be

```
add: accum := accum + operand;
     tyme := tyme + 1;
     go to no op;
```

and jump on overflow might be

```
jov: if overflow
     then overflow := false; go to jump;
     else go to no op;
     fi;
```

I still believe that this is the correct way to write such a program.

Such situations aren't restricted to interpreters and simulators, although the foregoing is a particularly dramatic example. Multiway branching is an important programming technique that is all too often replaced by an inefficient sequence of if tests. Peter Naur recently wrote me that he considers the use of tables to control program flow as a basic idea of computer science that has been nearly forgotten; but he expects it will be ripe for rediscovery any day now. It is the key to efficiency in all the best compilers I have studied.

Some hints of this situation, where one problem reduces to another, have occurred in the examples above. Thus, after searching for x and discovering that it is absent, the *not found* routine can insert x into the table, thereby reducing the problem to the *found* case. Consider also our decision-table Example 4, and suppose that each period was to be followed by a carriage return instead of by an extra space. Then it would be natural to reduce the post-processing of periods to the return-carriage part of the program. In each case, a **go to** would be easy to understand.

If we need to find a way to do this without saying **go to**, we could extend Zahn's situation indicator scheme so that some situations are allowed to appear in the **then** ... **fi** part after we have begun to process other situations. This accommodates the above-mentioned examples very nicely; but of course it can be dangerous when misused, since it gives us back all the power of **go to**. A restriction that allows $\langle$ statement list $\rangle_i$ to refer to $\langle$ situation $\rangle_j$ only for $j > i$ would be less dangerous.

With such a language feature, we can't "fall through" a label (i.e., a situation indicator) when the end of the preceding code is reached; we must explicitly name each situation when we **go to** its routine. Prohibiting "fall through" means forcing a programmer to write "**go to** *common*" just before the label "*common*:" in Example 7a; surprisingly, such a change actually makes that program more readable, since it makes the symmetry plain. Also, the program fragment

subtract: *operand* := −*operand*; **go to** *add*;
add: *accum* := *accum* + *operand*;

seems to be more readable than if "**go to** *add*" were deleted. It is interesting to ponder why this is so.

3. Conclusions

This has been a long discussion, and very detailed, but a few points stand out. First, there are several kinds of programming situations in which **go to** statements are harmless, even desirable, if we are programming in ALGOL or PL/I. But secondly, new types of syntax are being developed that provide good substitutes for these harmless **go to**'s, without encouraging a programmer to create "logical spaghetti." One thing we haven't spelled out clearly, however, is what makes some **go to**'s bad and others acceptable. The reason is that we've really been directing our attention to the wrong issue, to the objective question of **go to** elimination instead of the important subjective question of program structure. In the words of John Brown [8], "The act of focusing our mightiest intellectual resources on the elusive goal of **go to**-less programs has helped us get our minds off all those really tough and possibly unresolvable problems and issues with which today's professional programmer would otherwise have to grapple." By writing this long chapter I don't want to add fuel to the controversy about **go to** elimination, since that topic has already assumed entirely too much significance; my goal is to lay that controversy to rest, and to help direct the discussion towards more fruitful channels.

Structured Programming

The real issue is structured programming, but unfortunately the term structured programming has become a catch phrase whose meaning is rarely understood in the same way by different people. Everybody knows it is a Good Thing, but as McCracken [64] has said, "Few people would venture a definition. In fact, it is not clear that there exists a simple definition as yet." Only one thing is really clear: Structured programming is *not* the process of writing programs and then eliminating their **go to** statements. We should be able to define structured programming without referring to **go to** statements at all; then the fact that **go to** statements rarely need to be introduced as we write programs should follow as a corollary.

Indeed, Dijkstra's original article [23], which gave structured programming its name, never mentioned **go to** statements at all! He directed attention to the critical question, "For what program structures can we give correctness proofs without undue labor, even if the programs get large?" By correctness proofs he explained that he does not mean formal derivations from axioms, he means any sort of proof (formal or informal) that is "sufficiently convincing"; and a proof really means an understanding. By program structure he means data structure as well as control structure.

We understand complex things by systematically breaking them into successively simpler parts and understanding how these parts fit together locally. Thus, we have different levels of understanding, and each of those levels corresponds to an *abstraction* of the detail at the level from which it is composed. For example, at one level of abstraction, we deal with an integer without considering whether it is represented in binary notation or two's complement, etc., while at deeper levels this representation may be important. At more abstract levels the precise value of the integer is not important except as it relates to other data.

David J. Wheeler mentioned this principle as early as 1952, at the first ACM National Conference [94]:

> When a programme has been made from a set of sub-routines the breakdown of the code is more complete than it would otherwise be. This allows the coder to concentrate on one section of a programme at a time without the overall detailed programme continually intruding.

Abstraction is easily understood in terms of BNF notation. A metalinguistic category like ⟨ assignment statement ⟩ is an abstraction that is composed in turn of two abstractions (a ⟨ left part list ⟩ and an ⟨ arithmetic expression ⟩), each of which is composed of abstractions such as ⟨ identifier ⟩ or ⟨ term ⟩, etc. We understand the program syntax as a whole by knowing the structural details that relate these abstract parts. The most difficult things to understand about a program's syntax are the identifiers, since their meaning is passed across several levels of structure. If all identifiers of an ALGOL program were changed to random meaningless strings of symbols, we would have great difficulty seeing what the type of a variable is and what the program means, but we would still easily recognize the more local features, such as assignment statements, expressions, subscripts, etc. (This inability for our eyes to associate a type or mode with an identifier has led to what I believe are fundamental errors of human engineering in the design of ALGOL 68, but that's another story. My own notation for stacks in Example 6c suffers from the same problem; it works in that example chiefly because t is lower case and S is upper case.) Larger nested structures are harder for the eye to see unless they are indented, but indentation makes the structure plain.

It would probably be better still if we changed our source language concept so that the program wouldn't appear as one long string. John McCarthy says "I find it difficult to believe that whenever I see a tree I am really seeing a string of symbols." Instead, we should give meaningful names to the larger constructs in our program that correspond to meaningful levels of abstraction, and we should define those levels of abstraction in one place, and merely use their names (instead of including the detailed code) when they are used to build larger concepts. Procedure names do this, but the language could easily be designed so that no action of calling a subroutine is implied.

From these remarks it is clear that sequential composition, iteration, and conditional branching present syntactic structures that the eye can readily assimilate; but a **go to** statement does not. The visual structure of **go to** statements is like that of flowcharts, except reduced to *one* dimension in our source languages. In two dimensions it is possible to perceive **go to** structure in small examples, but we rapidly lose our ability to understand larger and larger flowcharts; some intermediate levels of abstraction are necessary. As an undergraduate, in 1959, I published an octopus flowchart which I sincerely hope is the most horribly complicated that will ever appear in print; anyone who believes that flowcharts are the best way to understand a program is urged to look at this example [47]. (See also [30, p. 54] for a nice illustration of how **go to** statements make a PL/I program obscure, and see R. Lawrence Clark's hilarious spoof about linear representation of flowcharts by means of a "**come from** statement" [12].

I have felt for a long time that a talent for programming consists largely of the ability to switch readily from microscopic to macroscopic views of things, i.e., to change levels of abstraction fluently. I mentioned this [53] to Dijkstra, and he replied [27] with an excellent analysis of the situation:

> I feel somewhat guilty when I have suggested that the distinction or introduction of "different levels of abstraction" allow you to think about only one level at a time, ignoring completely the other levels. This is not true. You are trying to organize your thoughts; that is, you are seeking to arrange matters in such a way that you can concentrate on some portion, say with 90% of your conscious thinking, while the rest is temporarily moved away somewhat towards the background of your mind. But that is something quite different from "ignoring completely": you allow yourself temporarily to

> ignore details, but some overall appreciation of what is supposed to be or to come there continues to play a vital role. You remain alert for little red lamps that suddenly start flickering in the corners of your eye.

I asked Hoare for a short definition of structured programming, and he replied that it is "the systematic use of abstraction to control a mass of detail, and also a means of documentation which aids program design." I hope that my remarks above have made the abstract concept of abstraction clear; the second part of Hoare's definition (which was also stressed by Dijkstra in his original paper [23]) states that a good way to express the abstract properties of an unwritten piece of program often helps us to write that program, and to "know" that it is correct as we write it.

Syntactic structure is just one part of the picture, and BNF would be worthless if the syntactic constructs did not correspond to semantic abstractions. Similarly, a good program will be composed in such a way that each semantic level of abstraction has a reasonably simple relation to its constituent parts. We noticed in our discussion of Jacopini's theorem that every program can trivially be expressed in terms of a simple iteration that simulates a computer; but the trivial iteration has to carry the entire behavior of the program through the loop, so it is worthless as a level of abstraction.

An iteration statement should have a purpose that is reasonably easy to state; typically, this purpose is to make a certain Boolean relation **true** while maintaining a certain invariant condition satisfied by the variables. The Boolean condition is stated in the program, while the invariant should be stated in a comment, unless it is easily supplied by the reader. For example, the invariant in Example 1 is that $A[k] \neq x$ for $1 \leq k < i$, and in Example 2 it is the same, plus the additional relation $A[m+1] = x$. Both of these are so obvious that I didn't bother to mention them; but in Examples 6e and 8, I stated the more complicated invariants that arose. In each of those cases the program almost wrote itself once the proper invariant was given. Notice that an "invariant assertion" actually does vary slightly as we execute statements of the loop, but it comes back to its original form when we repeat the loop.

Thus, an iteration makes a good abstraction if we can assign a meaningful invariant to describe the local states of affairs as it executes, and if we can describe its purpose (e.g., to change one state to another). Similarly, an **if** ... **then** ... **else** ... **fi** statement will be a good abstraction if we can state an overall purpose for the statement as a whole.

We also need well-structured *data*; i.e., as we write the program we should have an abstract idea of what each variable means. This idea is also usually describable as an invariant relation, e.g., "m is the number of items in the table" or "x is the search argument" or "$L[t]$ is the number of the root node of node t's left subtree, or 0 if this subtree is empty" or "the contents of stack S are postponed obligations to do such and such."

Now let's consider the slightly more complex case of a situation-driven construct. This should also correspond to a meaningful abstraction, and our examples show what is involved: For each situation we give an (invariant) assertion that describes the relations which must hold when that situation occurs, and for the **loop until** we also give an invariant for the loop. A situation statement typically corresponds to an abrupt change in conditions so that a different assertion from the loop invariant is necessary.

An error exit can be considered well-structured for precisely this reason—it corresponds to a situation that is impossible according to the local invariant assertions. It is easiest to formulate assertions that assume nothing will go wrong, rather than to make the invariants cover all contingencies. When we jump out to an error exit we **go to** another level of abstraction having different assumptions.

As another simple example, consider binary search in an ordered array using the invariant relation $A[i] < x < A[j]$:

```
loop while i + 1 < j;
  k := (i + j) ÷ 2;
  if A[k] < x then i := k;
  else if A[k] > x then j := k;
    else cannot preserve the invariant fi;
  fi;
repeat;
```

Upon normal exit from this loop, the conditions $i + 1 \geq j$ and $A[i] < x < A[j]$ imply that $A[i] < x < A[i+1]$, i.e., that x is not present. If the program comes to *cannot preserve the invariant* (because $x = A[k]$), it wants to **go to** another set of assumptions. The situation-driven construct provides a level at which it is appropriate to specify the other assumptions.

Another good illustration occurs in Example 6g; the purpose of the main **if** statement is to find the first node whose A value should be printed. If there is no such t, the situation *finished* has clearly occurred; it is better to regard the **if** statement as having the stated abstract purpose without considering that t might not exist.

With go to Statements

We can also consider **go to** statements from the same point of view; when do they correspond to a good abstraction? We've already mentioned that **go to**'s do not have a syntactic structure that the eye can grasp automatically; but in this respect they are no worse off than variables and other identifiers. When a variable or label is given a meaningful name corresponding to the abstraction (N.B. *not* a numeric label!), we need not apologize for the lack of syntactic structure. And the appropriate abstraction for a label is an invariant essentially like the assertions specified for a situation.

In other words, we can indeed consider **go to** statements as part of systematic abstraction; all we need is a clearcut notion of exactly what it means to **go to** each label. This should come as no great surprise. After all, a lot of computer programs have been written using **go to** statements during the last 25 years, and those programs haven't all been failures! Some programmers have clearly been able to master structure and exploit it; not as consistently, perhaps, as in modern-day structured programming, but not inflexibly either. By now, many people who have never had any special difficulty writing correct programs have naturally been somewhat upset after being branded as sinners, especially when they know perfectly well what they're doing; so they have understandably been less than enthusiastic about "structured programming" as it has been advertised to them.

My feeling is that it's certainly possible to write well-structured programs with **go to** statements. For example, Dijkstra's 1968 program about concurrent process control [22] used three **go to** statements, all of which were perfectly easy to understand; and I think at most two of these would have disappeared from his code if ALGOL 60 had had a **while** statement. But **go to** is hardly ever the best alternative now, since better language features are appearing. If the invariant for a label is closely related to another invariant, we can usually save complexity by combining those two into one abstraction, using something other than **go to** for the combination.

There is also another problem, namely, at what level of abstraction should we introduce a label? This however is like the analogous problem for variables, and the general answer is still unclear in both cases. Aspects of data structure are often postponed, but sometimes variables are defined and passed as "parameters" to other levels of abstraction. There seems to be no clearcut idea as yet about a set of syntax conventions, relating to the definition of variables, that would be most appropriate to structured programming methodology; but for each particular problem there seems to be an appropriate level.

Efficiency

In our previous discussion we concluded that premature emphasis on efficiency is a big mistake, which may well be the source of most programming complexity and grief. We should ordinarily keep efficiency considerations in the background when we formulate our programs. We need to be subconsciously aware of the data processing tools available to us, but we should strive most of all for a program that is easy to understand and almost sure to work. (Most programs are probably only run once; and I suppose in such cases we needn't be too fussy about even the structure, much less the efficiency, as long as we are happy with the answers.)

When efficiencies do matter, however, the good news is that only a very small fraction of the code is usually involved in any significant way. And when it is desirable to sacrifice clarity for efficiency, we have seen that it *is* possible to produce reliable programs that can be maintained over a period of time, if we start with a well-structured program and then use well-understood transformations that can be applied mechanically. We shouldn't attempt to understand the resulting program as it appears in its final form; it should be thought of as the result of the original program modified by specified transformations. We can envision program manipulation systems that will facilitate making and documenting these transformations.

In this regard I would like to quote some observations made recently by Pierre-Arnoul de Marneffe [61]:

> In civil engineering design, it is presently a mandatory concept known as the "Shanley Design Criterion" to collect several functions into one part ... If you make a cross-section of, for instance, the German V-2, you find external skin, structural rods, tank wall, etc. If you cut across the Saturn-B moon rocket, you find only an external skin which is at the same time a structural component and the tank wall. Rocketry engineers have used the "Shanley Principle" thoroughly when they use the fuel pressure inside the tank to improve the rigidity of the external skin! ... People can argue that structured programs, even if they work correctly, will look like laboratory prototypes where you can discern all the individual components, but which are not daily usable. Building "integrated" products is an engineering principle as valuable as structuring the design process.

He goes on to describe plans for a prototype system that will automatically assemble integrated programs from well-structured ones that have been written top-down by stepwise refinement.

Today's hardware designers certainly know the advantages of integrated circuitry, but of course they must first understand the separate circuits before the integration is done. The V-2 rocket would never have been airborne if its designers had originally tried to combine all its functions. Engineering has two phases, structuring and integration; we ought not to forget either one, but it is best to hold off the integration phase until a well-structured prototype is working and understood. As stated by Weinberg [93], the former regimen of analysis/coding/debugging should be replaced by analysis/coding/debugging/improving.

The Future

It seems clear that languages somewhat different from those in existence today would enhance the preparation of structured programs. We will perhaps eventually be writing only small modules that are identified by name as they are used to build larger ones, so that devices like indentation, rather than delimiters, might become feasible for expressing local structure in the source language. (See the discussion following Landin's paper [57].) Although our examples don't indicate this, it turns out that a given level of abstraction often involves several related routines and data definitions; for example, when we decide to represent a table in a certain way, we simultaneously want to specify the routines for storing and fetching information from that table. The next generation of languages will probably take into account such related routines.

Program manipulation systems appear to be a promising future tool that will help programmers to improve their programs and to enjoy making the improvements. The standard operating procedure nowadays is usually to hand code critical portions of a routine in assembly language. Let us hope such assemblers will die out, and we will see several levels of language instead: At the highest levels we will be able to write abstract programs, while at the lowest levels we will be able to control storage and register allocation, and to suppress subscript range checking, etc. With an integrated system it will be possible to do debugging and analysis of the transformed program using a higher level language for communication. All levels will, of course, exhibit program structure syntactically so that our eyes can grasp it.

I guess the big question, although it really shouldn't be so big, is whether or not the ultimate language will have **go to** statements in its higher levels, or whether **go to** will be confined to lower levels. I personally wouldn't mind having **go to** in the highest level, just in case I really need it; but I probably would never use it, if the general iteration and situation constructs suggested in this chapter were present. As soon as people learn to apply principles of abstraction consciously, they won't see the need for **go to**, and the issue will just fade away. On the other hand, W. W. Peterson told me about his experience teaching PL/I to beginning programmers: he taught them to use **go to** only in unusual special cases where **if** and **while** aren't right, but he found [78] that "A disturbingly large percentage of the students ran into situations that require **go to**'s, and sure enough, it was often because **while** didn't work well to their plan, but almost invariably because their plan was poorly thought out." Because of arguments like this, I'd say we should, indeed, abolish **go to** from the high-level language, at least as an experiment in training people to formulate their abstractions more carefully. This does have a beneficial effect on style, although I would not make such a prohibition if the new language features described above were not available. The question is whether we should ban it, or educate against it; should we attempt to legislate program morality? In this case I vote for legislation, with appropriate legal substitutes in place of the former overwhelming temptations.

A great deal of research must be done if we're going to have the desired language by 1984. Control structure is merely one simple issue, compared to questions of abstract data structure. It will be a major problem to keep the total number of language features within tight limits. And we must especially look at problems of input/output and data formatting, in order to provide a viable alternative to COBOL.

Acknowledgments

I've benefited from a truly extraordinary amount of help while preparing this chapter. The following individuals provided me with a total of 144 pages of single-spaced comments, plus six hours of conversation and four computer listings: Frances E. Allen, Forest Baskett, G. V. Bochmann, Per Brinch Hansen, R. M. Burstall, Vinton Cerf, T. E. Cheatham, Jr., John Cocke, Ole-Johan Dahl, Peter J. Denning, Edsger Dijkstra, James Eve, K. Friedenbach, Donald I. Good, Ralph E. Gorin, Leo Guibas, C. A. R. Hoare, Martin Hopkins, James J. Horning, B. M. Leavenworth, Henry F. Ledgard, Ralph L. London, Zohar Manna, W. M. McKeeman, Harlan D. Mills, Peter Naur, Kjell Overholt, James Peterson, W. Wesley Peterson, Mark Rain, John Reynolds, Barry K. Rosen, E. Satterthwaite, Jr., D. V. Schorre, Jacob T. Schwartz, Richard L. Sites, Richard Sweet, Robert D. Tennent, Niklaus Wirth, M. Woodger, William A. Wulf,

Charles T. Zahn. These people unselfishly devoted hundreds of hours to helping me revise the first draft; and I'm sorry that I wasn't able to reconcile all of their interesting points of view. In many places I have shamelessly used their suggestions without an explicit acknowledgment; this essay is virtually a joint paper with 30 to 40 co-authors! However, any mistakes it contains are my own.

Appendix

In order to make some quantitative estimates of efficiency, I have counted memory references for data and instructions, assuming a multiregister computer without cache memory. Thus, each instruction costs one unit, plus another if it refers to memory; small constants and base addresses are assumed to be either part of the instruction or present in a register. Here are the code sequences developed for the first two examples, assuming that a typical assembly-language programmer or a very good optimizing compiler is at work.

Label	*Instruction*	*Cost*	*Times*
Example 1	r1 ← 1	1	1
	r2 ← m	2	1
	r3 ← x	2	1
	to *test*	1	1
loop:	A[r1] : r3	2	$n - a$
	to *found* **if** =	1	$n - a$
	r1 ← r1 + 1	1	$n - 1$
test:	r1 : r2	1	n
	to *loop* **if** ≤	1	n
not found:	m ← r1	2	a
	A[r1] ← r3	2	a
	B[r1] ← 0	2	a
found:	r4 ← B[r1]	2	1
	r4 ← r4 + 1	1	1
	B[r1] ← r4	2	1
Example 2	r2 ← m	2	1
	r3 ← x	2	1
	A[r2 + 1] ← r3	2	1
	r1 ← 0	1	1
loop:	r1 ← r1 + 1	1	n
	A[r1] : r3	2	n
	to *loop* **if** ≠	1	n
	r1 : r2	1	1
	to *found* **if** ≤	1	1
not found:	m ← r1	etc., as in Example 1.	

A traditional "90% efficient compiler" would render the first example as follows:

Label	*Instruction*	*Cost*	*Times*
Example 1	$\mathrm{r1} \leftarrow 1$	1	1
	to *test*	1	1
incr:	$\mathrm{r1} \leftarrow i$	2	$n-1$
	$\mathrm{r1} \leftarrow \mathrm{r1}+1$	1	$n-1$
test:	$\mathrm{r1} : m$	2	n
	to *not found* **if** $>$	1	n
	$i \leftarrow \mathrm{r1}$	2	$n-a$
	$\mathrm{r2} \leftarrow A[\mathrm{r1}]$	2	$n-a$
	$\mathrm{r2} : x$	2	$n-a$
	to *found* **if** $=$	1	$n-a$
	to *incr*	1	$n-1$
not found:	$\mathrm{r1} \leftarrow m$	2	a
	$\mathrm{r1} \leftarrow \mathrm{r1}+1$	1	a
	$i \leftarrow \mathrm{r1}$	2	a
	$m \leftarrow \mathrm{r1}$	2	a
	$\mathrm{r1} \leftarrow x$	2	a
	$\mathrm{r2} \leftarrow i$	2	a
	$A[\mathrm{r2}] \leftarrow \mathrm{r1}$	2	a
	$B[\mathrm{r2}] \leftarrow 0$	2	a
found:	$\mathrm{r1} \leftarrow i$	2	1
	$\mathrm{r2} \leftarrow B[\mathrm{r1}]$	2	1
	$\mathrm{r2} \leftarrow \mathrm{r2}+1$	1	1
	$B[\mathrm{r1}] \leftarrow \mathrm{r2}$	2	1

Answer to PL/I Problem, Page 26.

The variable `I` is increased before `FOUND` is tested. One way to fix the program is to insert "`I = I - FOUND;`" before the last statement. (Unfortunately.)

References

[1] Edward Ashcroft and Zohar Manna, "The translation of **go to** programs to **while** programs," *Information Processing 71*, Proceedings of IFIP Congress 71, **1** (Amsterdam: North-Holland, 1972), 250–255.

[2] F. Terry Baker and Harlan D. Mills, "Chief programmer teams," *Datamation* **19**,12 (December 1973), 58–61.

[3] D. W. Barron, *Recursive techniques in programming* (New York: American Elsevier, 1968), 64 pp.

[4] F. L. Bauer, "A philosophy of programming," University of London Special Lectures in Computer Science (October 1973): Lecture notes published by Mathematics Institute, Technical University of Munich, Germany.

[5] Daniel M. Berry, "Loops with normal and abnormal exits," *Modeling and Measurement Note 23*, Computer Science Department, University of California, Los Angeles, CA (1974), 39 pp.

[6] G. V. Bochmann, "Multiple exits from a loop without the GOTO'," *Communications of the ACM* **16**,7 (July 1973), 443–444.

[7] Corrado Böhm and Giuseppe Jacopini, "Flow-diagrams, Turing machines, and languages with only two formation rules," *Communications of the ACM* **9**,5 (May 1966), 366–371.

[8] John R. Brown, "In memoriam ... ", unpublished note (January 1974).

[9] J. Bruno and K. Steiglitz, "The expression of algorithms by charts," *Journal of the ACM* **19**,3 (July 1972), 517–525.

[10] W. A. Burkhard, "Nonrecursive tree traversal algorithms," in *Proceedings of the 7th Annual Princeton Conference on Information Sciences and Systems*, (Princeton, New Jersey: Princeton University Press, 1973), 403–405.

[11] T. E. Cheatham, Jr., and Ben Wegbreit, "A laboratory for the study of automating programming," in *Proceedings of the AFIPS 1972 Spring Joint Computer Conference* **40** (Montvale, New Jersey: AFIPS Press, 1972), 11–21.

[12] R. Lawrence Clark, "A linguistic contribution to GOTO-less programming," *Datamation* **19**,12 (December 1973), 62–63.

[13] M. Clint and C. A. R. Hoare, "Program proving: jumps and functions," *Acta Informatica* **1** (1972), 214–224.

[14] D. C. Cooper, "The equivalence of certain computations," *The Computer Journal* **9**,1 (May 1966), 45–52.

[15] D. C. Cooper, "Böhm and Jacopini's reduction of flow charts," *Communications of the ACM* **10**,8 (August 1967), 463, 473.

[16] Ole-Johan Dahl, Edsger W. Dijkstra, and C. A. R. Hoare, *Structured programming* (London: Academic Press, 1972), 220 pp.

[17] J. Darlington and R. M. Burstall, "A system which automatically improves programs," in *Proceedings of the 3rd International Joint Conference on Artificial Intelligence*, 20–23 August 1973, Stanford University, Stanford, CA (Menlo Park, California: Stanford Research Institute, 1973), 479–485.

[18] E. W. Dijkstra, "Recursive programming," *Numerische Mathematik* **2**,5 (1960), 312–318.

[19] E. W. Dijkstra, "Programming considered as a human activity," *Information Processing 1965*, Proceedings of IFIP Congress 1965 (Washington, D.C.: Spartan, 1965), 213–217.

[20] E. W. Dijkstra, "A constructive approach to the problem of program correctness," *BIT* **8** (1968), 174–186. [Uses **go to**.]

[21] Edsger W. Dijkstra, "Go to statement considered harmful," *Communications of the ACM* **11**,3 (March 1968), 147–148, 538, 541. [There are two instances of pages 147–148 in this volume; the *second* 147–148 is relevant here.]

[22] E. W. Dijkstra, "Solution of a problem in concurrent programming control," *Communications of the ACM* **9**,9 (September 1968), 569.

[23] E. W. Dijkstra, "Structured programming," in *Software engineering techniques*, J. N. Buxton and B. Randell [Eds.], NATO Scientific Affairs Division (Brussels, 1970), 84–88.

[24] Edsger W. Dijkstra, *EWD316: A Short Introduction to the Art of Programming*, Technical University Eindhoven, Eindhoven, The Netherlands (August 1971), 97 pp.

[25] Edsger W. Dijkstra, "The humble programmer,' *Communications of the ACM* **15**,10 (October 1972), 859–866.

[26] E. W. Dijkstra, "Prospects for a better programming language," in *High Level Languages*, C. Boon [Ed]., Infotech State of the Art Report **7** (1972), 217–232.

[27] E. W. Dijkstra, Personal communication (3 January 1973).

[28] E. W. Dijkstra, Personal communication (19 November 1973).

[29] E. W. Dijkstra, Personal communication (30 January 1974).

[30] James R. Donaldson, "Structured programming," *Datamation* **19**, 12 (December 1973), 52–54.

[31] Bob Dylan, *Blonde on blonde*, record album produced by Bob Johnston (New York: Columbia Records, March 1966), Columbia C2S 841.

[32] Stanley Gill, "Automatic computing: Its problems and prizes," *The Computer Journal* **8**,3 (October 1965), 177–189.

[33] P. Henderson and R. Snowdon, "An experiment in structured programming," *BIT* **12** (1972), 38–53.

[34] C. A. R. Hoare, "Quicksort," *The Computer Journal* **5**,1 (1962), 10–15.

[35] C. A. R. Hoare, "An axiomatic approach to computer programming," *Communications of the ACM* **12**,10 (October 1969), 576–580, 583.

[36] C. A. R. Hoare, "Proof of a program: FIND," *Communications of the ACM* **14**,1 (January 1971), 39–45.

[37] C. A. R. Hoare, "A note on the for statement," *BIT* **12** (1972), 334–341.

[38] C. A. R. Hoare, "Prospects for a better programming language," in *High Level Languages*, C. Boon [Ed.], Infotech State of the Art Report **7** (1972), 327–343.

[39] C. A. R. Hoare and Niklaus Wirth, "An axiomatic definition of the programming language PASCAL," *Acta Informatica* **2** (1973), 335–355.

[40] C. A. R. Hoare, "Hints on programming language design," in *Computer systems Reliability*, C. J. Bunyan [Ed.], Infotech State of the Art Report **20** (1972), 505–534. Reprinted in *Essays in Computing Science*, C. B. Jones [Ed.] (Hemel Hempstead: Prentice-Hall International, 1989), 193–216.

[41] Martin E. Hopkins, "Computer aided software design," in *Software engineering techniques*, J. N. Buxton and B. Randell [Eds.], NATO Scientific Affairs Division (Brussels, 1970), 99–101.

[42] Martin E. Hopkins, "A case for the GOTO," *Proceedings of the ACM*, Boston, MA (August 1972), 787–790.

[43] T. E. Hull, "Would you believe structured FORTRAN?" *SIGNUM Newsletter* **8**,4 (October 1973), 13–16.

[44] Dan Ingalls, "The execution time profile as a programming tool," in *Compiler optimization*, 2nd Courant Computer Science Symposium, Randall Rustin [Ed.] (Englewood Cliffs, New Jersey: Prentice-Hall, 1972), 107–128.

[45] Robert A. Kelley and John R. Walters, "APLGOL-2, a structured programming system for APL," IBM Palo Alto Scientific Center report 320-3318 (August 1973), 29 pp.

[46] S. C. Kleene, "Representation of events in nerve nets," in *Automata Studies*, C. E. Shannon and J. McCarthy [Eds.] (Princeton, New Jersey: Princeton University Press, 1956), 3–40.

[47] Donald E. Knuth, "RUNCIBLE—Algebraic translation on a limited computer," *Communications of the ACM* **2**,11 (November 1959), 18–21. [There is a bug in the flowchart. The arc labeled "2" from the box labeled "θ:" in the upper left corner should go to the box labeled $R_M = 8003$.]

[48] Donald E. Knuth, Fundamental algorithms: *The Art of Computer Programming* **1** (Reading, Massachusetts: Addison-Wesley, 1968), 634 pp. Second edition, 1973.

[49] Donald E. Knuth, "An empirical study of FORTRAN programs," *Software—Practice and Experience* **1**,2 (April–June 1971), 105–133.

[50] Donald E. Knuth and Robert W. Floyd, "Notes on avoiding 'go to' statements," *Information Processing Letters* **1**,1 (February 1971), 23–31, 177.

[51] Donald E. Knuth, "George Forsythe and the development of Computer Science," *Communications of the ACM* **15**,8 (August 1972), 721–726.

[52] Donald E. Knuth, Sorting and Searching: *The Art of Computer Programming* **3** (Reading, Massachusetts: Addison-Wesley, 1973), 722 pp.

[53] Donald E. Knuth, *A review of 'Structured Programming'*, Stanford Computer Science Department report STAN-CS-73-371, Stanford University, Stanford, CA (June 1973), 25 pp.

[54] Donald E. Knuth and Jayme L. Szwarcfiter, "A structured program to generate all topological sorting arrangements," *Information Processing Letters* **2**,6 (April 1974), 153–157.

[55] S. Rao Kosaraju, "Analysis of structured programs," *Proceedings of the Fifth Annual ACM Symposium on Theory of Computation*

(May 1973), 240–252; *Journal of Computer and System Sciences* **9**,3 (December 1974), 232–255.

[56] P. J. Landin, "A correspondence between ALGOL 60 and Church's lambda-notation: part I," *Communications of the ACM* **8**,2 (February 1965), 89–101.

[57] P. J. Landin, "The next 700 programming languages," *Communications of the ACM* **9**,3 (March 1966), 157–166.

[58] B. M. Leavenworth, "Programming with(out) the GOTO," *Proceedings of the ACM*, Boston, MA (August 1972), 782–786.

[59] R. J. Lipton, S. C. Eisenstadt, and R. A. DeMillo, "The complexity of control structures and data structures," *Proceedings of the 7th ACM Symposium on Theory of Computation* (1975), 186–193. [Expanded versions published later in *Journal of the ACM* **23** (1976), 720–732; *Communications of the ACM* **21** (1978), 228–231; Journal of the ACM **27** (1980), 123–127.

[60] Zohar Manna and Richard J. Waldinger, "Towards automatic program synthesis," in Symposium on Semantics of Algorithmic Languages, E. Engeler [Ed.], *Lecture Notes in Mathematics* **188** (1971), 270–310.

[61] Pierre-Arnoul de Marneffe, *Holon programming: A survey*, Universite de Liege, Service Informatique, Liege, Belgium (1973), 135 pp.

[62] John McCarthy, "Recursive functions of symbolic expressions and their computation by machine, part I," *Communications of the ACM* **3**,4 (April 1960), 184–195.

[63] John McCarthy, "Towards a mathematical science of computation," *Information Processing 1962*, Proceedings of IFIP Congress 1962 (Amsterdam: North-Holland, 1963), 21–28.

[64] Daniel D. McCracken, "Revolution in programming," *Datamation* **19**,12 (December 1973), 50–52.

[65] W. M. McKeeman, J. J. Horning, and D. B. Wortman, *A compiler generator* (Englewood Cliffs, New Jersey: Prentice-Hall, 1970), 527 pp.

[66] Edna St. Vincent Millay, "Elaine"; cf. Bartlett's *Familiar Quotations*.

[67] Edward F. Miller, Jr., and George E. Lindamood, "Structured programming: top-down approach," *Datamation* **19**,12 (December 1973), 55–57.

[68] H. D. Mills, "Top-down programming in large systems," in *Debugging techniques in large systems*, Randall Rustin [Ed.] (Englewood Cliffs, New Jersey: Prentice-Hall, 1971), 41–55.

[69] H. D. Mills, "Mathematical foundations for structured programming," report FSC 72-6012, IBM Federal Systems Division, Gaithersburg, MD (February 1972), 62 pp.

[70] H. D. Mills, "How to write correct programs and know it," report FSC 73-5008, IBM Federal Systems Division, Gaithersburg, MD (1973), 26 pp.

[71] I. R. Nassi and E. A. Akkoyunlu, "Verification techniques for a hierarchy of control structures," Technical report 26, Department of Computer Science, State University of New York, Stony Brook, NY (January 1974), 48 pp. [See also Nassi's Ph.D. thesis, *Control Structure Semantics for Programming Languages* (Stony Brook, 1974), 98 pp.]

[72] Peter Naur [Ed.] et al., "Report on the algorithmic language ALGOL 60," *Communications of the ACM* **3**,5 (May 1960), 299–314.

[73] Peter Naur, "Go to statements and good Algol style," *BIT* **3** (1963), 204–205.

[74] Peter Naur, "Program translation viewed as a general data processing problem," *Communications of the ACM* **9**,3 (March 1966), 176–179.

[75] Peter Naur, "An experiment on program development," *BIT* **12** (1972), 347–365.

[76] D. Pager, "Some notes on speeding up certain loops by software, firmware, and hardware means," in *Computers and automata*, Jerome Fox [Ed.] (New York: John Wiley & Sons, 1972), 207–213; also in *IEEE Transactions on Computers* **C-21**,1 (January 1972), 97–100.

[77] W. W. Peterson, T. Kasami, and N. Tokura, "On the capabilities of **while**, **repeat**, and **exit** statements," *Communications of the ACM* **16**,8 (August 1973), 503–512.

[78] W. Wesley Peterson, Personal communication (2 April, 1974).

[79] Mark Rain and Per Holager, "The present most recent final word about labels in MARY," *Machine Oriented Languages Bulletin* **1** (Trondheim, Norway, October 1972), 18–26.

[80] Constance Reid, *Hilbert* (New YorkSpringer-Verlag, 1970), 290 pp.

[81] John Reynolds, "Fundamentals of structured programming," Systems and Information Science 555 course notes, Syracuse University, Syracuse, NY (Spring 1973).

[82] E. H. Satterthwaite, "Debugging tools for high level languages," *Software—Practice and Experience* **2**,3 (July–September 1972), 197–217.

[83] P. B. Schneck and Ellinor Angel, "A FORTRAN to FORTRAN optimizing compiler," *The Computer Journal* **16**,4 (1973), 322–330.

[84] D. V. Schorre, "META-II—a syntax-directed compiler writing language," *Proceedings of the ACM*, Philadelphia, PA (1964), paper D1.3.

[85] D. V. Schorre, "Improved organization for procedural languages," Tech memo TM 3086/002/00, Systems Development Corporation, Santa Monica, CA (8 September 1966), 8 pp.

[86] O. Shigo, T. Shimomura, S. Fujibayashi, and T. Maejima, "SPOT: an experimental system for structured programming" (in Japanese), *Conference Record*, Information Processing Society of Japan, 1973. [Translation available from the authors, Nippon Electric Company Ltd., Kawasaki, Japan.]

[87] C. Strachey, "Varieties of programming language," in *High Level Languages*, C. Boon [Ed.], Infotech State of the Art Report **7** (1972), 345–362.

[88] H. R. Strong, Jr., "Translating recursion equations into flowcharts," *Journal of Computer and System Sciences* **5** (1971), 254–285.

[89] W. Teitelman, "Toward a programming laboratory," in *Software Engineering Techniques*, J. N. Buxton and B. Randell [Eds.], NATO Scientific Affairs Division (Brussels, 1970), 137–149.

[90] W. Teitelman et al. "INTERLISP reference manual," Xerox Palo Alto Research Center, Palo Alto, CA, and Bolt Beranek and Newman, Inc. (1974).

[91] S. A. Walker and H. R. Strong, "Characterizations of flowchartable recursions," *Journal of Computer and System Sciences* **7** (1973), 404–447.

[92] Eberhard Wegner, "Tree-structured programs," *Communications of the ACM* **16**,11 (November 1973), 704–705.

[93] Gerald M. Weinberg, "The psychology of improved programming performance," *Datamation* **17**,11 (November 1972), 82–85.

[94] David J. Wheeler, "The use of subroutines in programmes," *Proceedings of the ACM*, Pittsburgh, PA (May 1952), 235–236.

[95] Niklaus Wirth, "On certain basic concepts of programming languages," Stanford Computer Science Report CS 65, Stanford, CA (May 1967), 30 pp.

[96] Niklaus Wirth, "PL360, a programming language for the 360 computers," *Journal of the ACM* **15**,1 (January 1968), 37–74.

[97] Niklaus Wirth, "Program development by stepwise refinement," *Communications of the ACM* **14**, 4 (April 1971), 221–227.

[98] N. Wirth, "The programming language Pascal," *Acta Informatica* **1**,1 (1971), 35–63.

[99] W. A. Wulf, D. B. Russell, and A. N. Habermann, "BLISS: A language for systems programming," *Communications of the ACM* **14**,12 (December 1971), 780–790.

[100] W. A. Wulf, "Programming without the goto," *Information Processing 71*, Proceedings of IFIP Congress 71, **1** (Amsterdam, North-Holland, 1972), 408–413.

[101] William A. Wulf, "A case against the GOTO," *Proceedings of the ACM*, Boston, MA (August 1972), 791–797.

[102] W. A. Wulf, Richard K. Johnson, Charles P. Weinstock, and Steven O. Hobbs, "The design of an optimizing compiler," Computer Science Department report, Carnegie-Mellon University, Pittsburgh, PA (December 1973), 103 pp.

[103] Charles T. Zahn, "A control statement for natural top-down structured programming," presented at Symposium on Programming Languages, Paris, 1974.

Chapter 3

A Structured Program to Generate All Topological Sorting Arrangements (1974)

[This paper by Donald E. Knuth and Jayme L. Szwarcfiter, originally published in Information Processing Letters (April 1974), deals with a problem that goes beyond the simple examples discussed in Chapter 2. Although this problem is still "academic" and rather small by comparison with a fullblown software system, it gives insight into the decomposition of large tasks into comprehensible subtasks.]

An algorithm for topological sorting was presented by Knuth [4] as an example of typical interaction between linked and sequential forms of data representation. The purpose of the present note is to extend the algorithm so that it generates *all* solutions of the topological sorting problem. The extended algorithm serves as an instructive example of several important general issues related to backtracking, procedures for changing recursion into iteration, manipulation of data structures, and the creation of well-structured programs.

Given a number n and a set of integer pairs (i, j), where $1 \le i,\ j \le n$, the problem of topological sorting is to find a permutation $x_1 x_2 \ldots x_n$ of $\{1, 2, \ldots, n\}$ such that i appears to the left of j for all pairs (i, j) that have been input. It is convenient to denote input pairs by writing the relation "$i \prec j$" and saying "i precedes j". The topological sorting problem is essentially equivalent to arranging the vertices of a directed graph into a straight line so that all arcs go from left to right. It is well known that such an arrangement is possible if and only if there are no oriented cycles in the graph, i.e., if and only if no relations of the form

$$i_1 \prec i_2, \quad i_2 \prec i_3, \quad \ldots, \quad i_k \prec i_1$$

exist in the input, for any $k \geq 1$. The problem in mathematical terms is to embed a given partial order into a linear (total) order.

A natural way to solve this problem is to let x_1 be an element having no predecessors, then to erase all relations of the form $x_1 \prec j$ and to let x_2 be an element $\neq x_1$ with no predecessors in the system as it now exists, then to erase all relations of the form $x_2 \prec j$, etc. It is not difficult to verify (cf. [4]) that this method will always succeed unless there is an oriented cycle in the input. Moreover, in a sense it is the *only* way to proceed, since x_1 must be an element without predecessors, and x_2 must be without predecessors when all relations $x_1 \prec j$ are deleted, etc. This observation leads naturally to an algorithm that finds *all* solutions to the topological sorting problem; it is a typical example of a "backtrack" procedure [2,3], where at every stage we consider a subproblem of the form "Find all ways to complete a given partial permutation $x_1 x_2 \ldots x_k$ to a topological sort $x_1 x_2 \ldots x_n$." The general method is to branch on all possible choices of x_{k+1}.

A central problem in backtrack applications is to find a suitable way to arrange the data so that it is easy to sequence through the possible choices of x_{k+1}; in this case we need an efficient way to discover the set of all elements $\neq \{x_1, \ldots, x_k\}$ which have no predecessors other than $x_1, \ldots, x_k$, and to maintain this knowledge efficiently as we move from one subproblem to another. It is not satisfactory merely to make a brute-force search through all n possibilities for x_{k+1}, since this typically makes the program on the order of n times slower than a method that avoids such searching.

The following procedure, written in an ALGOL-like language using "abstract" data structures (cf. Hoare [1]), shows how to solve the problem with only order n additional units of storage. The procedure is to be invoked by a main driver program of the form "read and prepare the input; *alltopsorts*(0)".

procedure *alltopsorts*(k); **integer** k; **value** k;
comment This procedure will output all topological sorting arrangements beginning with a sequence $x_1 \ldots x_k$ that has already been output. Let $R = \{1, 2, \ldots, n\} \backslash \{x_1, \ldots, x_k\}$ be the set of all vertices not yet output; the procedure assumes that, for all $y \in R$, the current value of global variable *count*[y] is the number of relations $z \prec y$ for $z \in R$, and that there is a linear list D containing precisely those elements $y \in R$ such that *count*[y] $= 0$. The execution of this procedure may cause temporary changes to the contents of D and the *count* array, but both will be restored to their entry values upon exit;

```
begin integer q, base;
  if D not empty then
    begin base := rightmost element of D;
      repeat set q to rightmost element of D and delete it from D;
        erase all relations of the form q ≺ j;
        output q in column k + 1;
        if k = n − 1 then newline;
        alltopsorts(k + 1);
        retrieve all relations of the form q ≺ j;
        insert q at the left of D;
      until rightmost element of D = base;
    end
end.
```

The operations of erasing and retrieving relations will respectively decrease and increase appropriate entries of the *count* array, and they will also respectively insert and delete elements at the *right* of list D.

Thus, if we suppose that D contains $y_1 \dots y_r$ on entry to *alltopsorts*, for $r \geq 1$, the procedure will first set $base := y_r$, then $q := y_r$. Then it will decrease $count[j]$ by 1 for each variable j such that $y_r \prec j$ was input; and if $z_1, \dots, z_s$ are the values of j whose count drops to zero at this time, D will be changed to $y_1 \dots y_{r-1} z_1 \dots z_s$. After outputting y_r, and doing *alltopsorts* beginning with $x_1 \dots x_k y_r$, the procedure will restore each *count* to its initial condition and will change D to $y_r y_1 \dots y_{r-1}$. The same process will then occur again with $q = y_{r-1}, y_{r-2} \dots, y_1$, until finally all sortings will have been produced and D will again be $y_1 \dots y_r$; then *alltopsorts* will exit. These remarks amount to a proof by recursion induction that the algorithm is correct, since termination is an obvious consequence of the fact that D contains at most $n - k$ entries.

Note that D operates as an *output-restricted deque*, since all deletions from D occur at its right and all insertions occur at its ends. Therefore we can represent D as a list with one-way linking. (It may be of interest to note that the authors' original algorithm took *base* and q from the left of D while inserting $z_1 \dots z_s$ and q at the right; this made D an input-restricted deque, so that two-way linking was originally needed. Thus, a slight perturbation of the algorithm removed the need for one link.) Our program below uses an array $link[0:n]$ to hold the pointers for D, which will be a circular list; a simple variable D points to the leftmost element, and $link[D]$ points to the rightmost.

The erasure and retrieval operations are not difficult but they require some comment. It is clear that a natural way to represent the input relations for this purpose is to have a list for each i of all j such that

$i \prec j$. If there are m input relations in all, entering in random order, we can handle this as in [4] by having integer arrays $top[1:n]$, $suc[1:m]$, $next[1:m]$, such that $top[i]$ is the index p of the first relation for i, and (if $p \neq 0$) $suc[p]$ is the corresponding j value and $next[p]$ is the index of the next such relation. The erasing operation is now easily programmed.

In order to convert the recursion to iteration, we will need a stack for the local variables q and *base*. (It is not necessary to save return addresses on the stack, since control always returns to one place when $k > 0$ and to another when $k = 0$; furthermore it is unnecessary to save k on the stack since it is easily updated across calls.) This suggests that we introduce arrays $q[1:n]$ and $base[1:n]$. However, since the *count* entries are zero for all items q on the stack, it is possible to save n locations by keeping an implicit "q stack" in the *count* array; thus, a simple variable t contains the value of q at the level just outside the current one, and $count[t]$ holds the value on the next level, etc.

Two more refinements will speed up the program. First, we can test D for emptiness before actually calling the procedure, thereby maintaining D as a nonempty list throughout the process; this is a big advantage, since empty circular lists are always very awkward. Second, we can realize that the procedure *alltopsorts* is called most often when $k = n-1$, and it can be greatly simplified in that case.

Putting these observations together yields the following efficient machine-oriented program.

```
procedure generate all topological sorting arrangements (m, n);
  integer m, n; value m, n; comment m relations on n elements;
begin integer array count, top[1 : n];
  integer array suc, next[1 : m];
  integer array link, base[0 : n];
  integer q, k, i, j, p, t, D, D1;
read and prepare the input:
  for j := 1 step 1 until n do count[j] := top[j] := 0;
  for k := 1 step 1 until m do
    begin read(i, j);
      suc[k] := j; next[k] := top[i];
      top[i] := k; count[j] := count[j] + 1;
    end;
  link[0] := D := 0;
  for j := 1 step 1 until n do
    begin if count[j] = 0 then
        begin link[D] := j; D := j end;
    end;
```

```
  if D = 0 then go to done else link[D] := link[0];
  k := 0; t := 0;
alltopsorts: if k = n − 1 then
    begin print(D) in column: (n); newline end
  else begin base[k] := link[D];
      repeat set q to rightmost and delete:
        q := link[D]; D1 := link[q];
      erase relations beginning with q:
        p := top[q];
        while p ≠ 0 do
          begin j := suc[p];   count[j] := count[j] − 1;
            if count[j] = 0 then
              begin if D = q then D := j else link[j] := D1;
                D1 := j;
              end;
              p := next[p];
            end;
          link[D] := D1;
          print(q) in column: (k + 1);
        recursive call:
          if D1 = q then
            begin comment input contains an oriented cycle, and
                    D is empty;
              go to done;
            end;
          count[q] := t;   t := q;
          k := k + 1;  go to alltopsorts;
        return when k positive: k := k − 1;
          q := t;   t := count[q];   count[q] := 0;
        retrieve relations beginning with q:
          p := top[q];
          while p ≠ 0 do
            begin j := suc[p];   count[j] := count[j] + 1;
            p := next[p];
            end;
        insert q at left: comment link[q] is still set properly;
          link[D] := q;   D := q;
        until link[D] = base[k];
      end;
    if k > 0 then go to return when k positive;
  done: end.
```

The example input

$$1 \prec 3, \quad 2 \prec 1, \quad 2 \prec 4, \quad 4 \prec 3, \quad 4 \prec 5$$

will cause this program to print the five solutions

```
2 1 4 3 5
      5 3
  4 5 1 3
    1 3 5
      5 3
```

Notice that redundant printing has been suppressed. Alternatively, of course, the statement "*print* (q) *in column*: $(k+1)$" could have been replaced by "*buffer*$[k+1] := q$", and "*newline*" replaced by "*printline*(*buffer*)".

This program is efficient in the sense that its inner loops are reasonably fast, it uses only $O(m+n)$ words of memory, and it takes at most $O(m+n)$ units of time per output. However, there may be tremendous amounts of output, since the number of topological sortings for large n is often very large. For example, when there are no input relations at all, all $n!$ permutations are produced. (Note that the number of digits printed in this worst case is not $n \cdot n!$, but $n+n(n-1)+n(n-1)(n-2)+\cdots+n! = \lfloor n!\,e \rfloor - 1$, about e per permutation on the average.)

The volume of output and the running time can be reduced to $O(n \cdot 2^n)$, if $O(2^n)$ more memory cells are allotted by modifying the recursive procedure so that it "remembers" similar situations. We can add a new global variable corresponding to the current value of the set $\{x_1, \ldots, x_k\}$, and have the procedure *alltopsorts* remember which sets it has seen before, and where this occurred in the output. Whenever a set is repeated, the output can now be replaced by a simple cross-reference to the appropriate line. Thus, the above example would reduce to

```
1: 2 1 4 3 5
2:       5 3
3:   4 5 1 3
4:     1 .. see line 1
```

Adding memory to recursive procedures is, of course, a standard way to speed them up. Compare the exponential running time of

integer procedure $F(n)$; **if** $n \le 1$ **then** n **else** $F(n-1)+F(n-2)$

to the linear running time of

for $n := 0$ **step** 1 **until** N **do**
  $F[n] :=$ **if** $n \le 1$ **then** n **else** $F[n-1]+F[n-2]$.

Our program contains the statement "**go to** return when k positive", which jumps *into* the **repeat** loop! Some people consider this disgraceful; but the detailed discussion in [5] [Chapter 2 of this volume] points out that this **go to** is not really harmful, because it has been obtained by straightforward modification of an original recursive program that was easily proved correct. The complete documentation of a program should include its abstract form and a discussion of the essentially mechanical transformations that led to the final optimized form. It is possible to remove this **go to**, but there would be no advantage in doing so. (See [5] for further examples and discussion.)

References

[1] Ole-Johan Dahl, Edsger W. Dijkstra, and C. A. R. Hoare, *Structured programming* (London: Academic Press, 1972), 220 pp.

[2] Robert W. Floyd, "Nondeterministic algorithms," *Journal of the ACM* **14** (1967), 636–644.

[3] Solomon W. Golomb and Leonard D. Baumert, "Backtrack programming," *Journal of the ACM* **12** (1965), 516–524.

[4] Donald E. Knuth, Fundamental algorithms: *The Art of Computer Programming* **1** (Reading, Massachusetts: Addison-Wesley, 1968), 634 pp. Second edition, 1973.

[5] Donald E. Knuth, "Structured programming with **go to** statements," *Computing Surveys* **6** (December 1974), 261–301. [Reprinted with minor changes in *Current Trends in Programming Methodology*, Raymond T. Yeh [Ed.], **1** (Englewood Cliffs, New Jersey: Prentice-Hall, 1977), 140–194; *Classics in Software Engineering*, Edward Nash Yourdon [Ed.] (New York: Yourdon Press, 1979), 259–321.]

[6] William M. Waite, "An efficient procedure for the generation of closed subsets," *Communications of the ACM* **10** (1967), 169–171.

Chapter 4

Literate Programming (1984)

[Ten years of additional experimentation led from the situation described in Chapters 1–3 to a new kind of system described in the following article, which was originally published in The Computer Journal, May 1984.]

Introduction

The past ten years have witnessed substantial improvements in programming methodology. This advance, carried out under the banner of "structured programming," has led to programs that are more reliable and easier to comprehend; yet the results are not entirely satisfactory. My purpose in the present paper is to propose another motto that may be appropriate for the next decade, as we attempt to make further progress in the state of the art. I believe that the time is ripe for significantly better documentation of programs, and that we can best achieve this by considering programs to be *works of literature*. Hence, my title: "Literate Programming."

Let us change our traditional attitude to the construction of programs. Instead of imagining that our main task is to instruct a *computer* what to do, let us concentrate rather on explaining to *human beings* what we want a computer to do.

The practitioner of literate programming can be regarded as an essayist, whose main concern is with exposition and excellence of style. Such an author, with thesaurus in hand, chooses the names of variables carefully and explains what each variable means. He or she strives for a program that is comprehensible because its concepts have been introduced in an order that is best for human understanding, using a mixture of formal and informal methods that nicely reïnforce each other.

I dare to suggest that such advances in documentation are possible because of the experiences I've had during the past several years while working intensively on software development. By making use of several ideas that have existed for a long time, and by applying them systematically in a slightly new way, I've stumbled across a method of composing programs that excites me very much. In fact, my enthusiasm is so great that I must warn the reader to discount much of what I shall say as the ravings of a fanatic who thinks he has just seen a great light.

Programming is a very personal activity, so I can't be certain that what has worked for me will work for everybody. Yet the impact of this new approach on my own style has been profound, and my excitement has continued unabated for more than two years. I enjoy the new methodology so much that it is hard for me to refrain from going back to every program that I've ever written and recasting it in "literate" form. I find myself unable to resist working on programming tasks that I would ordinarily have assigned to student research assistants; and why? Because it seems to me that at last I'm able to write programs as they should be written. My programs are not only explained better than ever before; they also are better programs, because the new methodology encourages me to do a better job. For these reasons I am compelled to write this paper, in hopes that my experiences will prove to be relevant to others.

I must confess that there may also be a bit of malice in my choice of a title. During the 1970s I was coerced like everybody else into adopting the ideas of structured programming, because I couldn't bear to be found guilty of writing *unstructured* programs. Now I have a chance to get even. By coining the phrase "literate programming," I am imposing a moral commitment on everyone who hears the term; surely nobody wants to admit writing an *illiterate* program.

The `WEB` System

I hope, however, to demonstrate in this paper that the title is not merely wordplay. The ideas of literate programming have been embodied in a language and a suite of computer programs that have been developed at Stanford University during the past few years as part of my research on algorithms and on digital typography. This language and its associated programs have come to be known as the `WEB` system. My goal in what follows is to describe the philosophy that underlies `WEB`, to present examples of programs in the `WEB` language, and to discuss what may be the future implications of this work.

I chose the name `WEB` partly because it was one of the few three-letter words of English that hadn't already been applied to computers. But as time went on, I've become extremely pleased with the name, because

I think that a complex piece of software is, indeed, best regarded as a *web* that has been delicately pieced together from simple materials. We understand a complicated system by understanding its simple parts, and by understanding the simple relations between those parts and their immediate neighbors. If we express a program as a web of ideas, we can emphasize its structural properties in a natural and satisfying way.

WEB itself is chiefly a combination of two other languages: (1) a document formatting language and (2) a programming language. My prototype WEB system uses TEX as the document formatting language and Pascal as the programming language, but the same principles would apply equally well if other languages were substituted. Instead of TEX, one could use a language like Scribe or Troff. Instead of Pascal, one could use ADA, ALGOL, LISP, COBOL, FORTRAN, APL, C, etc., or even assembly language. The main point is that WEB is inherently bilingual, and that such a combination of languages proves to be much more powerful than either single language by itself. WEB does not make the other languages obsolete; on the contrary, it enhances them.

I naturally chose TEX to be the document formatting language, in the first WEB system, because TEX is my own creation [6]; I wanted to acquire a lot of experience in harnessing TEX to a variety of different tasks. I chose Pascal as the programming language because it has received such widespread support from educational institutions all over the world; it is not my favorite language for system programming, but it has become a "second language" for so many programmers that it provides an exceptionally effective medium of communication. Furthermore WEB itself has a macro-processing ability that makes Pascal's limitations largely irrelevant.

Document formatting languages are newcomers to the computing scene, but their use is spreading rapidly. Therefore I'm confident that we will be able to expect each member of the next generation of programmers to be familiar with a document language as well as a programming language, as part of their basic education. Once a person knows both of the underlying languages, there's no trick at all to learning WEB, because the WEB user's manual is fewer than ten pages long.

A WEB user writes a program that serves as the source language for two different system routines. (See Figure 1.) One line of processing is called *weaving* the web; it produces a document that describes the program clearly and that facilitates program maintenance. The other line of processing is called *tangling* the web; it produces a machine-executable program. The program and its documentation are both generated from the same source, so they are consistent with each other.

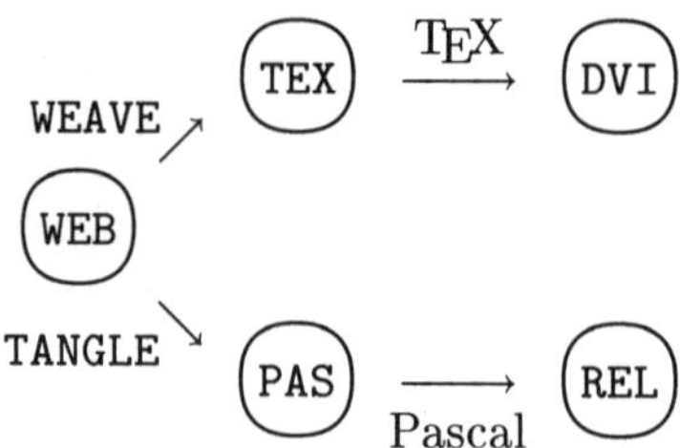

Figure 1. Dual usage of a WEB file.

Let's look at this process in slightly more detail. Suppose you have written a WEB program and put it into a computer text file called COB.WEB (say). To generate hardcopy documentation for your program, you can run the WEAVE processor; this is a system program that takes the file COB.WEB as input and produces another file COB.TEX as output. Then you run the TeX processor, which takes COB.TEX as input and produces COB.DVI as output. The latter file, COB.DVI, is a "device-independent" binary description of how to typeset the documentation, so you can get printed output by applying one more system routine to this file.

You can also follow the other branch of Figure 1, by running the TANGLE processor; this is a system program that takes the file COB.WEB as input and produces a new file COB.PAS as output. Then you run the Pascal compiler, which converts COB.PAS to a binary file COB.REL (say). Finally, you can run your program by loading and executing COB.REL. The process of "compile, load, and go" has been slightly lengthened to "tangle, compile, load, and go."

A Complete Example

Now it's time for me to stop presenting general platitudes and to move on to something tangible. Let us look at a real program that has been written in WEB. The numbered paragraphs that follow are the actual output of a WEB file that has been "woven" into a document; a computer has also generated the indexes that appear at the program's end. If my claims for the advantages of literate programming have any merit, you should be able to understand the following description more easily than you could have understood the same program when presented in a more conventional way. However, I am trying here to explain the format of WEB documentation at the same time as I am discussing the details of a nontrivial algorithm, so the description below is slightly longer than it would be if it were written for people who already have been introduced to WEB.

Here, then, is the computer-generated output:

1. Printing primes: An example of WEB. The following program is essentially the same as Edsger Dijkstra's "first example of step-wise program composition," found on pages 26–39 of his *Notes on Structured Programming* [1], but it has been translated into the WEB language.

⟦Double brackets will be used in what follows to enclose comments relating to WEB itself, because the chief purpose of this program is to introduce the reader to the WEB style of documentation. WEB programs are always broken into small sections, each of which has a serial number; the present section is number 1.⟧

Dijkstra's program prints a table of the first thousand prime numbers. We shall begin as he did, by reducing the entire program to its top-level description. ⟦Every section in a WEB program begins with optional *commentary* about that section, and ends with optional *program text* for the section. For example, you are now reading part of the commentary in §1, and the program text for §1 immediately follows the present paragraph. Program texts are specifications of Pascal programs; they either use Pascal language directly, or they use angle brackets to represent Pascal code that appears in other sections. For example, the angle-bracket notation '⟨ Program to print ... numbers 2 ⟩' is WEB's way of saying the following: "The Pascal text to be inserted here is called 'Program to print ... numbers', and you can find out all about it by looking at section 2." One of the main characteristics of WEB is that different parts of the program are usually abbreviated, by giving them such an informal top-level description.⟧

⟨ Program to print the first thousand prime numbers 2 ⟩

2. This program has no input, because we want to keep it rather simple. The result of the program will be to produce a list of the first thousand prime numbers, and this list will appear on the *output* file.

Since there is no input, we declare the value $m = 1000$ as a compile-time constant. The program itself is capable of generating the first m prime numbers for any positive m, as long as the computer's finite limitations are not exceeded.

⟦The program text below specifies the "expanded meaning" of '⟨ Program to print ... numbers 2 ⟩'; notice that it involves the top-level descriptions of three other sections. When those top-level descriptions are replaced by their expanded meanings, a syntactically correct Pascal program will be obtained.⟧

⟨ Program to print the first thousand prime numbers 2 ⟩ ≡
program *print_primes*(*output*);
  const $m = 1000$; ⟨ Other constants of the program 5 ⟩
  var ⟨ Variables of the program 4 ⟩
    begin ⟨ Print the first m prime numbers 3 ⟩;
    end.

This code is used in section 1.

---

3. Plan of the program. We shall proceed to fill out the rest of the program by making whatever decisions seem easiest at each step; the idea will be to strive for simplicity first and efficiency later, in order to see where this leads us. The final program may not be optimum, but we want it to be reliable, well motivated, and reasonably fast.

Let us decide at this point to maintain a table that includes all of the prime numbers that will be generated, and to separate the generation problem from the printing problem.

⟦The WEB description you are reading once again follows a pattern that will soon be familiar: A typical section begins with comments and ends with program text. The comments motivate and explain noteworthy features of the program text.⟧

⟨ Print the first m prime numbers 3 ⟩ ≡
  ⟨ Fill table p with the first m prime numbers 11 ⟩;
  ⟨ Print table p 8 ⟩

This code is used in section 2.

4. How should table p be represented? Two possibilities suggest themselves: We could construct a sufficiently large array of boolean values in which the kth entry is *true* if and only if the number k is prime; or we could build an array of integers in which the kth entry is the kth prime number. Let us choose the latter alternative, by introducing an integer array called $p[1\,..\,m]$.

In the documentation below, the notation '$p[k]$' will refer to the kth element of array p, while 'p_k' will refer to the kth prime number. If the program is correct, $p[k]$ will either be equal to p_k or it will not yet have been assigned any value.

⟦Incidentally, our program will eventually make use of several more variables as we refine the data structures. All of the sections where variables are declared will be called '⟨ Variables of the program 4 ⟩'; the number '4' in this name refers to the present section, which is the first section to specify the expanded meaning of '⟨ Variables of the program ⟩'. The note 'See also ...' refers to all of the other sections that have the same top-level description. The expanded meaning of '⟨ Variables of the program 4 ⟩' consists of all the program texts for this name, not just the text found in §4.⟧

⟨ Variables of the program 4 ⟩ ≡
p: **array** [1 .. *m*] **of** *integer*;
  { the first *m* prime numbers, in increasing order }

See also sections 7, 12, 15, 17, 23, and 24.

This code is used in section 2.

---

5. The output phase. Let's work on the second part of the program first. It's not as interesting as the problem of computing prime numbers; but the job of printing must be done sooner or later, and we might as well do it sooner, since it will be good to have it done. ⟦And it is easier to learn WEB when reading a program that has comparatively few distracting complications.⟧

Since *p* is simply an array of integers, there is little difficulty in printing the output, except that we need to decide upon a suitable output format. Let us print the table on separate pages, with *rr* rows and *cc* columns per page, where every column is *ww* character positions wide. In this case we shall choose $rr = 50$, $cc = 4$, and $ww = 10$, so that the first 1000 primes will appear on five pages. The program will not assume that *m* is an exact multiple of $rr \cdot cc$.

⟨ Other constants of the program 5 ⟩ ≡
  $rr = 50$; { this many rows will be on each page in the output }
  $cc = 4$; { this many columns will be on each page in the output }
  $ww = 10$;
    { this many character positions will be used in each column }

See also section 19.

This code is used in section 2.

6. In order to keep this program reasonably free of notations that are uniquely Pascalesque, ⟦and in order to illustrate more of the facilities of WEB,⟧ a few macro definitions for low-level output instructions are introduced here. All of the output-oriented commands in the remainder of the program will be stated in terms of five simple primitives called *print_string*, *print_integer*, *print_entry*, *new_line*, and *new_page*.

⟦Sections of a WEB program are allowed to contain *macro definitions* between the opening comments and the closing program text. The general format for each section is actually tripartite: commentary, then definitions, then program. Any of the three parts may be absent; for example, the present section contains no program text.⟧

⟦Simple macros simply substitute a bit of Pascal code for an identifier. Parametric macros are similar, but they also substitute an argument wherever '#' occurs in the macro definition. The first three macro definitions here are parametric; the other two are simple.⟧

define *print_string*(#) ≡ *write*(#)
{ put a given string into the *output* file }
define *print_integer*(#) ≡ *write*(# : 1) { put a given integer into the *output* file, in decimal notation, using only as many digit positions as necessary }
define *print_entry*(#) ≡ *write*(# : *ww*) { like *print_integer*, but *ww* character positions are filled, inserting blanks at the left }
define *new_line* ≡ *write_ln*
{ advance to a new line in the *output* file }
define *new_page* ≡ *page* { advance to a new page in the *output* file }

7. Several variables are needed to govern the output process. When we begin to print a new page, the variable *page_number* will be the ordinal number of that page, and *page_offset* will be such that *p*[*page_offset*] is the first prime to be printed. Similarly, *p*[*row_offset*] will be the first prime in a given row.

⟦Notice the notation '+≡' below; this indicates that the present section has the same name as a previous section, so the program text will be appended to some text that was previously specified.⟧

⟨ Variables of the program 4 ⟩ +≡
page_number: *integer*;
{ one more than the number of pages printed so far }
page_offset: *integer*;
{ index into *p* for the first entry on the current page }
row_offset: *integer*;
{ index into *p* for the first entry in the current row }
c: 0 .. *cc*; { runs through the columns in a row }

8. Now that appropriate auxiliary variables have been introduced, the process of outputting table *p* almost writes itself.

⟨ Print table *p* 8 ⟩ ≡
begin *page_number* ← 1; *page_offset* ← 1;
while *page_offset* ≤ *m* **do**
begin ⟨ Output a page of answers 9 ⟩;

```
    page_number ← page_number + 1;
    page_offset ← page_offset + rr * cc;
    end;
  end
```

This code is used in section 3.

9. A simple heading is printed at the top of each page.

```
⟨Output a page of answers 9⟩ ≡
  begin print_string('The␣First␣'); print_integer(m);
  print_string('␣Prime␣Numbers␣---␣Page␣');
  print_integer(page_number); new_line; new_line;
      {there's a blank line after the heading}
  for row_offset ← page_offset to page_offset + rr − 1 do
    ⟨Output a line of answers 10⟩;
  new_page;
  end
```

This code is used in section 8.

10. The first row will contain

$$p[1],\ p[1 + rr],\ p[1 + 2 * rr],\ \ldots;$$

a similar pattern holds for each value of the *row_offset*.

```
⟨Output a line of answers 10⟩ ≡
  begin for c ← 0 to cc − 1 do
    if row_offset + c * rr ≤ m then print_entry(p[row_offset + c * rr]);
  new_line;
  end
```

This code is used in section 9.

---

11. Generating the primes. The remaining task is to fill table *p* with the correct numbers. Let us do this by generating its entries one at a time: Assuming that we have computed all primes that are *j* or less, we will advance *j* to the next suitable value, and continue doing this until the table is completely full.

The program includes a provision to initialize the variables in certain data structures that will be introduced later.

```
⟨Fill table p with the first m prime numbers 11⟩ ≡
  ⟨Initialize the data structures 16⟩;
  while k < m do
    begin ⟨Increase j until it is the next prime number 14⟩;
    k ← k + 1; p[k] ← j;
    end
```

This code is used in section 3.

12. We need to declare the two variables j and k that were just introduced.

⟨ Variables of the program 4 ⟩ +≡
j: *integer*; { all primes $\leq j$ are in table p }
k: $0\,..\,m$; { this many primes are in table p }

13. So far we haven't needed to confront the issue of what a prime number is. But everything else has been taken care of, so we must delve into a bit of number theory now.

By definition, a number is called prime if it is an integer greater than 1 that is not evenly divisible by any smaller prime number. Stating this another way, the integer $j > 1$ is not prime if and only if there exists a prime number $p_n < j$ such that j is a multiple of p_n.

Therefore the section of the program that is called '⟨ Increase j until it is the next prime number ⟩' could be coded very simply: '**repeat** $j \leftarrow j + 1$; ⟨ Give to *j_prime* the meaning: j is a prime number ⟩; **until** *j_prime*'. And to compute the boolean value *j_prime*, the following would suffice: '*j_prime* ← *true*; **for** $n \leftarrow 1$ **to** k **do** ⟨ If $p[n]$ divides j, set *j_prime* ← *false* ⟩'.

14. However, it is possible to obtain a much more efficient algorithm by using more facts of number theory. In the first place, we can speed things up a bit by recognizing that $p_1 = 2$ and that all subsequent primes are odd; therefore we can let j run through odd values only. Our program now takes the following form:

⟨ Increase j until it is the next prime number 14 ⟩ ≡
  repeat $j \leftarrow j + 2$; ⟨ Update variables that depend on j 20 ⟩;
    ⟨ Give to *j_prime* the meaning: j is a prime number 22 ⟩;
  until *j_prime*

This code is used in section 11.

15. The **repeat** loop in the previous section introduces a boolean variable *j_prime*, so that it will not be necessary to resort to a **goto** statement. (We are following Dijkstra [1], not Knuth [5].)

⟨ Variables of the program 4 ⟩ +≡
j_prime: *boolean*; { is j a prime number? }

16. In order to make the odd-even trick work, we must of course initialize the variables j, k, and $p[1]$ as follows.

⟨ Initialize the data structures 16 ⟩ ≡
  $j \leftarrow 1$; $k \leftarrow 1$; $p[1] \leftarrow 2$;

See also section 18.

This code is used in section 11.

17. Now we can apply more number theory in order to obtain further economies. If j is not prime, its smallest prime factor p_n will be $\sqrt{j}$ or less. Thus if we know a number *ord* such that

$$p[ord]^2 > j,$$

and if j is odd, we need only test for divisors in the set $\{p[2], \ldots, p[ord-1]\}$. This is much faster than testing divisibility by the full set $\{p[2], \ldots, p[k]\}$, since *ord* tends to be much smaller than k. (Indeed, when k is large, the celebrated "prime number theorem" implies that the value of *ord* will be approximately $2\sqrt{k/\ln k}$.)

Let us therefore introduce *ord* into the data structure. A moment's thought makes it clear that *ord* changes in a simple way when j increases, and that another variable *square* facilitates the updating process.

⟨ Variables of the program 4 ⟩ +≡
ord: 2 .. *ord_max*; { the smallest index ≥ 2 such that $p_{ord}^2 > j$ }
square: *integer*; { $square = p_{ord}^2$ }

18. ⟨ Initialize the data structures 16 ⟩ +≡
ord ← 2; *square* ← 9;

19. The value of *ord* will never get larger than a certain value *ord_max*, which must be chosen sufficiently large. It turns out that *ord* never exceeds 30 when $m = 1000$.

⟨ Other constants of the program 5 ⟩ +≡
ord_max = 30; { $p_{ord\_max}^2$ must exceed p_m }

20. When j has been increased by 2, we must increase *ord* by unity when $j = p_{ord}^2$, i.e., when $j = square$.

⟨ Update variables that depend on j 20 ⟩ ≡
if $j = square$ **then**
begin *ord* ← *ord* + 1; ⟨ Update variables that depend on *ord* 21 ⟩;
end

This code is used in section 14.

21. At this point in the program, *ord* has just been increased by unity, and we want to set $square := p_{ord}^2$. A surprisingly subtle point arises here: How do we know that p_{ord} has already been computed, i.e., that $ord \leq k$? If there were a gap in the sequence of prime numbers, such that $p_{k+1} > p_k^2$ for some k, then this part of the program would refer to the yet-uncomputed value $p[k+1]$ unless some special test were made.

Fortunately, there are no such gaps. But no simple proof of this fact is known. For example, Euclid's famous demonstration that there are infinitely many prime numbers is strong enough to prove only that $p_{k+1} \le p_1 \ldots p_k + 1$. Advanced books on number theory come to our rescue by showing that much more is true; for example, "Bertrand's postulate" states that $p_{k+1} < 2p_k$ for all k.

⟨ Update variables that depend on *ord* 21 ⟩ ≡
  square ← *p*[*ord*] ∗ *p*[*ord*]; { at this point *ord* ≤ *k* }

See also section 25.

This code is used in section 20.

---

22. The inner loop. Our remaining task is to determine whether or not a given integer j is prime. The general outline of this part of the program is quite simple, using the value of *ord* as described above.

⟨ Give to *j_prime* the meaning: *j* is a prime number 22 ⟩ ≡
  n ← 2; *j_prime* ← *true*;
  while (*n* < *ord*) ∧ *j_prime* **do**
    begin ⟨ If *p*[*n*] is a factor of *j*, set *j_prime* ← *false* 26 ⟩;
    n ← *n* + 1;
    end

This code is used in section 14.

23. ⟨ Variables of the program 4 ⟩ +≡
n: 2 .. *ord_max*; { runs from 2 to *ord* when testing divisibility }

24. Let's suppose that division is very slow or nonexistent on our machine. We want to detect nonprime odd numbers, which are odd multiples of the set of primes $\{p_2, \ldots, p_{ord-1}\}$.

Since *ord_max* is small, it is reasonable to maintain an auxiliary table of the smallest odd multiples that haven't already been used to show that some j is nonprime. In other words, our goal is to "knock out" all of the odd multiples of each p_n in the set $\{p_2, \ldots, p_{ord-1}\}$, and one way to do this is to introduce an auxiliary table that serves as a control structure for a set of knock-out procedures that are being simulated in parallel. (The so-called "sieve of Eratosthenes" generates primes by a similar method, but it knocks out the multiples of each prime serially.)

The auxiliary table suggested by these considerations is a *mult* array that satisfies the following invariant condition: For $2 \le n < ord$, $mult[n]$ is an odd multiple of p_n such that $mult[n] < j + 2p_n$.

⟨ Variables of the program 4 ⟩ +≡
mult: **array** [2 .. *ord_max*] **of** *integer*;
    { runs through multiples of primes }

25. When *ord* has been increased, we need to initialize a new element of the *mult* array. At this point $j = p[ord - 1]^2$, so there is no need for an elaborate computation.

⟨Update variables that depend on *ord* 21⟩ +≡
  $mult[ord - 1] \leftarrow j$;

26. The remaining task is straightforward, given the data structures already prepared. Let us recapitulate the current situation: The goal is to test whether or not j is divisible by p_n, without actually performing a division. We know that j is odd, and that $mult[n]$ is an odd multiple of p_n such that $mult[n] < j + 2p_n$. If $mult[n] < j$, we can increase $mult[n]$ by $2p_n$ and the same conditions will hold. On the other hand if $mult[n] \geq j$, the conditions imply that j is divisible by p_n if and only if $j = mult[n]$.

⟨If $p[n]$ is a factor of j, set *j_prime* ← *false* 26⟩ ≡
  while $mult[n] < j$ **do** $mult[n] \leftarrow mult[n] + p[n] + p[n]$;
  if $mult[n] = j$ **then** *j_prime* ← *false*

This code is used in section 22.

---

27. Index. Every identifier used in this program is shown here together with a list of the section numbers where that identifier appears. The section number is underlined if the identifier was defined in that section. However, one-letter identifiers are indexed only at their point of definition, since such identifiers tend to appear almost everywhere. ⟦An index like this is prepared automatically by the `WEB` software, and it is appended to the final section of the program. However, underlining of section numbers is not automatic; the user is supposed to mark identifiers at their point of definition in the `WEB` source file.⟧

This index also refers to some of the places where key elements of the program are treated. For example, the entries for 'output format' and 'page headings' indicate where details of the output format are discussed. Several other topics that appear in the documentation (e.g., 'Bertrand's postulate') have also been indexed. ⟦Special instructions within a `WEB` source file can be used to insert essentially anything into the index.⟧

How the Example Was Specified

Everything reproduced above, from the table of contents preceding the program to the indexes of identifiers and section names at the end, was generated by applying the program `WEAVE` to a source file `PRIMES.WEB` written in the `WEB` language. Let us now look at that file `PRIMES.WEB`, in order to get an idea of what a `WEB` user actually types.

There's no need to show very much of `PRIMES.WEB`, however, because that file is reflected quite faithfully by the formatted output. Figure 2 contains enough of the `WEB` source to indicate the general flavor; a reader

```
% Prime example
\font\ninerm=cmr9
\let\mc=\ninerm % medium caps
\def\WEB{{\tt WEB}}
\def\[{\ifhmode\ \fi$[\mkern-2mu[$}
\def\]{$]\mkern-2mu]$\ }
    ⋮
\hyphenation{Dijk-stra}

@* Printing primes: An example of \WEB.
The following program is essentially the same
as Edsger Dijkstra's @^Dijkstra, Edsger@>
``first example of step-wise program
composition,'' found on pages 26--39
of his {\sl Notes on Structured
Programming} [1], but it has been
translated into the \WEB\ language. @.WEB@>

\[Double brackets will be used in what
follows to enclose comments relating to \WEB\
    ⋮
an informal top-level description.\]

@p @<Program to print the first thousand
prime numbers@>
```

Figure 2a. The beginning of PRIMES.WEB.

who is familiar with the rudiments of TEX will be able to reconstruct all of PRIMES.WEB by looking only at the formatted output and Figure 2.

Figure 2a starts with TEX commands (not shown in full) that make it convenient to typeset double brackets ⟦...⟧ and to give special typographic treatment to names like 'WEB'. A WEB user generally begins by declaring such special aspects of the document format; for example, if nonstandard fonts of type are needed, they are usually stated first. It may also be necessary to specify the correct hyphenation of non-English words that appear in the document.

Then comes '@*', which starts the program proper. WEB uses the symbol '@' as an escape character for special instructions to the WEAVE and TANGLE processors. Everything between such special commands is either expressed in TeX language or in Pascal language, depending on the context.

Each section of the program begins either with '@ ' (i.e., at-sign and space) or '@*' (i.e., at-sign and asterisk); WEB supplies the section numbers automatically. The latter case, '@*', denotes a *major section* of the program, for which a special title is given. This title will appear in boldface type, and it will also appear in the table of contents, and as a running headline on all pages of the woven documentation until another major section begins. Each major section starts at the top of a page. (Such page beginnings have been indicated by horizontal lines in our example, because WEB's normal output format has been adapted to the format of this book. The output of WEAVE usually has a lot more white space, and the individual lines of text are usually a bit wider.)

The lines that follow in Figure 2a show a few more WEB instructions: '@^' marks the beginning of an index entry to be set in roman type; '@>' marks the end of an argument to a WEB command; '@.' marks the beginning of an index entry to be set in typewriter type; '@p' marks the beginning of the Pascal program; and '@<' marks the beginning of a top-level description, i.e., of a section name in the WEB program.

Figure 2b immediately follows Figure 2a in the WEB file. This material is what generated §2 of the documentation, and it illustrates the bilingual nature of WEB: The commentary at the beginning of each section is typed in TeX language, and the program text at the end is typed in Pascal language.

Language-switching between TeX and Pascal is occasionally desirable. For example, when you refer to technical details about the program, you usually want to describe them in Pascal, hence you want WEAVE to format them with the typographic conventions it uses for Pascal programs. Conversely, when you put comments in a Pascal program, you want the text of those comments to be formatted by TeX in the normal way. WEB files use vertical bars to introduce Pascal formatting in the midst of TeX formatting; for example, Figure 2b says 'the |output| file' in order to typeset 'the *output* file'.

The program text in Figure 2b begins with '@<' instead of with the '@p' command used in Figure 2a, because the program text in §2 is the expansion of a specific top-level description. Notice that the top-level description has been abbreviated to '@<Program to print...@>'. Since the names of sections tend to be rather long, it is a nuisance to type them in full each time; WEB allows you to type '...' after you have given enough text to identify the remainder uniquely.

```
@ This program has no input, because we want
to keep it rather simple.  The result of the
program will be to produce a list of the
first thousand prime numbers, and this list
will appear on the |output| file.

Since there is no input, we declare the value
|m=1000| as a compile-time constant. The
program itself is capable of generating the
first |m| prime numbers for any positive |m|,
as long as the computer's finite limitations
are not exceeded.

\[The program text below specifies the
``expanded meaning'' of `\X2:Program to print
$\ldots$ numbers\X'; notice that it involves
the top-level descriptions of three other
sections. When those top-level descriptions
are replaced by their expanded meanings, a
syntactically correct Pascal program will
be obtained.\]

@<Program to print...@>=
program print_primes(output);
const @!m=1000;
@<Other constants of the program@>@;
var @<Variables of the program@>@;
begin @<Print the first |m| prime numbers@>;
end.
```

Figure 2b. The WEB code that generated §2.

The '@!' operation in the program text of Figure 2b governs the underlining of index entries. The '@;' specifies an invisible symbol that has the effect of a semicolon in Pascal syntax. Commands such as these are comparatively unimportant, but they are available for polishing up the final documentation when you want to maintain fine control.

Figure 2c shows key portions of the WEB text that generated §6. Notice that the command '@d' introduces a macro definition. All features of WEB that appear in our example program are illustrated in Figures 2a, 2b, and 2c; the remainder of PRIMES.WEB simply uses the same conventions

```
@ In order to keep this program reasonably
free of notations that are uniquely
Pascalesque, \[and in order to illustrate
more of the facilities of \WEB,\] a few
macro definitions for low-level output
    ⋮
\[Simple macros simply substitute a bit of
Pascal code for an identifier. Parametric
macros are similar, but they also substitute
an argument wherever `|#|' occurs in the macro
definition. The first three macro definitions
here are parametric; the other two are simple.\]

@d print_string(#)==write(#)
 {put a given string into the |output| file}
@d print_integer(#)==write(#:1)
 {put a given integer into the |output|
  file, in decimal notation, using only as
  many digit positions as necessary}
@d print_entry(#)==write(#:ww)
 {like |print_integer|, but
  |ww| character positions are filled,
  inserting blanks at the left}
@d new_line==write_ln
 {advance to a new line in the |output| file}
@d new_page==page
 {advance to a new page in the |output| file}
```

Figure 2c. The WEB code that generated §6.

again and again. In fact, most of the WEB file is much simpler than the examples shown here; Figure 2 has illustrated only the difficult parts.

The Tangled Output

Figure 3 shows the Pascal program PRIMES.PAS that results when TANGLE is applied to PRIMES.WEB. This program is not intended for human consumption—it's only supposed to be readable by a Pascal compiler—so TANGLE does not go to great pains to produce a beautiful format. Notice that underlines have been removed from the identifier names, and that all of the letters have been converted to uppercase (except in strings); TANGLE tries to produce a format that will be acceptable to every Pascal compiler.

TANGLE removes all of the commentary in the WEB file, but it inserts new comments of its own. If for some reason you need to correlate the tangled Pascal code with the woven documentation, you can find the program text for, say, §8 by looking between the comments '{8:}' and '{:8}'.

A comparison of Figure 3 to Figure 2 should make it clear why the TANGLE processor has acquired its name.

```
{1:}{2:}PROGRAM PRINTPRIMES(OUTPUT);CONST M=1000;{5:}
RR=50;CC=4;WW=10;{:5}{19:}ORDMAX=30;{:19}VAR{4:}
P:ARRAY[1..M]OF INTEGER;{:4}{7:}PAGENUMBER:INTEGER;
PAGEOFFSET:INTEGER;ROWOFFSET:INTEGER;C:0..CC;{:7}{12:}
J:INTEGER;K:0..M;{:12}{15:}JPRIME:BOOLEAN;{:15}{17:}
ORD:2..ORDMAX;SQUARE:INTEGER;{:17}{23:}N:2..ORDMAX;{:23}
{24:}MULT:ARRAY[2..ORDMAX]OF INTEGER;{:24}BEGIN{3:}{11:}
{16:}J:=1;K:=1;P[1]:=2;{:16}{18:}ORD:=2;SQUARE:=9;{:18};
WHILE K<M DO BEGIN{14:}REPEAT J:=J+2;{20:}
IF J=SQUARE THEN BEGIN ORD:=ORD+1;{21:}
SQUARE:=P[ORD]*P[ORD];{:21}{25:}MULT[ORD-1]:=J;{:25};
END{:20};{22:}N:=2;JPRIME:=TRUE;
WHILE(N<ORD)AND JPRIME DO BEGIN{26:}
WHILE MULT[N]<J DO MULT[N]:=MULT[N]+P[N]+P[N];
IF MULT[N]=J THEN JPRIME:=FALSE{:26};N:=N+1;END{:22};
UNTIL JPRIME{:14};K:=K+1;P[K]:=J;END{:11};{8:}
BEGIN PAGENUMBER:=1;PAGEOFFSET:=1;
WHILE PAGEOFFSET<=M DO BEGIN{9:}
BEGIN WRITE('The First ');WRITE(M:1);
WRITE(' Prime Numbers --- Page ');WRITE(PAGENUMBER:1);
WRITELN;WRITELN;
FOR ROWOFFSET:=PAGEOFFSET TO PAGEOFFSET+RR-1 DO{10:}
BEGIN FOR C:=0 TO CC-1 DO IF ROWOFFSET+C*RR<=M THEN WRITE
(P[ROWOFFSET+C*RR]:WW);WRITELN;END{:10};PAGE;END{:9};
PAGENUMBER:=PAGENUMBER+1;PAGEOFFSET:=PAGEOFFSET+RR*CC;
END;END{:8}{:3};END.{:2}{:1}
```

Figure 3. Pascal program generated from the WEB file.

The Woven Output

I mentioned earlier that WEAVE is a program that converts a file like PRIMES.WEB into a file PRIMES.TEX, which is a syntactically correct source file for TeX. Figure 4 gives a sampling of PRIMES.TEX; the TeX file turns out to be even more unreadable than PRIMES.PAS, but again it is not supposed to be read by human beings. The instructions that cause TeX to produce formatted Pascal programs, with appropriate typefaces and indentation, etc., are somewhat complex because they are supposed to give decent results regardless of the page size.

There is no need to discuss Figure 4 further in the present paper, because the details of "pretty printing" are not relevant to my main theme. I have shown this much of PRIMES.TEX only to make the point that it is nice to have a program like WEAVE to do all the formatting; computer programs are not easy to typeset.

Additional Bells and Whistles

A system like WEB can be successful only if it is capable of handling large programs as well as small ones, and only if it is complete enough to take care of all the practical requirements that arise when many different kinds of programs are considered. A small example like PRIMES.WEB is a satisfactory vehicle for illustrating the general ideas, but it cannot be convincing as a demonstration of WEB's ability to produce quality software in the "real world." My original design of WEB in September, 1981, was followed by a year of extensive experiments, so that by the time Version 1 was released in September, 1982, I could be fairly confident that the language was reasonably complete. Since then only one or two small extensions have proved to be necessary; and although numerous enhancements can easily be imagined, I believe that a useful stopping point for a working system called WEB83 has been reached.

A full description of WEB83 appears in a Stanford report [7], which also contains the complete WEB programs for WEAVE and TANGLE. The full language contains only a few features that do not show up in the PRIMES example considered above:

1) There are facilities to override WEAVE's automatic formatting of Pascal programs. For example, it is possible to force a statement to begin on a new line, or to force several statements to appear on the same line, or to suggest a desirable breakpoint in the middle of a long expression. In unusual cases, WEAVE must parse program fragments that are not syntactically complete—for example, there

```
\input webmac
% Prime example
\font\ninerm=cmr9
    ⋮
descriptions are replaced by their expanded meanings, a
syntactically correct \PASCAL\ program will be obtained.\]

\Y\P$\4\X2:Program to print the first thousand prime
numbers\X\S$\6\
4\&{program}\1\  \37$\\{print\_primes}(\\{output})$;\6
\4\&{const} \37$\|m=1000$;\5
\X5:Other constants of the program\X\6
\4\&{var} \37\X4:Variables of the program\X\6
\&{begin} \37\X3:Print the first \|m prime numbers\X;\6
\&{end}.\par
\U section~1.\fi
    ⋮
The first three macro definitions here are parametric;
the other two are simple.\]

\Y\P\D \37$\\{print\_string}(\#)\S\\{write}(\#)$\C{put %
a given string into the \\{output} file}\par
\P\D \37$\\{print\_integer}(\#)\S\\{write}(\#:1)$\C{put %
a given integer into the \\{output} file, in decimal %
    ⋮
\inx
\:{Bertrand, Joseph, postulate}, 21.
\:\\{boolean}, 15.
    ⋮
\:\.{WEB}, 1.
\:\\{write}, 6.
\:\\{write\_ln}, 6.
\:\\{ww}, \[5], 6.
\fin
    ⋮
\:\X4, 7, 12, 15, 17, 23, 24:Variables of the program\X
\U section~2.
\con
```

Figure 4. TeX program generated from the WEB file.

may be a **begin** without a matching **end**—so a WEB user must be given a chance to control the results. Furthermore there is a facility for changing WEAVE's formatting rules by declaring that a certain identifier should be treated as a certain Pascal reserved word, or by declaring that a certain reserved word should be treated as an ordinary identifier.

2) There is a way to force TANGLE to omit a space between two adjacent pieces of text, so that a name like '*x3*' can be manufactured from '*x*' and '*3*'. Similarly, there is a way to pass an arbitrary sequence of characters through TANGLE so that the same sequence will appear "verbatim" in the Pascal file; and there is a way to force beginning-of-line in that file. The latter extensions have proved to be necessary to deal with various nonstandard conventions of different Pascal compilers.

3) There are facilities for octal and hexadecimal constants in WEB source files. TANGLE converts such constants to decimal form; WEAVE gives them an appropriate typographic treatment.

4) There is a facility for dealing with alphabetic constants. When a program contains a double-quoted character like "A", TANGLE converts this to an integer between 0 and 255 that equals the corresponding ASCII code (in this case 65). The use of ASCII code facilitates the construction of software that is readily portable from one machine to another, independent of the actual character set in use.

5) Furthermore, if a double-quoted constant is a string of several characters, like "cat", TANGLE converts it into a unique integer that is 256 or more. A special *string pool file* is written, containing all of the strings that have been specially encoded in this way. I have used this general mechanism only in large programs, but experience has shown that it makes quite a nice substitute for the string-processing capabilities that Pascal lacks. (Incidentally, I learned an interesting thing after several months of experimenting: A program needs to have some indication that the string-pool file it is reading contains the same strings that TANGLE generated when the program itself was tangled. Therefore a "check sum" is included in the string pool file; each program is able to refer to its own check sum and to compare it with the value in the file. This check-sum extension was one of the last features to be added to WEB83.)

6) The PRIMES example illustrates macros with parameters and macros without parameters. WEB also allows "numeric" macros, which are

small integer constants; TANGLE is capable of doing simple arithmetic on such constants. This feature of WEB was introduced specifically to overcome Pascal's unfortunate inability to do compile-time arithmetic. For example, it is impossible to have a Pascal array whose bounds are '0 .. $n-1$', or to write '$20+3$:' as the label of one of the cases in '**case** $x+y$'; WEB's numeric macros make it possible for TANGLE to preprocess such constants.

Occam's Razor

I would also like to mention several things that were intentionally left out of WEB, since I have tried to keep the language as simple as I could.

There are no "conditional macros," nor does TANGLE evaluate Boolean expressions that might influence the output. I found that everything I needed could be done satisfactorily by commenting out the optional code.

For example, a system program is often designed to gather statistics about its own operation, but such statistics-gathering is pointless unless someone is actually going to use the results. In order to make the instrumentation code optional, I include the word '**stat**' just before any special code for statistics, and '**tats**' just after such code; and I tell WEAVE to regard **stat** and **tats** as if they were **begin** and **end**. But **stat** and **tats** are actually simple macros. When I do want to gather the statistics, I define **stat** and **tats** to be null; but in a production version of the software, I make **stat** expand to '@{' and **tats** expand to '@}', where @{ and @} are special braces that TANGLE does not remove. Thus the optional code appears as a harmless comment in the Pascal program. When a comment in braces is sent to the Pascal file, TANGLE is careful not to introduce further braces inside the comment.

WEB's macros are allowed to have at most one parameter. Again, I did this in the interests of simplicity, because I noticed that most applications of multiple parameters could in fact be reduced to the one-parameter case. For example, suppose that you want to define something like

```
mac(#1,#2) == m[#1*r+#2]
```

which WEB doesn't permit. You can get essentially the same result with two one-parameter macros

```
mac_tail(#) == #]
mac(#) == m[#*r+mac_tail
```

since, e.g., 'mac(a)(b)' will expand into 'm[a*r+b]'.

Here is another example that indicates some of the surprising generality of one-parameter macros: Consider the two definitions

```
define two_cases(#)==case j of
                1:#(1); 2:#(2); end
define reset_file(#)==reset(file@&#)
```

where '@&' in the second definition is the concatenation operation, which pastes two texts together. You can now say

```
two_cases(reset_file)
```

and the resulting Pascal output will be

```
case j of
1:reset(file1);
2:reset(file2);
end
```

In other words, the name of one macro can usefully be a parameter to another macro. This particular trick makes it possible to live with Pascal compilers that do not allow arrays of files.

Portability

One of the goals of my TEX research has been to produce portable software, and the WEB system has been extremely helpful in this respect. Although my own work is done on a DEC-10 computer with Stanford's one-of-a-kind operating system, the software developed with WEB has already been transported successfully to a wide variety of computers made by other manufacturers (including IBM, Control Data, XEROX, Hewlett-Packard), and to a variety of different operating systems for those machines. To my knowledge, no other software of such complexity has ever been transported to so many different machines. It seems likely that TEX will soon be operating on all but the smallest of the world's computer systems.

To my surprise, the main bottleneck to portability of the TEXware has been the lack of suitable Pascal compilers, because Pascal has often been implemented without system programming in mind. Anybody who has a decent Pascal compiler can install WEB (and all programs written in WEB) without great difficulty, essentially as follows:

1) Start with the three files WEAVE.WEB, TANGLE.WEB, and TANGLE.PAS. (The programs are in the public domain, so these files are not difficult to obtain.)

2) Run `TANGLE.PAS` through your Pascal compiler to get a working `TANGLE` program.
3) Check your `TANGLE` by applying it to `TANGLE.WEB`; your output file should match `TANGLE.PAS`.
4) Apply your `TANGLE` to the file `WEAVE.WEB`, obtaining `WEAVE.PAS`; then apply Pascal to `WEAVE.PAS` and you'll have a working `WEAVE` system.
5) The same process applies to any software written in `WEB`, notably to TeX itself. (However, you need fonts and suitable output equipment in order to make proper use of TeX; that may be another bottleneck.) Once you have TeX working, you can apply `WEAVE` and TeX to your `WEB` files, thereby getting program documents as illustrated above.

Notice that a `TANGLE.PAS` file is needed in order to get this "bootstrapping" process started. If you have just `WEAVE.WEB` and `TANGLE.WEB`, you can't do the first step.

However, anybody who has looked seriously into the question of software portability will realize that my comments in the preceding paragraphs have been oversimplified. I have glossed over some serious problems that arise: Character sets are different; file naming conventions are different; special conventions are needed to interact with a user's terminal; data is packed differently on different machines; floating-point arithmetic is always nonstandard and sometimes nonexistent; users want "friendly" interaction with existing programs for editing and spooling; etc., etc. Furthermore, many of the world's Pascal compilers are incredibly bizarre. Therefore it is quite naïve to believe that a single program `TANGLE.PAS` could actually work on very many different machines, or even that one single source file `TANGLE.WEB` could be adequate; some system-dependent changes are inevitable.

The `WEB` system caters to system-dependent changes in a simple but surprisingly effective way that I neglected to mention when I listed its other features. Both `TANGLE` and `WEAVE` are designed to work with *two* input files, not just one: In addition to a `WEB` source file like `TEX.WEB`, there is also a "change file" `TEX.CH` that contains whatever changes are needed to customize TeX for a particular system. (Similarly, the source files `WEAVE.WEB` and `TANGLE.WEB` are accompanied by `WEAVE.CH` and `TANGLE.CH`.)

Here's how change files work: Each change has the form "replace $x_1 \ldots x_m$ by $y_1 \ldots y_n$," for some $m \geq 1$ and $n \geq 0$; here x_i and y_j represent lines in the change file. The `WEAVE` and `TANGLE` programs read data from the `WEB` input file until finding a line that matches x_1; this line, and the $m - 1$ following lines, are replaced by $y_1 \ldots y_n$. An error message is given if the m lines replaced did not match $x_1 \ldots x_m$ perfectly.

For example, the program PRIMES.WEB invokes a *page* procedure to begin a new page; but *page* was not present in Wirth's original Pascal and it is defined rather vaguely in the Pascal standard. Therefore a system-dependent change may be needed here. A change file PRIMES.CH could be made by copying the line

```
@d new_page==page
```

from Figure 2c and specifying one or more appropriate replacement lines.

The program TANGLE itself contains about 190 sections, and a typical installation will have to change about 15 of these. If you want to transport TANGLE to a new environment, you therefore need to create a suitable file TANGLE.CH that modifies 15 or so parts of TANGLE.WEB. (Examples of TANGLE.CH are provided to all people who receive TANGLE.WEB, so that each implementor has a model of what to do.) You need to insert your changes by hand into TANGLE.PAS, until you have a TANGLE program that works sufficiently well to support further bootstrapping. But you never actually change the master file TANGLE.WEB.

This approach has two important advantages. First, the same master file TANGLE.WEB is used by everybody, and it contains the basic logic of TANGLE that really defines the essence of tangling. The system-dependent changes do not affect any of the subtle parts of TANGLE's control structures or data structures. Second, when the official TANGLE has been upgraded to a newer version, a brand new TANGLE.WEB will almost always work with the old TANGLE.CH, since changes are rarely made to the system-dependent parts. In other words, this dual-input-file scheme works when the WEB file is constant and the CH file is modified, and it also works when the CH file is constant but the WEB file is modified.

Change files were added to WEB about three months after the system was initially designed, based on our initial experiences with people who had volunteered to participate in portability experiments. We realized about a year later that WEAVE could be modified so that only the changed parts of a program would (optionally) be printed; thus, it's now possible to document the changes by listing only the sections that are actually affected by the CH file that WEAVE has processed. We also generalized the original format of CH files, which permitted only changes that extended to the end of a section. These two important ideas were among the final enhancements incorporated into WEB83.

Programs as Webs

When I first began to work with the ideas that eventually became the WEB system, I thought that I would be designing a language for "top-down" programming, where a top-level description is given first and successively refined. On the other hand I knew that I often created major parts of programs in a "bottom-up" fashion, starting with the definitions of basic procedures and data structures and gradually building more and more powerful subroutines. I had the feeling that top-down and bottom-up were opposing methodologies: one more suitable for program exposition and the other more suitable for program creation.

But after gaining experience with WEB, I have come to realize that there is no need to choose once and for all between top-down and bottom-up, because a program is best thought of as a web instead of as a tree. A hierarchical structure is present, but the most important thing about a program is its structural relationships. A complex piece of software consists of simple parts and simple relations between those parts; the programmer's task is to state those parts and those relationships, in whatever order is best for human comprehension—not in some rigidly determined order like top-down or bottom-up.

When I'm writing a longish program like TANGLE.WEB or WEAVE.WEB or TEX.WEB, I invariably have strong feelings about what part of the whole should be tackled next. For example, I'll come to a point where I need to define a major data structure and its conventions, before I'll feel happy about going further. My experiences have led me to believe that a person reading a program is, likewise, ready to comprehend it by learning its various parts in approximately the order in which it was written. The PRIMES.WEB example illustrates this principle on a small scale; the decisions that Dijkstra made as he composed the original program [1] appear in the WEB documentation in the same order.

Top-down programming gives you a strong idea of where you are going, but it forces you to keep a lot of plans in your head; suspense builds up because nothing is really nailed down until the end. Bottom-up programming has the advantage that you continually wield a more and more powerful pencil, as more and more subroutines have been constructed; but it forces you to postpone the overall program organization until the last minute, so you might flounder aimlessly.

When I tear up the first draft of a program and start over, my second draft usually considers things in almost the same order as the first one did. Sometimes the "correct" order is top-down, sometimes it is bottom-up, and sometimes it's a mixture; but always it's an order that makes sense on expository grounds.

Thus the WEB language allows a person to express programs in a "stream of consciousness" order. TANGLE is able to scramble everything up into the arrangement that a Pascal compiler demands. This feature of WEB is perhaps its greatest asset; it makes a WEB-written program much more readable than the same program written purely in Pascal, even if the latter program is well commented. And the fact that there's no need to be hung up on the question of top-down versus bottom-up—since a programmer can now view a large program as a web, to be explored in a psychologically correct order—is perhaps the greatest lesson I have learned from my recent experiences.

Another surprising thing that I learned while using WEB was that traditional programming languages had been causing me to write inferior programs, although I hadn't realized what I was doing. My original idea was that WEB would be merely a tool for documentation, but I actually found that my WEB programs were better than the programs I had been writing in other languages. How could this be?

Well, imagine that you are writing a small subroutine that updates part of a data structure, and suppose that the updating takes only one or two lines of code. In practical programs, there's often something that can go wrong, if the user's input is incorrect, so the subroutine has to check that the input is correct before doing the update. Thus, the subroutine has the general form

> **procedure** *update*;
> **begin if** ⟨ input data is invalid ⟩ **then**
>   ⟨ Issue an error message and try to recover ⟩;
> ⟨ Update the data structure ⟩;
> **end**.

A subtle phenomenon occurs in traditional programming languages: While writing the program for '⟨ Issue an error message and try to recover ⟩', a programmer subconsciously tries to get by with the fewest possible lines of code, in cases where the program for '⟨ Update the data structure ⟩' is quite short. For if an extensive error recovery were actually programmed, the subroutine would appear to have error-message printing as its main purpose. The programmer knows that the error is really an exceptional case that arises only rarely; therefore a lengthy error recovery doesn't look right, and most programmers will minimize it (without realizing that they are doing so) in order to make the subroutine's appearance match its intended behavior. On the other hand when the same task is programmed with WEB, the purpose of *update* is manifestly clear, and the possibility of error recovery can be reduced to a mere mention when *update* is defined. When another section entitled '⟨ Issue an error message and try to recover ⟩' is subsequently written, the whole point of that section is to do the best error recovery, and it becomes quite natural to write a better program as a result.

This fact—that WEB allows you to let each part of the program have its appropriate size, without distorting the readability of other parts—means that good programmers find their WEB programs better than their Pascal programs, even though their Pascal programs once looked like the work of an expert.

Stylistic Issues

I found that my style of using WEB evolved quite a bit during the first year. The general format, in which each section begins with commentary and ends with a formal program fragment, is extremely versatile; you have the freedom to say anything you want, yet you must make a decision about how you'll do it. I imagine that different programmers will converge to quite different styles, but I would like to note down some of the things that have seemed to work best for me.

Consider first the question of macros versus section names. A named section, like '⟨ Issue an error message and try to recover ⟩', is essentially the same as a parameterless macro; WEB provides both. I prefer to use parameterless macros for "small" things that can be embodied in a word or two, but named sections for longer portions of the program that merit a fuller description.

I usually start the name of a section with an imperative verb, but I give a declarative commentary at the beginning of a section. Thus, PRIMES.WEB says '**8.** Now that appropriate ... ⟨ Print table p 8 ⟩ ≡ ... '; I wouldn't do the opposite and say '**8.** Print the table. ⟨ Code for printing 8 ⟩ ≡ ... '.

The name of a section, enclosed in angle brackets, should be long enough to encapsulate the essential characteristics of the code in that section, but it should not be too verbose. I found very early that it would be a mistake to include all of the assumptions about local and global variables in the name of each section, even though such information would strictly be necessary to isolate that section as an independent module. The trick is to find a balance between formal and informal exposition so that a reader can grasp what is happening without being overwhelmed with detail. (See Naur [14].)

Another lesson I learned early in the game was that the name of a section should explicitly mention any nonstandard control structures, even though its data structures can often be left implied. Furthermore, if the control flow is properly explained, you can avoid the usual errors associated with **goto** statements; such statements can safely be introduced in a restrained but natural manner.

For example, §14 of the prime-printing example could be reprogrammed as follows, using '**loop**' as a macro abbreviation for '**while** *true* **do**':

⟨ Increase j until it is the next prime number 14 ⟩ ≡
  loop begin $j \leftarrow j + 2$;
    ⟨ Update variables that depend on j 20 ⟩;
    ⟨ If j is prime, **goto** *found* 22 ⟩;
    end;
found:

With this change, §22 could become

⟨ If j is prime, **goto** *found* 22 ⟩ ≡
  $n \leftarrow 2$;
  while $n < ord$ **do**
    begin ⟨ If $p[n]$ is a factor of j, **goto** *not_found* 26 ⟩;
    $n \leftarrow n + 1$;
    end;
  goto *found*;
not_found:

if §26 changes in the obvious way. The resulting program will be more efficient on most machines; and I believe that it is actually easier to read and to write, in spite of the fact that two **goto** statements appear, because the labels have been used with appropriate interpretations of their abstract significance.

Of course, Pascal makes it difficult to use **goto** statements, because Wirth decided that labels should be numeric, and that they should be declared in advance. If I were to introduce the **goto** statements as suggested, I would have to define numeric macros *found* and *not_found*, and I would have to insert '**label** *found*, *not_found*' into the program at the right place. Such extra work is a bit of a nuisance, but it can be done in WEB without spoiling the exposition.

Pascal has a few other misfeatures that prove to be inconvenient with respect to WEB exposition. The worst of these is the inability to declare local variables in the midst of a program or procedure. For example, a programmer often finds it most natural to define an integer variable when a **for** loop is introduced, but the rules of Pascal insist that such a variable be declared rather far away from that **for** loop. My WEB programs overcome this problem by having sections like '⟨ Local variables for *xyzzy* ⟩' whenever there's a rather lengthy procedure '*xyzzy*' whose local variables should not be declared all at once. But when a procedure is short, say only half a dozen sections long, there's usually no harm in declaring its local variables in Pascal style, because the entire text of the procedure will tend to appear on one or two adjacent pages of the documentation.

Another slightly awkward aspect of Pascal is its treatment of semicolons. If you look closely at the prime-number example, you'll see that I had to be a bit careful about where I put semicolons; sometimes they occur at the end of the expanded text of a section, but usually they don't. With a little self discipline, a person can learn to do this quite satisfactorily, but it is a nuisance until you get used to it.

Economic Issues

What does it cost to use WEB? Let's look first at the lowest level, where computer costs are considered, because it is easy to make quantitative statements at this level. The running time to TANGLE a WEB file is approximately the same as the time needed to compile the resulting Pascal program with a fast compiler; hence the extra preprocessing does not cost much. Similarly, WEAVE doesn't take long to produce a file for TeX. However, TeX needs a comparatively large amount of time to typeset the final document. For example, if we assume that each page requires four seconds, it will take four minutes to produce a 60-page document. The running time for WEAVE-plus-TeX is quite reasonable when you consider that your program is effectively being converted into a fairly substantial booklet; but the costs are sufficiently large to discourage remaking and reprinting such a booklet more than once or twice a day. When a new program is being developed, it is therefore customary to work with hardcopy documentation that is slightly obsolete, and to read the WEB source file itself when up-to-date information is required; the source file is sufficiently easy to read for such purposes.

The costs of WEB are more difficult to estimate at higher levels, but I have found to my surprise that the total time of writing and debugging a WEB program is no greater than the total time of writing and debugging an ALGOL or Pascal program, even though my WEB programs are much better, and even though I am putting substantially more documentation into the programs. Therefore I have lately been using WEB for all of my programming, even for one-off jobs that I write "for my eyes only" just to explore occasional problems. The extra time I spend in preparing additional commentary is regained because the debugging time is reduced.

In retrospect, the fact that a "literate" program takes much less time to debug is not surprising, because the WEB language encourages a discipline that I was previously unwilling to impose on myself. I had known for a long time that the programs I construct for publication in a book, or the programs that I construct in front of a class, have tended to be comparatively free of errors, because I am forced to clarify my thoughts as I do the programming. By contrast, when writing for myself alone, I have often taken shortcuts that proved later to be dreadful mistakes. It's harder for me to fool myself in such ways when I'm writing a WEB program, because I'm in "expository mode" (analogous to classroom lecturing) whenever a WEB is being spun. Ergo, less debugging time.

Now that I am writing all my programs in WEB, an unforeseen problem has, however, arisen: I suddenly have a collection of programs that seem quite beautiful in my own eyes, and I have a compelling urge to publish all of them so that everybody can admire these works of art. A nice little 10-page program can easily be written and debugged in an afternoon and evening; if I keep accumulating such gems, I'll soon run out of storage space, and my office will be encrusted with webs of my own making. There is no telling what will happen if lots of other people catch WEB fever and start foisting their creations on each other. I can already envision the appearance of a new journal, to be entitled *Webs*, for the publication of literate programs; I imagine that it will have a large backlog and a large group of dedicated editors and referees.

Related Work

Nothing about WEB is really new; I have simply combined a bunch of ideas that have been in the air for a long time. I would like to summarize in the next few paragraphs the things that had the greatest influence on my thinking as I put those pieces together.

George Forsythe wrote in 1966 that "A useful algorithm is a substantial contribution to knowledge. Its publication constitutes an important piece of scholarship [2]." His comments have always inspired me to strive for excellence in programming, and they have played a major rôle in shaping my present view that it is worthwhile to consider *every* program as a work of literature.

The design of WEB was influenced primarily by the pioneering work of Pierre-Arnoul de Marneffe [10], [11], whose research on what he called "Holon Programming" has not received the attention it deserves. His work was, in turn, inspired by Arthur Koestler's excellent treatise on the structure of complex systems and organisms [8]; thus we have another connection between programming and literature. A somewhat similar system was independently created by Edwin Towster [18].

I owe a great debt to Edsger Dijkstra, Tony Hoare, Ole-Johan Dahl, and Niklaus Wirth for opening my eyes to the importance of abstraction in the reading and writing of programs, and to Peter Naur for stressing the importance of a balance between formal and informal methods.

Tony Hoare provided a special impetus for WEB when he suggested in 1978 that I should publish my program for TeX. Since very few large-scale software systems were documented in the literature, he had been trying to promote the publication of well-written programs. Hoare's suggestion was actually rather terrifying to me, and I'm sure he knew that he was posing quite a challenge. As a professor of computer science, I was quite comfortable publishing papers about toy problems that could be polished up nicely and presented in an elegant manner; but I had no idea how to take a piece of real software, with all the compromises necessary to make it useful to a large class of people on a wide variety of systems, and to open it up to public scrutiny. How could a supposedly respectable academic, like me, reveal the way he actually writes large programs? And could a large program be made intelligible? My previous attempts along these lines [4] were by now hopelessly out of date. I decided that this would be a good time to try out de Marneffe's ideas; furthermore, the TeX system itself provided me with new tools for printing and format control, so I suspected that it would be possible to obtain state-of-the-art documentation by making proper use of typography.

It is interesting to reread some of the comments that Tony made ten years ago in his keynote address to the first ACM symposium on Principles of Programming Languages [3]:

> Documentation must be regarded as an integral part of the process of design and coding. A good programming language will encourage and assist the programmer to write clear, self-documenting code, and even perhaps to develop and display a pleasant style of writing.

He foresaw many future trends, but not the impending improvements in typesetting quality:

> It is of course possible for a compiler or service program to expand the abbreviations, fill in the defaults, and make explicit the assumptions. But in practice, experience shows that it is very unlikely that the output of a computer will ever be more readable than

its input, except in such trivial but important aspects as improved indentation.

Typographic formatting of computer programs has a long tradition, originating with ALGOL and its immediate precursors. I'm not sure who made the first experiments, but I believe that the lion's share of the credit for developing excellent programming-language typography belongs to two people: Peter Naur, who edited the ALGOL 60 report [13] and gave special care to its presentation; and Myrtle Kellington, who served for many years as executive editor of ACM publications and set the standards that have been adopted by other journals. The computing profession owes much to these people, who made published programs so much more readable than they would otherwise have been; the magnitude of their contribution can only be appreciated by people who submit computer programs to journals like *Acta Arithmetica* whose editors are unfamiliar with computer science. Bill McKeeman called attention to formatting issues when he published Algorithm 268, "ALGOL 60 reference language editor," in 1965 [12]. There has been a flowering of such algorithms in recent years; the papers by Oppen [15] and by Rose and Welsh [16] are particularly noteworthy.

I began to design `WEB` in the spring of 1979, when I constructed a prototype system that was called `DOC`. Luis Trabb Pardo helped me to develop a suitable style of exposition at that time; then Ignacio Zabala Salelles gave `DOC` a thorough test when he prepared a full implementation of TeX in Pascal. Zabala's implementation was successfully transported to many different computers [19]–[22] and this experience was of immense value to me when I cast `WEB` into its present form in 1981. Since then many significant improvements have been suggested by my colleague David R. Fuchs, and I have also benefited from the experiences of a large number of outstanding people who volunteered to be guinea pigs for pre-released versions of TeX. It's impossible for me to name everyone who has helped, but I would like to give special thanks to Arthur Samuel, Howard Trickey, Joe Weening, and Pierre MacKay for important contributions. I'm fortunate indeed to share a working environment with such stimulating people.

When I originally designed the `WEB` system, I spent about six weeks preparing the files `TANGLE.WEB` and `WEAVE.WEB`, during which time I was continually changing the language and trying different styles of exposition. (The programs were neither long nor complicated, but this was rather intensive work, so I didn't get much else done during those six weeks. The first two weeks were actually spent drafting the first ten per cent of what is now `TEX.WEB`.) Then I spent about six tedious hours with a text editor, hand-simulating the behavior of `TANGLE` on `TANGLE.WEB`, so that I had a program `TANGLE.PAS` that was ripe for debugging. At first I had to correct errors both in `TANGLE.WEB` and `TANGLE.PAS`, but soon `TANGLE` was working well enough that I needed only `TANGLE.WEB` as a source file. Then `WEAVE.WEB` could be tangled and debugged too. The total time to create "Version 0" of the `WEB` system, including the language design and the time to debug the programs and write a brief manual for users, was about eight weeks; then enhancements were added at the rate of about one per month for the next 18 months. As a result of this experience I think it's reasonable to state that a `WEB`-like system can be created from scratch in a fairly short time, for some other pair of languages besides TeX and Pascal, by an expert system programmer who is conversant with both languages. Indeed, I spoke about `WEB` on a recent visit to London and one of the people in the audience decided to test this hypothesis; shortly afterwards I received an elegant report from Harold Thimbleby, who had just constructed an excellent system called `Cweb`, based on Troff/Nroff and C instead of TeX and Pascal [17].

Retrospect and Prospects

Enthusiastic reports about new computer languages, by the authors of those languages, are commonplace. Hence I'm well aware of the fact that my own experiences cannot be extrapolated too far. I also realize that, whenever I have encountered a problem with `WEB`, I've simply changed the system; other users of `WEB` cannot operate under the same ground rules.

However, I believe that I have stumbled on a way of programming that produces better programs that are more portable and more easily understood and maintained than ever before; furthermore, the system seems to work with large programs as well as with small ones. I'm pleased that my work on typography, which began as an application of computers to another field, has come full circle and become an application of typography to the heart of computer science; I like to think of `WEB` as a neat "spinoff" of my research on TeX. However, all of my experiences with this system have been highly colored by my own tastes, and only time will tell if a large number of other people will find `WEB` to be equally attractive and useful.

I made a conscious decision not to design a language that would be suitable for everybody. My goal was to provide a tool for system programmers, not for high school students or for hobbyists. I don't have anything against high school students and hobbyists, but I don't believe every computer language should attempt to offer all things to all people.

A user of WEB needs to be good enough at computer science that he or she is comfortable dealing with several languages simultaneously. Since WEB combines TEX and Pascal with a few rules of its own, WEB programs can contain WEB syntax errors, TEX syntax errors, Pascal syntax errors, and algorithmic errors; in practice, all four types of errors occur, and a bit of sophistication is needed to sort out which is which. Computer specialists tend to be better at such things than other people. I have found that WEB programs can be debugged rapidly in spite of the profusion of languages, but I'm sure that many other intelligent people will find such a task difficult.

In other words, WEB seems to be specifically for the peculiar breed of people who are called computer scientists. And I'm pretty sure that there are also a lot of computer scientists who will not enjoy using WEB; some of us are glad that traditional programming languages have comparatively primitive capabilities for inserted comments, because such difficulties provide a good excuse for not documenting programs well. Thus, WEB may be only for the subset of computer scientists who like to write and to explain what they are doing. My hope is that the ability to make explanations more natural will cause more programmers to discover the joys of literate programming, because I believe it's quite a pleasure to combine verbal and mathematical skills; but perhaps I'm hoping for too much. The fact that at least one paper has been written that is a syntactically correct ALGOL 68 program [9] encourages me to persevere in my hopes for the future. Perhaps we will even one day find Pulitzer prizes awarded to computer programs.

And what about the future of WEB? If the next year or so of trial use shows that a lot of other people besides myself become "hooked" on this method of programming, there will be many ways to incorporate the WEB philosophy into a really effective programming environment. For example, it will be worthwhile to produce a unified system that does both tangling and compiling, instead of using separate programs as in Figure 1; and it will also be worthwhile to carry the unification one step further, so that run-time debugging as well as syntactic debugging can be done entirely in terms of the WEB source language. Furthermore, a WEB-like system could be designed to incorporate additional modularization, so that it would be easier to compile different parts of a program independently. The new generation of graphic workstations makes it desirable to display selected program sections on demand, by using TEX only on the sections that are of current interest, instead of producing hardcopy for an entire document. And so on; a considerable amount of additional research and development will be appropriate if the idea of literate programming catches on.

References

[1] Ole-Johan Dahl, Edsger W. Dijkstra, and C. A. R. Hoare, *Structured programming* (London: Academic Press, 1972), 220 pp.

[2] George E. Forsythe, "Algorithms for scientific computation," *Communications of the ACM* **9** (1966), 255–256.

[3] C. A. R. Hoare, "Hints on programming language design," in *Computer systems Reliability*, C. J. Bunyan [Ed.], Infotech State of the Art Report **20** (1972), 505–534. Reprinted in *Essays in Computing Science*, C. B. Jones [Ed.] (Hemel Hempstead: Prentice-Hall International, 1989), 193–216.

[4] Donald E. Knuth, "Computer-drawn flow charts," *Communications of the ACM* **6** (1963), 555–563.

[5] Donald E. Knuth, "Structured programming with **go to** statements," *Computing Surveys* **6**,4 (December 1974), 261–301. [Reprinted with minor changes in *Current Trends in Programming Methodology*, Raymond T. Yeh [Ed.], **1** (Englewood Cliffs, New Jersey: Prentice-Hall, 1977), 140–194; *Classics in Software Engineering*, Edward Nash Yourdon [Ed.] (New York: Yourdon Press, 1979), 259–321.]

[6] Donald E. Knuth, *The TEXbook* (Reading, Massachusetts: Addison-Wesley, 1984), 483 pp.

[7] Donald E. Knuth, *The WEB System of Structured Documentation*, Computer Science Department Report STAN-CS-83-980, Stanford University, Stanford, CA (September 1983), 206 pp.

[8] Arthur Koestler, *The Ghost in the Machine* (New York: Macmillan, 1968).

[9] C. H. Lindsey, "ALGOL 68 with fewer tears," *The Computer Journal* **15** (1972), 176–188.

[10] Pierre Arnoul de Marneffe, *Holon Programming*, Univ. de Liege, Service D'Informatique (December, 1973).

[11] P. A. de Marneffe and D. Ribbens, "Holon Programming," in A. Günther et al. (Eds.), *International Computing Symposium 1973* (Amsterdam: North-Holland, 1974).

[12] William M. McKeeman, "Algorithm 268," *Communications of the ACM* **8** (1965), 667–668.

[13] Peter Naur [Ed.] et al., "Report on the algorithmic language ALGOL 60," *Communications of the ACM* **3**,5 (May 1960), 299–314.

[14] Peter Naur, “Formalization in program development,” *BIT* **22** (1982), 437–453.

[15] Derek Oppen, “Prettyprinting,” *ACM Transactions on Programming Languages and Systems* **2** (1980), 465–483.

[16] G. A. Rose and J. Welsh, “Formatted programming languages,” *Software—Practice & Experience* **11** (1981), 651–669.

[17] H. Thimbleby, *Cweb*, Preprint, University of York (August 1983).

[18] Edwin Towster, “A convention for explicit declaration of environments and top-down refinement of data,” *IEEE Transactions on Software Engineering* **SE–5** (1979), 374–386.

[19] Ignacio Zabala and Luis Trabb Pardo, “The status of the PASCAL implementation of TEX,” *TUGboat* **1** (1980), 16–17.

[20] I. Zabala, “TEX-PASCAL and PASCAL compilers,” *TUGboat* **2**,1 (February 1981), 11–12.

[21] I. Zabala, “Some feedback from PTEX installations,” *TUGboat* **2**,2 (July 1981), 16–19.

[22] I. Zabala, “How portable is PASCAL?” draft of paper in preparation (1982).

Chapter 5

Programming Pearls, by Jon Bentley: Sampling (1986)

[Jon Bentley devoted his popular columns entitled Programming Pearls to the topic of Literate Programming, in the May and June 1986 Communications of the ACM. These columns are reprinted here and in the next chapter.]

When was the last time you spent a pleasant evening in a comfortable chair, reading a good program? I don't mean the slick subroutine you wrote last summer, nor even the big system you have to modify next week. I'm talking about cuddling up with a classic, and starting to read on page one. Sure, you may spend more time studying this elegant routine or worrying about that questionable decision, and everybody skims over a few parts they find boring. But let's get back to the question: When was the last time you read an excellent program?

Until recently, my answer to that question was, "Never." I'm ashamed of that. I wouldn't have much respect for an aeronautical engineer who had never admired a superb airplane, nor for a structural engineer who had never studied a beautiful bridge. Yet I, like most programmers, was in roughly that position with respect to programs. That's tragic, because good writing requires good reading—you can't write a novel if you've never read one. But the fault doesn't rest entirely with us programmers: Most programs are written to be executed, a few are written to be maintained, but almost no programs are written so someone else can read them.

Don Knuth is changing that. I recently spent a couple of pleasant evenings reading the five-hundred-page implementation of the TEX document compiler. I have no intention of modifying the code, nor am I much more interested in document compilers than the average programmer-on-the-street. I read the code, rather, for the same reason that a student of architecture would spend an afternoon admiring one of Frank Lloyd Wright's buildings. There was a lot to admire in Knuth's work: the decomposition of the large task into subroutines, elegant algorithms and data structures, and a coding style that gives a robust, portable, and maintainable system. I'm a better programmer for having read the program, and I had a lot of fun doing it.

At this point, of course, I hope that you'll run out and read the TEX program yourself; the Further Reading tells you where to find it. As a temporary substitute, this column introduces the programming style that Knuth used to create his program, and the `WEB` programming system that supports the approach. He calls the style "literate programming"; his goal is to produce programs that are works of literature. My dictionary defines literature as "writings having excellence of form or expression and expressing ideas of permanent or universal interest." I think that Knuth has met his goal.

This column describes the style and presents a small example that Don Knuth was kind enough to write; next month's column is devoted to a more substantial literate program by Knuth.

The Vision

When I wrote my first program, the only reader I had in mind was the computer that ran it. The "structured programming" revolution of the early 1970s taught us that we should keep in mind several other purposes of a program:

Design. As I write a program, I should use a language that minimizes the distance between the problem-solving strategies I have in my head and the program text I eventually write on paper.

Analysis. When I develop particularly subtle code, I should use a language that helps me to reason about its correctness.

Maintenance. When I write a program, I should keep in mind that its next reader might be someone who is totally unfamiliar with it (such as myself, a year later).

These insights had a tremendous impact. A few principles of programming style and a little discipline led to COBOL, FORTRAN, and assembly routines that were easier to understand. By the early 1980s, most of us had stopped debating whether **go to** statements were acceptable and had started programming in a high-level language that encouraged cleanliness of expression.

This raised the problem one level: We can understand any given procedure, but it's still hard to make sense of the system as a whole ("I see the trees, but where is the forest?"). Researchers have worked on many kinds of solutions to this problem, such as documentation techniques and module specification and interconnection languages.

Knuth's insight is to focus on the program as a message from its author to its readers. While typical programs are organized for the convenience of their compilers, literate programs are designed for their human readers. At some point, of course, the program must be executed by a computer. Knuth's system allows the programmer to think at a high level, and has the computer do the dirty work of translating the literate description into an executable program.

Before we move on to the details of the system, take a few minutes to enjoy Knuth's Program 1 on pages 144–149. In addition to illustrating literate programming, it is also a particularly efficient solution to a problem posed in an earlier column.

The WEB System

O what a tangled web we weave
When first we practice to deceive!
—Walter Scott

Program 1 may look too good to be true, but it is indeed the genuine article: when Knuth wrote, tested, and debugged the program, he did so from a listing almost exactly like the one presented here [only "almost exactly" because his program was re-typeset to conform to the style of this publication]. This section will sketch the mechanics of the WEB system and the programming style it encourages.

The major components of a WEB program named PROG are shown in this figure:

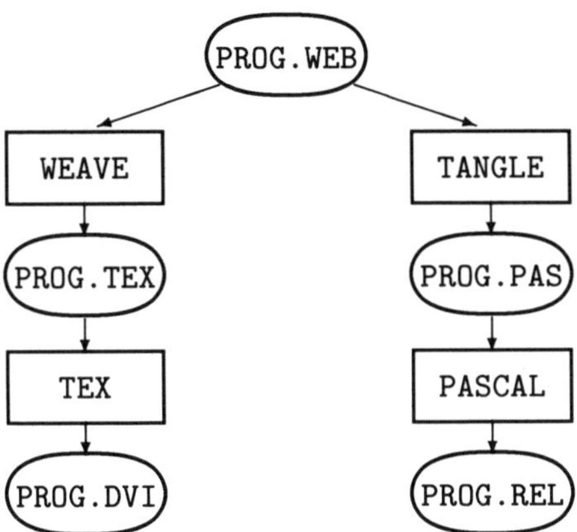

The programmer writes the "source file" PROG.WEB. The WEAVE program transforms that file into the TEX input PROG.TEX, which is in turn fed to the TEX compiler. The output of this process (the process is the left branch in the figure) is the file PROG.DVI, a device-independent output file that can be printed on a typesetter or laser printer. Program 1 was produced in this fashion.

The same PROG.WEB file can also serve as input to the TANGLE program, which produces the Pascal file PROG.PAS; the Pascal compiler then transforms that to the executable program PROG.REL. Thus the right-hand branch in the above figure yields running code.

Knuth chose the names carefully. The WEB source file is an intricate structure that describes the program both in text and Pascal code. The WEAVE program spins that into a beautiful document: It unites the parts into a coherent whole that can be readily understood by human readers. The TANGLE program, on the other hand, produces a Pascal program that can be processed by a machine, but it is totally unfit for human consumption. (In the bad old days well-intentioned programmers "patched" binary object code: TANGLE output is as ugly as possible to ensure that programmers deal only with WEB files.)

There isn't space enough in this column to give details on the WEB input file PROG.WEB. Parts of it are pure TEX typesetting commands, and other parts are pure Pascal source text. The vast majority, though, is a straightforward combination of English text and program text and a few simple commands to tell which is which. For more details, consult the Further Reading.

But more important than the mechanics of the WEB system is its philosophy. The system does not force one to write in any particular style. Rather, it provides the ability to present the code and text in the order desired by the programmer/author.

The Challenge

When I first read Knuth's "Literate Programming" paper referenced under Further Reading, I was quite impressed by his approach. When I read the large programs referenced there, I was overwhelmed: For the first time, somebody was proud enough of a substantial piece of code to publish it for public viewing, in a way that is inviting to read. I was so fascinated that I wrote Knuth a letter, asking whether he had any spare programs handy that I might publish as a "Programming Pearl."

But that was too easy for Knuth. He responded, "Why should you let me choose the program? My claim is that programming is an artistic endeavor and that the WEB system gives me the best way to write beautiful programs. Therefore I should be able to meet a stiffer test: I should be able to write a superliterate program that will be noticeably better than an ordinary one, whatever the topic. So how about this: You tell me what sort of program you want me to write, and I'll try to prove the merits of literate programming by finding the best possible solution to whatever problem you pose[1]—at least the best by current standards."

He laid some ground rules for the task. The program had to be short enough to fit comfortably in a column, say, an afternoon's worth of programming. It had to be a complete program (not just a fragment), and could not stress input and output (Knuth has boilerplate to handle that problem, but that isn't of interest to most readers). Because his "Literate Programming" article is built around a program to print prime numbers, this assignment should avoid number-theoretic problems.

I chose a problem that I had assigned to several classes on data structures.

> Given a text file and an integer K, you are to print the K most common words in the file (and the number of their occurrences) in decreasing frequency.

I left open a number of issues, such as the precise definition of words and limits on sizes such as maximum number of words. I did impose an efficiency constraint: A user should be able to find the 100 most frequent words in a twenty-page technical paper without undue emotional trauma.

This problem has several pleasant attributes: It combines simple text manipulation with searching (to increment the count of this input word) and sorting (for output in decreasing frequency). Furthermore, it's useful: I run such a program on documents I write, to find overused words.

Next month's column presents Knuth's literate solution to this problem. Problem 1 encourages you to tackle the problem yourself to increase your appreciation of Knuth's program.

---

[1] Although I assigned the program to be described next month, Knuth chose Program 1 himself. When I sent him the "assignment," he returned both the requested solution and a solution to a problem described in an earlier column. He has kindly allowed both programs to be published.

Principles

An Important Problem. Most real programs are written to be executed but not read; many published programs are written to be read but have never been executed.[2] Knuth's work on literate programs is an important step towards programs fit for both man and computing beast. That's good news for writers as well as readers: Rob Pike writes, "Publishing programs is a healthy habit. Every program I've written knowing it was to be published was improved by that knowledge. I think more clearly when I'm writing for an audience, and find it helps to pretend there always is one."

An Important Solution. In addition to defining (and naming) the area, Knuth has made two fundamental contributions to literate programming. The first is his `WEB` system, which has been used to develop several large (and widely used) programs. His insights, though, transcend the particular system: his "Literate Programming" paper describes `WEB` lookalikes implemented for other programming and document-production languages. The second fundamental contribution is a body of literate programs written in `WEB`, several of which are referenced under Further Reading. Most computer scientists are as cowardly as I am; our published programs are rarely more than tiny (and highly polished) subroutines. Knuth is almost unique in publishing the code to workhorse programs. He even believes that it is correct: in the book *TEX: The Program* he writes that "I believe that the final bug in TEX was discovered and removed on November 27, 1985" and offers the princely sum of $20.48 to the finder of any errors still lurking in the code.

Problems in Paradise. Because it is based on Pascal, `WEB` inherits all the universality and some of the problems of the language (although it nicely patches several serious defects of Pascal). A `WEB` program is written in a mixture of `WEB`, TEX, and Pascal; that can be a barrier both for learning to use the system and for debugging a program. And the very name "literate programming" implies that its practitioners must be competent in both literature and programming; it is hard enough to find people with one of those skills, let alone both (though `WEB` does amplify one's abilities).

---

[2] There are exceptions. The programs in Kernighan and Plauger's *Software Tools* are widely used and were included in the text directly from their executable form (the book and the programs were published by Addison-Wesley in 1976; a Pascal version appeared in 1981). I am less exacting with the small programs that appear in this column: I usually test and debug them in a real language (typically C or `AWK`), then transliterate the trusted code into the Pascal-like pseudocode that I use in the column.

Problems

1. Knuth's programming problem (finding the K most common words in a document) can be interpreted in several ways; Knuth's assignment is somewhere between a and b. Try the problem yourself in one or more of these versions.
   a. *An exercise in simple programming.* In an Algol-like language, implement the simplest program to solve the problem (simplicity might be measured by lines of source code).
   b. *An exercise in efficient programming.* In an Algol-like language, implement the most efficient program to solve the problem (measured in terms of time and/or space).
   c. *An exercise in text processing.* The February column discussed novel solutions to hard problems. Can you find a way to use existing text processing tools to solve this problem with very little new code?
2. Implement Knuth's Program 1 in your favorite language, using the best documentation style that you know. How does it compare to Program 1 in length and comprehensibility?
3. Analyze the run time taken by Program 1 either mathematically or experimentally.
4. Knuth's Program 1 solves the sampling problem in $O(M)$ expected time and $O(M)$ space; show how it can be solved in $O(M)$ expected time and $O(1)$ space.
5. [H. Trickey] One can view `WEB` as providing two levels of macros: one can define a short string or use the ⟨ Do this now ⟩ notation for longer pieces of code. Is this mechanism qualitatively better than that provided by other programming environments?
6. [H. Trickey] `TANGLE` intentionally produces unreadable code. Are there any potential problems?
7. [D. E. Knuth] A program for "set equality" must determine whether two input sequences of integers determine the same set. Show how to use ordered hash tables to solve this problem.

Appendix: `sample.web`

1. Introduction. Jon Bentley recently discussed the following interesting problem as one of his "Programming Pearls" [*Communications of the ACM* **27** (December, 1984), 1179–1182]:

> The input consists of two integers M and N, with $M < N$. The output is a sorted list of M random numbers in the range $1\,..\,N$ in which no integer occurs more than once. For probability buffs, we desire a sorted selection without replacement in which each selection occurs equiprobably.

The present program illustrates what I think is the best solution to this problem, when M is reasonably large yet small compared to N. It's the method described tersely in the answer to exercise 3.4.2–15 of my book *Seminumerical Algorithms*, pp. 141 and 555.

2. For simplicity, all input and output in this program is assumed to be handled at the terminal. The `WEB` macros *read_terminal*, *print*, and *print_ln* defined here can easily be changed to accommodate other conventions.

define *read_terminal*(#) ≡ *read*(*tty*, #)
  { input a value from the terminal }
define *print*(#) ≡ *write*(*tty*, #) { output to the terminal }
define *print_ln*(#) ≡ *write_ln*(*tty*, #)
  { output to the terminal and end the line }

3. Here's an outline of the entire Pascal program:

program *sample*;
  var ⟨ Global variables 4 ⟩
  ⟨ The random number generation procedure 5 ⟩
  begin ⟨ The main program 6 ⟩;
  end.

4. The global variables M and N have already been mentioned; we had better declare them. Other global variables will be declared later.

define $M\_max = 5000$
{ maximum value of M allowed in this program }

⟨ Global variables 4 ⟩ ≡
M: *integer*; { size of the sample }
N: *integer*; { size of the population }

See also sections 7, 9, and 13.

This code is used in section 3.

5. We assume the existence of a system routine called $rand\_int(i, j)$ that returns a random integer chosen uniformly in the range $i \mathrel{..} j$.

⟨ The random number generation procedure 5 ⟩ ≡
function $rand\_int(i, j : integer)$: *integer*; *extern*;

This code is used in section 3.

---

6. A plan of attack. After the user has specified M and N, we compute the sample by following a general procedure recommended by Bentley:

⟨ The main program 6 ⟩ ≡
  ⟨ Establish the values of M and N 8 ⟩;
  $size \leftarrow 0$; ⟨ Initialize set S to empty 10 ⟩;
  while $size < M$ **do**
    begin $T \leftarrow rand\_int(1, N)$;
    ⟨ If T is not in S, insert it and increase *size* 11 ⟩;
    end;
  ⟨ Print the elements of S in sorted order 14 ⟩

This code is used in section 3.

7. The main program just sketched has introduced several more global variables. There's a set S of integers, whose representation will be deferred until later; but we can declare two auxiliary integer variables now.

⟨ Global variables 4 ⟩ +≡
size: *integer*; { the number of elements in set S }
T: *integer*; { new candidate for membership in S }

8. The first order of business is to have a short dialog with the user.

⟨ Establish the values of M and N 8 ⟩ ≡
```
repeat print('population␣size:␣N␣=␣'); read_terminal(N);
  if N ≤ 0 then print_ln('N␣should␣be␣positive!');
until N > 0;
repeat print('sample␣size:␣M␣=␣'); read_terminal(M);
  if M < 0 then print_ln('M␣shouldn''t␣be␣negative!')
  else if M > N then print_ln('M␣shouldn''t␣exceed␣N!')
    else if M > M_max then
        print_ln('(Sorry,␣M␣must␣be␣at␣most␣', M_max : 1, '.)');
until (M ≥ 0) ∧ (M ≤ N) ∧ (M ≤ M_max)
```
This code is used in section 6.

---

9. An ordered hash table. The key idea to an efficient solution of this sampling problem is to maintain a set whose entries are easily sorted. The method of "ordered hash tables" [Amble and Knuth, *The Computer Journal* **17** (May 1974), 135–142] is ideally suited to this task, as we shall see.

Ordered hashing is similar to ordinary linear probing, except that the relative order of keys is taken into account. The cited paper derives theoretical results that will not be rederived here, but we shall use the following fundamental property: *The entries of an ordered hash table are independent of the order in which its keys were inserted.* Thus, an ordered hash table is a "canonical" representation of its set of entries.

We shall represent S by an array of $2M$ integers. Since Pascal doesn't permit arrays of variable size, we must leave room for the largest possible table.

⟨ Global variables 4 ⟩ +≡
```
hash: array [0 .. M_max + M_max − 1] of integer;
        { the ordered hash table }
H: 0 .. M_max + M_max − 1;   { an index into hash }
H_max: 0 .. M_max + M_max − 1;   { the current hash size }
alpha: real;   { the ratio of table size to N }
```

10. ⟨ Initialize set S to empty 10 ⟩ ≡
```
H_max ← 2 * M − 1; alpha ← 2 * M/N;
for H ← 0 to H_max do hash[H] ← 0
```
This code is used in section 6.

11. Now we come to the interesting part, where the algorithm tries to insert T into an ordered hash table. We use the hash address $H = \lfloor 2M(T-1)/N \rfloor$ as a starting point, since this quantity is monotonic in T and almost uniformly distributed in the range $0 \le H < 2M$.

⟨ If T is not in S, insert it and increase *size* 11 ⟩ ≡
  $H \leftarrow trunc(alpha * (T-1))$;
  while $hash[H] > T$ **do**
    if $H = 0$ **then** $H \leftarrow H\_max$ **else** $H \leftarrow H - 1$;
  if $hash[H] < T$ **then** { T is not present }
    begin $size \leftarrow size + 1$; ⟨ Insert T into the ordered hash table 12 ⟩;
    end

This code is used in section 6.

12. The heart of ordered hashing is the insertion process. In general, the new key T will be inserted in place of a previous key $T_1 < T$, which is then reinserted in place of $T_2 < T_1$, etc., until an empty slot is discovered.

⟨ Insert T into the ordered hash table 12 ⟩ ≡
  while $hash[H] > 0$ **do**
    begin $TT \leftarrow hash[H]$; { we have $0 < TT < T$ }
    $hash[H] \leftarrow T$; $T \leftarrow TT$;
    repeat if $H = 0$ **then** $H \leftarrow H\_max$ **else** $H \leftarrow H - 1$;
    until $hash[H] < T$;
    end;
  $hash[H] \leftarrow T$

This code is used in section 11.

13. ⟨ Global variables 4 ⟩ +≡
TT: *integer*; { a key that's being moved }

---

14. Sorting in linear time. The climax of this program is the fact that the entries in our ordered hash table can easily be read out in increasing order.

Why is this true? Well, we know that the final state of the table is independent of the order in which the elements entered. Furthermore it's easy to understand what the table looks like when the entries are inserted in decreasing order, because we have used a monotonic hash function. Therefore we know that the table must have an especially simple form.

Suppose the nonzero entries are $T_1 < \cdots < T_M$. If k of these have "wrapped around" in the insertion process (i.e., if H passed from 0 to H_max, k times), table position $hash[0]$ will either be zero (in which case k must also be zero) or it will contain T_{k+1}. In the latter case, the entries $T_{k+1} < \cdots < T_M$ and $T_1 < \cdots < T_k$ will appear in order from left to right. Thus the output can be sorted with at most two passes over the table!

define *print_it* $\equiv$ *print_ln*(*hash*[*H*] : 10)

⟨Print the elements of S in sorted order 14⟩ $\equiv$

```
if hash[0] = 0 then   { there was no wrap-around }
  begin for H ← 1 to H_max do
    if hash[H] > 0 then print_it;
  end
else begin for H ← 1 to H_max do
        { print the wrapped-around entries }
    if hash[H] > 0 then
      if hash[H] < hash[0] then print_it;
  for H ← 0 to H_max do
    if hash[H] ≥ hash[0] then print_it;
  end
```

This code is used in section 6.

---

15. Index. The uses of single-letter variables aren't indexed by WEB, so this list is quite short. (And an index is quite pointless anyway, for a program of this size.)

⟨ Insert T into the ordered hash table 12 ⟩ Used in section 11.
⟨ Print the elements of S in sorted order 14 ⟩ Used in section 6.
⟨ The main program 6 ⟩ Used in section 3.
⟨ The random number generation procedure 5 ⟩ Used in section 3.

Further Reading

"Literate programming" is the title and the topic of Knuth's article in the May 1984 *Computer Journal* (Volume 27, Number 2, pp. 97–111) [Chapter 4 of this volume]. It introduces a literate style of programming with the example of printing the first 1,000 prime numbers. Complete documentation of "The `WEB` System of Structured Documentation" is available as Stanford Computer Science technical report 980 (September 1983, 206 pages); it contains the `WEB` source code for `TANGLE` and `WEAVE`.

The small programs in this column and next month's hint at the benefits of literate programming: Its full power can only be appreciated when you see it applied to substantial programs. Two large `WEB` programs appear in Knuth's five-volume *Computers & Typesetting*, just published by Addison-Wesley. The source code for TeX is Volume B, entitled *TeX: The Program* (xvi + 594 pages). Volume D is *METAFONT: The Program* (xvi + 560 pages) [excerpts from Volumes B and D are included in the present book as Chapter 8]. Volume A is *The TeXbook*, Volume C is *The METAFONTbook*, and Volume E is *Computer Modern Typefaces.*

In a subsequent "Programming Pearl," David Gries contributed his own version of the sampling program above, with independent proofs of the properties of ordered hashing for which §9 had simply given a brief reference to the literature. See *Communications of the ACM* **30** (April 1987), 284–289.

Chapter 6

Programming Pearls, Continued: Common Words (1986)

Last month's column [Chapter 5] introduced Don Knuth's style of "Literate Programming" and his `WEB` *system for building programs that are works of literature. This column presents a literate program by Knuth (its origins are sketched in last month's column) and, as befits literature, a review. So without further ado, here is Knuth's program, retypeset for this publication. —Jon Bentley*

1. Introduction. The purpose of this program is to solve the following problem posed by Jon Bentley:

> Given a text file and an integer k, print the k most common words in the file (and the number of their occurrences) in decreasing frequency.

Jon intentionally left the problem somewhat vague, but he stated that "a user should be able to find the one hundred most frequent words in a twenty-page technical paper (roughly a 50K byte file) without undue emotional trauma."

Let us agree that a *word* is a sequence of one or more contiguous letters; `"Bentley"` is a word, but `"ain't"` isn't. The sequence of letters should be maximal, in the sense that it cannot be lengthened without including a nonletter. Uppercase letters are considered equivalent to their lowercase counterparts, so that the words `"Bentley"` and `"BENTLEY"` and `"bentley"` are essentially identical.

The given problem still isn't well defined, for the file might contain more than k words, all of the same frequency; or there might not even be as many as k words. Let's be more precise: The most common words are to be printed in order of decreasing frequency, with words of equal frequency listed in alphabetic order. Printing should stop after k words have been output, if more than k words are present.

2. The *input* file is assumed to contain the given text. If it begins with a positive decimal number (preceded by optional blanks), that number will be the value of k; otherwise we shall assume that $k = 100$. Answers will be sent to the *output* file.

define *default_k* = 100
{ use this value if k isn't otherwise specified }

3. Besides solving the given problem, this program is supposed to be an example of the `WEB` system, for people who know some Pascal but who have never seen `WEB` before. Here is an outline of the program to be constructed:

program *common_words*(*input*, *output*);
type ⟨ Type declarations 17 ⟩
var ⟨ Global variables 4 ⟩
⟨ Procedures for initialization 5 ⟩
⟨ Procedures for input and output 9 ⟩
⟨ Procedures for data manipulation 20 ⟩
begin ⟨ The main program 8 ⟩;
end.

4. The main idea of the `WEB` approach is to let the program grow in natural stages, with its parts presented in roughly the order that they might have been written by a programmer who isn't especially clairvoyant.

For example, each global variable will be introduced when we first know that it is necessary or desirable; the `WEB` system will take care of collecting these declarations into the proper place. We already know about one global variable, namely the number that Bentley called k. Let us give it the more descriptive name *max_words_to_print*.

⟨ Global variables 4 ⟩ ≡
max_words_to_print: *integer*;
    { at most this many words will be printed }

See also sections 11, 13, 18, 22, 32, and 36.

This code is used in section 3.

5. As we introduce new global variables, we'll often want to give them certain starting values. This will be done by the *initialize* procedure, whose body will consist of various pieces of code to be specified when we think of particular kinds of initialization.

⟨ Procedures for initialization 5 ⟩ ≡
procedure *initialize*;
  var *i*: *integer*; { all-purpose index for initializations }
  begin ⟨ Set initial values 12 ⟩
  end;

This code is used in section 3.

6. The `WEB` system, which may be thought of as a preprocessor for Pascal, includes a macro definition facility so that portable programs are easier to write. For example, we have already defined '*default_k*' to be 100. Here are two more examples of `WEB` macros; they allow us to write, e.g., '*incr*(*count*[*p*])' as a convenient abbreviation for the statement '*count*[*p*] ← *count*[*p*] + 1'.

  define *incr*(#) ≡ # ← # + 1 { increment a variable }
  define *decr*(#) ≡ # ← # − 1 { decrement a variable }

7. Some of the procedures we shall be writing come to abrupt conclusions; hence it will be convenient to introduce a '**return**' macro for the operation of jumping to the end of the procedure. A symbolic label '*exit*' will be declared in all such procedures, and '*exit*:' will be placed just before the final **end**. (No other labels or **goto** statements are used in the present program, but the author would find it painful to eliminate these particular ones.)

  define *exit* = 30 { the end of a procedure }
  define *return* ≡ **goto** *exit* { quick termination }
  format *return* ≡ *nil* { typeset '**return**' in boldface }

---

8. Strategic considerations. What algorithms and data structures should be used for Bentley's problem? Clearly we need to be able to recognize different occurrences of the same word, so some sort of internal dictionary is necessary. There's no obvious way to decide that a particular word of the input cannot possibly be in the final set, until we've gotten very near the end of the file; so we might as well remember every word that appears.

There should be a frequency count associated with each word, and we will eventually want to run through the words in order of decreasing frequency. But there's no need to keep these counts in order as we read through the input, since the order matters only at the end.

Therefore it makes sense to structure our program as follows:

⟨ The main program 8 ⟩ ≡
  initialize;
  ⟨ Establish the value of *max_words_to_print* 10 ⟩;
  ⟨ Input the text, maintaining a dictionary with frequency counts 34 ⟩;
  ⟨ Sort the dictionary by frequency 39 ⟩;
  ⟨ Output the results 41 ⟩

This code is used in section 3.

---

9. Basic input routines. Let's switch to a bottom-up approach now, by writing some of the procedures that we know will be necessary sooner or later. Then we'll have some confidence that our program is taking shape, even though we haven't decided yet how to handle the searching or the sorting. It will be nice to get the messy details of Pascal input out of the way and off our minds.

Here's a function that reads an optional positive integer, returning zero if none is present at the beginning of the current line.

⟨ Procedures for input and output 9 ⟩ ≡
function *read_int*: *integer*;
  var *n*: *integer*; { the accumulated value }
  begin $n \leftarrow 0$;
  if $\neg eof$ **then**
    begin while $(\neg eoln) \land (input\uparrow = \text{'␣'})$ **do** *get*(*input*);
    while $(input\uparrow \ge \text{'0'}) \land (input\uparrow \le \text{'9'})$ **do**
      begin $n \leftarrow 10 * n + ord(input\uparrow) - ord(\text{'0'})$;
      get(*input*);
      end;
    end;

```
  read_int ← n;
  end;
```

See also sections 15, 35, and 40.

This code is used in section 3.

10. We invoke *read_int* only once.

```
⟨ Establish the value of max_words_to_print 10 ⟩ ≡
  max_words_to_print ← read_int;
  if max_words_to_print = 0 then max_words_to_print ← default_k
```

This code is used in section 8.

11. To find words in the *input* file, we want a quick way to distinguish letters from nonletters. Pascal has conspired to make this problem somewhat tricky, because it leaves many details of the character set undefined. We shall define two arrays, *lowercase* and *uppercase*, that specify the letters of the alphabet. A third array, *lettercode*, maps arbitrary characters into the integers 0 . . 26.

If c is a value of type *char* that represents the kth letter of the alphabet, then $lettercode[ord(c)] = k$; but if c is a nonletter, $lettercode[ord(c)] = 0$. We assume that $0 \le ord(c) \le 255$ whenever c is of type *char*.

```
⟨ Global variables 4 ⟩ +≡
lowercase, uppercase: array [1 .. 26] of char;  { the letters }
lettercode: array [0 .. 255] of 0 .. 26;  { the input conversion table }
```

12. A somewhat tedious set of assignments is necessary for the definition of *lowercase* and *uppercase*, because letters need not be consecutive in Pascal's character set.

```
⟨ Set initial values 12 ⟩ ≡
  lowercase[1] ← ´a´; uppercase[1] ← ´A´;
  lowercase[2] ← ´b´; uppercase[2] ← ´B´;
  lowercase[3] ← ´c´; uppercase[3] ← ´C´;
  lowercase[4] ← ´d´; uppercase[4] ← ´D´;
  lowercase[5] ← ´e´; uppercase[5] ← ´E´;
  lowercase[6] ← ´f´; uppercase[6] ← ´F´;
  lowercase[7] ← ´g´; uppercase[7] ← ´G´;
  lowercase[8] ← ´h´; uppercase[8] ← ´H´;
  lowercase[9] ← ´i´; uppercase[9] ← ´I´;
  lowercase[10] ← ´j´; uppercase[10] ← ´J´;
  lowercase[11] ← ´k´; uppercase[11] ← ´K´;
  lowercase[12] ← ´l´; uppercase[12] ← ´L´;
  lowercase[13] ← ´m´; uppercase[13] ← ´M´;
```

```
lowercase[14] ← 'n'; uppercase[14] ← 'N';
lowercase[15] ← 'o'; uppercase[15] ← 'O';
lowercase[16] ← 'p'; uppercase[16] ← 'P';
lowercase[17] ← 'q'; uppercase[17] ← 'Q';
lowercase[18] ← 'r'; uppercase[18] ← 'R';
lowercase[19] ← 's'; uppercase[19] ← 'S';
lowercase[20] ← 't'; uppercase[20] ← 'T';
lowercase[21] ← 'u'; uppercase[21] ← 'U';
lowercase[22] ← 'v'; uppercase[22] ← 'V';
lowercase[23] ← 'w'; uppercase[23] ← 'W';
lowercase[24] ← 'x'; uppercase[24] ← 'X';
lowercase[25] ← 'y'; uppercase[25] ← 'Y';
lowercase[26] ← 'z'; uppercase[26] ← 'Z';
for i ← 0 to 255 do lettercode[i] ← 0;
for i ← 1 to 26 do
  begin lettercode[ord(lowercase[i])] ← i;
  lettercode[ord(uppercase[i])] ← i;
  end;
```

See also sections 14, 19, 23, and 33.

This code is used in section 5.

13. Each new word found in the input will be placed into a *buffer* array. We shall assume that no words are more than 60 letters long; if a longer word appears, it will be truncated to 60 characters, and a warning message will be printed at the end of the run.

```
define max_word_length = 60
            { words shouldn't be longer than this }
⟨ Global variables 4 ⟩ +≡
buffer: array [1 .. max_word_length] of 1 .. 26;  { the current word }
word_length: 0 .. max_word_length;
      { the number of active letters currently in buffer }
word_truncated: boolean;
      { was some word longer than max_word_length? }
```

14. ⟨ Set initial values 12 ⟩ +≡

```
word_truncated ← false;
```

15. We're ready now for the main input routine, which puts the next word into the buffer. If no more words remain, *word_length* is set to zero; otherwise *word_length* is set to the length of the new word.

```
⟨ Procedures for input and output 9 ⟩ +≡
procedure get_word;
```

```
  label exit;  { enable a quick return }
  begin word_length ← 0;
  if ¬eof then
    begin while lettercode[ord(input↑)] = 0 do
      if ¬eoln then get(input)
      else begin read_ln;
        if eof then return;
        end;
    ⟨ Read a word into buffer 16 ⟩;
    end;
exit: end;
```

16. At this point *lettercode*[*ord*(*input*↑)] > 0, hence *input*↑ contains the first letter of a word.

```
⟨ Read a word into buffer 16 ⟩ ≡
  repeat if word_length = max_word_length then
      word_truncated ← true
    else begin incr(word_length);
      buffer[word_length] ← lettercode[ord(input↑)];
      end;
    get(input);
  until lettercode[ord(input↑)] = 0
```

This code is used in section 15.

---

17. Dictionary lookup. Given a word in the buffer, we will want to look for it in a dynamic dictionary of all words that have appeared so far. We expect many words to occur often, so we want a search technique that will find existing words quickly. Furthermore, the dictionary should accommodate words of variable length, and (ideally) it should also facilitate the task of alphabetic ordering.

These constraints suggest a variant of the data structure introduced by Frank M. Liang in his Ph.D. thesis [*Word Hy-phen-a-tion by Com-pu-ter*, Stanford University, 1983]. Liang's structure, which we may call a *hash trie*, requires comparatively few operations to find a word that is already present, although it may take somewhat longer to insert a new entry. Some space is sacrificed—we will need two pointers, a count, and another 5-bit field for each character in the dictionary, plus extra space to keep the hash table from becoming congested—but relatively large memories are commonplace nowadays, so the method seems ideal for the present application.

A trie represents a set of words and all prefixes of those words [cf. Knuth, *Sorting and Searching*, Section 6.3]. For convenience, we shall say that all nonempty prefixes of the words in our dictionary are also words, even though they may not occur as "words" in the input file. Each word (in this generalized sense) is represented by a *pointer*, which is an index into four large arrays called *link*, *sibling*, *count*, and *ch*.

define *trie_size* = 32767 { the largest pointer value }

⟨ Type declarations 17 ⟩ ≡
pointer = 0 . . *trie_size*;

This code is used in section 3.

18. One-letter words are represented by the pointers 1 through 26. The representation of longer words is defined recursively: If p represents word w and if $1 \leq c \leq 26$, then the word w followed by the cth letter of the alphabet is represented by $link[p] + c$.

For example, suppose that $link[2] = 1000$, $link[1005] = 2000$, and $link[2014] = 3000$. Then the word `"b"` is represented by the pointer value 2; `"be"` is represented by $link[2] + 5 = 1005$; `"ben"` is represented by 2014; and `"bent"` by 3020. If no longer word beginning with `"bent"` appears in the dictionary, $link[3020]$ will be zero.

The hash trie also contains redundant information to facilitate traversal and updating. If $link[p]$ is nonzero, then $link[link[p]] = p$. Furthermore if $q = link[p] + c$ is a "child" of p, we have $ch[q] = c$; this additional information makes it possible to go from child to parent, since $link[q - ch[q]] = link[link[p]] = p$.

Children of the same parent are linked together cyclically by *sibling* pointers: The largest child of p is $sibling[link[p]]$, and the next largest is $sibling[sibling[link[p]]]$; the smallest child's *sibling* pointer is $link[p]$. Continuing our earlier example, if all words in the dictionary beginning with `"be"` start with either `"ben"` or `"bet"`, then $sibling[2000] = 2020$, $sibling[2020] = 2014$, and $sibling[2014] = 2000$.

Notice that children of different parents might appear next to each other. For example, we might have $ch[2019] = 6$, for the child of some word such that $link[p] = 2013$.

If $link[p] \neq 0$, the table entry in position $link[p]$ is called the "header" of p's children. The special code value *header* appears in the *ch* field of each header entry.

If p represents a word, $count[p]$ is the number of times that the word has occurred in the input so far. The *count* field in a header entry is undefined.

Unused positions p have $ch[p] = empty\_slot$. In this case $link[p]$, $sibling[p]$, and $count[p]$ are undefined.

```
define empty_slot = 0
define header = 27
define move_to_prefix(#) ≡ # ← link[# − ch[#]]
define move_to_last_suffix(#) ≡
        while link[#] ≠ 0 do # ← sibling[link[#]]
⟨Global variables 4⟩ +≡
link, sibling: array [pointer] of pointer;
ch: array [pointer] of empty_slot .. header;
```

19. ⟨Set initial values 12⟩ +≡

```
for i ← 27 to trie_size do ch[i] ← empty_slot;
for i ← 1 to 26 do
  begin ch[i] ← i; link[i] ← 0; count[i] ← 0; sibling[i] ← i − 1;
  end;
ch[0] ← header; link[0] ← 0; sibling[0] ← 26;
```

20. Here's the basic subroutine that finds a given word in the dictionary. The word will be inserted (with a *count* of zero) if it isn't already present.

More precisely, the *find_buffer* function looks for the contents of *buffer*, and returns a pointer to the appropriate dictionary location. If the dictionary is so full that a new word cannot be inserted, the pointer 0 is returned.

```
define abort_find ≡
        begin find_buffer ← 0; return; end
⟨Procedures for data manipulation 20⟩ ≡
function find_buffer: pointer;
  label exit; {enable a quick return}
  var i: 1 .. max_word_length; {index into buffer}
    p: pointer; {the current word position}
    q: pointer; {the next word position}
    c: 1 .. 26; {current letter code}
    ⟨Other local variables of find_buffer 26⟩
  begin i ← 1; p ← buffer[1];
  while i < word_length do
    begin incr(i); c ← buffer[i];
    ⟨Advance p to its child number c 21⟩;
    end;
  find_buffer ← p;
exit: end;
```

See also section 37.

This code is used in section 3.

21. ⟨ Advance p to its child number c 21 ⟩ ≡

```
if link[p] = 0 then
    ⟨ Insert the firstborn child of p and move to it, or abort_find 27 ⟩
else begin q ← link[p] + c;
    if ch[q] ≠ c then
        begin if ch[q] ≠ empty_slot then ⟨ Move p's family to a place
                where child c will fit, or abort_find 29 ⟩;
        ⟨ Insert child c into p's family 28 ⟩;
        end;
    p ← q;
    end
```

This code is used in section 20.

22. Each "family" in the trie has a header location $h = link[p]$ such that child c is in location $h + c$. We want these values to be spread out in the trie, so that families don't often interfere with each other. Furthermore we will need to have $26 < h \le trie\_size - 26$ if the search algorithm is going to work properly.

One of the main tasks of the insertion algorithm is to find a place for a new header. The theory of hashing tells us that it is advantageous to put the nth header near the location $x_n = \alpha n \bmod t$, where $t = trie\_size - 52$ and where α is an integer relatively prime to t such that α/t is approximately equal to $(\sqrt{5} - 1)/2 \approx .61803$. [These locations x_n are about as "spread out" as you can get; see *Sorting and Searching*, pp. 510–511.]

define *alpha* = 20219 $\{\approx .61803(trie\_size - 52)\}$

⟨ Global variables 4 ⟩ +≡
x: *pointer*; $\{\alpha n \bmod (trie\_size - 52)\}$

23. ⟨ Set initial values 12 ⟩ +≡
$x \leftarrow 0$;

24. We will give up trying to find a vacancy if 1000 trials have been made without success. This will happen only if the table is quite full, at which time the most common words will probably already appear in the dictionary.

define *tolerance* = 1000

⟨ Get set for computing header locations 24 ⟩ ≡
  if $x < trie\_size - 52 - alpha$ **then** $x \leftarrow x + alpha$
  else $x \leftarrow x + alpha - trie\_size + 52$;
  $h \leftarrow x + 27$; { now $26 < h \le trie\_size - 26$ }
  if $h \le trie\_size - 26 - tolerance$ **then** $last\_h \leftarrow h + tolerance$
  else $last\_h \leftarrow h + tolerance - trie\_size + 52$;

This code is used in sections 27 and 31.

25. ⟨ Compute the next trial header location h, or *abort_find* 25 ⟩ ≡
  if $h = last\_h$ **then** *abort_find*;
  if $h = trie\_size - 26$ **then** $h \leftarrow 27$
  else $incr(h)$

This code is used in sections 27 and 31.

26. ⟨ Other local variables of *find_buffer* 26 ⟩ ≡
h: *pointer*; { trial header location }
last_h: *integer*; { the final one to try }

See also section 30.

This code is used in section 20.

27. ⟨ Insert the firstborn child of p and move to it, or *abort_find* 27 ⟩ ≡
  begin ⟨ Get set for computing header locations 24 ⟩;
  repeat ⟨ Compute the next trial header location h, or *abort_find* 25 ⟩;
  until $(ch[h] = empty\_slot) \land (ch[h + c] = empty\_slot)$;
  $link[p] \leftarrow h$; $link[h] \leftarrow p$; $p \leftarrow h + c$;
  $ch[h] \leftarrow header$; $ch[p] \leftarrow c$;
  $sibling[h] \leftarrow p$; $sibling[p] \leftarrow h$; $count[p] \leftarrow 0$; $link[p] \leftarrow 0$;
  end

This code is used in section 21.

28. The decreasing order of *sibling* pointers is preserved here. We assume that $q = link[p] + c$.

⟨ Insert child c into p's family 28 ⟩ ≡
  begin $h \leftarrow link[p]$;
  while $sibling[h] > q$ **do** $h \leftarrow sibling[h]$;
  $sibling[q] \leftarrow sibling[h]$; $sibling[h] \leftarrow q$;
  $ch[q] \leftarrow c$; $count[q] \leftarrow 0$; $link[q] \leftarrow 0$;
  end

This code is used in section 21.

29. There's one complicated case, which we have left for last. Fortunately this step doesn't need to be done very often in practice, and the families that need to be moved are generally small.

⟨ Move *p*'s family to a place where child *c* will fit, or *abort_find* 29 ⟩ ≡
begin ⟨ Find a suitable place *h* to move, or *abort_find* 31 ⟩;
$q \leftarrow h + c$; $r \leftarrow link[p]$; $delta \leftarrow h - r$;
repeat $sibling[r + delta] \leftarrow sibling[r] + delta$; $ch[r + delta] \leftarrow ch[r]$;
$ch[r] \leftarrow empty\_slot$; $count[r + delta] \leftarrow count[r]$;
$link[r + delta] \leftarrow link[r]$;
if $link[r] \neq 0$ **then** $link[link[r]] \leftarrow r + delta$;
$r \leftarrow sibling[r]$;
until $ch[r] = empty\_slot$;
end

This code is used in section 21.

30. ⟨ Other local variables of *find_buffer* 26 ⟩ +≡
r: *pointer*; { family member to be moved }
delta: *integer*; { amount of motion }
slot_found: *boolean*; { have we found a new homestead? }

31. ⟨ Find a suitable place *h* to move, or *abort_find* 31 ⟩ ≡
$slot\_found \leftarrow false$; ⟨ Get set for computing header locations 24 ⟩;
repeat ⟨ Compute the next trial header location *h*, or *abort_find* 25 ⟩;
if $ch[h + c] = empty\_slot$ **then**
begin $r \leftarrow link[p]$; $delta \leftarrow h - r$;
while $(ch[r + delta] = empty\_slot) \land (sibling[r] \neq link[p])$ **do**
$r \leftarrow sibling[r]$;
if $ch[r + delta] = empty\_slot$ **then** $slot\_found \leftarrow true$;
end;
until *slot_found*

This code is used in section 29.

---

32. The frequency counts. It is, of course, a simple matter to combine dictionary lookup with the *get_word* routine, so that all the word frequencies are counted. We may have to drop a few words in extreme cases (when the dictionary is full or the maximum count has been reached).

define *max_count* = 32767 { counts won't go higher than this }

⟨ Global variables 4 ⟩ +≡
count: **array** [*pointer*] **of** 0 .. *max_count*;
word_missed: *boolean*; { did the dictionary get too full? }
p: *pointer*; { location of the current word }

33. ⟨ Set initial values 12 ⟩ +≡
word_missed ← *false*;

34. ⟨ Input the text, maintaining a dictionary with frequency counts 34 ⟩ ≡

```
get_word;
while word_length ≠ 0 do
  begin p ← find_buffer;
  if p = 0 then word_missed ← true
  else if count[p] < max_count then incr(count[p]);
  get_word;
  end
```

This code is used in section 8.

35. While we have the dictionary structure in mind, let's write a routine that prints the word corresponding to a given pointer, together with the corresponding frequency count.

For obvious reasons, we put the word into the buffer backwards during this process.

⟨ Procedures for input and output 9 ⟩ +≡

```
procedure print_word(p : pointer);
  var q: pointer;  { runs through ancestors of p }
    i: 1 .. max_word_length;  { index into buffer }
  begin word_length ← 0; q ← p; write('␣');
  repeat incr(word_length); buffer[word_length] ← ch[q];
    move_to_prefix(q);
  until q = 0;
  for i ← word_length downto 1 do write(lowercase[buffer[i]]);
  if count[p] < max_count then write_ln('␣', count[p] : 1)
  else write_ln('␣', max_count : 1, '␣or␣more');
  end;
```

---

36. Sorting a trie. Almost all of the frequency counts will be small, in typical situations, so we needn't use a general-purpose sorting method. It suffices to keep a few linked lists for the words with small frequencies, with one other list to hold everything else.

define *large_count* = 200 { smaller counts are in separate lists }

⟨ Global variables 4 ⟩ +≡

```
sorted: array [1 .. large_count] of pointer;  { list heads }
total_words: integer;  { the number of words sorted }
```

37. If we walk through the trie in reverse alphabetical order, it is a simple matter to change the sibling links so that the words of frequency f are pointed to by *sorted*[f], *sibling*[*sorted*[f]], ... in alphabetical order. When f = *large_count*, the words must also be linked in decreasing order of their *count* fields.

The restructuring operations are slightly subtle here, because we are modifying the *sibling* pointers while traversing the trie.

```
⟨Procedures for data manipulation 20⟩ +≡
procedure trie_sort;
  var k: 1 .. large_count;  {index to sorted}
    p: pointer;  {current position in the trie}
    f: 0 .. max_count;  {current frequency count}
    q, r: pointer;  {list manipulation variables}
  begin total_words ← 0;
  for k ← 1 to large_count do sorted[k] ← 0;
  p ← sibling[0]; move_to_last_suffix(p);
  repeat f ← count[p]; q ← sibling[p];
    if f ≠ 0 then ⟨Link p into the list sorted[f] 38⟩;
    if ch[q] ≠ header then
      begin p ← q; move_to_last_suffix(p); end
    else p ← link[q];  {move to prefix}
  until p = 0;
  end;
```

38. Here we use the fact that *count*[0] = 0.

```
⟨Link p into the list sorted[f] 38⟩ ≡
  begin incr(total_words);
  if f < large_count then  {easy case}
    begin sibling[p] ← sorted[f]; sorted[f] ← p; end
  else begin r ← sorted[large_count];
    if count[p] ≥ count[r] then
      begin sibling[p] ← r; sorted[large_count] ← p; end
    else begin while count[p] < count[sibling[r]] do r ← sibling[r];
      sibling[p] ← sibling[r]; sibling[r] ← p;
      end;
    end;
  end
```

This code is used in section 37.

39. ⟨Sort the dictionary by frequency 39⟩ ≡

```
  trie_sort
```

This code is used in section 8.

40. After *trie_sort* has done its thing, the sequence of linked lists *sorted*[*large_count*], ..., *sorted*[1] collectively contain all the words of the input file, in decreasing order of frequency. Words of equal frequency appear in alphabetic order. The individual lists are linked by means of the *sibling* array.

Therefore the following procedure will print the first k words, as required in Bentley's problem.

```
⟨ Procedures for input and output 9 ⟩ +≡
procedure print_common(k : integer);
  label exit;  { enable a quick return }
  var f: 1 .. large_count;  { current frequency }
    p: pointer;  { current or next word }
  begin f ← large_count; p ← sorted[f];
  repeat while p = 0 do
      begin if f = 1 then return;
      decr(f); p ← sorted[f];
      end;
    print_word(p); decr(k); p ← sibling[p];
  until k = 0;
exit: end;
```

---

41. The endgame. We have recorded *total_words* different words. Furthermore the variables *word_missed* and *word_truncated* tell whether or not any storage limitations were exceeded. So the remaining task is simple:

```
⟨ Output the results 41 ⟩ ≡
  if total_words = 0 then
    write_ln('There␣are␣no␣words␣in␣the␣input!')
  else begin if total_words < max_words_to_print then
          { we will print all words }
      write_ln('Words␣of␣the␣input␣file,',
          '␣ordered␣by␣frequency:')
    else if max_words_to_print = 1 then
        write('The␣most␣common␣word␣and␣its␣frequency:')
      else write_ln('The␣', max_words_to_print : 1,
          '␣most␣common␣words,␣and␣their␣frequencies:');
    print_common(max_words_to_print);
    if word_truncated then
      write_ln('(At␣least␣one␣word␣had␣to␣be',
          '␣shortened␣to␣', max_word_length : 1, '␣letters.)');
```

```
if word_missed then
  write_ln('(Some␣input␣data␣was␣skipped,',
      '␣due␣to␣memory␣limitations.)');
end
```

This code is used in section 8.

---

42. Index. Here is a list of all uses of all identifiers, underlined at the point of definition.

A Review by M. D. McIlroy

My dictionary defines criticism as "the art of evaluating or analyzing with knowledge and propriety, especially works of art or literature." Knuth's program deserves criticism on two counts. He was the one, after all, who put forth the analogy of programming as literature, so what is more deserved than a little criticism? This program also merits criticism by its intrinsic interest; although Knuth set out only to display `WEB`*, he has produced a program that is fascinating in its own right. Doug McIlroy of Bell Labs was kind enough to provide this review.—J. B.*

I found Don Knuth's program convincing as a demonstration of `WEB` and fascinating for its data structure, but I disagree with it on engineering grounds. The problem is to print the K most common words in an input file (and the number of their occurrences) in decreasing frequency. Knuth's solution is to tally in an associative data structure each word as it is read from the file. The data structure is a trie, with 26-way (for technical reasons actually 27-way) fanout at each letter. To avoid wasting space all the (sparse) 26-element arrays are cleverly interleaved in one common arena, with hashing used to assign homes. Homes may move underfoot as new words cause old arrays to collide. The final sorting is done by distributing counts less than 200 into buckets and insertion-sorting larger counts into a list.

The presentation is engaging and clear. In `WEB` one deliberately writes a paper, not just comments, along with code. This of course helps readers. I am sure that it also helps writers: Reflecting upon design choices sufficiently to make them explainable must help clarify and refine one's thinking. Moreover, because an explanation in `WEB` is intimately combined with the hard reality of implementation, it is qualitatively different from, and far more useful than, an ordinary "specification" or "design" document. It can't gloss over the tough places.

Perhaps the greatest strength of `WEB` is that it allows almost any sensible order of presentation. Even if you did not intend to include any documentation, and even if you had an ordinary cross-referencer at your disposal, it would make sense to program in `WEB` simply to circumvent the unnatural order forced by the syntax of Pascal. Knuth's exercise amply demonstrates the virtue of doing so.

Mere use of `WEB`, though, won't assure the best organization. In the present instance the central idea of interleaving sparsely populated arrays is not mentioned until far into the paper. Upon first reading that, with hash tries, "some space is sacrificed," I snorted to myself that some understatement had been made of the wastage. Only much later was

I disabused of my misunderstanding. I suspect that this oversight in presentation was a result of documenting on the fly. With this sole exception, the paper eloquently attests that the discipline of simultaneously writing and describing a program pays off handsomely.

A few matters of style: First, the program is studded with instances of an obviously important constant, which variously take the guise of "26", "27", and "52." Though it is unobjectionable to have such a familiar number occur undocumented in a program about words, it is impossible to predict all its disguised forms. Just how might one confidently change it to handle, say, Norwegian or, more mundanely, alphanumeric "words"? A more obscure example is afforded by a constant *alpha*, calculated as the golden ratio times another constant, *triesize*. Signaled only by a comment deep inside the program, this relationship would surely be missed in any quick attempt to change the table size. WEB, unlike Pascal, admits dependent constants. They should have been used.

Second, small assignment statements are grouped several to the line with no particularly clear rationale. This convention saves space; but the groupings impose a false and distracting phrasing, like "poetry" produced by randomly breaking prose into lines.

Third, a picture would help the verbal explanation of the complex data structure. Indeed, pictures in listings are another strong reason to combine programming with typesetting; see Figure 1[1].

Like any other scheme of commentary, WEB can't guarantee that the documentation agrees perfectly with the program. For example, the procedure *read_int* expects an integer possibly preceded by blanks, although a literal reading of the description would require the integer to appear at the exact beginning of the text. This, however, was the only such case I noticed. The accuracy of the documentation compliments both the author and his method.

The WEB description led me pleasantly through the program and contained excellent cross references to help me navigate in my own ways. It provided important guideposts to the logical structure of the program, which are utterly unavailable in straight Pascal. For no matter how conscientiously commented or stylishly expressed programs in Pascal may

---

[1] I typeset this picture in an hour or two of my time using the PIC language; Knuth could have used TEX features to include such a figure in his WEB program. The figure contains a slight mistake for consistency with an off-by-one slip in §18 of Knuth's program: he assumed that "N" was the 15th letter of the alphabet, while it is really the 14th. Knuth insisted that we publish his program as he wrote it, warts and all, since it shows that WEB does not totally eliminate mistakes.—J. B.

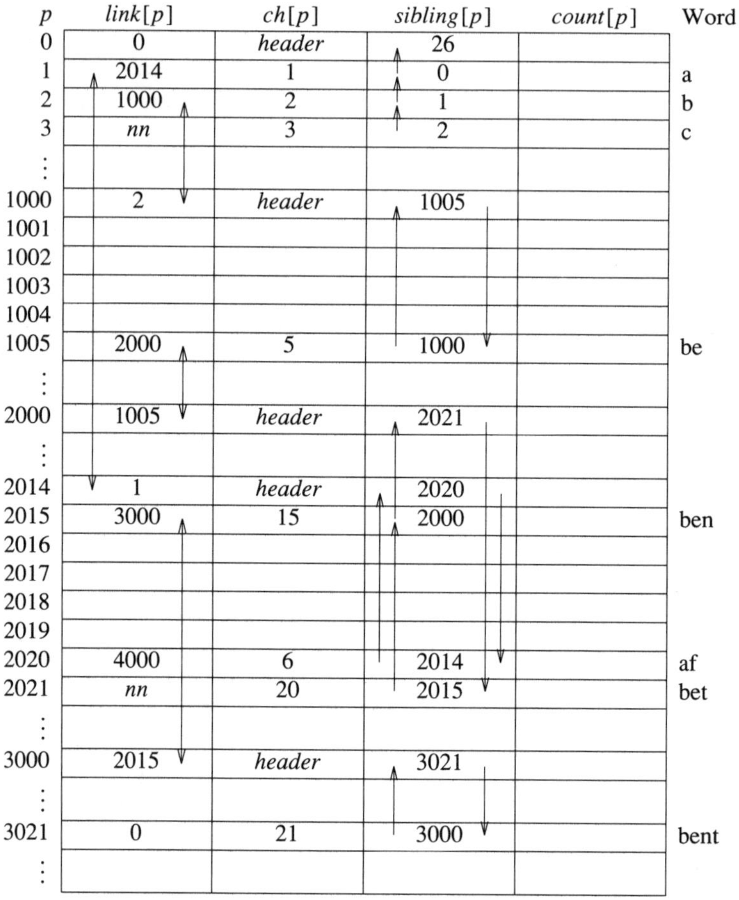

p	$link[p]$	$ch[p]$	$sibling[p]$	$count[p]$	Word
0	0	*header*	26		
1	2014	1	0		a
2	1000	2	1		b
3	*nn*	3	2		c
⋮					
1000	2	*header*	1005		
1001					
1002					
1003					
1004					
1005	2000	5	1000		be
⋮					
2000	1005	*header*	2021		
⋮					
2014	1	*header*	2020		
2015	3000	15	2000		ben
2016					
2017					
2018					
2019					
2020	4000	6	2014		af
2021	*nn*	20	2015		bet
⋮					
3000	2015	*header*	3021		
⋮					
3021	0	21	3000		bent
⋮					

Figure 1. A picture to accompany Knuth's §18.

be, the language forces an organization convenient for translating, not for writing or reading. In the WEB presentation variables were introduced where needed, rather than where permitted, and procedures were presented top-down as well as bottom-up according to pedagogical convenience rather than syntactic convention. I was able to skim the dull parts and concentrate on the significant ones, learning painlessly about a new data structure. Although I could have learned about hash tries without the program, it was truly helpful to have it there, if only to taste the practical complexity of the idea. Along the way I even learned some math: the equidistribution (mod 1) of multiples of the golden mean. Don Knuth's ideas and practice mix into a whole greater than the parts.

Although WEB circumvents Pascal's rigid rules of order, it makes no attempt to remedy other defects of Pascal (and rightly so, for the idea of WEB transcends the particulars of one language). Knuth tiptoes around the tarpits of Pascal I/O—as I do myself. To avoid multiple input files, he expects a numerical parameter to be tacked on to the beginning of otherwise pure text. Besides violating the spirit of Bentley's specification, where the file was clearly distinguished from the parameter, this clumsy convention could not conceivably happen in any real data. Worse still, how is the parameter, which Knuth chose to make optional, to be distinguished from the text proper? Finally, by overtaxing Pascal's higher-level I/O capabilities, the convention compels Knuth to write a special, but utterly mundane, read routine.

Knuth's purpose was to illustrate WEB. Nevertheless, it is instructive to consider the program at face value as a solution to a problem. A first engineering question to ask is: How often is one likely to have to do this exact task? Not at all often, I contend. It is plausible, though, that similar, but not identical, problems might arise. A wise engineering solution would produce—or better, exploit—reusable parts.

If the application were so big as to need the efficiency of a sophisticated solution, the question of size should be addressed before plunging in. Bentley's original statement suggested middling size input, perhaps 10,000 words. But a major piece of engineering built for the ages, as Knuth's program is, should have a large factor of safety. Would it, for example, work on the Bible? A quick check of a concordance reveals that the Bible contains some 15,000 distinct words, with typically 3 unshared letters each (supposing a trie solution, which squeezes out common prefixes). At 4 integers per trie node, that makes 180,000 machine integers. Allowing for gaps in the hash trie, we may reasonably round up to half a million. Knuth provided for 128K integers: the prospects for scaling the trie store are not impossible.

Still, unless the program were run in a multi-megabyte memory, it would likely have to ignore some late-arriving words, and not necessarily the least frequent ones, either: the word "Jesus" doesn't appear until three-fourths of the way through the Bible.

Very few people can obtain the virtuoso services of Knuth (or afford the equivalent person-weeks of lesser personnel) to attack nonce problems such as Bentley's from the ground up. But old UNIX hands know instinctively how to solve this one in a jiffy. (So do users of SNOBOL and other programmers who have associative tables[2] readily at hand—for almost any small problem, there's some language that makes it a snap.) The following shell script[3] was written on the spot and worked on the first try. It took 30 seconds to handle a 10,000-word file on a VAX–11/750.

```
(1) tr -cs A-Za-z '
    ' |
(2) tr A-Z a-z |
(3) sort |
(4) uniq -c |
(5) sort -rn |
(6) sed ${1}q
```

If you are not a UNIX adept, you may need a little explanation, but not much, to understand this pipeline of processes. The plan is easy:

1. Make one-word lines by transliterating the complement (`-c`) of the alphabet into newlines (note the quoted newline), and squeezing out (`-s`) multiple newlines.
2. Transliterate upper case to lower case.
3. Sort to bring identical words together.
4. Replace each run of duplicate words with a single representative and include a count (`-c`).
5. Sort in reverse (`-r`) numeric (`-n`) order.
6. Pass through a stream editor; quit (`q`) after printing the number of lines designated by the script's first parameter (`${1}`).

The utilities employed in this trivial solution are UNIX staples. They grew up over the years as people noticed useful steps that tended to recur in real problems. Every one was written first for a particular need, but untangled from the specific application.

---

[2] The June 1985 column describes associative arrays as they are implemented in the `AWK` language; page 572 contains a 6-line `AWK` program to count how many times each word occurs in a file.—J. B.

[3] This shell script is similar to a prototype spelling checker described in the May 1985 column. (That column also described a production-quality spelling checker designed and implemented by one-and-the-same Doug McIlroy.) This shell script runs on a descendant of the "seventh edition" UNIX system: trivial syntactic changes would adapt it for System V.—J. B.

With time they accreted a few optional parameters to handle variant, but closely related, tasks. The `sort` routine, for example, did not at first admit reverse or numeric ordering, but these options were eventually identified as worth adding.

As an aside on programming methodology, let us compare the two approaches. At a sufficiently abstract level both may be described in the same terms: Partition the words of a document into equivalence classes by spelling and extract certain information about the classes. Of two familiar strategies for constructing equivalence classes, tabulation and sorting, Knuth used the former, and I chose the latter. In fact, the choice seems to be made preconsciously by most people. Everybody has an instinctive idea how to solve this problem, but the instinct is very much a product of culture: In a small poll of programming luminaries, all (and only) the people with UNIX experience suggested sorting as a quick-and-easy technique.

The tabulation method, which gets right to the equivalence classes, deals more directly with the data of interest than does the sorting method, which keeps the members much longer. The sorting method, being more concerned with process than with data, is less natural and, in this instance, potentially less efficient. Yet in many practical circumstances it is a clear winner. The causes are not far to seek: We have succeeded in capturing generic processes in a directly usable way far better than we have data structures. One may hope that the new crop of more data-centered languages will narrow the gap. But for now, good old process-centered thinking still has a place in the sun.

Program transformations between the two approaches are interesting to contemplate, but only one direction seems reasonable: sorting to tabulation. The reverse transformation is harder because the elaboration of the tabulation method obscures the basic pattern. In the context of standard software tools, sorting is the more primitive, less irrevocably committed method from which piecewise refinements more easily flow.

To return to Knuth's paper: Everything there—even input conversion and sorting—is programmed monolithically and from scratch. In particular the isolation of words, the handling of punctuation, and the treatment of case distinctions are built in. Even if data-filtering programs for these exact purposes were not at hand, these operations would well be implemented separately: for separation of concerns, for easier development, for piecewise debugging, and for potential reuse. The small gain in efficiency from integrating them is not likely to warrant the resulting loss of flexibility. And the worst possible eventuality—being forced to combine programs—is not severe.

The simple pipeline given above will suffice to get answers right now, not next week or next month. It could well be enough to finish the job. But even for a production project, say for the Library of Congress, it would make a handsome down payment, useful for testing the value of the answers and for smoking out follow-on questions.

If we do have to get fancier, what should we do next? We first notice that all the time goes into sorting. It might make sense to look into the possibility of modifying the sort utility to cast out duplicates as it goes (UNIX `sort` already can) and to keep counts. A quick experiment shows that this would throw away 85 percent of a 10,000-word document, even more of a larger file. The second sort would become trivial. Perhaps half the time of the first would be saved, too. Thus the idea promises an easy 4–to–1 speedup overall—provided the sort routine is easy to modify. If it isn't, the next best thing to try is to program the tallying using some kind of associative memory—just as Knuth did. Hash tables come to mind as easy to get right. So do simple tries (with list fanout to save space, except perhaps at the first couple of levels where the density of fanout may justify arrays). And now that Knuth has provided us with the idea and the code, we would also consider hash tries. It remains sensible, though, to use utilities for case transliteration and for the final sort by count. With only 15 percent as much stuff to sort (even less on big jobs) and only one sort instead of two, we can expect an order of magnitude speedup, probably enough relief to dispel further worries about sorting.

Knuth has shown us here how to program intelligibly, but not wisely. I buy the discipline. I do not buy the result. He has fashioned a sort of industrial-strength Fabergé egg—intricate, wonderfully worked, refined beyond all ordinary desires, a museum piece from the start.

Principles—*J. B.*

Literate Programming. Last month's column sketched the mechanics of literate programming. This month's column provides a large example—by far the most substantial pearl described in detail in this column. I'm impressed by Knuth's methods and his results; I hope that this small sample has convinced you to explore the Further Reading [at the end of Chapter 5] to see his methods applied to real software.

A New Data Structure. I asked Knuth to provide a textbook solution to a textbook problem; he went far beyond that request by inventing, implementing and lucidly describing a fascinating new data structure—the hash trie.

Criticism of Programs. The role of any critic is to give the reader insight, and McIlroy does that splendidly. He first looks inside this gem, then sets it against a background to help us see it in context. He admires the execution of the solution, but faults the problem on engineering grounds. (That is, of course, my responsibility as problem assigner; Knuth solved the problem he was given, on grounds that are important to most engineers—the paychecks provided by their problem assigners.) Book reviews tell you what is in the book; good reviews go beyond that to give you insight into the environment that molded the work. As Knuth has set high standards for future authors of programming literature, McIlroy has shown us how to analyze those works.

Problems

1. Design and implement programs for finding the K most common words. Characterize the tradeoffs among code length, problem definition, resource utilization (time and space), and implementation language and system.
2. The problem of the K most common words can be altered in many ways. How do solutions to the original problem handle these new twists? Instead of finding the K most common words, suppose you want to find the single most frequent word, the frequency of all words in decreasing order, or the K least frequent words. Instead of dealing with words, suppose you wish to study the frequency of letters, letter pairs, letter triples, word pairs, or sentences.
3. Quantify the time and space required by Knuth's version of Liang's hash tries: use either experimental or mathematical tools (see Problem 4). Knuth's *dynamic* implementation allows insertions into hash tries: How would you use the data structure in a *static* problem in which the entire set of words was known before any lookups (consider representing an English dictionary)?
4. Both Knuth and McIlroy made assumptions about the distribution of words in English documents. For instance, Knuth assumed that most frequent words tend to occur near the front of the document, and McIlroy pointed out that a few frequent words may not appear until relatively late.
   a. Run experiments to test the various assumptions. For instance, does reducing the memory size of Knuth's program cause it to miss any frequent words?
   b. Gather data on the distribution of words in English documents to help one answer questions like this; can you summarize that statistical data in a probabilistic model of English text?

Solutions to May's Problems

4. J. S. Vitter's "Faster Methods for Random Sampling" in the July 1984 *Communications* shows how to generate M sorted random integers in $O(M)$ expected time and constant space: Those resource bounds are within a constant factor of optimal.
5. WEB provides two kinds of macros: **define** for short strings and the ⟨ Do this now ⟩ notation for longer pieces of code. Howard Trickey writes that "this facility is qualitatively better than the C preprocessor macros, because the syntax for naming and defining C macros is too awkward for use-once code fragments. Even in languages with the ability to declare procedures 'inline', I think most people would resist using procedures as prolifically as WEB users use modules. Somehow the ability to describe modules with sentences instead of having to make up a name helps me a lot in using lots of modules. Also, WEB macros can be used before they are defined, and they can be defined in pieces (e.g., ⟨ Global variables ⟩), and that isn't allowed in any macro language I know."
6. Howard Trickey observes that "the fact that TANGLE produces unreadable code can make it hard to use debuggers and other source-level software. Knuth's rejoinder is that if people like WEB enough they will modify such software to work with the WEB source. In practice, I never had much difficulty debugging TANGLE output run through a filter to break lines at statement boundaries."
7. [Knuth] To determine whether two input sequences define the same set of integers, insert each into an ordered hash table. The two ordered hash tables are equal if and only if the two sets are equal.

Solutions to June's Problems *[from the August column]*

1. Most programs for computing the K most common words in a file spend a great deal of effort on words that occur only a few times; in the text of both May and June's columns, for instance, over half the distinct words occurred just once. A two-pass program saves time and space by reading the file twice: The first pass identifies infrequent words, and the second pass concentrates on other words. The two passes share information in an array named *Count*, which is initialized to zero. As the first pass reads word X, it increments $Count[Hash(X)]$; no information is stored about the words themselves. After the first pass, frequent words must have high *Count*s, but some high *Count* values could be the result of several rare words.

The second pass deals with word X only if $Count[Hash(X)]$ is appropriately large, using any of the techniques discussed in the June column.

4. When Knuth ran his program with reduced memory to find the 100 most common words in Section 3.5 of his *Seminumerical Algorithms*, it missed just two words that were used frequently at the end of the section.

Chapter 7

How to Read a WEB (1986)

[The following "reader's manual" for WEB was written at the same time as Chapter 4, but first published with the programs for TeX and METAFONT in 1986. It is intended to be a stand-alone introduction to literate programming for people who will be reading but not necessarily writing WEB programs.]

The programs for TeX and METAFONT were prepared with the WEB system of structured documentation. A WEB program is a Pascal program that has been cut up into pieces and rearranged into an order that is easier for a human being to understand. A Pascal program is a WEB program that has been rearranged into an order that is easier for a computer to understand.

In other words, WEB programs and Pascal programs are essentially the same kinds of things, but their parts are arranged differently. You should be able to understand a Pascal program better when you see it in its WEB form, if the author of the WEB form has chosen a good order of presentation.

Before you try to read a WEB program, you should be familiar with the Pascal language. The following paragraphs describe how a WEB document can be mechanically translated into Pascal code. Thus, the WEB form serves as a high-level description that can be converted to ordinary Pascal by a preprocessing routine. The preprocessor expands macros and does a few other things that compensate for Pascal's limitations; although Pascal was not originally designed to be a language for system programming, WEB enriches it so that production software can be constructed and documented in a pleasant way.

A WEB program consists of numbered sections: First comes §1, then §2, and so on. Each section is intended to be small enough that it can be understood by itself, and the WEB format indicates how each section relates to other sections. In this way, an entire program can be regarded as a web or network, consisting of little pieces and interconnections between pieces. The complex whole can be understood by understanding each simple part and by understanding the simple relationships between neighboring parts.

Large software programs are inherently complex, and there is no "royal road" to instant comprehension of their subtle features. But if you read a well-written `WEB` program one section at a time, starting with §1, you will find that its ideas are not difficult to assimilate.

Every section of a `WEB` program begins with commentary about the purpose of that section, or about some noteworthy feature of that part of the program; such comments are in English, and informality is the rule. Then the section concludes with a formal part that is expressed in Pascal language; this is what actually counts, and you should be able to convince yourself that the formal Pascal code actually does what the informal comments imply.

Between the introductory comments and the Pascal code, there may also be one or more macro definitions, which are explained below. Thus, each section has three parts:

- informal commentary;
- macro definitions;
- Pascal code;

and these three parts always occur in the stated order. In practice, the individual parts are sometimes empty: Some sections have no opening comments, some have no macro definitions, and some have no Pascal code.

Every section is either *named* or *unnamed*. The Pascal code in a named section begins with '⟨ Name of section ⟩ ≡' in angle brackets, and the section name is followed by its so-called replacement text. For example, the Pascal code in §23 might be

⟨ Clear the arrays 23 ⟩ ≡
  for $k \leftarrow 1$ **to** n **do**
    begin $a[k] \leftarrow 0$; $b[k] \leftarrow 0$;
    end

and this means that the section name is 'Clear the arrays' while the replacement text is '`FOR K:=1 TO N DO BEGIN A[K]:=0; B[K]:=0;END`'.

This example illustrates the fact that `WEB` descriptions of replacement texts are formatted in a special way, intended to make the Pascal code easy to read. For example, lowercase letters are used instead of uppercase; reserved words like '**begin**' are set in boldface type, while identifiers like '*k*' are set in italics. Program structure is shown by indentation. A few special symbols are also used to enhance readability:

'←'	stands for	':=';
'≤'	stands for	'<=';
'≥'	stands for	'>=';
'≠'	stands for	'<>';
'∧'	stands for	'AND';
'∨'	stands for	'OR';
'¬'	stands for	'NOT';
'∈'	stands for	'IN';
'$5 \cdot 10^{20}$'	stands for	'5E20'.

When the name of a section appears in another section, it stands for the corresponding replacement text. For example, suppose the Pascal code for §20 is

⟨ Initialize the data structures 20 ⟩ ≡
  sum ← 0; ⟨ Clear the arrays 23 ⟩;

this means that the replacement text for 'Clear the arrays' should be inserted as part of the replacement text for 'Initialize the data structures'. The name of a section generally provides a short summary of what that section does; therefore the full details won't distract your attention unless you need to know them. But if you do need further details, the subscript '23' in '⟨ Clear the arrays 23 ⟩' makes it easy for you to locate the subsidiary replacement text. Incidentally, §23 in our example will contain a footnote that says 'This code is used in section 20'; thus you can move easily from a replacement text to its context or vice versa.

The process of converting a WEB program to a Pascal program is quite simple, at least conceptually: First you put together all the Pascal code that appears in *unnamed* sections, preserving the relative order. Then you substitute the replacement texts for all macros and named sections that appear in the resulting code; and you continue to do this until only pure Pascal remains.

It's possible to give the same name to several different sections. Continuing our example, let's suppose that the Pascal code of §30 is

⟨ Initialize the data structures 20 ⟩ +≡
  reset(*source_file*);

The '+≡' here indicates that the name 'Initialize the data structures' has appeared before; the Pascal code following '+≡' will be *appended* to the previous replacement text for that name. Thus, if 'Initialize the data structures' is defined only in §20 and §30, the actual replacement text for ⟨Initialize the data structures 20⟩ will be

sum ← 0; ⟨Clear the arrays 23⟩; *reset*(*source_file*);

Section 20 will also contain a footnote: 'See also section 30'.

Incidentally, the identifier '*source_file*' in this example contains an *underline* symbol; but its Pascal equivalent is just 'SOURCEFILE', because Pascal doesn't allow underlines to appear in names. When you're reading a WEB program, you might as well imagine that the underlines are really present, since they make the program more readable; but you should realize that '*write_ln*' is the same as Pascal's 'WRITELN'.

Macros in WEB are introduced by the keyword '**define**', and they act rather like section names but on a smaller scale. For example, the definitions

define *exit* ≡ 10 { go here to leave a procedure }
define *return* ≡ **goto** *exit* { terminate a procedure call }

say that the identifier '*return*' should be replaced by 'GOTO 10' when it appears in Pascal code. A macro might also have a parameter, denoted by '#'; for example, after

define *print_ln*(#) ≡ *write_ln*(*print_file*, #)

the preprocessor will expand a text like '*print_ln*('Hello.')' into

```
WRITELN(PRINTFILE,'Hello.')
```

Macros with parameters must be followed by an argument in parentheses whenever they are used. This argument is substituted for all #'s in the right-hand side of the macro definition.

WEB also has *numeric macros*, which are defined with an '=' sign instead of '≡'. For example, definitions like

define *buf_size* = 80
define *double_buf_size* = *buf_size* + *buf_size*

associate numbers with identifiers; the numbers are substituted for later appearances of the identifiers in subsequent Pascal texts. The preprocessor also adds and subtracts adjacent numbers before generating Pascal code. For example, '**array** [0 .. *double_buf_size* − 1] **of** *char*' will become 'ARRAY[0..159]OF CHAR' after the definitions above.

Hundreds of identifiers generally appear in a long program, and it's hard to keep them straight. Therefore the WEB system provides a comprehensive index that lists all sections where a given identifier appears. Entries in the index are underlined if the identifier was defined in the corresponding section. Furthermore, the right-hand pages of this book contain mini-indexes that will make it unnecessary for you to look at the big index very often. Every identifier that is used somewhere on a pair of facing pages is listed in a footnote on the right-hand page, unless it is explicitly defined or declared somewhere on the left-hand or right-hand page you are reading. These footnote entries tell you whether the identifier is a procedure or a macro or a boolean, etc.

Constants in a WEB program might be specified in octal or hexadecimal notation; the preprocessor will convert them into decimal form as required by Pascal. An octal constant starts with a single prime symbol followed by digits in italics; a hexadecimal constant starts with a double prime symbol followed by digits in typewriter type. For example, *´10000* and ″1000 both represent the number 2^{12}, which is 4096 in decimal notation.

Alphabetic constants for ASCII codes can be represented in WEB programs by double-quoted strings of length 1. For example, "A" stands for 65 and "a" stands for 97. Double-quoted strings of other lengths are also permitted; the preprocessor converts these into numeric constants that are 256 or more. This makes it possible to circumvent Pascal's limited string-manipulation capabilities.

OK! You know enough now about WEB conventions to understand 99% of the programs for TeX and METAFONT. Just a few more rules are needed to make the systems work in practice and to make your knowledge 100% complete. These remaining technicalities are given here in fine print so that you can come back to them if necessary; but you should really turn now to the programs and start reading them first, so that you can see how natural the WEB format turns out to be. Then you'll find it easy to understand the few nitty-gritty details that remain.

Detail #1, forced comments. Comments that appear in braces within Pascal code are not included in the Pascal program output by the preprocessor. But the special symbols @{ and @} stand for braces that do get through to the Pascal program. This makes it possible to "comment out" certain code that is not necessary in a production system, using WEB's primitive macro capabilities.

Detail #2, verbatim text. A string of symbols that's enclosed in a box, e.g., '`verbatim`', is included in the Pascal program without any preprocessing.

Detail #3, concatenation. Two consecutive identifiers or constants are usually separated by spaces in the Pascal program. This space is suppressed if the symbol `@&` appears between them in the `WEB` program.

Detail #4, the string pool. The preprocessor creates a file that lists all the double-quoted strings of length $\neq 1$, so that the program can manipulate these strings. This file contains one line per string, starting with string number 256, then number 257, and so on. Each line begins with a two-digit number `nn`, which is followed by `nn` characters for the string in question. After the final string, the file ends with a special line containing an asterisk in the first column, followed by a nine-digit "check sum." For example, suppose that the `WEB` program uses only two special strings, namely `""` (the empty string) and `"This longer string"`. Then the pool file will contain a total of three lines,

```
00
18This longer string
*519788345
```

In this case, occurrences of `""` in the `WEB` program will be replaced by 256; occurrences of `"This longer string"` will be replaced by 257. The symbol `@$` stands for the numeric value of the check sum (in this case 519788345); a program can test if it has read the correct string pool by comparing the file's check sum with `@$`.

Detail #5, format changes. The macro-definition part of a `WEB` section might contain '**format**' specifications mixed in with the instructions that '**define**' macros. Format specs have no effect on the corresponding Pascal program, but they do influence the appearance of the `WEB` program. For example, the specification

format *return* $\equiv$ *nil*

means that the identifier '*return*' should get the same typographic treatment as Pascal's reserved word '**nil**'. Therefore we will henceforth see '**return**' in boldface type, even though it is not a reserved word of Pascal. Format specifications are appropriate for macros that don't behave as ordinary variables in the Pascal program.

Chapter 8

Excerpts from the Programs for TEX and METAFONT (1986)

Introduction

[A practical programming methodology must be useful for large programs as well as small ones. Thus, the WEB *system passed its most crucial test when it was first used to produce the programs for TEX and for METAFONT. The complete texts of those programs have been published as books: Computers & Typesetting, Volumes B and D (Addison-Wesley, 1986). Although each book is nearly 600 pages long, hundreds of people have read them carefully, and it is not unreasonable to suppose that the programs for TEX and METAFONT are now understood better and more widely than any other computer programs of comparable size.*

The following reasonably self-contained excerpts from those books are reprinted here so that readers can get a taste of the ways in which small examples of literate programming can be scaled up to larger ones. Special software was written to provide a "mini-index" at the bottom of each right-hand page, thereby helping readers of the books to find their way more easily. The program sections reprinted here include several techniques of general interest that are useful in a wide variety of applications.

Familiarity with TEX and METAFONT is not a prerequisite for reading these excerpts, except that the very last portion involves some acquaintance with TEX's approach to hyphenation. We begin with excerpts from METAFONT because its program is the most interesting. METAFONT brings together arithmetic, linear algebra, parsing, raster graphics, typography, and recursive macro processing all under one roof.]

Excerpts from the Program for METAFONT (1986)

15. Labels are given symbolic names by the following definitions, so that occasional **goto** statements will be meaningful. We insert the label '*exit*:' just before the '**end**' of a procedure in which we have used the '**return**' statement defined below. Loops that are set up with the **loop** construction defined below are commonly exited by going to '*done*' or to '*found*' or to '*not_found*', and they are sometimes repeated by going to '*continue*'.

define *exit* = 10 { go here to leave a procedure }
define *continue* = 22 { go here to resume a loop }
define *done* = 30 { go here to exit a loop }
define *found* = 40 { go here when you've found it }
define *not_found* = 45 { go here when you've found nothing }

16. Here are some macros for common programming idioms.

define *incr*(#) ≡ # ← # + 1 { increase a variable by unity }
define *decr*(#) ≡ # ← # − 1 { decrease a variable by unity }
define *negate*(#) ≡ # ← −# { change the sign of a variable }
define *double*(#) ≡ # ← # + # { multiply a variable by two }
define *loop* ≡ **while** *true* **do**
{ repeat over and over until a **goto** happens }
format *loop* ≡ *xclause* { WEB's **xclause** acts like '**while** *true* **do**' }
define *do_nothing* ≡ { empty statement }
define *return* ≡ **goto** *exit* { terminate a procedure call }
format *return* ≡ *nil* { WEB will henceforth say **return** instead of *return* }

⋮

95. Arithmetic with scaled numbers. The principal computations performed by METAFONT are done entirely in terms of integers less than 2^{31} in magnitude; thus, the arithmetic specified in this program can be carried out in exactly the same way on a wide variety of computers, including some small ones.

But Pascal does not define the **div** operation fully in the case of negative dividends; for example, the result of $(-2*n-1)$**div**2 is $-(n+1)$ on some computers and $-n$ on others. There are two principal types of arithmetic: "translation-preserving," in which the identity $(a + q * b)$ **div** $b = (a$ **div** $b) + q$ is valid; and "negation-preserving," in which $(-a)$ **div** $b = -(a$ **div** $b)$. This leads to two METAFONTs, which can produce different results, although the differences should be negligible when the language is being used properly. The TEX processor has been defined carefully so that both varieties of arithmetic will produce identical output, but it would be too inefficient to constrain METAFONT in a similar way.

define *el_gordo* ≡ *'17777777777*
{ $2^{31} - 1$, the largest value that METAFONT likes }

96. One of METAFONT's most common operations is the calculation of $\lfloor \frac{a+b}{2} \rfloor$, the midpoint of two given integers a and b. The only decent way to do this in Pascal is to write '$(a+b)$ **div** 2'; but on most machines it is far more efficient to calculate '$(a+b)$ right shifted one bit'.

Therefore the midpoint operation will always be expressed in macro notation as '*half*$(a+b)$' below. If METAFONT is being implemented with languages that permit binary shifting, the *half* macro should be changed to make this operation as efficient as possible.

define *half*(#) ≡ (#) **div** 2

97. A single computation might use several subroutine calls, and it is desirable to avoid producing multiple error messages in case of arithmetic overflow. So the routines below set the global variable *arith_error* to *true* instead of reporting errors directly to the user.

⟨ Global variables 13 ⟩ +≡
arith_error: *boolean*; { has arithmetic overflow occurred recently? }

98. ⟨ Set initial values of key variables 21 ⟩ +≡
arith_error ← *false*;

99. At crucial points the program will say *check_arith*, to test if an arithmetic error has been detected.

```
define check_arith ≡
        begin if arith_error then clear_arith; end
procedure clear_arith;
  begin print_err("Arithmetic␣overflow");
  help4("Uh,␣oh.␣A␣little␣while␣ago␣one␣of␣the␣quantities␣that␣I")
  ("was␣computing␣got␣too␣large,␣so␣I´m␣afraid␣your␣answers␣will")
  ("be␣somewhat␣askew.␣You´ll␣probably␣have␣to␣adopt␣different")
  ("tactics␣next␣time.␣But␣I␣shall␣try␣to␣carry␣on␣anyway."); error;
  arith_error ← false;
  end;
```

100. Addition is not always checked to make sure that it doesn't overflow, but in places where overflow isn't too unlikely the *slow_add* routine is used.

```
function slow_add(x, y : integer): integer;
  begin if x ≥ 0 then
    if y ≤ el_gordo − x then slow_add ← x + y
    else begin arith_error ← true; slow_add ← el_gordo;
      end
  else if −y ≤ el_gordo + x then slow_add ← x + y
    else begin arith_error ← true; slow_add ← −el_gordo;
      end;
  end;
```

101. Fixed-point arithmetic is done on *scaled integers* that are multiples of 2^{-16}. In other words, a binary point is assumed to be sixteen bit positions from the right end of a binary computer word.

```
define quarter_unit ≡ ´40000   { 2^14, represents 0.250000 }
define half_unit ≡ ´100000   { 2^15, represents 0.50000 }
define three_quarter_unit ≡ ´140000   { 3 · 2^14, represents 0.75000 }
define unity ≡ ´200000   { 2^16, represents 1.00000 }
define two ≡ ´400000   { 2^17, represents 2.00000 }
define three ≡ ´600000   { 2^17 + 2^16, represents 3.00000 }
⟨ Types in the outer block 18 ⟩ +≡
  scaled = integer;   { this type is used for scaled integers }
  small_number = 0 . . 63;   { this type is self-explanatory }
```

102. The following function is used to create a scaled integer from a given decimal fraction $(.d_0d_1\ldots d_{k-1})$, where $0 \le k \le 17$. The digit d_i is given in *dig*[*i*], and the calculation produces a correctly rounded result.

function *round_decimals*(*k* : *small_number*): *scaled*;
{ converts a decimal fraction }
var *a*: *integer*; { the accumulator }
begin $a \leftarrow 0$;
while $k > 0$ **do**
begin *decr*(*k*); $a \leftarrow (a + dig[k] * two)$ **div** 10;
end;
round_decimals ← *half*$(a + 1)$;
end;

---

arith_error: *boolean*, §97.
decr = macro, §16.
dig: **array**, §54.
el_gordo = macro, §95.
error: **procedure**, §77.
half = macro, §96.
help4 = macro, §74.
print_err = macro, §68.

103. Conversely, here is a procedure analogous to *print_int*. If the output of this procedure is subsequently read by METAFONT and converted by the *round_decimals* routine above, it turns out that the original value will be reproduced exactly. A decimal point is printed only if the value is not an integer. If there is more than one way to print the result with the optimum number of digits following the decimal point, the closest possible value is given.

The invariant relation in the **repeat** loop is that a sequence of decimal digits yet to be printed will yield the original number if and only if they form a fraction f in the range $s - \delta \leq 10 \cdot 2^{16} f < s$. We can stop if and only if $f = 0$ satisfies this condition; the loop will terminate before s can possibly become zero.

[For further details about this routine, see "A simple program whose proof isn't," in *Beauty is Our Business*, edited by W. H. J. Feijen et al. (Springer, 1990), 233–242.]

```
⟨Basic printing procedures 57⟩ +≡
procedure print_scaled(s : scaled);
        { prints scaled real, rounded to five digits }
  var delta: scaled;  { amount of allowable inaccuracy }
  begin if s < 0 then
    begin print_char("-"); negate(s); { print the sign, if negative }
    end;
  print_int(s div unity); { print the integer part }
  s ← 10 * (s mod unity) + 5;
  if s ≠ 5 then
    begin delta ← 10; print_char(".");
    repeat if delta > unity then s ← s + '100000 − (delta div 2);
             { round the final digit }
      print_char("0" + (s div unity)); s ← 10 * (s mod unity);
      delta ← delta * 10;
    until s ≤ delta;
    end;
  end;
```

105. The *scaled* quantities in METAFONT programs are generally supposed to be less than 2^{12} in absolute value, so METAFONT does much of its internal arithmetic with 28 significant bits of precision. A *fraction* denotes a scaled integer whose binary point is assumed to be 28 bit positions from the right.

```
define fraction_half ≡ '1000000000  { 2^27, represents 0.50000000 }
define fraction_one ≡ '2000000000  { 2^28, represents 1.00000000 }
define fraction_two ≡ '4000000000  { 2^29, represents 2.00000000 }
```

define *fraction_three* ≡ *'6000000000* { $3 \cdot 2^{28}$, represents 3.00000000 }
define *fraction_four* ≡ *'10000000000* { 2^{30}, represents 4.00000000 }

⟨ Types in the outer block 18 ⟩ +≡
fraction = *integer*; { this type is used for scaled fractions }

---

negate = macro, §16.
print_char: **procedure**, §58.
print_int: **procedure**, §64.
round_decimals: **function**, §102.
scaled = *integer*, §101.
unity = macro, §101.

107. The *make_fraction* routine produces the *fraction* equivalent of p/q, given integers p and q; it computes the integer $f = \lfloor 2^{28}p/q + \frac{1}{2} \rfloor$, when p and q are positive. If p and q are both of the same scaled type t, the "type relation" $make\_fraction(t, t) = fraction$ is valid; and it's also possible to use the subroutine "backwards," using the relation $make\_fraction(t, fraction) = t$ between scaled types.

If the result would have magnitude 2^{31} or more, *make_fraction* sets $arith\_error \leftarrow true$. Most of METAFONT's internal computations have been designed to avoid this sort of error.

If this subroutine were programmed in assembly language on a typical machine, we could simply compute $(2^{28}*p)\,\mathbf{div}\,q$, since a double-precision product can often be input to a fixed-point division instruction. But when we are restricted to Pascal arithmetic it is necessary either to resort to multiple-precision maneuvering or to use a simple but slow iteration. The multiple-precision technique would be about three times faster than the code adopted here, but it would be comparatively long and tricky, involving about sixteen additional multiplications and divisions.

This operation is part of METAFONT's "inner loop"; indeed, it will consume nearly 10% of the running time (exclusive of input and output) if the code below is left unchanged. A machine-dependent recoding will therefore make METAFONT run faster. The present implementation is highly portable, but slow; it avoids multiplication and division except in the initial stage. System wizards should be careful to replace it with a routine that is guaranteed to produce identical results in all cases.

As noted below, a few more routines should also be replaced by machine-dependent code, for efficiency. But when a procedure is not part of the "inner loop," such changes aren't advisable; simplicity and robustness are preferable to trickery, unless the cost is too high.

```
function make_fraction(p, q : integer): fraction;
  var f: integer;  { the fraction bits, with a leading 1 bit }
    n: integer;  { the integer part of |p/q| }
    negative: boolean;  { should the result be negated? }
    be_careful: integer;  { disables certain compiler optimizations }
  begin if p ≥ 0 then negative ← false
  else begin negate(p); negative ← true;
    end;
  if q ≤ 0 then
    begin debug if q = 0 then confusion("/"); gubed
    negate(q); negative ← ¬negative; end;
  n ← p div q; p ← p mod q;
  if n ≥ 8 then
```

```
    begin arith_error ← true;
    if negative then
      make_fraction ← −el_gordo else make_fraction ← el_gordo;
    end
  else begin n ← (n − 1) ∗ fraction_one;
    ⟨Compute f = ⌊2^28(1 + p/q) + 1/2⌋ 108⟩;
    if negative then make_fraction ← −(f + n) else make_fraction ← f + n;
    end;
  end;
```

108. The **repeat** loop here preserves the following invariant relations between f, p, and q: (i) $0 \le p < q$; (ii) $fq + p = 2^k(q + p_0)$, where k is an integer and p_0 is the original value of p.

Notice that the computation specifies $(p-q)+p$ instead of $(p+p)-q$, because the latter could overflow. Let us hope that optimizing compilers do not miss this point; a special variable *be_careful* is used to emphasize the necessary order of computation. Optimizing compilers should keep *be_careful* in a register, not store it in memory.

```
⟨Compute f = ⌊2^28(1 + p/q) + 1/2⌋ 108⟩ ≡
  f ← 1;
  repeat be_careful ← p − q; p ← be_careful + p;
    if p ≥ 0 then f ← f + f + 1
    else begin double(f); p ← p + q;
      end;
  until f ≥ fraction_one;
  be_careful ← p − q;
  if be_careful + p ≥ 0 then incr(f)
```

This code is used in section 107.

---

arith_error: *boolean*, §97.
confusion: **procedure**, §90.
double = macro, §16.
el_gordo = macro, §95.
fraction = *integer*, §105.
fraction_one = macro, §105.
incr = macro, §16.
negate = macro, §16.

109. The dual of *make_fraction* is *take_fraction*, which multiplies a given integer q by a fraction f. When the operands are positive, it computes $p = \lfloor qf/2^{28} + \frac{1}{2} \rfloor$, a symmetric function of q and f.

This routine is even more "inner loopy" than *make_fraction*; the present implementation consumes almost 20% of METAFONT's computation time during typical jobs, so a machine-language substitute is advisable.

```
function take_fraction(q : integer; f : fraction): integer;
  var p: integer; { the fraction so far }
    negative: boolean; { should the result be negated? }
    n: integer; { additional multiple of q }
    be_careful: integer; { disables certain compiler optimizations }
  begin ⟨Reduce to the case that f ≥ 0 and q > 0 110⟩;
  if f < fraction_one then n ← 0
  else begin n ← f div fraction_one; f ← f mod fraction_one;
    if q ≤ el_gordo div n then n ← n * q
    else begin arith_error ← true; n ← el_gordo;
      end;
    end;
  f ← f + fraction_one; ⟨Compute p = ⌊qf/2^28 + 1/2⌋ − q 111⟩;
  be_careful ← n − el_gordo;
  if be_careful + p > 0 then
    begin arith_error ← true; n ← el_gordo − p;
    end;
  if negative then take_fraction ← −(n + p)
  else take_fraction ← n + p;
  end;
```

110. ⟨Reduce to the case that $f \geq 0$ and $q > 0$ 110⟩ ≡

```
  if f ≥ 0 then negative ← false
  else begin negate(f); negative ← true;
    end;
  if q < 0 then
    begin negate(q); negative ← ¬negative;
    end;
```

This code is used in section 109.

111. The invariant relations in this case are (i) $\lfloor (qf + p)/2^k \rfloor = \lfloor qf_0/2^{28} + \frac{1}{2} \rfloor$, where k is an integer and f_0 is the original value of f; (ii) $2^k \leq f < 2^{k+1}$.

⟨Compute $p = \lfloor qf/2^{28} + \frac{1}{2} \rfloor - q$ 111⟩ ≡

```
  p ← fraction_half; { that's 2^27; the invariants hold now with k = 28 }
```

```
if q < fraction_four then
   repeat if odd(f) then p ← half(p + q) else p ← half(p);
      f ← half(f);
   until f = 1
else repeat if odd(f) then p ← p + half(q − p) else p ← half(p);
      f ← half(f);
   until f = 1
```

This code is used in section 109.

117. The following somewhat different subroutine uses single-precision arithmetic to test rigorously if ab is greater than, equal to, or less than cd, given integers (a, b, c, d). In most cases a quick decision is reached. The result is $+1$, 0, or -1 in the three respective cases.

```
define return_sign(#) ≡
         begin ab_vs_cd ← #; return;
         end

function ab_vs_cd(a, b, c, d : integer): integer;
   label exit;
   var q, r: integer; {temporary registers}
   begin ⟨Reduce to the case that a, c ≥ 0 and b, d > 0 118⟩;
   loop begin q ← a div d; r ← c div b;
      if q ≠ r then
         if q > r then return_sign(1) else return_sign(−1);
      q ← a mod d; r ← c mod b;
      if r = 0 then
         if q = 0 then return_sign(0) else return_sign(1);
      if q = 0 then return_sign(−1);
      a ← b; b ← q; c ← d; d ← r;
      end; {now a > d > 0 and c > b > 0}
exit: end;
```

---

arith_error: *boolean*, §97.
b: *integer*, §124.
c: *ASCII_code*, §77.
d: *integer*, §333.
el_gordo = macro, §95.
exit = 10, §15.
fraction = *integer*, §105.
fraction_four = macro, §105.
fraction_half = macro, §105.
fraction_one = macro, §105.
half = macro, §96.
make_fraction: **function**, §107.
negate = macro, §16.

118. ⟨Reduce to the case that $a, c \ge 0$ and $b, d > 0$ 118⟩ ≡

```
if a < 0 then
   begin negate(a); negate(b); end;
if c < 0 then
   begin negate(c); negate(d); end;
if d ≤ 0 then
   begin if b ≥ 0 then
      if ((a = 0) ∨ (b = 0)) ∧ ((c = 0) ∨ (d = 0)) then return_sign(0)
      else return_sign(1);
   if d = 0 then
      if a = 0 then return_sign(0) else return_sign(−1);
   q ← a; a ← c; c ← q; q ← −b; b ← −d; d ← q;
   end
else if b ≤ 0 then
      begin if b < 0 then
         if a > 0 then return_sign(−1);
      if c = 0 then return_sign(0)
      else return_sign(−1);
      end
```

This code is used in section 117.

119. We conclude this set of elementary routines with some simple rounding and truncation operations that are coded in a machine-independent fashion. The routines are slightly complicated because we want them to work without overflow whenever $-2^{31} \le x < 2^{31}$.

```
function floor_scaled(x : scaled): scaled;  { 2^16 ⌊x/2^16⌋ }
   var be_careful: integer;  { temporary register }
   begin if x ≥ 0 then floor_scaled ← x − (x mod unity)
   else begin be_careful ← x + 1;
      floor_scaled ← x + ((−be_careful) mod unity) + 1 − unity;
      end;
   end;

function floor_unscaled(x : scaled): integer;  { ⌊x/2^16⌋ }
   var be_careful: integer;  { temporary register }
   begin if x ≥ 0 then floor_unscaled ← x div unity
   else begin be_careful ← x + 1;
      floor_unscaled ← −(1 + ((−be_careful) div unity));
      end;
   end;

function round_unscaled(x : scaled): integer;  { ⌊x/2^16 + .5⌋ }
   var be_careful: integer;  { temporary register }
   begin if x ≥ half_unit then
      round_unscaled ← 1 + ((x − half_unit) div unity)
```

```
else if x ≥ −half_unit then round_unscaled ← 0
  else begin be_careful ← x + 1;
    round_unscaled ← −(1 + ((−be_careful − half_unit) div unity));
    end;
end;
```

---

a: *integer*, §117.
b: *integer*, §124.
c: *ASCII_code*, §77.
d: *integer*, §333.
half_unit = macro, §101.
negate = macro, §16.
q: *integer*, §117.
return_sign = macro, §117.
scaled = *integer*, §101.
unity = macro, §101.

120. Algebraic and transcendental functions. METAFONT computes all of the necessary special functions from scratch, without relying on *real* arithmetic or system subroutines for sines, cosines, etc.

121. To get the square root of a *scaled* number x, we want to calculate $s = \lfloor 2^8\sqrt{x} + \frac{1}{2}\rfloor$. If $x > 0$, this is the unique integer such that $2^{16}x - s \le s^2 < 2^{16}x + s$. The following subroutine determines s by an iterative method that maintains the invariant relations $x = 2^{46-2k}x_0 \bmod 2^{30}$, $0 < y = \lfloor 2^{16-2k}x_0\rfloor - s^2 + s \le q = 2s$, where x_0 is the initial value of x. The value of y might, however, be zero at the start of the first iteration.

```
function square_rt(x : scaled): scaled;
  var k: small_number;  { iteration control counter }
    y, q: integer;  { registers for intermediate calculations }
  begin if x ≤ 0 then
    ⟨Handle square root of zero or negative argument 122⟩
  else begin k ← 23; q ← 2;
    while x < fraction_two do  { i.e., while x < 2^29 }
      begin decr(k); x ← x + x + x + x;
      end;
    if x < fraction_four then y ← 0
    else begin x ← x − fraction_four; y ← 1;
      end;
    repeat ⟨Decrease k by 1, maintaining the invariant relations between x,
          y, and q 123⟩;
    until k = 0;
    square_rt ← half(q);
    end;
  end;
```

122. ⟨Handle square root of zero or negative argument 122⟩ ≡

```
begin if x < 0 then
  begin print_err("Square␣root␣of␣"); print_scaled(x);
  print("␣has␣been␣replaced␣by␣0");
  help2("Since␣I␣don´t␣take␣square␣roots␣of␣negative␣numbers,")
  ("I´m␣zeroing␣this␣one.␣Proceed,␣with␣fingers␣crossed."); error;
  end;
square_rt ← 0;
end
```

This code is used in section 121.

123. ⟨ Decrease k by 1, maintaining the invariant relations between x, y, and q 123 ⟩ ≡

double(x); *double*(y);
if $x \ge$ *fraction_four* **then** { note that *fraction_four* $= 2^{30}$ }
  begin $x \leftarrow x -$ *fraction_four*; *incr*(y); **end**;
double(x); $y \leftarrow y + y - q$; *double*(q);
if $x \ge$ *fraction_four* **then**
  begin $x \leftarrow x -$ *fraction_four*; *incr*(y); **end**;
if $y > q$ **then**
  begin $y \leftarrow y - q$; $q \leftarrow q + 2$; **end**
else if $y \le 0$ **then**
    begin $q \leftarrow q - 2$; $y \leftarrow y + q$; **end**;
decr(k)

This code is used in section 121.

---

decr = macro, §16.
double = macro, §16.
error: **procedure**, §77.
fraction_four = macro, §105.
fraction_two = macro, §105.
half = macro, §96.
help2 = macro, §74.
incr = macro, §16.
print: **procedure**, §59.
print_err = macro, §68.
print_scaled: **procedure**, §103.
scaled = *integer*, §101.
small_number = 0 . . 63, §101.

124. Pythagorean addition $\sqrt{a^2+b^2}$ is implemented by an elegant iterative scheme due to Cleve Moler and Donald Morrison [*IBM Journal of Research and Development* **27** (1983), 577–581]. It modifies a and b in such a way that their pythagorean sum remains invariant, while the smaller argument decreases.

```
function pyth_add(a, b : integer): integer;
  label done;
  var r: fraction;  { register used to transform a and b }
    big: boolean;  { is the result dangerously near 2^31? }
  begin a ← abs(a); b ← abs(b);
  if a < b then
    begin r ← b; b ← a; a ← r;
    end;  { now 0 ≤ b ≤ a }
  if a > 0 then
    begin if a < fraction_two then big ← false
    else begin a ← a div 4; b ← b div 4; big ← true;
      end;  { we reduced the precision to avoid arithmetic overflow }
    ⟨Replace a by an approximation to √(a² + b²) 125⟩;
    if big then
      if a < fraction_two then a ← a + a + a + a
      else begin arith_error ← true; a ← el_gordo;
        end;
    end;
  pyth_add ← a;
  end;
```

125. The key idea here is to reflect the vector (a,b) about the line through $(a,b/2)$.

```
⟨Replace a by an approximation to √(a² + b²) 125⟩ ≡
  loop begin r ← make_fraction(b, a); r ← take_fraction(r, r);
        { now r ≈ b²/a² }
    if r = 0 then goto done;
    r ← make_fraction(r, fraction_four + r); a ← a + take_fraction(a + a, r);
    b ← take_fraction(b, r);
    end;
done:
```

This code is used in section 124.

126. Here is a similar algorithm for $\sqrt{a^2-b^2}$. It converges slowly when b is near a, but otherwise it works fine.

```
function pyth_sub(a, b : integer): integer;
  label done;
  var r: fraction;  { register used to transform a and b }
    big: boolean;  { is the input dangerously near 2^31? }
  begin a ← abs(a); b ← abs(b);
  if a ≤ b then ⟨Handle erroneous pyth_sub and set a ← 0 128⟩
  else begin if a < fraction_four then big ← false
    else begin a ← half(a); b ← half(b); big ← true;
      end;
    ⟨Replace a by an approximation to √(a^2 − b^2) 127⟩;
    if big then a ← a + a;
    end;
  pyth_sub ← a;
  end;
```

127. ⟨Replace a by an approximation to $\sqrt{a^2-b^2}$ 127⟩ ≡

```
  loop begin r ← make_fraction(b, a); r ← take_fraction(r, r);
        { now r ≈ b^2/a^2 }
    if r = 0 then goto done;
    r ← make_fraction(r, fraction_four − r); a ← a − take_fraction(a + a, r);
    b ← take_fraction(b, r);
    end;
done:
```

This code is used in section 126.

128. ⟨Handle erroneous *pyth_sub* and set $a \leftarrow 0$ 128⟩ ≡

```
  begin if a < b then
    begin print_err("Pythagorean␣subtraction␣"); print_scaled(a);
    print("+-+"); print_scaled(b); print("␣has␣been␣replaced␣by␣0");
    help2("Since␣I␣don´t␣take␣square␣roots␣of␣negative␣numbers,")
    ("I´m␣zeroing␣this␣one.␣Proceed,␣with␣fingers␣crossed."); error;
    end;
  a ← 0;
  end
```

This code is used in section 126.

---

arith_error: *boolean*, §97.
done = 30, §15.
el_gordo = macro, §95.
error: **procedure**, §77.
fraction = *integer*, §105.
fraction_four = macro, §105.
fraction_two = macro, §105.
half = macro, §96.
help2 = macro, §74.
make_fraction: **function**, §107.
print: **procedure**, §59.
print_err = macro, §68.
print_scaled: **procedure**, §103.
take_fraction: **function**, §109.

⋮

303. Generating discrete moves. The purpose of the next part of METAFONT is to compute discrete approximations to curves described as parametric polynomial functions $z(t)$. We shall start with the low level first, because an efficient "engine" is needed to support the high-level constructions.

Most of the subroutines are based on variations of a single theme, namely the idea of *bisection*. Given a Bernshteĭn polynomial

$$B(z_0, z_1, \ldots, z_n; t) = \sum_k \binom{n}{k} t^k (1-t)^{n-k} z_k,$$

we can conveniently bisect its range as follows:

1) Let $z_k^{(0)} = z_k$, for $0 \le k \le n$.

2) Let $z_k^{(j+1)} = \frac{1}{2}(z_k^{(j)} + z_{k+1}^{(j)})$, for $0 \le k < n - j$, for $0 \le j < n$.

Then

$$\begin{aligned} B(z_0, z_1, \ldots, z_n; t) &= B(z_0^{(0)}, z_0^{(1)}, \ldots, z_0^{(n)}; 2t) \\ &= B(z_0^{(n)}, z_1^{(n-1)}, \ldots, z_n^{(0)}; 2t - 1). \end{aligned}$$

This formula gives us the coefficients of polynomials to use over the ranges $0 \le t \le \frac{1}{2}$ and $\frac{1}{2} \le t \le 1$.

In our applications it will usually be possible to work indirectly with numbers that allow us to deduce relevant properties of the polynomials without actually computing the polynomial values. We will deal with coefficients $Z_k = 2^l(z_k - z_{k-1})$ for $1 \le k \le n$, instead of the actual numbers z_0, z_1, …, z_n, and the value of l will increase by 1 at each bisection step. This technique reduces the amount of calculation needed for bisection and also increases the accuracy of evaluation (since one bit of precision is gained at each bisection). Indeed, the bisection process now becomes one level shorter:

1′) Let $Z_k^{(1)} = Z_k$, for $1 \le k \le n$.

2′) Let $Z_k^{(j+1)} = \frac{1}{2}(Z_k^{(j)} + Z_{k+1}^{(j)})$, for $1 \le k < n - j$, for $1 \le j < n$.

The relevant coefficients $(Z'_1, \ldots, Z'_n)$ and $(Z''_1, \ldots, Z''_n)$ for the two subintervals after bisection are respectively $(Z_1^{(1)}, Z_1^{(2)}, \ldots, Z_1^{(n)})$ and $(Z_1^{(n)}, Z_2^{(n-1)}, \ldots, Z_n^{(1)})$. And the values of z_0 appropriate for the bisected interval are $z'_0 = z_0$ and $z''_0 = z_0 + (Z_1 + Z_2 + \cdots + Z_n)/2^{l+1}$.

Step 2′ involves division by 2, which introduces computational errors of at most $\frac{1}{2}$ at each step; thus after l levels of bisection the integers Z_k will differ from their true values by at most $(n-1)l/2$. This error rate is quite acceptable, considering that we have l more bits of precision in the Z's by comparison with the z's. Note also that the Z's remain bounded; there's no danger of integer overflow, even though we have the identity $Z_k = 2^l(z_k - z_{k-1})$ for arbitrarily large l.

In fact, we can show not only that the Z's remain bounded, but also that they become nearly equal, since they are control points for a polynomial of one less degree. If $|Z_{k+1} - Z_k| \le M$ initially, it is possible to prove that $|Z_{k+1} - Z_k| \le \lceil M/2^l \rceil$ after l levels of bisection, even in the presence of rounding errors. Here's the proof [cf. Lane and Riesenfeld, *IEEE Trans. on Pattern Analysis and Machine Intelligence* **PAMI-2** (1980), 35–46]: Assuming that $|Z_{k+1} - Z_k| \le M$ before bisection, we want to prove that $|Z_{k+1} - Z_k| \le \lceil M/2 \rceil$ afterward. First we show that $|Z_{k+1}^{(j)} - Z_k^{(j)}| \le M$ for all j and k, by induction on j; this follows from the fact that

$$\bigl|\mathit{half}(a+b) - \mathit{half}(b+c)\bigr| \le \max\bigl(|a-b|, |b-c|\bigr)$$

holds for both of the rounding rules $\mathit{half}(x) = \lfloor x/2 \rfloor$ and $\mathit{half}(x) = \operatorname{sign}(x)\lfloor |x/2| \rfloor$. (If $|a-b|$ and $|b-c|$ are equal, then $a+b$ and $b+c$ are both even or both odd. The rounding errors either cancel or round the numbers toward each other; hence

$$\begin{aligned}\bigl|\mathit{half}(a+b) - \mathit{half}(b+c)\bigr| &\le \bigl|\tfrac{1}{2}(a+b) - \tfrac{1}{2}(b+c)\bigr| \\ &= \bigl|\tfrac{1}{2}(a-b) + \tfrac{1}{2}(b-c)\bigr| \\ &\le \max\bigl(|a-b|, |b-c|\bigr),\end{aligned}$$

as required. A simpler argument applies if $|a-b|$ and $|b-c|$ are unequal.) Now it is easy to see that $|Z_1^{(j+1)} - Z_1^{(j)}| \le \bigl\lfloor \frac{1}{2}|Z_2^{(j)} - Z_1^{(j)}| + \frac{1}{2} \bigr\rfloor \le \bigl\lfloor \frac{1}{2}(M+1) \bigr\rfloor = \lceil M/2 \rceil$.

Another interesting fact about bisection is the identity

$$Z_1' + \cdots + Z_n' + Z_1'' + \cdots + Z_n'' = 2(Z_1 + \cdots + Z_n + E),$$

where E is the sum of the rounding errors in all of the halving operations ($|E| \le n(n-1)/4$).

⋮

391. Now here's a subroutine that's handy for subdivision: Given a quadratic polynomial $B(a, b, c; t)$, the *crossing_point* function returns the unique *fraction* value t between 0 and 1 at which $B(a, b, c; t)$ changes from positive to negative, or returns $t = \textit{fraction\_one} + 1$ if no such value exists. If $a < 0$ (so that $B(a, b, c; t)$ is already negative at $t = 0$), *crossing_point* returns the value zero.

```
define no_crossing ≡
        begin crossing_point ← fraction_one + 1; return;
        end
define one_crossing ≡
        begin crossing_point ← fraction_one; return;
        end
define zero_crossing ≡
        begin crossing_point ← 0; return;
        end
function crossing_point(a, b, c : integer): fraction;
  label exit;
  var d: integer; {recursive counter}
    x, xx, x0, x1, x2: integer; {temporary registers for bisection}
  begin if a < 0 then zero_crossing;
  if c ≥ 0 then
    begin if b ≥ 0 then
      if c > 0 then no_crossing
      else if (a = 0) ∧ (b = 0) then no_crossing
        else one_crossing;
    if a = 0 then zero_crossing;
    end
  else if a = 0 then
      if b ≤ 0 then zero_crossing;
  ⟨Use bisection to find the crossing point, if one exists 392⟩;
exit: end;
```

392. The general bisection method is quite simple when $n = 2$, hence *crossing_point* does not take much time. At each stage in the recursion we have a subinterval defined by l and j such that $B(a, b, c; 2^{-l}(j+t)) = B(x_0, x_1, x_2; t)$, and we want to "zero in" on the subinterval where $x_0 \geq 0$ and $\min(x_1, x_2) < 0$.

It is convenient for purposes of calculation to combine the values of l and j in a single variable $d = 2^l + j$, because the operation of bisection then corresponds simply to doubling d and possibly adding 1. Furthermore it proves to be convenient to modify our previous conventions for bisection slightly, maintaining the variables $X_0 = 2^l x_0$, $X_1 = 2^l(x_0 - x_1)$, and $X_2 = 2^l(x_1 - x_2)$. With these variables the conditions $x_0 \geq 0$ and $\min(x_1, x_2) < 0$ are equivalent to $\max(X_1, X_1 + X_2) > X_0 \geq 0$.

The following code maintains the invariant relations $0 \leq x0 < \max(x1, x1 + x2)$, $|x1| < 2^{30}$, $|x2| < 2^{30}$; it has been constructed in such a way that no arithmetic overflow will occur if the inputs satisfy $a < 2^{30}$, $|a - b| < 2^{30}$, and $|b - c| < 2^{30}$.

```
⟨Use bisection to find the crossing point, if one exists 392⟩ ≡
  d ← 1; x0 ← a; x1 ← a − b; x2 ← b − c;
  repeat x ← half(x1 + x2);
    if x1 − x0 > x0 then
      begin x2 ← x; double(x0); double(d);
      end
    else begin xx ← x1 + x − x0;
      if xx > x0 then
        begin x2 ← x; double(x0); double(d);
        end
      else begin x0 ← x0 − xx;
        if x ≤ x0 then
          if x + x2 ≤ x0 then no_crossing;
        x1 ← x; d ← d + d + 1;
        end;
      end;
  until d ≥ fraction_one;
  crossing_point ← d − fraction_one
```

This code is used in section 391.

---

double = macro, §16.
exit = 10, §15.
fraction = *integer*, §105.
fraction_one = macro, §105.
half = macro, §96.
j: *integer*, §378.
l: *integer*, §311.

Excerpts from the Program for TeX (1986)

38. String handling. Control sequence names and diagnostic messages are variable-length strings of eight-bit characters. Since Pascal does not have a well-developed string mechanism, TeX does all of its string processing by homegrown methods.

Elaborate facilities for dynamic strings are not needed, so all of the necessary operations can be handled with a simple data structure. The array *str_pool* contains all of the (eight-bit) ASCII codes in all of the strings, and the array *str_start* contains indices of the starting points of each string. Strings are referred to by integer numbers, so that string number s comprises the characters *str_pool*[j] for *str_start*[s] $\le j <$ *str_start*[$s+1$]. Additional integer variables *pool_ptr* and *str_ptr* indicate the number of entries used so far in *str_pool* and *str_start*, respectively; locations *str_pool*[*pool_ptr*] and *str_start*[*str_ptr*] are ready for the next string to be allocated.

String numbers 0 to 255 are reserved for strings that correspond to single ASCII characters. This is in accordance with the conventions of `WEB`, which converts single-character strings into the ASCII code number of the single character involved, while it converts other strings into integers and builds a string pool file. Thus, when the string constant `"."` appears in the program below, `WEB` converts it into the integer 46, which is the ASCII code for a period, while `WEB` will convert a string like `"hello"` into some integer greater than 255. String number 46 will presumably be the single character '`.`'; but some ASCII codes have no standard visible representation, and TeX sometimes needs to be able to print an arbitrary ASCII character, so the first 256 strings are used to specify exactly what should be printed for each of the 256 possibilities.

Elements of the *str_pool* array must be ASCII codes that can actually be printed; i.e., they must have an *xchr* equivalent in the local character set. (This restriction applies only to preloaded strings, not to those generated dynamically by the user.)

Some Pascal compilers won't pack integers into a single byte unless the integers lie in the range $-128\,..\,127$. To accommodate such systems we access the string pool only via macros that can easily be redefined.

define *si*(#) ≡ # { convert from *ASCII_code* to *packed_ASCII_code* }
define *so*(#) ≡ # { convert from *packed_ASCII_code* to *ASCII_code* }

⟨ Types in the outer block 18 ⟩ +≡
pool_pointer = 0 .. *pool_size*; { for variables that point into *str_pool* }

str_number = 0 .. *max_strings*; { for variables that point into *str_start* }
packed_ASCII_code = 0 .. 255; { elements of *str_pool* array }

39. ⟨ Global variables 13 ⟩ +≡
str_pool: **packed array** [*pool_pointer*] **of** *packed_ASCII_code*;
{ the characters }
str_start: **array** [*str_number*] **of** *pool_pointer*; { the starting pointers }
pool_ptr: *pool_pointer*; { first unused position in *str_pool* }
str_ptr: *str_number*; { number of the current string being created }
init_pool_ptr: *pool_pointer*; { the starting value of *pool_ptr* }
init_str_ptr: *str_number*; { the starting value of *str_ptr* }

40. Several of the elementary string operations are performed using WEB macros instead of Pascal procedures, because many of the operations are done quite frequently and we want to avoid the overhead of procedure calls. For example, here is a simple macro that computes the length of a string.

define *length*(#) ≡ (*str_start*[# + 1] − *str_start*[#])
{ the number of characters in string number # }

41. The length of the current string is called *cur_length*:

define *cur_length* ≡ (*pool_ptr* − *str_start*[*str_ptr*])

ASCII_code = 0 .. 255, §18.
max_strings = **const**, §11.
pool_size = **const**, §11.
xchr: **array**, §20.

42. Strings are created by appending character codes to *str_pool*. The *append_char* macro, defined here, does not check to see if the value of *pool_ptr* has gotten too high; this test is supposed to be made before *append_char* is used. There is also a *flush_char* macro, which erases the last character appended.

To test if there is room to append l more characters to *str_pool*, we shall write *str_room*(l), which aborts TEX and gives an apologetic error message if there isn't enough room.

```
define append_char(#) ≡ { put ASCII_code # at the end of str_pool }
        begin str_pool[pool_ptr] ← si(#); incr(pool_ptr);
        end
define flush_char ≡ decr(pool_ptr)
            { forget the last character in the pool }
define str_room(#) ≡ { make sure that the pool hasn't overflowed }
        begin if pool_ptr + # > pool_size then
          overflow("pool␣size", pool_size − init_pool_ptr);
        end
```

43. Once a sequence of characters has been appended to *str_pool*, it officially becomes a string when the function *make_string* is called. This function returns the identification number of the new string as its value.

```
function make_string: str_number; { current string enters the pool }
  begin if str_ptr = max_strings then
    overflow("number␣of␣strings", max_strings − init_str_ptr);
  incr(str_ptr); str_start[str_ptr] ← pool_ptr; make_string ← str_ptr − 1;
  end;
```

44. To destroy the most recently made string, we say *flush_string*.

```
define flush_string ≡
          begin decr(str_ptr); pool_ptr ← str_start[str_ptr]; end
```

45. The following subroutine compares string s with another string of the same length that appears in *buffer* starting at position k; the result is *true* if and only if the strings are equal. Empirical tests indicate that *str_eq_buf* is used in such a way that it tends to return *true* about 80 percent of the time.

```
function str_eq_buf(s : str_number; k : integer): boolean;
        { test equality of strings }
  label not_found; { loop exit }
  var j: pool_pointer; { running index }
    result: boolean; { result of comparison }
  begin j ← str_start[s];
  while j < str_start[s + 1] do
```

```
    begin if so(str_pool[j]) ≠ buffer[k] then
      begin result ← false; goto not_found;
      end;
    incr(j); incr(k);
    end;
  result ← true;
not_found: str_eq_buf ← result;
  end;
```

ASCII_code = 0 .. 255, §18.
buffer: **array**, §30.
decr = macro, §16.
incr = macro, §16.
init_pool_ptr: *pool_pointer*, §39.
init_str_ptr: *str_number*, §39.
max_strings = **const**, §11.
not_found = 45, §15.
overflow: **procedure**, §94.
pool_pointer = 0 .. *pool_size*, §38.
pool_ptr: *pool_pointer*, §39.
pool_size = **const**, §11.
si = macro, §38.
so = macro, §38.
str_number = 0 .. *max_strings*, §38.
str_pool: **packed array**, §39.
str_ptr: *str_number*, §39.
str_start: **array**, §39.

⋮

110. Packed data. In order to make efficient use of storage space, TEX bases its major data structures on a *memory_word*, which contains either a (signed) integer, possibly scaled, or an (unsigned) *glue_ratio*, or a small number of fields that are one half or one quarter of the size used for storing integers.

If x is a variable of type *memory_word*, it contains up to four fields that can be referred to as follows:

$x.int$	(an *integer*)
$x.sc$	(a *scaled* integer)
$x.gr$	(a *glue_ratio*)
$x.hh.lh$, $x.hh.rh$	(two halfword fields)
$x.hh.b0$, $x.hh.b1$, $x.hh.rh$	(two quarterword fields, one halfword field)
$x.qqqq.b0$, $x.qqqq.b1$, $x.qqqq.b2$, $x.qqqq.b3$	(four quarterword fields)

This is somewhat cumbersome to write, and not very readable either, but macros will be used to make the notation shorter and more transparent. The Pascal code below gives a formal definition of *memory_word* and its subsidiary types, using packed variant records. TEX makes no assumptions about the relative positions of the fields within a word.

Since we are assuming 32-bit integers, a halfword must contain at least 16 bits, and a quarterword must contain at least 8 bits. But it doesn't hurt to have more bits; for example, with enough 36-bit words you might be able to have *mem_max* as large as 262142, which is eight times as much memory as anybody had during the first four years of TEX's existence.

N.B.: Valuable memory space will be dreadfully wasted unless TEX is compiled by a Pascal that packs all of the *memory_word* variants into the space of a single integer. This means, for example, that *glue_ratio* words should be *short_real* instead of *real* on some computers. Some Pascal compilers will pack an integer whose subrange is '0 .. 255' into an eight-bit field, but others insist on allocating space for an additional sign bit; on such systems you can get 256 values into a quarterword only if the subrange is '−128 .. 127'.

The present implementation tries to accommodate as many variations as possible, so it makes few assumptions. If integers having the subrange '*min_quarterword* .. *max_quarterword*' can be packed into a quarterword, and if integers having the subrange '*min_halfword* ..

max_halfword' can be packed into a halfword, everything should work satisfactorily.

It is usually most efficient to have *min_quarterword* = *min_halfword* = 0, so one should try to achieve this unless it causes a severe problem. The values defined here are recommended for most 32-bit computers.

define *min_quarterword* = 0 { smallest allowable value in a *quarterword* }
define *max_quarterword* = 255
{ largest allowable value in a *quarterword* }
define *min_halfword* ≡ 0 { smallest allowable value in a *halfword* }
define *max_halfword* ≡ 65535 { largest allowable value in a *halfword* }

112. The operation of adding or subtracting *min_quarterword* occurs quite frequently in TEX, so it is convenient to abbreviate this operation by using the macros *qi* and *qo* for input and output to and from quarterword format.

The inner loop of TEX will run faster with respect to compilers that don't optimize expressions like '$x + 0$' and '$x - 0$', if these macros are simplified in the obvious way when *min_quarterword* = 0.

define *qi*(#) ≡ # + *min_quarterword*
{ to put an *eight_bits* item into a quarterword }
define *qo*(#) ≡ # − *min_quarterword*
{ to take an *eight_bits* item out of a quarterword }
define *hi*(#) ≡ # + *min_halfword*
{ to put a sixteen-bit item into a halfword }
define *ho*(#) ≡ # − *min_halfword*
{ to take a sixteen-bit item from a halfword }

---

eight_bits = 0 .. 255, §25.
halfword = *min_halfword* .. *max_halfword*, §113.
mem_max = **const**, §11.
memory_word = **record**, §113.
quarterword = 0 .. 255, §113.

113. The reader should study the following definitions closely:

define $sc \equiv int$ { *scaled* data is equivalent to *integer* }

⟨ Types in the outer block 18 ⟩ +≡

quarterword = *min_quarterword* .. *max_quarterword*; { 1/4 of a word }
halfword = *min_halfword* .. *max_halfword*; { 1/2 of a word }
two_choices = 1 .. 2; { used when there are two variants in a record }
four_choices = 1 .. 4; { used when there are four variants in a record }
two_halves = **packed record** *rh*: *halfword*;
  case *two_choices* **of**
  1: (*lh* : *halfword*);
  2: (*b0* : *quarterword*; *b1* : *quarterword*);
  end;
four_quarters = **packed record** *b0*: *quarterword*;
  b1: *quarterword*;
  b2: *quarterword*;
  b3: *quarterword*;
  end;
memory_word = **record**
  case *four_choices* **of**
  1: (*int* : *integer*);
  2: (*gr* : *glue_ratio*);
  3: (*hh* : *two_halves*);
  4: (*qqqq* : *four_quarters*);
  end;
word_file = **file of** *memory_word*;

⋮

919. Hyphenation. When a word $hc[1 \mathinner{..} hn]$ has been set up to contain a candidate for hyphenation, TEX first looks to see if it is in the user's exception dictionary. If not, hyphens are inserted based on patterns that appear within the given word, using an algorithm due to Frank M. Liang.

Let's consider Liang's method first, since it is much more interesting than the exception-lookup routine. The algorithm begins by setting $hyf[j]$ to zero for all j, and invalid characters are inserted into $hc[0]$ and $hc[hn+1]$ to serve as delimiters. Then a reasonably fast method is used to see which of a given set of patterns occurs in the word $hc[0 \mathinner{..} (hn+1)]$. Each pattern $p_1 \ldots p_k$ of length k has an associated sequence of $k+1$ numbers $n_0 \ldots n_k$; and if the pattern occurs in $hc[(j+1) \mathinner{..} (j+k)]$, TEX will set $hyf[j+i] \leftarrow \max(hyf[j+i], n_i)$ for $0 \le i \le k$. After this has been done for each pattern that occurs, a discretionary hyphen will be inserted between $hc[j]$ and $hc[j+1]$ when $hyf[j]$ is odd.

The set of patterns $p_1 \ldots p_k$ and associated numbers $n_0 \ldots n_k$ depends, of course, on the language whose words are being hyphenated, and on the degree of hyphenation that is desired. A method for finding appropriate p's and n's, from a given dictionary of words and acceptable hyphenations, is discussed in Liang's Ph.D. thesis (Stanford University, 1983); TEX simply starts with the patterns and works from there.

---

glue_ratio = *real*, §109.
hc: **array**, §892.
hn: *small_number*, §892.
hyf: **array**, §900.
max_halfword = macro, §110.
max_quarterword = 255, §110.
min_halfword = macro, §110.
min_quarterword = 0, §110.
scaled = *integer*, §101.

920. The patterns are stored in a compact table that is also efficient for retrieval, using a variant of "trie memory" [cf. *The Art of Computer Programming* **3** (1973), 481–505]. We can find each pattern $p_1 \ldots p_k$ by letting z_0 be one greater than the relevant language index and then, for $1 \le i \le k$, setting $z_i \leftarrow \mathit{trie\_link}(z_{i-1}) + p_i$; the pattern will be identified by the number z_k. Since all the pattern information is packed together into a single *trie_link* array, it is necessary to prevent confusion between the data from inequivalent patterns, so another table is provided such that $\mathit{trie\_char}(z_i) = p_i$ for all i. There is also a table $\mathit{trie\_op}(z_k)$ to identify the numbers $n_0 \ldots n_k$ associated with $p_1 \ldots p_k$.

Comparatively few different number sequences $n_0 \ldots n_k$ actually occur, since most of the n's are generally zero. Therefore the number sequences are encoded in such a way that $\mathit{trie\_op}(z_k)$ is only one byte long. If $\mathit{trie\_op}(z_k) \ne \mathit{min\_quarterword}$, when $p_1 \ldots p_k$ has matched the letters in $hc[(l - k + 1) \,..\, l]$ of language t, we perform all of the required operations for this pattern by carrying out the following little program: Set $v \leftarrow \mathit{trie\_op}(z_k)$. Then set $v \leftarrow v + \mathit{op\_start}[t]$, $\mathit{hyf}[l - \mathit{hyf\_distance}[v]] \leftarrow \max(\mathit{hyf}[l - \mathit{hyf\_distance}[v]], \mathit{hyf\_num}[v])$, and $v \leftarrow \mathit{hyf\_next}[v]$; repeat, if necessary, until $v = \mathit{min\_quarterword}$.

⟨Types in the outer block 18⟩ +≡
trie_pointer = 0 .. *trie_size*; { an index into *trie* }

921. **define** *trie_link*(#) ≡ *trie*[#].*rh* { "downward" link in a trie }
define *trie_char*(#) ≡ *trie*[#].*b1*
{ character matched at this trie location }
define *trie_op*(#) ≡ *trie*[#].*b0*
{ program for hyphenation at this trie location }

⟨Global variables 13⟩ +≡
trie: **array** [*trie_pointer*] **of** *two_halves*; { *trie_link*, *trie_char*, *trie_op* }
hyf_distance: **array** [1 .. *trie_op_size*] **of** *small_number*;
{ position $k - j$ of n_j }
hyf_num: **array** [1 .. *trie_op_size*] **of** *small_number*; { value of n_j }
hyf_next: **array** [1 .. *trie_op_size*] **of** *quarterword*; { continuation code }
op_start: **array** [*ASCII_code*] **of** 0 .. *trie_op_size*;
{ offset for current language }

922. ⟨Local variables for hyphenation 901⟩ +≡
z: *trie_pointer*; { an index into *trie* }
v: *integer*; { an index into *hyf_distance*, etc. }

923. Assuming that these auxiliary tables have been set up properly, the hyphenation algorithm is quite short. In the following code we set $hc[hn+2]$ to the impossible value 256, in order to guarantee that $hc[hn+3]$ will never be fetched.

```
⟨Find hyphen locations for the word in hc, or return 923⟩ ≡
  for j ← 0 to hn do hyf[j] ← 0;
  ⟨Look for the word hc[1 .. hn] in the exception table, and goto found
      (with hyf containing the hyphens) if an entry is found 930⟩;
  if trie_char(cur_lang + 1) ≠ qi(cur_lang) then return;
        { no patterns for cur_lang }
  hc[0] ← 0; hc[hn + 1] ← 0; hc[hn + 2] ← 256;  { insert delimiters }
  for j ← 0 to hn − r_hyf + 1 do
    begin z ← trie_link(cur_lang + 1) + hc[j]; l ← j;
    while hc[l] = qo(trie_char(z)) do
      begin if trie_op(z) ≠ min_quarterword then
        ⟨Store maximum values in the hyf table 924⟩;
      incr(l); z ← trie_link(z) + hc[l];
      end;
    end;
found: for j ← 0 to l_hyf − 1 do hyf[j] ← 0;
  for j ← 0 to r_hyf − 1 do hyf[hn − j] ← 0
```

This code is used in section 895.

924. ⟨Store maximum values in the *hyf* table 924⟩ ≡

```
  begin v ← trie_op(z);
  repeat v ← v + op_start[cur_lang]; i ← l − hyf_distance[v];
    if hyf_num[v] > hyf[i] then hyf[i] ← hyf_num[v];
    v ← hyf_next[v];
  until v = min_quarterword;
  end
```

This code is used in section 923.

ASCII_code = 0 .. 255, §18.
b0: *quarterword*, §113.
b1: *quarterword*, §113.
cur_lang: *ASCII_code*, §892.
found = 40, §15.
hc: **array**, §892.
hn: *small_number*, §892.
hyf: **array**, §900.
i: 0 .. 65, §901.
incr = macro, §16.
j: 0 .. 65, §901.
l: 0 .. 65, §901.
l_hyf: *integer*, §892.
min_quarterword = 0, §110.
qi = macro, §112.
qo = macro, §112.
quarterword = 0 .. 255, §113.
r_hyf: *integer*, §892.
rh: *halfword*, §113.
small_number = 0 .. 63, §101.
trie_op_size = **const**, §11.
trie_size = **const**, §11.
two_halves = **packed record**, §113.

925. The exception table that is built by TeX's `\hyphenation` primitive is organized as an ordered hash table [cf. Amble and Knuth, *The Computer Journal* **17** (1974), 135–142] using linear probing. If α and β are words, we will say that $\alpha < \beta$ if $|\alpha| < |\beta|$ or if $|\alpha| = |\beta|$ and α is lexicographically smaller than β. (The notation $|\alpha|$ stands for the length of α.) The idea of ordered hashing is to arrange the table so that a given word α can be sought by computing a hash address $h = h(\alpha)$ and then looking in table positions h, $h-1$, ..., until encountering the first word $\leq \alpha$. If this word is different from α, we can conclude that α is not in the table.

The words in the table point to lists in *mem* that specify hyphen positions in their *info* fields. The list for $c_1 \ldots c_n$ contains the number k if the word $c_1 \ldots c_n$ has a discretionary hyphen between c_k and c_{k+1}.

⟨Types in the outer block 18⟩ +≡
hyph_pointer = 0 .. *hyph_size*; { an index into the ordered hash table }

926. ⟨Global variables 13⟩ +≡
hyph_word: **array** [*hyph_pointer*] **of** *str_number*; { exception words }
hyph_list: **array** [*hyph_pointer*] **of** *pointer*; { list of hyphen positions }
hyph_count: *hyph_pointer*;
{ the number of words in the exception dictionary }

927. ⟨Local variables for initialization 19⟩ +≡
z: *hyph_pointer*; { runs through the exception dictionary }

928. ⟨Set initial values of key variables 21⟩ +≡
for *z* ← 0 **to** *hyph_size* **do**
begin *hyph_word*[*z*] ← 0; *hyph_list*[*z*] ← *null*;
end;
hyph_count ← 0;

929. The algorithm for exception lookup is quite simple, as soon as we have a few more local variables to work with.

⟨Local variables for hyphenation 901⟩ +≡
h: *hyph_pointer*; { an index into *hyph_word* and *hyph_list* }
k: *str_number*; { an index into *str_start* }
u: *pool_pointer*; { an index into *str_pool* }

930. First we compute the hash code h, then we search until we either find the word or we don't. Words from different languages are kept separate by appending the language code to the string.

⟨Look for the word $hc[1\,..\,hn]$ in the exception table, and **goto** *found* (with *hyf* containing the hyphens) if an entry is found 930⟩ ≡
  $h \leftarrow hc[1]$; $incr(hn)$; $hc[hn] \leftarrow cur\_lang$;
  for $j \leftarrow 2$ **to** hn **do** $h \leftarrow (h + h + hc[j])$ **mod** $hyph\_size$;
  loop begin ⟨If the string $hyph\_word[h]$ is less than $hc[1\,..\,hn]$, **goto** *not_found*; but if the two strings are equal, set *hyf* to the hyphen positions and **goto** *found* 931⟩;
    if $h > 0$ **then** $decr(h)$ **else** $h \leftarrow hyph\_size$;
    end;
not_found: $decr(hn)$

This code is used in section 923.

931. ⟨If the string $hyph\_word[h]$ is less than $hc[1\,..\,hn]$, **goto** *not_found*; but if the two strings are equal, set *hyf* to the hyphen positions and **goto** *found* 931⟩ ≡
  $k \leftarrow hyph\_word[h]$;
  if $k = 0$ **then goto** *not_found*;
  if $length(k) < hn$ **then goto** *not_found*;
  if $length(k) = hn$ **then**
    begin $j \leftarrow 1$; $u \leftarrow str\_start[k]$;
    repeat if $so(str\_pool[u]) < hc[j]$ **then goto** *not_found*;
      if $so(str\_pool[u]) > hc[j]$ **then goto** *done*;
      $incr(j)$; $incr(u)$;
    until $j > hn$;
    ⟨Insert hyphens as specified in $hyph\_list[h]$ 932⟩;
    $decr(hn)$; **goto** *found*;
    end;
done:

This code is used in section 930.

---

cur_lang: *ASCII_code*, §892.
decr = macro, §16.
done = 30, §15.
found = 40, §15.
hc: **array**, §892.
hn: *small_number*, §892.
hyf: **array**, §900.
hyph_size = 307, §12.
incr = macro, §16.
info = macro, §118.
j: 0 .. 65, §901.
length = macro, §40.
mem: **array**, §116.
not_found = 45, §15.
null = macro, §115.
pointer = macro, §115.
pool_pointer = 0 .. *pool_size*, §38.
so = macro, §38.
str_number = 0 .. *max_strings*, §38.
str_pool: **packed array**, §39.
str_start: **array**, §39.

932. ⟨Insert hyphens as specified in *hyph_list*[*h*] 932⟩ ≡
   $s \leftarrow$ *hyph_list*[*h*];
   while $s \neq$ *null* **do**
      begin *hyf*[*info*(*s*)] ← 1; *s* ← *link*(*s*);
      end

This code is used in section 931.

933. ⟨Search *hyph_list* for pointers to *p* 933⟩ ≡
   for *q* ← 0 **to** *hyph_size* **do**
      begin if *hyph_list*[*q*] = *p* **then**
         begin *print_nl*("HYPH("); *print_int*(*q*); *print_char*(")");
         end;
      end

This code is used in section 172.

⋮

942. Initializing the hyphenation tables. The trie for TeX's hyphenation algorithm is built from a sequence of patterns following a `\patterns` specification. Such a specification is allowed only in `INITEX`, since the extra memory for auxiliary tables and for the initialization program itself would only clutter up the production version of TeX with a lot of deadwood.

The first step is to build a trie that is linked, instead of packed into sequential storage, so that insertions are readily made. After all patterns have been processed, `INITEX` compresses the linked trie by identifying common subtries. Finally the trie is packed into the efficient sequential form that the hyphenation algorithm actually uses.

⟨Declare subprocedures for *line_break* 826⟩ +≡
   init ⟨Declare procedures for preprocessing hyphenation patterns 944⟩
   tini

943. Before we discuss trie building in detail, let's consider the simpler problem of creating the *hyf_distance*, *hyf_num*, and *hyf_next* arrays.

Suppose, for example, that TeX reads the pattern '`ab2cde1`'. This is a pattern of length 5, with $n_0 \ldots n_5 = 0\,0\,2\,0\,0\,1$ in the notation above. We want the corresponding *trie_op* code *v* to have *hyf_distance*[*v*] = 3, *hyf_num*[*v*] = 2, and *hyf_next*[*v*] = *v′*, where the auxiliary *trie_op* code *v′* has *hyf_distance*[*v′*] = 0, *hyf_num*[*v′*] = 1, and *hyf_next*[*v′*] = *min_quarterword*.

TEX computes an appropriate value v with the *new_trie_op* subroutine below, by setting

$$v' \leftarrow new\_trie\_op(0, 1, min\_quarterword), \qquad v \leftarrow new\_trie\_op(3, 2, v').$$

This subroutine looks up its three parameters in a special hash table, assigning a new value only if these three have not appeared before for the current language.

The hash table is called *trie_op_hash*, and the number of entries it contains is *trie_op_ptr*.

⟨ Global variables 13 ⟩ +≡
init
trie_op_hash: **array** [−*trie_op_size* .. *trie_op_size*] **of** 0 .. *trie_op_size*;
{ trie op codes for quadruples }
trie_used: **array** [*ASCII_code*] **of** *quarterword*;
{ largest opcode used so far for this language }
trie_op_lang: **array** [1 .. *trie_op_size*] **of** *ASCII_code*;
{ language part of a hashed quadruple }
trie_op_val: **array** [1 .. *trie_op_size*] **of** *quarterword*;
{ opcode corresponding to a hashed quadruple }
trie_op_ptr: 0 .. *trie_op_size*; { number of stored ops so far }
tini

ASCII_code = 0 .. 255, §18.
h: *hyph_pointer*, §929.
hyf: **array**, §900.
hyf_distance: **array**, §921.
hyf_next: **array**, §921.
hyf_num: **array**, §921.
hyph_list: **array**, §926.
hyph_size = 307, §12.
info = macro, §118.
line_break: **procedure**, §815.
link = macro, §118.
min_quarterword = 0, §110.
new_trie_op: **function**, §944.
null = macro, §115.
p: *pointer*, §172.
print_char: **procedure**, §58.
print_int: **procedure**, §65.
print_nl: **procedure**, §62.
q: *integer*, §172.
quarterword = 0 .. 255, §113.
s: *pointer*, §901.
trie_op = macro, §921.
trie_op_size = **const**, §11.
v: *pool_pointer*, §934.

944. It's tempting to remove the *overflow* stops in the following procedure; *new_trie_op* could return *min_quarterword* (thereby simply ignoring part of a hyphenation pattern) instead of aborting the job. However, that would lead to different hyphenation results on different installations of TEX using the same patterns. The *overflow* stops are necessary for portability of patterns.

⟨Declare procedures for preprocessing hyphenation patterns 944⟩ ≡
function *new_trie_op*(*d*, *n* : *small_number*; *v* : *quarterword*): *quarterword*;
  label *exit*;
  var *h*: −*trie_op_size* .. *trie_op_size*; { trial hash location }
    u: *quarterword*; { trial op code }
    l: 0 .. *trie_op_size*; { pointer to stored data }
  begin $h \leftarrow abs(n + 313 * d + 361 * v + 1009 * cur\_lang)$ **mod** (*trie_op_size* + *trie_op_size*) − *trie_op_size*;
  loop begin *l* ← *trie_op_hash*[*h*];
    if *l* = 0 **then** { empty position found for a new op }
      begin if *trie_op_ptr* = *trie_op_size* **then**
        overflow("pattern␣memory␣ops", *trie_op_size*);
      u ← *trie_used*[*cur_lang*];
      if *u* = *max_quarterword* **then**
        overflow("pattern␣memory␣ops␣per␣language",
          max_quarterword − *min_quarterword*);
      incr(*trie_op_ptr*); *incr*(*u*); *trie_used*[*cur_lang*] ← *u*;
      hyf_distance[*trie_op_ptr*] ← *d*; *hyf_num*[*trie_op_ptr*] ← *n*;
      hyf_next[*trie_op_ptr*] ← *v*; *trie_op_lang*[*trie_op_ptr*] ← *cur_lang*;
      trie_op_hash[*h*] ← *trie_op_ptr*; *trie_op_val*[*trie_op_ptr*] ← *u*;
      new_trie_op ← *u*; **return**;
      end;
    if (*hyf_distance*[*l*] = *d*) ∧ (*hyf_num*[*l*] = *n*) ∧ (*hyf_next*[*l*] = *v*) ∧ (*trie_op_lang*[*l*] = *cur_lang*) **then**
      begin *new_trie_op* ← *trie_op_val*[*l*]; **return**;
      end;
    if *h* > −*trie_op_size* **then** *decr*(*h*) **else** *h* ← *trie_op_size*;
    end;
exit: **end**;

See also sections 948, 949, 953, 957, 959, 960, and 966.

This code is used in section 942.

945. After *new_trie_op* has compressed the necessary opcode information, plenty of information is available to unscramble the data into the final form needed by our hyphenation algorithm.

⟨Sort the hyphenation op tables into proper order 945⟩ ≡
  op_start[0] ← −*min_quarterword*;

```
for j ← 1 to 255 do op_start[j] ← op_start[j − 1] + qo(trie_used[j − 1]);
for j ← 1 to trie_op_ptr do
  trie_op_hash[j] ← op_start[trie_op_lang[j]] + trie_op_val[j];
      { destination }
for j ← 1 to trie_op_ptr do
  while trie_op_hash[j] > j do
    begin k ← trie_op_hash[j];
    t ← hyf_distance[k]; hyf_distance[k] ← hyf_distance[j];
    hyf_distance[j] ← t;
    t ← hyf_num[k]; hyf_num[k] ← hyf_num[j]; hyf_num[j] ← t;
    t ← hyf_next[k]; hyf_next[k] ← hyf_next[j]; hyf_next[j] ← t;
    trie_op_hash[j] ← trie_op_hash[k]; trie_op_hash[k] ← k;
    end
```

This code is used in section 952.

946. Before we forget how to initialize the data structures that have been mentioned so far, let's write down the code that gets them started.

```
⟨Initialize table entries (done by INITEX only) 164⟩ +≡
  for k ← −trie_op_size to trie_op_size do trie_op_hash[k] ← 0;
  for k ← 0 to 255 do trie_used[k] ← min_quarterword;
  trie_op_ptr ← 0;
```

---

cur_lang: *ASCII_code*, §892.
decr = macro, §16.
exit = 10, §15.
hyf_distance: **array**, §921.
hyf_next: **array**, §921.
hyf_num: **array**, §921.
incr = macro, §16.
j: *integer*, §966.
k: *integer*, §163.
k: *integer*, §966.
max_quarterword = 255, §110.
min_quarterword = 0, §110.
op_start: **array**, §921.
overflow: **procedure**, §94.
qo = macro, §112.
quarterword = 0 .. 255, §113.
small_number = 0 .. 63, §101.
t: *integer*, §966.
trie_op_hash: **array**, §943.
trie_op_lang: **array**, §943.
trie_op_ptr: 0 .. *trie_op_size*, §943.
trie_op_size = **const**, §11.
trie_op_val: **array**, §943.
trie_used: **array**, §943.

947. The linked trie that is used to preprocess hyphenation patterns appears in several global arrays. Each node represents an instruction of the form "if you see character c, then perform operation o, move to the next character, and go to node l; otherwise go to node r." The four quantities c, o, l, and r are stored in four arrays *trie_c*, *trie_o*, *trie_l*, and *trie_r*. The root of the trie is *trie_l*[0], and the number of nodes is *trie_ptr*. Null trie pointers are represented by zero. To initialize the trie, we simply set *trie_l*[0] and *trie_ptr* to zero. We also set *trie_c*[0] to some arbitrary value, since the algorithm may access it.

The algorithms maintain the condition

$$\mathit{trie\_c}[\mathit{trie\_r}[z]] > \mathit{trie\_c}[z] \qquad \text{whenever } z \neq 0 \text{ and } \mathit{trie\_r}[z] \neq 0;$$

in other words, sibling nodes are ordered by their c fields.

define *trie_root* ≡ *trie_l*[0] { root of the linked trie }

⟨ Global variables 13 ⟩ +≡
init *trie_c*: **packed array** [*trie_pointer*] **of** *packed_ASCII_code*;
{ characters to match }
trie_o: **packed array** [*trie_pointer*] **of** *quarterword*;
{ operations to perform }
trie_l: **packed array** [*trie_pointer*] **of** *trie_pointer*; { left subtrie links }
trie_r: **packed array** [*trie_pointer*] **of** *trie_pointer*; { right subtrie links }
trie_ptr: *trie_pointer*; { the number of nodes in the trie }
trie_hash: **packed array** [*trie_pointer*] **of** *trie_pointer*;
{ used to identify equivalent subtries }
tini

948. Let us suppose that a linked trie has already been constructed. Experience shows that we can often reduce its size by recognizing common subtries; therefore another hash table is introduced for this purpose, somewhat similar to *trie_op_hash*. The new hash table will be initialized to zero.

The function *trie_node*(p) returns p if p is distinct from other nodes that it has seen, otherwise it returns the number of the first equivalent node that it has seen.

Notice that we might make subtries equivalent even if they correspond to patterns for different languages, in which the trie ops might mean quite different things. That's perfectly all right.

⟨ Declare procedures for preprocessing hyphenation patterns 944 ⟩ +≡
function *trie_node*(p : *trie_pointer*): *trie_pointer*;
{ converts to a canonical form }

```
  label exit;
  var h: trie_pointer; { trial hash location }
    q: trie_pointer; { trial trie node }
  begin h ← abs(trie_c[p] + 1009 * trie_o[p] +
        2718 * trie_l[p] + 3142 * trie_r[p]) mod trie_size;
  loop begin q ← trie_hash[h];
    if q = 0 then
      begin trie_hash[h] ← p; trie_node ← p; return;
      end;
    if (trie_c[q] = trie_c[p]) ∧ (trie_o[q] = trie_o[p]) ∧
          (trie_l[q] = trie_l[p]) ∧ (trie_r[q] = trie_r[p]) then
      begin trie_node ← q; return;
      end;
    if h > 0 then decr(h) else h ← trie_size;
    end;
exit: end;
```

949. A neat recursive procedure is now able to compress a trie by traversing it and applying *trie_node* to its nodes in "bottom up" fashion. We will compress the entire trie by clearing *trie_hash* to zero and then saying '*trie_root* ← *compress_trie*(*trie_root*)'.

```
⟨ Declare procedures for preprocessing hyphenation patterns 944 ⟩ +≡
function compress_trie(p : trie_pointer): trie_pointer;
  begin if p = 0 then compress_trie ← 0
  else begin trie_l[p] ← compress_trie(trie_l[p]);
    trie_r[p] ← compress_trie(trie_r[p]); compress_trie ← trie_node(p);
    end;
  end;
```

---

decr = macro, §16.
exit = 10, §15.
packed_ASCII_code = 0 .. 255, §38.
quarterword = 0 .. 255, §113.
trie_op_hash: **array**, §943.
trie_pointer = 0 .. *trie_size*, §920.
trie_size = **const**, §11.

950. The compressed trie will be packed into the *trie* array using a "top-down first-fit" procedure. This is a little tricky, so the reader should pay close attention: The *trie_hash* array is cleared to zero again and renamed *trie_ref* for this phase of the operation; later on, *trie_ref* [*p*] will be nonzero only if the linked trie node *p* is the smallest character in a family and if the characters *c* of that family have been allocated to locations *trie_ref* [*p*] + *c* in the *trie* array. Locations of *trie* that are in use will have *trie_link* = 0, while the unused holes in *trie* will be doubly linked with *trie_link* pointing to the next larger vacant location and *trie_back* pointing to the next smaller one. This double linking will have been carried out only as far as *trie_max*, where *trie_max* is the largest index of *trie* that will be needed. To save time at the low end of the trie, we maintain array entries *trie_min*[*c*] pointing to the smallest hole that is greater than *c*. Another array *trie_taken* tells whether or not a given location is equal to *trie_ref* [*p*] for some *p*; this array is used to ensure that distinct nodes in the compressed trie will have distinct *trie_ref* entries.

define *trie_ref* ≡ *trie_hash* { where linked trie families go into *trie* }
define *trie_back*(#) ≡ *trie*[#].*lh* { backward links in *trie* holes }

⟨ Global variables 13 ⟩ +≡
init *trie_taken*: **packed array** [1 .. *trie_size*] **of** *boolean*;
{ does a family start here? }
trie_min: **array** [*ASCII_code*] **of** *trie_pointer*;
{ the first possible slot for each character }
trie_max: *trie_pointer*; { largest location used in *trie* }
trie_not_ready: *boolean*; { is the trie still in linked form? }
tini

951. Each time `\patterns` appears, it contributes further patterns to the future trie, which will be built only when hyphenation is attempted or when a format file is dumped. The boolean variable *trie_not_ready* will change to *false* when the trie is compressed; this will disable further patterns.

⟨ Initialize table entries (done by `INITEX` only) 164 ⟩ +≡
trie_not_ready ← *true*; *trie_root* ← 0; *trie_c*[0] ← *si*(0); *trie_ptr* ← 0;

952. Here is how the trie-compression data structures are initialized. If storage is tight, it would be possible to overlap *trie_op_hash*, *trie_op_lang*, and *trie_op_val* with *trie*, *trie_hash*, and *trie_taken*, because we finish with the former just before we need the latter.

⟨ Get ready to compress the trie 952 ⟩ ≡
⟨ Sort the hyphenation op tables into proper order 945 ⟩;
for $p \leftarrow 0$ **to** *trie_size* **do** $trie\_hash[p] \leftarrow 0$;
$trie\_root \leftarrow compress\_trie(trie\_root)$; { identify equivalent subtries }
for $p \leftarrow 0$ **to** *trie_ptr* **do** $trie\_ref[p] \leftarrow 0$;
for $p \leftarrow 0$ **to** 255 **do** $trie\_min[p] \leftarrow p + 1$;
$trie\_link(0) \leftarrow 1$; $trie\_max \leftarrow 0$

This code is used in section 966.

ASCII_code = 0 . . 255, §18.
compress_trie: **function**, §949.
lh: *halfword*, §113.
p: *trie_pointer*, §966.
si = macro, §38.
trie: **array**, §921.
trie_c: **packed array**, §947.
trie_hash: **packed array**, §947.
trie_link = macro, §921.
trie_op_hash: **array**, §943.
trie_op_lang: **array**, §943.
trie_op_val: **array**, §943.
trie_pointer = 0 . . *trie_size*, §920.
trie_ptr: *trie_pointer*, §947.
trie_root = macro, §947.
trie_size = **const**, §11.

953. The *first_fit* procedure finds the smallest hole z in *trie* such that a trie family starting at a given node p will fit into vacant positions starting at z. If $c = trie\_c[p]$, this means that location $z - c$ must not already be taken by some other family, and that $z-c+c'$ must be vacant for all characters c' in the family. The procedure sets $trie\_ref[p]$ to $z - c$ when the first fit has been found.

⟨Declare procedures for preprocessing hyphenation patterns 944⟩ +≡
procedure *first_fit*(*p* : *trie_pointer*); { packs a family into *trie* }
  label *not_found*, *found*;
  var *h*: *trie_pointer*; { candidate for *trie_ref*[*p*] }
    z: *trie_pointer*; { runs through holes }
    q: *trie_pointer*; { runs through the family starting at *p* }
    c: *ASCII_code*; { smallest character in the family }
    l, *r*: *trie_pointer*; { left and right neighbors }
    ll: 1 .. 256; { upper limit of *trie_min* updating }
  begin $c \leftarrow so(trie\_c[p])$; $z \leftarrow trie\_min[c]$;
      { get the first conceivably good hole }
  loop begin $h \leftarrow z - c$;
    ⟨Ensure that $trie\_max \geq h + 256$ 954⟩;
    if *trie_taken*[*h*] **then goto** *not_found*;
    ⟨If all characters of the family fit relative to *h*, then **goto** *found*,
        otherwise **goto** *not_found* 955⟩;
  not_found: $z \leftarrow trie\_link(z)$; { move to the next hole }
    end;
found: ⟨Pack the family into *trie* relative to *h* 956⟩;
  end;

954. By making sure that *trie_max* is at least $h + 256$, we can be sure that $trie\_max > z$, since $h = z - c$. It follows that location *trie_max* will never be occupied in *trie*, and we will have $trie\_max \geq trie\_link(z)$.

⟨Ensure that $trie\_max \geq h + 256$ 954⟩ ≡
  if $trie\_max < h + 256$ **then**
    begin if $trie\_size \leq h + 256$ **then**
      overflow("pattern␣memory", *trie_size*);
    repeat *incr*(*trie_max*); *trie_taken*[*trie_max*] ← *false*;
      $trie\_link(trie\_max) \leftarrow trie\_max + 1$;
      $trie\_back(trie\_max) \leftarrow trie\_max - 1$;
    until $trie\_max = h + 256$;
    end

This code is used in section 953.

955. ⟨If all characters of the family fit relative to h, then **goto** *found*, otherwise **goto** *not_found* 955⟩ ≡

```
q ← trie_r[p];
while q > 0 do
  begin if trie_link(h + so(trie_c[q])) = 0 then goto not_found;
  q ← trie_r[q];
  end;
goto found
```

This code is used in section 953.

956. ⟨Pack the family into *trie* relative to h 956⟩ ≡

```
trie_taken[h] ← true; trie_ref[p] ← h; q ← p;
repeat z ← h + so(trie_c[q]); l ← trie_back(z); r ← trie_link(z);
  trie_back(r) ← l; trie_link(l) ← r; trie_link(z) ← 0;
  if l < 256 then
    begin if z < 256 then ll ← z else ll ← 256;
    repeat trie_min[l] ← r; incr(l); until l = ll;
    end;
  q ← trie_r[q];
until q = 0
```

This code is used in section 953.

957. To pack the entire linked trie, we use the following recursive procedure.

⟨Declare procedures for preprocessing hyphenation patterns 944⟩ +≡

```
procedure trie_pack(p : trie_pointer); { pack subtries of a family }
  var q: trie_pointer;
        { a local variable that need not be saved on recursive calls }
  begin repeat q ← trie_l[p];
    if (q > 0) ∧ (trie_ref[q] = 0) then
      begin first_fit(q); trie_pack(q); end;
    p ← trie_r[p];
  until p = 0;
  end;
```

ASCII_code = 0 .. 255, §18.
found = 40, §15.
incr = macro, §16.
not_found = 45, §15.
overflow: **procedure**, §94.
so = macro, §38.
trie: **array**, §921.
trie_back = macro, §950.
trie_c: **packed array**, §947.
trie_l: **packed array**, §947.
trie_link = macro, §921.
trie_max: *trie_pointer*, §950.
trie_min: **array**, §950.
trie_pointer = 0 .. *trie_size*, §920.
trie_r: **packed array**, §947.
trie_ref = macro, §950.
trie_size = **const**, §11.
trie_taken: **packed array**, §950.

958. When the whole trie has been allocated into the sequential table, we must go through it once again so that *trie* contains the correct information. Null pointers in the linked trie will be represented by the value 0, which properly implements an "empty" family.

⟨Move the data into *trie* 958⟩ ≡
```
h.rh ← 0; h.b0 ← min_quarterword; h.b1 ← min_quarterword;
      { trie_link ← 0, trie_op ← min_quarterword, trie_char ← qi(0) }
  if trie_root = 0 then   { no patterns were given }
    begin for r ← 0 to 256 do trie[r] ← h;
    trie_max ← 256;
    end
  else begin trie_fix(trie_root);   { this fixes the non-holes in trie }
    r ← 0;   { now we will zero out all the holes }
    repeat s ← trie_link(r); trie[r] ← h; r ← s;
    until r > trie_max;
    end;
  trie_char(0) ← qi("?");   { make trie_char(c) ≠ c for all c }
```
This code is used in section 966.

959. The fixing-up procedure is, of course, recursive. Since the linked trie usually has overlapping subtries, the same data may be moved several times; but that causes no harm, and at most as much work is done as it took to build the uncompressed trie.

⟨Declare procedures for preprocessing hyphenation patterns 944⟩ +≡
```
procedure trie_fix(p : trie_pointer);   { moves p and its siblings into trie }
  var q: trie_pointer;
        { a local variable that need not be saved on recursive calls }
    c: ASCII_code;   { another one that need not be saved }
    z: trie_pointer;   { trie reference; this local variable must be saved }
  begin z ← trie_ref[p];
  repeat q ← trie_l[p]; c ← so(trie_c[p]); trie_link(z + c) ← trie_ref[q];
    trie_char(z + c) ← qi(c); trie_op(z + c) ← trie_o[p];
    if q > 0 then trie_fix(q);
    p ← trie_r[p];
  until p = 0;
  end;
```

960. Now let's go back to the easier problem, of building the linked trie. When `INITEX` has scanned the '`\patterns`' control sequence, it calls on *new_patterns* to do the right thing.

⟨Declare procedures for preprocessing hyphenation patterns 944⟩ +≡
```
procedure new_patterns;   { initializes the hyphenation pattern data }
```

```
label done, done1;
var k, l: small_number; { indices into hc and hyf }
  digit_sensed: boolean; { should the next digit be treated as a letter? }
  v: quarterword; { trie op code }
  p, q: trie_pointer; { nodes of trie traversed during insertion }
  first_child: boolean; { is p = trie_l[q]? }
  c: ASCII_code; { character being inserted }
begin if trie_not_ready then
  begin set_cur_lang; scan_left_brace;
      { a left brace must follow \patterns }
  ⟨ Enter all of the patterns into a linked trie, until coming to a right
      brace 961 ⟩;
  end
else begin print_err("Too␣late␣for␣"); print_esc("patterns");
  help1("All␣patterns␣must␣be␣given␣before␣typesetting␣begins.");
  error; link(garbage) ← scan_toks(false, false); flush_list(def_ref);
  end;
end;
```

ASCII_code = 0 .. 255, §18.
b0: *quarterword*, §113.
b1: *quarterword*, §113.
c: *ASCII_code*, §953.
def_ref: *pointer*, §305.
done = 30, §15.
done1 = 31, §15.
error: **procedure**, §82.
flush_list: **procedure**, §123.
garbage = macro, §162.
h: *two_halves*, §966.
hc: **array**, §892.
help1 = macro, §79.
hyf: **array**, §900.
link = macro, §118.
min_quarterword = 0, §110.
print_err = macro, §73.
print_esc: **procedure**, §63.
qi = macro, §112.
quarterword = 0 .. 255, §113.
r: *trie_pointer*, §966.
rh: *halfword*, §113.
s: *trie_pointer*, §966.
scan_left_brace: **procedure**, §403.
scan_toks: **function**, §473.
set_cur_lang = macro, §934.
small_number = 0 .. 63, §101.
so = macro, §38.
trie: **array**, §921.
trie_c: **packed array**, §947.
trie_char = macro, §921.
trie_l: **packed array**, §947.
trie_link = macro, §921.
trie_max: *trie_pointer*, §950.
trie_not_ready: *boolean*, §950.
trie_o: **packed array**, §947.
trie_op = macro, §921.
trie_pointer = 0 .. *trie_size*, §920.
trie_r: **packed array**, §947.
trie_ref = macro, §950.
trie_root = macro, §947.

961. Novices are not supposed to be using `\patterns`, so the error messages are terse. (Note that all error messages appear in TEX's string pool, even if they are used only by `INITEX`.)

```
⟨Enter all of the patterns into a linked trie, until coming to a right
      brace 961⟩ ≡
  k ← 0; hyf[0] ← 0; digit_sensed ← false;
  loop begin get_x_token;
    case cur_cmd of
    letter, other_char: ⟨Append a new letter or a hyphen level 962⟩;
    spacer, right_brace: begin if k > 0 then
        ⟨Insert a new pattern into the linked trie 963⟩;
      if cur_cmd = right_brace then goto done;
      k ← 0; hyf[0] ← 0; digit_sensed ← false;
      end;
    othercases begin print_err("Bad␣"); print_esc("patterns");
      help1("(See␣Appendix␣H.)"); error;
      end
    endcases;
    end;
done:
```

This code is used in section 960.

962.
```
⟨Append a new letter or a hyphen level 962⟩ ≡
  if digit_sensed ∨ (cur_chr < "0") ∨ (cur_chr > "9") then
    begin if cur_chr = "." then cur_chr ← 0  {edge-of-word delimiter}
    else begin cur_chr ← lc_code(cur_chr);
      if cur_chr = 0 then
        begin print_err("Nonletter"); help1("(See␣Appendix␣H.)");
        error;
        end;
      end;
    if k < 63 then
      begin incr(k); hc[k] ← cur_chr; hyf[k] ← 0; digit_sensed ← false;
      end;
    end
  else if k < 63 then
      begin hyf[k] ← cur_chr − "0"; digit_sensed ← true;
      end
```

This code is used in section 961.

963. When the following code comes into play, the pattern $p_1 \ldots p_k$ appears in $hc[1\,..\,k]$, and the corresponding sequence of numbers $n_0 \ldots n_k$ appears in $hyf[0\,..\,k]$.

⟨Insert a new pattern into the linked trie 963⟩ ≡

```
begin ⟨Compute the trie op code, v, and set l ← 0 965⟩; q ← 0;
hc[0] ← cur_lang;
while l ≤ k do
  begin c ← hc[l]; incr(l); p ← trie_l[q]; first_child ← true;
  while (p > 0) ∧ (c > so(trie_c[p])) do begin q ← p; p ← trie_r[q];
    first_child ← false; end;
  if (p = 0) ∨ (c < so(trie_c[p])) then
    ⟨Insert a new trie node between q and p, and make p point to it 964⟩;
  q ← p; { now node q represents p1 ... pl }
  end;
if trie_o[q] ≠ min_quarterword then
  begin print_err("Duplicate␣pattern"); help1("(See␣Appendix␣H.)");
  error; end;
trie_o[q] ← v;
end
```

This code is used in section 961.

---

c: *ASCII_code*, §960.
cur_chr: *halfword*, §297.
cur_cmd: *eight_bits*, §297.
cur_lang: *ASCII_code*, §892.
digit_sensed: *boolean*, §960.
done = 30, §15.
error: **procedure**, §82.
first_child: *boolean*, §960.
get_x_token: **procedure**, §380.
hc: **array**, §892.
help1 = macro, §79.
hyf: **array**, §900.
incr = macro, §16.
k: *small_number*, §960.
l: *small_number*, §960.
lc_code = macro, §230.
letter = 11, §207.
min_quarterword = 0, §110.
other_char = 12, §207.
p: *trie_pointer*, §960.
print_err = macro, §73.
print_esc: **procedure**, §63.
q: *trie_pointer*, §960.
right_brace = 2, §207.
so = macro, §38.
spacer = 10, §207.
trie_c: **packed array**, §947.
trie_l: **packed array**, §947.
trie_o: **packed array**, §947.
trie_r: **packed array**, §947.
v: *quarterword*, §960.

964. ⟨ Insert a new trie node between q and p, and make p point to it 964 ⟩ ≡

```
begin if trie_ptr = trie_size then overflow("pattern␣memory", trie_size);
incr(trie_ptr); trie_r[trie_ptr] ← p; p ← trie_ptr; trie_l[p] ← 0;
if first_child then trie_l[q] ← p else trie_r[q] ← p;
trie_c[p] ← si(c); trie_o[p] ← min_quarterword;
end
```

This code is used in section 963.

965. ⟨ Compute the trie op code, v, and set $l \leftarrow 0$ 965 ⟩ ≡

```
if hc[1] = 0 then hyf[0] ← 0; if hc[k] = 0 then hyf[k] ← 0;
l ← k; v ← min_quarterword;
loop begin if hyf[l] ≠ 0 then v ← new_trie_op(k − l, hyf[l], v);
  if l > 0 then decr(l) else goto done1; end;
done1:
```

This code is used in section 963.

966. Finally we put everything together: Here is how the trie gets to its final, efficient form. The following packing routine is rigged so that the root of the linked tree gets mapped into location 1 of *trie*, as required by the hyphenation algorithm. This happens because the first call of *first_fit* will "take" location 1.

⟨ Declare procedures for preprocessing hyphenation patterns 944 ⟩ +≡

```
procedure init_trie;
  var p: trie_pointer; { pointer for initialization }
    j, k, t: integer; { all-purpose registers for initialization }
    r, s: trie_pointer; { used to clean up the packed trie }
    h: two_halves; { template used to zero out trie's holes }
  begin ⟨ Get ready to compress the trie 952 ⟩;
  if trie_root ≠ 0 then begin first_fit(trie_root); trie_pack(trie_root); end;
  ⟨ Move the data into trie 958 ⟩; trie_not_ready ← false;
  end;
```

c: *ASCII_code*, §960.
decr = macro, §16.
done1 = 31, §15.
first_child: *boolean*, §960.
first_fit: **procedure**, §953.
hc: **array**, §892.
hyf: **array**, §900.
incr = macro, §16.
k: *small_number*, §960.
l: *small_number*, §960.
min_quarterword = 0, §110.
new_trie_op: **function**, §944.
overflow: **procedure**, §94.
p: *trie_pointer*, §960.
q: *trie_pointer*, §960.
si = macro, §38.
trie: **array**, §921.
trie_c: **packed array**, §947.
trie_l: **packed array**, §947.
trie_not_ready: *boolean*, §950.
trie_o: **packed array**, §947.
trie_pack: **procedure**, §957.
trie_pointer = 0 .. *trie_size*, §920.
trie_ptr: *trie_pointer*, §947.
trie_r: **packed array**, §947.
trie_root = macro, §947.
trie_size = **const**, §11.
two_halves = **packed record**, §113.
v: *quarterword*, §960.

Chapter 9

Mathematical Writing (1987)

[This chapter contains excerpts from Mathematical Writing, a booklet based on a course of the same name given at Stanford University during autumn quarter, 1987. Informal discussions of programming style, during two of the class sessions, are summarized here by Paul Roberts.]

Notes from class, October 21

Returning to the subject of "Literate Programming," Don said that it takes a while to find a new style to suit a new system like `WEB`. When he was trying to write the `WEB` program in its own language he tore up his first 25 pages of code and started again, having finally found a comfortable style.

He digressed to talk about the vicious circle involved in writing a program in its own language. To break it, he hand-simulated the program on itself to produce a Pascal program that could then be used to compile `WEB` programs. The task was eased because there is obviously no need for error-handling routines when dealing with code that you have to debug anyway. But there is also another kind of bootstrapping going on; you can evolve a style to write these programs only by sitting down and writing programs. Don told us that he wrote `WEB` in just two months, as it was never intended to be a polished product like TeX.

We spent the rest of the class looking at `WEB` programs that had been written by undergraduates doing independent research with Don during the spring. We saw how they had (or had not) adapted to its style. Don said that he had got a lot of feedback and sometimes found it hard to be dispassionate about stylistic questions, but that some things were clearly wrong. He showed us an example that looked for all the world just like a Pascal program; the student had obviously not changed his ways of thinking or writing at all, and so had failed to make any use of the features of the system. The English in his introductory paragraph also left a lot to be desired.

Don showed us his thick book *TEX: The Program*—a listing of the code for TEX, written in `WEB`. It consists of almost 1400 modules. The guiding principle behind `WEB` is that each module is introduced at the psychologically right moment. This means that the program can be written in such a way as to motivate the reader, leaving `TANGLE` to sort everything out later on. [The `TANGLE` processor converts `WEB` programs to Pascal programs.] After all, we don't need to worry about motivating the compiler. (Don added the aside that contrary to superstition, the machine doesn't spend most of its time executing those parts of the code that took us the longest to write.) It seems to be true that the best way in which to present program constructs to the reader is to use the same order in which the creator of the program found himself making decisions about them. Don himself always felt it was quite clear what had to be presented next, throughout the entire composition of this huge program. There was at all points a natural order of exposition, and it seems that the natural orderings for reading and writing are very much the same.

The first student hadn't used this new flexibility at all; he had essentially just used `WEB` to throw in comments here and there.

A general problem of exposition arose: How are we to describe the behavior of a computer program? Do we see the program as essentially autonomous, "running itself," or are we participants in the action? Our attitude to this determines whether we are going to say 'we insert the element in the heap' or 'it inserts the element ... '. Don favours 'we'; at any rate one should be consistent.

Students used descriptors and imperatives for the names of their modules; Don said he favours the latter, as in ⟨ Store the word in the dictionary ⟩, which works much better than ⟨ Stores the word in the dictionary ⟩. On the other hand, where a module is essentially a piece of text with a declarative function—a list of declarations, say—we should use a descriptor to name it: ⟨ Procedures for sorting ⟩.

Incidentally, it is natural to capitalize the first letter of a module name.

One student used the identifier '*FindInNewWords*'. This looks comparatively bad in print: Uppercase letters were not designed to appear immediately following lowercase ones. Since the use of compound nouns is almost inevitable, `WEB` provides a neat solution. It allows a short underscore to be used to conjoin words like *get_word*. (Since the Pascal compiler will not accept identifiers like this, `TANGLE` quietly removes the underscore.) Don told us that Jim Dunlap of Digitek, who made some of the best early compilers, invariably used identifiers forty-or-so characters long. The meaning was always quite clear although no comments appeared in any of Dunlap's code.

Each module should contain an informal but clear description of what it actually does. A play-by-play account of an algorithm, a simple stepping through of the process, does not qualify. We are trying to convey an intuition of what is going on, so a high-level account is much more helpful.

We saw several modules that were much too long. Don thinks that a dozen lines of code is about the right length for a module. Often he simply recommended that the students cut the offending specimens into several pieces, each of more manageable size. The whole philosophy behind `WEB` is to break a complex thing into tractable parts, so the code should reflect this. Once you get the idea, you begin writing code piecewise, and it's easier.

We saw an example in which the student had slipped into "engineerese" in his descriptive text—all conjunctions and no punctuation. This worked for James Joyce, but it doesn't make for good documentation. One student had apparently managed to break `WEB`—the formatting of **begin**s and **end**s came out all wrong. Heaven knows what he did.

One student put comments after each **end** to show what was being ended, as **end** {**while**}. This is a good idea when writing ordinary Pascal, but it's unnecessary in `WEB`. Thus it's a good example of a convention that is no longer appropriate to the new style; when you change style you needn't carry excess baggage along.

Don had more to say about the anthropomorphization of computer systems. Why prompt the user with '`Name of file to process?`' when we can have the computer say '`What file should I process?`'? Don generally likes the use of '`I`' by the computer when referring to itself, and thinks this makes it easier for users to conceptualize what is going on. Perhaps humans can think of complex processes best in terms of demons in boxes, so why not acknowledge this? Eliza, the AI program that simulates a certain type of psychiatrist, managed to fool virtually everyone by an extension of this approach. Eliza may or may not be a recommendation for anthropomorphisms, or for psychiatry. There are those, such as Dijkstra, who think such use of 'I' to be a bad thing.

As in the case of maths, don't start a sentence with a symbol. So don't say '*data* assumes that ... '—it can easily be rewritten.

We saw several programs by one student who had developed a very distinctive and (Don thought) colourful style. His prose is littered with phrases like "Oooops! How can we fix this?" and "Now to get down to the nitty-gritty." This stream-of-consciousness style really does seem to motivate reading, and helps infect the reader with the author's obvious enthusiasm. There were a few small nits to pick with this guy though: His descriptions could often be more descriptive. Why not call a variable *caps_range* instead of just *range*? Don also had to point out to him that 'complement' and 'component' are in fact two different words.

In `WEB` you can declare your variables at any point in the program. Don thinks it is always a good idea to add some comment when you do so, even if only a very cursory explanation is needed.

A note about asterisks: Be warned that typeset asterisks tend to appear higher above the line than typewritten ones, so your multiplication formulæ may come out looking strange. Better to use × for multiplication, and to use a typewriter-style font with body-centered '`*`' symbols instead of the '*' in normal typographic fonts.

Another freshman was digitizing the Mona Lisa for reasons best known to insiders of Don's research project. Don pointed out that since the program uses a somewhat specialized data structure (the heap) that might be unknown to the readers, the author should keep all the heap routines together in the text so that they can be read as a group while fresh in the reader's mind. In `WEB` we are not constrained by top-down, bottom-up, or any other order.

This student capitalized the first letter of every word in titles of modules, even 'And' and the like. This looks rather unnatural—it is better to follow the newspaper-headlines convention by leaving such words entirely in lowercase, and even better to capitalize only the first word.

Don thought it a good idea to use typewriter type for hexadecimal numbers, for instance when saying '`3F` represents 63'. But leave the '63' in normal type. This convention looks appropriate and provides a kind of subliminal type-checking.

The words used in the documentation should match the words used in the formal program—you will only confuse the reader by using two different terms for the same thing.

It's a good idea to develop the habit of putting your **begin**s and **end**s inside the called modules, not putting them in the calling module. That is, do it like this:

```
if down = 4 then ⟨ Punt ⟩;
    ⋮
⟨ Punt ⟩ =
    begin snap;
    place;
    kick;
    end
```

Not like this:

```
if down = 4 then
    begin ⟨ Punt ⟩;
    end
    ⋮
⟨ Punt ⟩ =
    snap;
    place;
    kick
```

Incidentally, appalling bugs will occur if we mix the two conventions!

Notes from class, October 23

One of the chief aspects of WEB is to encourage better programming, not just better exposition of programs. For example, many people say that around 25% of any piece of software should be devoted to error handling and user guidance. But this will typically mean that a subroutine might have 15 lines of 'what to do if the data is faulty' followed by one or two lines of 'what to do in the normal course of events'. The subroutine then looks very much like an error-handling routine. This fails to motivate the writer to do a good job; his heart just isn't in the error handling. WEB provides a solution to this. The procedure can have a single line near the beginning that says ⟨ Check if the data is wrong 28 ⟩ and points to another module. Thus the proper focus is maintained: In the main module we have code devoted to handling the normal cases, and elsewhere we have all the error-case instructions. The programmer never feels that he's writing a whole lot of stuff where he'd really much rather be writing something else; in module 28, it feels right to do the best error detection and recovery. Don showed us an example of this from his undergraduate class in which a routine had two references of the form

if ... **then** ... **else** *char_error*

pointing to a very brief error-reporting module.

We looked at a program written by another student who had the temerity to include some comments critical of WEB. Don struck back with the following:

> It is good practice to use italics for the names of variables when they appear in comments.
>
> Let the variables in the module title correspond to the local parameters in the module itself.

> According to this student's comments, his algorithm uses 'tail recursion'. This is an impressive phrase, helpful in the proper context; but unfortunately that is not the kind of recursion his program uses.

However, Don did grant that his exposition was good, and said that it gave a nice intuition about the functions of the modules.

We saw a second program by the same student. It had the usual sprinkling of "wicked whiches"—'which's that should have been 'that's. The purpose of the program was to "enforce" the triangle inequality on a table of data that specified the distances between pairs of large cities in the US. Don commented here that his project (from which these programs came) intends to publish interesting data sets so that researchers in different places can replicate each other's results. He also observed that a program running on a table of "real data," as here (the actual "official" distances between the cities in question) is a lot more interesting than the same program running on "random data." Returning to the nitty-gritty of the program, Don observed that the student had made a good choice of variable names—for instance '*villains*' for those parts of the data that were causing inconsistencies. This fitted in nicely with the later exposition; he could talk about 'cut throats' and so forth. (Don added that we nearly always find villainy pretty unamusing in real life, but the word makes for a witty exposition in artificial life; the English language has lots of vocabulary just waiting for such applications.)

Don wondered aloud why it is that people talk about "the nth and m^{th} positions" (as this student had) thereby reversing the natural (or at any rate alphabetical) order?

He also pointed to an issue that arises with the move from typewriters to computer typesetting—the fact that we now distinguish between opening and closing quotes. We saw an example where the student had written "main program". To add to the confusion, different languages have different conventions for quotes; in German they appear like this: „The Name of the Rose“. How to represent this in a standard ASCII file remains a mystery.

Back to the triangle inequality. Don pointed out that one obvious check for bad data in the distance table follows from the fact that the road distance can not be less than a Great Circle route. ("It could, if you had a tunnel" commented a New Yorker in the audience.) The student had written a nice group of modules based on this fact, and it illustrated the `WEB` facility of being able to put displayed equations into comments.

"So WEB effectively just does macro substitution?" asked another member of the class. Exactly, said Don. In fact the macros he uses are not very general—they really allow only one parameter. This means he doesn't need a complex parser, but in fact one can do a great deal within this restriction. For instance, it is not difficult to simulate two-parameter macros if we wish.

Someone in the class commented that it seemed a little strange to put variable declarations in a different module from their use. Don said that this was OK as long as they are close to their use, but large procedures should have their local variables "distributed" as the exposition proceeds.

Don recalled that older versions of Algol allowed you to declare a variable in the middle of a block. This fits in nicely with the WEB philosophy, but unfortunately cannot be done in modern Pascal. Indeed, Don became painfully aware of the limitations of Pascal for system programming when he was writing WEB—you can't have an array of file names, for example. He got around them, though, with macros.

One example of improving Pascal via macros is to define (in WEB)

$$\textit{string\_type}(\#) \equiv \textbf{packed array } [1\,..\,\#] \textbf{ of } \textit{char}$$

so that you can say things like

$$\textit{name\_code}\colon\ \textit{string\_type}(2)$$

when declaring a two-letter string variable.

Don commented that the student had given a certain variable the name '*scan*'. Since this variable was essentially a place marker, Don thought that a noun would be much better than a verb—'*place*', perhaps. Let the function determine the part of speech; think of it as a kind of Truth in Naming. Verbs are for procedures, not data.

The last student had written a program to handle graph structures based on encounters between the characters in novels. He too had made the "quote mistake". The student gave a nice characterization of the input and output of the program, using the typewriter font to illustrate data as it appears in a file.

This student also showed a bit of inconsistency in the use of 'it' and 'we' as the personification of his program. We seem to be finding the same old faults over and over now, Don said, so perhaps that indicates that we have found them all. Discuss.

Chapter 10

The Errors of TEX (1989)

[Software creation involves much more than the writing of programs. The present chapter describes the milieu of literate programming, by tracing the history of all changes made to TEX as that system evolved. Knuth was asked by the editors of Software—Practice & Experience to prepare an article discussing the development of TEX; his response is reprinted here from the July 1989 issue of that journal.]

Introduction

I make mistakes. I always have, and I probably always will. But I like to think that I learn something, every time I go astray. In fact, one of my favorite poems consists of the following lines by Piet Hein [7]:

> The road to wisdom? Well, it's plain
> and simple to express:
> Err
> and err
> and err again
> but less
> and less
> and less.

The date today, as I begin to write this paper, is May 5, 1987, exactly ten years since I began to work intensively on software systems for typesetting. I have certainly learned a lot during those ten years, judging from the number of mistakes I made; and I would like to share what I've learned with other people who are developing software. The best way to do this, as far as I know, is to present a list of all the errors that were corrected in TEX while it was being developed, and to attempt to analyze those errors.

When I mentioned my plan for this paper to Paul M. B. Vitányi, he told me about a best-selling book that his grand-uncle had written for civil engineers, devoted entirely to descriptions of foundation work that had proved to be defective. The preface to that book [25] says

> It is natural that engineers should not wish to draw attention to their mistakes, but failures are sometimes due to causes of which there has been no previous experience or of which no information is available. An engineer cannot be blamed for not foreseeing the unknown, and in such cases his reputation would not be harmed if full details of the design and of the phenomena that caused the failure were published for the guidance of others. ... To be forewarned is to be forearmed.

In my own case I cannot claim that "unknown" factors lay behind my blunders, since I was totally in control of my programming environment. I can justly be blamed for every mistake I made, and I'm certainly not proud of the record. But I see no harm in admitting the horrible truth about my tendency to err, when such details might shed light on the problem of writing large programs. (Besides, I'm lucky enough to have a secure job.)

Empirical studies of programming errors, conducted by Endres [5] and by Basili and Perricone [1], have already led to interesting results and to the conclusion that "more data must be collected on different projects." I can't claim that the data presented below will be as generally applicable as theirs, because all of the programming I shall discuss was done by one person (me). Insightful models of truly large-scale software development and program evolution have been introduced by Belady and Lehman [3]. However, I do have one advantage that the authors of previous studies did not have; namely, the entire program for TEX has been published [23]. Hence I can give fairly precise information about the type and location of each error. The concept of scale cannot easily be communicated by means of numeric data alone; I believe that a detailed list gives important insights that cannot be gained from statistical summaries.

Types of Error

Some people undoubtedly think that everything I did on TEX was an error, from start to finish. But I shall consider only a limited class of errors here, based on the log books I kept while I was developing the program. Whenever I made a change, I noted it down for future reference, and it is these changes that I shall discuss in detail. Edited forms of my log books are appended below [Chapter 11].

I guess I could say that this paper is about 'changes', not 'errors', because many of the changes were made in order to introduce new features rather than to correct malfunctions. However, new features are necessary only when a design is deficient (or at least non-optimal). Hence, I'll continue to say that each change represents an error, even though I know that no complex system will ever be error-free in this extended sense.

The errors in my log books have each been assigned to one of fifteen general categories for purposes of analysis:

- **A**, an algorithm awry. Here my original method proved to be incorrect or inadequate, so I needed to change the procedure. For example, error **#212** fixed a problem in which footnotes appeared on a page backwards: The last footnote came out first.

- **B**, a blunder or botch. Here I knew what I ought to do, but I wrote something else that was syntactically correct—sort of a mental typo. For example, in error **#126** I wrote '*before*' when I meant '*after*' and vice versa. I was thinking so much of the Big Picture that I didn't have enough brainpower left to get the small details right.

- **C**, a cleanup for consistency or clarity. Here I changed the rules of the language to make things easier to remember and/or more logical. Sometimes this was just a surface change to TEX's "syntactic sugar," as in **#16** where I decided that `\input` would be a better name than `\require`.

- **D**, a data structure debacle. Here I didn't properly update the representation of information to preserve the appropriate invariants. For example, in error **#105** I failed to return nodes to available memory when they were no longer accessible.

- **E**, an efficiency enhancement. Here I changed the program so that it would run faster; the existing code was correct but slow. For example, in error **#287** I decided to give TEX the ability to preload font information, since it took awhile to read thirty short files at the beginning of every run.

- **F**, a forgotten function. Here I didn't remember to do everything I had intended, when I actually got around to writing a particular part of the code. It was a simple error of omission, rather than commission. For example, in error **#11** and again in **#172** I had a loop of the form '**while** $p \neq null$ **do**', and I forgot to advance the pointer p inside the loop! This seems to be one of my favorite mistakes: I often forget the most obvious things.

• **G**, a generalization or growth of ability. Here I realized that some extension of the existing specifications was desirable. For example, error **#303** generalized my original primitive command '`\ifT` ⟨char⟩', which tested if a given character was '`T`' or not, to the primitive '`\if` ⟨char⟩⟨char⟩', which tested if two given characters were equal. Eventually, in **#666**, I decided to generalize further and allow '`\if` ⟨token⟩⟨token⟩'.

• **I**, an interactive improvement. Here I made TEX respond better to the user's needs. Sometimes I saw how to help TEX identify and recover from errors in the documents it was processing. I also kept searching for better ways to communicate the reasons underlying TEX's behavior, by making diagnostic information available in symbolic form. For example, error **#54** introduced '`...`' into the display of context lines so that users could easily tell when information was truncated.

• **L**, a language liability. Here I misused or misunderstood the programming language or system hardware I was working with. For example, in error **#24** I wanted to reduce a counter modulo 8, so I wrote '$t := (t-1)$ **mod** 8'; this unfortunately made t negative because of the way '**mod**' was defined. Sometimes I forgot the precedence of operators, etc.

• **M**, a mismatch between modules. Here I forgot the conventions I had built into a subroutine when I actually got around to using that subroutine. For example, in error **#64** I had a macro with four parameters (x_0, y_0, x_1, y_1) that define a rectangle; but when I used it, I gave the parameters in different order, (x_0, x_1, y_0, y_1). Such "interface errors" included cases when a procedure had unwanted side effects (like clobbering a global variable) that I failed to take into account. Some mismatches (like incorrect data types) were caught by the compiler and not entered in my log.

• **P**, a promotion of portability. Here I changed the organization or documentation of the program; this affected only a person who would try to read or modify the code, not a person who tried to run it. For example, in error **#59**, one of my comments about how to set the size of memory had '$\geq$' where I meant to say '$\leq$'. (Most changes of this kind were not recorded in my log; I noted only the noteworthy ones.)

• **Q**, a quest for quality. Here I changed the specifications of what the program should output from given input, when I learned how to improve the typographic appearance of the output. For example, error #187 changed TEX's behavior when typesetting formulas that have an unusually complex superscript; as a result, TEX now produces

$$e^{\frac{1}{1-q_j^2}} \qquad \text{instead of} \qquad e^{\frac{1}{1-q_j^2}}\,.$$

• **R**, a reinforcement of robustness. Whenever I realized that TEX could loop or crash in the presence of certain erroneous input, I tried to make the code bulletproof. For example, error #200 made sure that a user-supplied character number was between 0 and 127; otherwise parts of TEX's memory could be wiped out.

• **S**, a surprising scenario. Errors of type S were particularly bad bugs that forced me to change my original ideas, because of unforeseen interactions between various parts of the program. For example, error #25 was logged when I first discovered a consequence of TEX's convention about blank lines denoting the end of a paragraph: There's often a blank space in TEX's internal data structure just before a paragraph ends, because a space is usually supplied at the end of the line just preceding a blank line. Thus I had to write new code to delete the unwanted space. Whenever such unexpected phenomena showed up, I had to go back to the drawing board and fix the design.

• **T**, a trivial typo. Sometimes I didn't type the right thing when I entered the program into the computer, although my original pencil draft was correct. For example, in error #48 I had typed '−' instead of '+'. If a typing mistake was detected by the compiler as a syntax error, I didn't log it, because bad syntax can easily be corrected.

Nine of these categories (A, B, D, F, L, M, R, S, T) represent "bugs"; such errors absolutely had to be corrected. The other six categories (C, E, G, I, P, Q) represent "enhancements"; I could have refused to consider the existing situation erroneous. As remarked earlier, I'm considering all items in the log to be indications of error. But there is a significant difference between errors of these two kinds: I felt guilty when fixing the bugs, but I felt virtuous when making the enhancements.

My classification of errors into fifteen categories is ad hoc, but at the moment it's the best way I can think of to make sense out of my experiences. Some of the bug categories refer to simple flaws in the basic mechanics of programming: Writing the right thing but typing it wrong (T); thinking the right thing but writing it wrong (B); knowing the right thing but forgetting to think it (F); imperfectly knowing the tools (L) or the specifications (M). Such bugs are easy to fix once they've been identified. Categories A and D represent the next level of difficulty, as we get into technical aspects of what programming is all about. (As Niklaus Wirth has said, Algorithms + Data Structures = Programs.) Category R covers the special situation in which we want a program to survive even when its input is incorrect. Finally, category S accounts for higher-level surprises; these are the subtle bugs that result from complex interactions between different parts of a system. Thus the nine types of bugs have a somewhat logical structure. The remaining six categories—cleanliness (C), efficiency (E), generalization (G), interaction (I), portability (P), and quality (Q)—seem to provide a reasonable way to classify the various kinds of enhancements that were made to TeX during its development.

My classification scheme relies more on essential functionality than on the external form of the program. Thus it isn't easy to use my statistics about the number of errors per category to answer questions like "How many bugs were due to improper use of **goto** statements?" Such questions are interesting to teachers of programming, but I no longer think that they are extremely important. If I had indexed my errors by syntactic categories, I would have found that errors #45, #91, #119, #155, #231, #352, #354, #419, #523, #581, and #801 could be ascribed to my use or abuse of **goto**; also #512 could be added to this list, since **return** and **goto** are analogous. Thus we can conclude from my experience with TeX that **goto** statements can indeed be harmful. On the other hand we must balance this fact with the realization that bad **goto**s account for only 1.4% of my errors; we must identify *other* culprits if we're going to do away with the other 98.6%. Sure enough, several other errors were caused by lapses in my use of other control structures: A **case** statement got me in trouble in #21; a **while** confused me in #29; **if-then-else** led me astray in #467, #471, #680, and #843. (See also #796 and #845, where efficiency of control was important.) I conclude that *every* feature of a programming language can be harmful, if it is misused.

Some of the errors noted in my log book were much more devastating than others. In certain cases the changes were far-reaching, affecting dozens of different parts of the program; several days of "hacking" were necessary before such changes had been made and verified. For example, change #110 required major surgery to the program, because my original ideas were incapable of handling aligned tables inside of aligned tables. On the other hand, some of my errors were only venial sins, and some of the changes were merely twiddles; for example, #87 simply improved the wording of a diagnostic message. Although the log doesn't give an explicit weighting to the errors, the "heavy" errors tend to cancel with the "light" ones, so we can still get a reasonable insight into the stability of the program if we calculate, say, the number of errors logged per year.

Chronology

The development of TEX has taken place over a period of ten years, and the lessons I learned can best be understood when they're put into the context of the other things I was doing during that time. Typography has many facets, hence TEX itself was only one of the projects I decided to work on. The two most significant companion systems were METAFONT (a system for typeface design) and Computer Modern (a family of typefaces defined in terms of the METAFONT language); these programs had to be debugged just as TEX did, and their debugging logs show a similar development history. I also needed a dozen or so utility routines to support TEX and METAFONT; the most notable of these are TANGLE and WEAVE, which constitute the WEB system of structured documentation [20,18].

Beginnings

The genesis of TEX probably took place on February 1, 1977, when I first chanced to see the output of a high-resolution typesetting machine. I was told that this fine typography (the galley proofs of a book by Winston [26], which our faculty was considering for inclusion on an exam syllabus) was produced by entirely digital methods; yet I could see no difference between the digital type and "real" type. Therefore I realized that a central aspect of printing had been reduced to bit manipulation. As a computer scientist, I couldn't resist the challenge of improving print quality by manipulating those bits better. Therefore my diary entry for February 8 says that, already at that time, I began discussing the possibility of new typesetting software with people at Stanford's Artificial Intelligence Lab. By February 13 I had changed my plan to spend a forthcoming sabbatical year in South America; instead of traveling to an exotic place and working on Volume 4 of *The Art of Computer Programming*, I had decided to stay at Stanford and work on digital typography.

I mentioned earlier that the design of TEX was begun on May 5, 1977. A week later, I wrote a draft report containing what I thought was a pretty complete design, and I stayed up until 5 a.m. typing it into the computer. The problem of typesetting seemed quite straightforward, so I soon started thinking about fonts instead; I spent the next 45 days writing a program that was destined to evolve into METAFONT. By June 28, I had 25 lowercase letters in various styles that looked reasonably good to me at the time; and three days later I figured out how to handle the 26th letter, which required some new ideas [15].

I went back to thinking about TEX on July 3. Several people had made thoughtful comments on my earlier draft, and I prepared a thoroughly revised language definition after two weeks of further study. (This included two days of working with dictionaries in order to develop an algorithm for hyphenation of English.) The resulting document, I thought, was a reasonably complete specification of a language for typesetting, and I left it in the capable hands of two graduate students who were my research assistants that summer (Frank Liang and Michael Plass). Their job was to implement TEX while I flew off for a visit to China. I returned on August 25 and had just one day to meet with them before leaving on another three-week trip. On September 14 I returned and they presented me with a sheet of paper that had been typeset by their proto-TEX program! They had implemented only about 15% of the language, and they had used data structures that were not general enough or efficient enough to support the remaining 85%; but they had chosen their subset wisely so that a small test program could run from start to finish. Hence it was easy for me to imagine what a complete system would entail.

Now it was time for Liang and Plass to go back to school, and time for my sabbatical year to begin. I started coding the "final version of TEX" (or so I thought) on September 16, and immediately I discovered that their summer work represented a truly heroic achievement. Although I had thought that my specification of TEX was quite complete, I encountered loose ends every 15 minutes or so when I was actually faced with writing the code. I soon realized that if I had been in my students' shoes—having to implement this language when the author was completely unreachable—I would have thrown up my hands in despair; important policy decisions had to be made at every turn.

That was the first big lesson I learned during my work with TEX: *The designer of a new kind of system must participate fully in the implementation.* Even if I had been available for consultation with my students, they would have had to come to me so often with questions that the work would have dragged on forever. I can imagine them having to spend a half hour or so explaining each particular problem to me, and we would have needed literally hundreds of those meetings. Now I knew why other projects I'd heard about, in which the language designer had decided not be the compiler writer, had failed.

By October 14 I had coded all of TEX except for the parts that typeset mathematics, and except for the routines that convert from TEX's internal representation into codes for an output device. At this point I had to leave for three weeks of travel in Europe. This European trip had been planned long before, so it was mostly unrelated to typesetting; but I did have some interesting discussions about curve-drawing with mathematicians I met in Oberwolfach, Germany, and in Oslo, Norway. I also was able to arrange a visit to the headquarters of Monotype Corporation in Redhill, England.

After returning I spent November finishing the numerals, uppercase letters, and punctuation marks of the first-draft Computer Modern types. I needed to have a complete font because I had been invited to give a lecture about this work to the American Mathematical Society, and I didn't want to have only lowercase examples to show. I prepared the AMS lecture [12] during December and presented it in January, so I didn't have a chance to resume the coding of TEX until January 14. But finally I was able to write the following in my diary on February 10, 1978:

> Finished the TEX programs including all loose ends and got them all compiled without syntax errors (4 a.m.).

TEX was the first fairly large program I had written since 1970; so it was my first nontrivial "structured program," in the sense that I wrote it while consciously applying the methodology I had learned in the early 70s from Dijkstra, Hoare, Dahl, and others. I found that structured programming greatly increased my confidence in the correctness of the code, while the code still existed only on paper. Therefore I could wait until the whole program was written, before trying to debug any of it. This saved lots of time, because I didn't have to prepare "dummy" versions of nonexistent modules while testing modules that were already written; I could test everything in its final environment. Of course I had a few qualms in January about whether my code from September would really work; but that gave me more of an incentive to finish the whole thing sooner.

Even on February 10, when TEX had been compiled and was ready to be tested, I didn't feel any compelling need to try it immediately. I knew that the program was fairly readable and "informally proved correct," so I spent the next month making italic, greek, script, symbols, and large delimiter fonts. My test program for TEX required those fonts, so I didn't want to start testing until everything was in place. Again, I knew I was saving time by not having to prepare prototypes that would merely simulate the real thing; structured programming gave me the courage to wait until the whole system was ready. I finished the large symbols on March 8, and I happily penned the following in my diary on March 9:

> Entered all accumulated corrections to TEX program and compiled it—tomorrow the debugging begins!

My log book for errors in TeX began that next day, March 10; the debugging process will be discussed below. By March 29 I had decided that TeX was essentially working,

> ... (except perhaps for error recovery)—it's time to celebrate!

I began tuning up the fonts and drafting ideas for a user manual; then I spent a few days at Alphatype Corporation in Illinois, from whom Stanford had decided to purchase a phototypesetter. From April 11 to May 11, I took time off from typography to work on dozens of updates to *Seminumerical Algorithms*, which is Volume 2 of *The Art of Computer Programming* [10]; I wanted to incorporate new research results into that text, which was to be TeX's first big application. Then on May 14 I began to get TeX running again; proof copies of pages iv through 8 of Volume 2 came out of our Xerox Graphics Printer on May 15.

My work was cut out for me during the next weeks: I became a production user of TeX, typing the manuscript of Volume 2. This proved to be an invaluable experience, as explained below. By the time my sabbatical year ended, on September 24, I had finished the typing up to page 441 of that 700-page book. Improvements to TeX kept occurring to me all during that time, of course—except during a month-long vacation trip with my family. (Even on vacation I kept seeing fonts everywhere and thinking about how to draw such letterforms by computer. I spent one morning sitting by one of the trails in the Grand Canyon designing the algebraic notation for METAFONT; my fonts had previously been written in a primitive macro language and compiled directly into machine code, not interpreted.) I also spent three weeks that summer writing the first manual for TeX.

Although my sabbatical year was over, I kept working on typography in odd moments between classes in the fall; the text of Volume 2 was completed on the morning of November 15. On November 17 I began writing METAFONT, and my diary entry for December 31, 1978 was this:

> Finished the METAFONT interpreter, just in time to celebrate New Year's eve (11:59 p.m.).

Other people had begun to use TeX in August of 1978, and I was surprised to see how fast the system was propagating. I spent my spare time during the first three months of 1979 thinking about how to make TeX available in Pascal form. (The original program was written in SAIL, a language that was available on only a few computers.) During this period I began to experiment with the typesetting of Pascal programs; I wrote a program called BLAISE that converted Pascal source code into a TEX file for pretty-printing. BLAISE soon developed into a system called DOC for structured documentation, completed on March 31, 1979; programs in DOC format could be converted either to Pascal or to TEX. Luis Trabb Pardo and Ignacio Zabala subsequently used DOC to prepare a highly portable version of TEX in Pascal, completed in April of 1980.

About this time I learned another big lesson: *Writing software is much harder than writing books.* I couldn't simultaneously teach classes well and finish what needed to be done on typography. So I asked to be excused from teaching in the spring of 1979; my diary for March 22 said,

> Now my obligations are fairly well cleared away and it's back to the stalled research on TEX.

(It turned out that I was able to teach during only 13 of the 21 academic quarters between my sabbatical years in that period. I continued to supervise graduate students, but I gave no classroom lectures during 1983 when the work on TEX and METAFONT was at its peak; I also missed three months in 82, 84, and 85. I really enjoy teaching, but I couldn't see any way to finish the TEX project without relinquishing almost all of my other duties.)

On April 1, 1979, I returned to METAFONT, which had been written but not debugged. METAFONT began to work on April 28. Then I began to design software for the Alphatype machine; that took about three months. During the summer I wrote the METAFONT manual, which gave me further experience with TEX. And TEX also received an important stimulus from the American Mathematical Society that summer, when several people (including Barbara Beeton and Michael Spivak) were given the opportunity to spend some time at Stanford developing TEX macros. The AMS people introduced me to several important applications, such as the indexes to *Mathematical Reviews*, which stretched TEX to its limits and led to substantial improvements.

Endings

By August 14, 1979, I felt that TEX was essentially complete and fairly stable. I lectured that evening to about 100 participants of the Western Institute for Computer Science in Santa Cruz, telling about my experiences developing and debugging the program. At that time my log book of errors had accumulated 420 items; little did I know that the final total would be more than twice that! But already I knew that I had learned a lot by keeping the log, and I must have been enthusiastic because I lectured from 7:30 to 9:30 p.m. (The audience was equally enthusiastic—they kept asking me questions until 11:30 p.m. So I resolved to write a paper about the errors of TEX, and at last I am able to do so.)

I devoted the last months of 1979 and the first months of 1980 to Computer Modern, which needed to be rewritten in terms of the new METAFONT. Then I needed to update Volume 2 again—computer science marches inexorably forward—until I finally had finished producing camera-ready copy on our Alphatype. This was the goal I had hoped to achieve during my sabbatical year; I reached it at 2 a.m. on July 29, 1980, about two years late. During the rest of 1980 I wrote papers about what I thought were the most novel ideas in TEX [16] and in METAFONT [17].

But my research on TEX was by no means finished. About 50 people from all over the USA met at Stanford on February 22, 1980, and established the TEX Users Group (TUG). I asked them if they would mind my cleaning up the language in several upward-incompatible ways, even though this would make the user manual and their existing computer files obsolete; and nobody objected to such changes! Soon TUG grew dramatically, under the able chairmanship of Richard Palais, and it became international. I realized that I could not disappoint all these people by leaving TEX in its current state and returning immediately to work on subsequent volumes of *The Art of Computer Programming.*

I needed to work out a better "endgame strategy," and it soon became clear what ought to be done: The original versions of TEX and METAFONT should be scrapped, once they had served their purpose of accumulating enough user experience to indicate what such languages ought to be. New versions of TEX and METAFONT should be written, designed to last a long time and to be highly portable between computers and typesetting devices of all kinds. Moreover, these new programs should be published, because TEX was making it possible to improve the state of the art of program documentation. I decided to do my best to produce a stable system and to explain all I knew about it, so that other people could take it over and maintain it if it proved to be important. This way I could return to other pursuits in good conscience, knowing that if my typographic research had any merit it would be carried on by others in whatever ways would prove to be necessary.

So that was my new goal; I thought I could achieve it in one or two more years. The original TEX program was renamed TEX78, and the new one was to be called TEX82.

Classes and miscellaneous chores kept me too busy to do much else during the first half of 1981, but I began to write TeX82 on August 22. By September 9 I realized that the DOC system needed to be completely revised, so I spent two months replacing it by a much better system called WEB [18]. Since then my programming language of choice has been WEB (which, unlike DOC, was written in its own language). After a month in Europe, I was able to resume writing TeX82 on December 1, 1981. The draft of TeX82 was completed on June 29, 1982; as before, I wrote the entire program before trying to run any of it.

Meanwhile I had other problems to worry about. When my new copy of *Seminumerical Algorithms* arrived in January of 1981, I had expected to be filled with joy at the consummation of so much hard work. Instead, I burned with disappointment, as I realized that I still had a great deal to learn about fonts. The early Computer Modern typefaces were not at all what I had hoped to achieve, when I first saw them in print. They had looked reasonably good at low resolution, so I had blithely assumed that high resolution would be much better. Not so. My education in typefaces was barely beginning. I met Richard Southall later in 1981, a professor of type design who had exactly the expertise I was lacking; so I invited him to visit Stanford. We spent the entire month of April, 1982, working about 16 hours a day, revising Computer Modern from A to z.

I debugged TeX82 in the summer of '82, then began to write the new manual—called *The TeXbook* [21]—in October. The first manual had been written hastily and finished in 21 days, but I wanted *The TeXbook* to meet much higher standards. Therefore I wasn't able to finish it until a full year later.

It was during this period, October '82 to October '83, that TeX became a mature system. I had to rethink every aspect of its design as I rewrote the manual. Fortunately I was aided by a wonderful group of knowledgeable volunteers, who would meet with me for two or three hours every Friday noon and we would discuss the tradeoffs of every important decision. The diverse backgrounds of these people provided an important counterweight to my one-sided views. Finally, on December 9, 1983, I decided that the first phase of my endgame strategy was complete; I gratefully hosted a coming-of-age party for TeX, with 36 guests of honor, at the Fuki-Sushi restaurant in Palo Alto.

The rest is history. I wrote METAFONT in WEB between December, 1983 and July, 1984; I wrote *The METAFONTbook* between August, 1984, and October, 1985, taking off five months (February through July) to rewrite Computer Modern in terms of the new METAFONT. I began another sabbatical year in October, 1985, just after the TeX project disbanded. Finally, after adding a few more finishing touches, I was able to celebrate the long-planned completion of my "endgame" on May 21, 1986, when my publishers sponsored a reception at the Computer Museum in Boston; that was the day I first saw the five hardcover volumes of *Computers & Typesetting*, the books that summarized my nine years of work on TeX, METAFONT, and Computer Modern.

Another year has gone by and I would like to report that TeX has proved to be 100% correct. But I cannot, not yet. For I stumbled across a hidden TeX anomaly last January. And I've just been teaching a course about software development based on the internal structure of TeX; students in the class have noticed a few things that should be improved. So I suppose there is still at least one bug lurking there. I plan to hold off publishing this paper until another year or so has gone by, so that I'll have more reason to believe that my log book of errors is complete.

Contents of the Log Books

As I said, an appendix to this paper [Chapter 11] reproduces the entire list of errors that I kept as TeX was changing. The best way to comprehend how TeX evolved is to peruse this list. The first 519 items refer to the original program TeX78, which was written in SAIL, from the time I began to debug it to the time I stopped maintaining it. The remaining items, numbered 520–849 (as of May 1987), refer to the "real" program TeX82, which was written in WEB. I didn't keep any record of errors removed during the hectic period when TeX82 was being debugged,[1] but items 520 and following include every change that was made to TeX82 after it passed its first test. The differences between TeX78 and TeX82, seen from a user's standpoint, have been listed elsewhere [2].

I've tried to edit the log entries so that they can be understood in terms of the published listing [23] of TeX82. For example,

15 Add the forgotten case '*set_font*:' to *eq_destroy*. §275 F

[1] (Footnote added July 1991) When I wrote the above I had forgotten about another log book that I had in fact kept during those hectic days. A complete list of the changes made while I debugged my first large-scale "literate program" has just turned up in the Stanford University Archives. I am inserting those entries into Chapter 11, so that the record is now complete. The newly discovered entries are numbered X1–X343.

is entry #15. My original log entry actually referred to case '`[font]`' in '`eqdestroy`' using SAIL syntax, but I've changed to Pascal syntax in the edited log. Similarly, the 1978 identifier `font` eventually became *set_font*, so I've adopted the published equivalent. TEX82 contains a procedure called *eq_destroy* in §275 of the program, and this procedure is quite similar to the `eqdestroy` of TEX78; so I've supplied §275 as a program reference. (It turns out that *eq_destroy* no longer needs a '*set_font:*' subcase, but it did in 1978.) The 'F' after §275 means that this was a bug of type F, a forgotten function.

Changes to a program often spawn other changes later. I've tried to indicate that phenomenon in the appendix by prefixing the number of a prior error when it was an important part of the reason for a subsequent error. Thus #67 is

> 25 ↦ **67** Replace the space at paragraph end by fillglue, not by zero. §816 B

Error #25 was logged when I had been surprised to find a space at the end of TEX's internal representation of a paragraph. I had "cured" the problem by converting the space from a normal interword space to a space of width zero. But that wasn't good enough, since it was possible for TEX to try breaking a line at the zero-width space. A better solution was to replace the space by the glue that is always added to fill out the end of a paragraph.

Figure 1 shows a time chart of the first 519 log entries—the errors of TEX78. There's a burst of activity right near the beginning, since I logged the first 237 errors during the three weeks of initial debugging. Thus the main line in Figure 1, which shows the cumulative number of errors as a function of time, is nearly horizontal at the beginning. But it's nearly vertical at the end, since only 13 changes were made during the last year of TEX78's activity.

Another line also appears in Figure 1: It represents the total number of different pages I typeset with TEX78 as I was experimenting with the first version. The dotted line in July 1978 stands for the 200 pages of the first TEX manual, and the dotted line in June 1979 stands for the 100 pages of the first METAFONT manual; the remaining solid lines stand for the 700 pages of Volume 2 and some experiments with DOC.

Figure 1 shows that four different phases can be distinguished in the development of TEX78. First came the debugging phase (Phase 0), already mentioned. Then came a longer period of time (Phase 1) when I typeset several hundred pages of Volume 2 and the first user manual; this experience suggested many amendments to my original design.

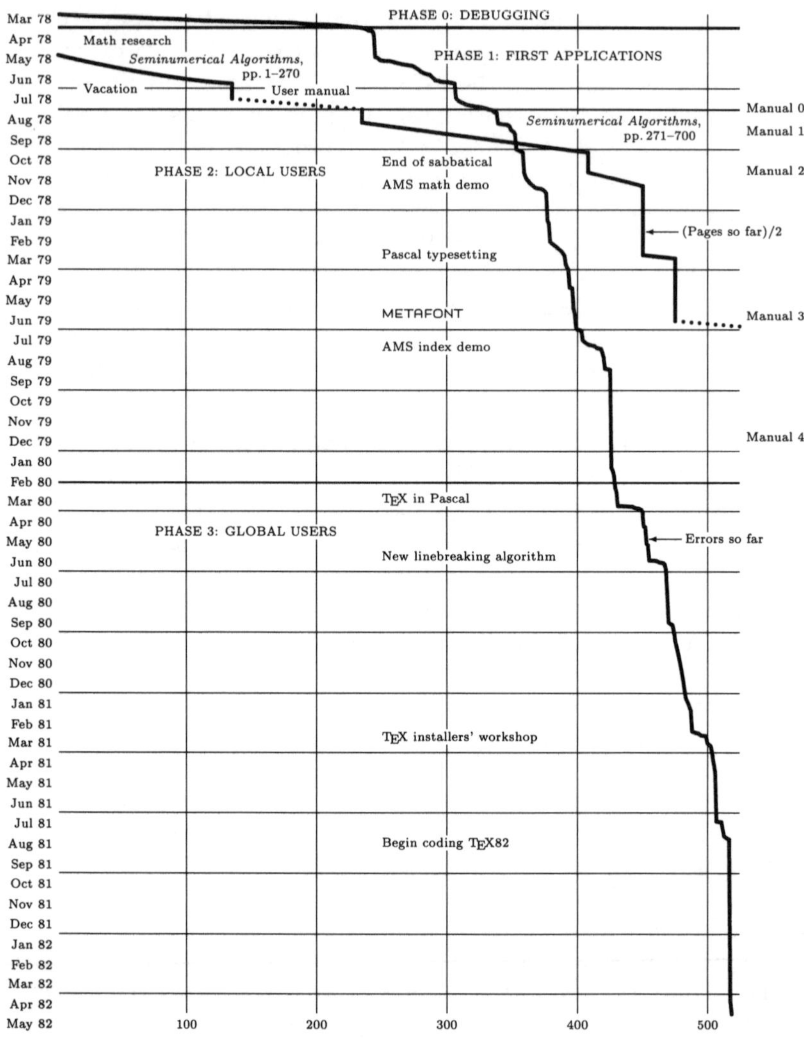

Figure 1. The rise and fall of TeX78.

Then TeX suddenly had more than one user, and different kinds of errors began to show up. *New users find new bugs.* This coming-out phase (Phase 2) included small bursts of changes when I faced new applications—a suite of difficult test cases posed by the American Mathematical Society, then the application to Pascal formatting, then the complex index to *Math Reviews*. Finally there was Phase 3, when changes were made in anticipation of a future TeX82; I wanted several new ideas to be well tested before I programmed the "ultimate" TeX.

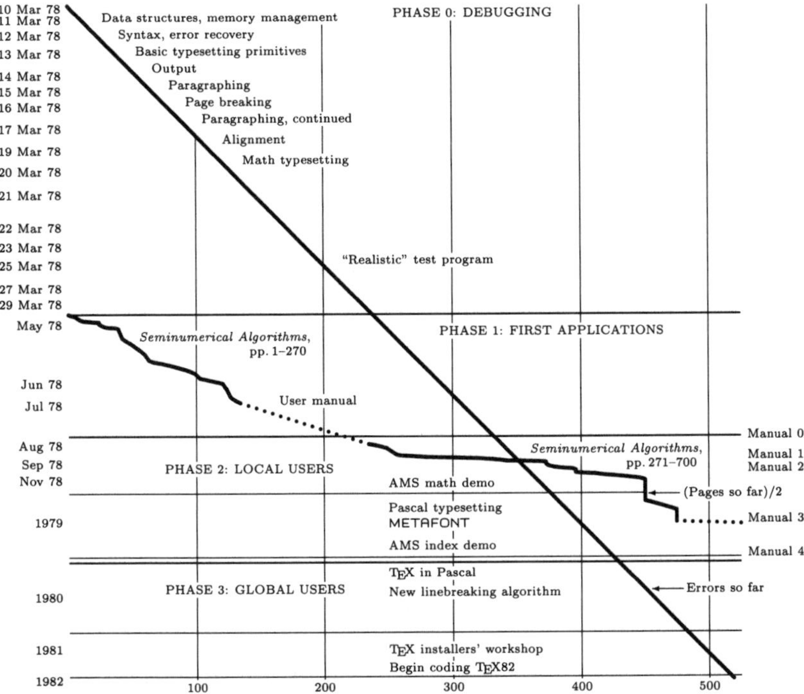

Figure 2. The errors of TEX78.

The Initial Debugging Stage

Let's roll the clock back now and look more closely at the earliest days of TEX78. In some ways this was the most interesting time, because the whole concept of TEX was just beginning to take shape. Figure 2 is a modified version of Figure 1, redrawn with a time warp. There's now exactly one error per time unit, so the 18-day debugging phase has been slowed down to almost half of the total development time; on the other hand, the years 1981–1982 at the bottom go by so fast as to be barely visible.

I mentioned that TEX78 was entirely coded before I first tried to run it on March 10. My debugging strategy was to walk through the program using the `BAIL` debugger, a system program by John Reiser that allowed me to execute the statements of my program one at a time; `BAIL` would also interpret additional SAIL statements that I entered online. Whenever I came to a section of program that I'd seen before, I could set a breakpoint and continue at high speed until coming to new material. Watching the program execute itself in this "dynamic order" has always been insightful for me, after I've desk-checked it in the "static order" of my original code.

Figure 2 shows that I got through the program initialization the first day; then I was gradually able to check out the routines for basic data management, parsing, and error reporting. On the fourth day TEX began to combine boxes and glue, and there was visible output on the fifth day. During the following three days I tested the algorithms for breaking paragraphs into lines and breaking lines into pages. All this went rather smoothly; I logged 101 errors during this first week, but all of the problems were comparatively minor oversights, to be expected in any program of this size.

On the ninth day I tackled alignment of tables, and got a big shock: My original algorithms were quite wrong. I had greatly misunderstood this aspect of TEX, because I'd greatly underestimated the complications of nested alignments. (The log mentions some of the puzzlement and frustration I felt at the time.) I wrestled with alignment for two days before finding a solution.

Then I looked at the last remaining part of TEX, the code for typesetting mathematics; this took another four days. (Well, the "days" were nights actually; I worked during the night to avoid delays due to time-sharing.) Finally I had seen essentially all of TEX in operation, and I could let it run at full speed instead of relying on single-step mode. I spent six more days helping TEX get through its first test data; finally the test was passed. Whew! The debugging phase was over, 18 days and 237 log-book entries after it began.

I kept track of how long this process took, so that I'd be better able to estimate the duration of future programming projects. Here are the figures:

Day	*Time (hours)*	*Day*	*Time (hours)*
10 Mar 1978	6	19 Mar 1978	7.5
11 Mar 1978	7	20 Mar 1978	10
12 Mar 1978	8	21 Mar 1978	8
13 Mar 1978	7	22 Mar 1978	6
14 Mar 1978	8	23 Mar 1978	7.5
15 Mar 1978	8	25 Mar 1978	7
16 Mar 1978	7	26 Mar 1978	6
17 Mar 1978	7	27 Mar 1978	8
18 Mar 1978	8	29 Mar 1978	6

The total debugging time, 132 hours, was extremely encouraging to me, because it was much less than the 41 days it had taken me to write the program. Previously I had needed to devote about 70% of program development time to debugging, but now the figure had dropped to about 30%. I considered this to be a tremendous victory for structured programming, since my programming time had also decreased from what it had been with old habits. Later, with the `WEB` system, I noticed even further gains in productivity.

How big was TeX at the time? I estimated this by counting the number of semicolons (4857) and the number of occurrences of the SAIL reserved words **comment** (480) and **else** (223). Since I always put semicolons before **end**, the total number of statements in the program could be computed as

$$; - \textbf{comment} + \textbf{else} = 4857 - 480 + 223 = 4600.$$

Thus the debugging strategy I used allowed me to verify about 35 statements per hour.

The fact that I made 237 log entries in 132 hours means that I was logging things only about once every 33 minutes; thus the total time needed to keep the log was negligible. I can definitely recommend the practice to everybody. During most of the debugging time I was clicking away at the keys of my terminal, getting to know exactly what TeX was doing; I needed only a few extra minutes to make the log entries, which helped me get to know myself.

Early Typesetting Experience

Now that TeX was able to typeset its test program, I could proceed to my main goal, the typesetting of Volume 2. This was a somewhat tedious task—the keyboarding of a 700-page book is not one of life's greatest pleasures—but the regular appearance of nice-looking pages kept me happy. The jagged line in Figure 2 shows my progress in terms of pages typeset versus errors in the TeX log; a similar (even more jagged) line appears in Figure 1, showing pages typeset as a function of time.

The most striking thing about the jagged line in Figure 2 is that it's almost straight. Ideas about how to improve TeX kept occurring to me quite regularly as I typed the manuscript. Between May 13 and June 22 I processed about 250 pages, and added 69 new entries to the log. Those 69 entries included 29 "bugs" and 40 "enhancements"; thus, I thought of a new way to improve TeX at a regular rate of about one enhancement for every six pages typed.

I mentioned earlier my firm conviction that I could not have correctly delegated the coding of TeX to another person; I had to be doing it myself, because writing a new sort of program implies continually revising the specifications. Similarly, I could not have correctly delegated these initial typing experiments to another person. I had to put myself in the rôle of a regular user; there's no substitute for such experience, when a new system is being designed.

But at the time I wasn't thinking about creating a system that would be used widely; I was designing TeX primarily for my own use. The idea that TeX could or should be generalized to other applications besides *The Art of Computer Programming* dawned on me only gradually, as people kept noticing what I was doing and expressing an interest in it.

John McCarthy observed during this period that TeX was doing a reasonable job with respect to traditional mathematical copy, but he suspected that I'd have a tough time typesetting a book about TeX itself. "That will be the real test," he said, "because you'll have to shut off many of TeX's automatic features in order to handle problems of self-reference."

In July I succumbed to John's challenge and prepared a user manual for TeX. Sure enough, this experience helped me identify quite a few weaknesses in the existing design, things that I probably wouldn't have noticed if I had confined my attention to *The Art of Computer Programming* alone. Again I thought of enhancements at the rate of about one for every six or seven pages, as I wrote the manual; but these weren't really occasioned by defects in TeX's ability to be self-referential, as John had predicted. The new enhancements came about because the process of manual-writing forced me to think about TeX as a whole, in a new way. The perspective of a teacher/expositor helped me to notice several inconsistencies and shortcomings.

Thus, I came to the conclusion that the designer of a new system must not only be the implementor and the first large-scale user; *the designer should also write the first user manual.* The separation of any of these four components would have hurt TeX significantly. If I had not participated fully in all these activities, literally hundreds of improvements would never have been made, because I would never have thought of them or perceived why they were important.

Phases 2 and 3: Users

But a system cannot be successful if it is too strongly influenced by a single person. Once the initial design is complete and fairly robust, the real test begins as people with many different viewpoints undertake their own experiments. At the beginning of August, I distributed 45 copies of the draft manual to people who had expressed interest in using TeX and who had promised to give me feedback before the "real" user manual would be issued in September. So TeX had a multitude of users for the first time, and I began to learn about a wide variety of new applications and perceptions.

I continued to typeset the remaining 450 pages of Volume 2, and my personal experiences with those pages continued to suggest regular improvements to TEX until I got up to about page 500. But the final 200 pages were just drudgework, not really inspirational to me in any way as far as TEX was concerned. Nor did I learn much more, except about page layout, when I typed the METAFONT manual some months later. The really important influences on TEX after the first manual was published were the users, first because they made different kinds of mistakes than I had anticipated, and later because they had important suggestions about how to improve TEX's capabilities.

Guy Steele was visiting Stanford that summer; he took a copy of TEX back to MIT with him, and I began to get feedback from two coasts. One of Guy's suggestions, which I staunchly resisted at the time, was to include some sort of mini-programming language in TEX so that users could do numerical calculations. Slowly but surely I began to understand the need for such features, which eventually became a basic part of TEX82. Another early user was Terry Winograd, who pushed TEX's early macro capabilities to their limits. He and Michael Spivak, who began to work with TEX in the summer of 1979, taught me a lot about the peculiar properties of macro expansion. Researchers at Xerox PARC also had a significant influence on TEX at this time; Lyle Ramshaw modified the program to work with Xerox's new fonts and new output devices, while Leo Guibas and Doug Wyatt undertook to rewrite TEX in the MESA language.

Figures 1 and 2 indicate that the first TEX user manual was issued in five versions. "Manual 0" was the preliminary draft, handed out to 45 guinea pigs who agreed to help me test the very first system. "Manual 1" was a Stanford technical report issued a month later; it was reprinted as "Manual 2" in November, using the higher-resolution printing devices at Xerox PARC. The American Mathematical Society published a paperback version [13] of Manual 2 in the summer of 1979; that was "Manual 3." Then Digital Press published "Manual 4," which included the METAFONT manual and some background information, in December of 1979 [14].

The publishers of manuals 3 and 4 asked readers to mail a reply card if they were interested in forming a TEX Users Group, and more than 100 people answered Yes. So the first TUG meeting, in February 1980, marked the beginning of yet another phase in the life of the SAIL program TEX78. A great influx of new users and new applications made me strive for a more complete language. Hence there was a flurry of activity at the end of March, 1980, when I decided to extend TEX in more than a dozen ways. These extensions represented only a fraction of the ideas that had been suggested, but they seemed to provide all the requested functionality in a clean way. The time was ripe to make the extensions now or never, because the first versions of TEX in Pascal were due to be released in April.

The last significant batch of changes to TEX78 were made in the summer of 1980, when TEX acquired the ability to typeset paragraphs with arbitrary shapes. Still, the error log shows that I kept adding enhancements regularly as the worldwide use of TEX continued to grow. It turned out that the final bugs corrected in TEX78 were all introduced by recent enhancements; they were not present in the program of 1978.

The most significant pattern to be found among the enhancements made to TEX78 after its earliest days is the "unbundling" of things that used to be frozen inside the code. At first I had fairly rigid ideas about how much space to put in certain places, about how much penalty to charge for certain line breaks, about how to interpret various characters in the input, and even about where to find certain characters in fonts. One by one, starting already at change #104, these things became parameters that could be changed by users who had different requirements and/or different preferences.

The Real TEX

I had vastly underestimated the complexities and subtleties of typesetting when I'd naïvely expected to work out a complete system during a single sabbatical year. But once I began, it became clear by 1980 that I had acquired almost a moral obligation to advance the art and science of typography in a more substantial way. I realized that I could never be happy with the monster I had created unless I started over and built an entirely new system, using the experience I had gained from TEX78.

I began writing the new system in the summer of 1981, and I decided to call it TEX82 because I knew it would take a year to complete. Once again I couldn't delegate the job to an associate; I wanted to rethink every detail of TEX, and I wanted to have a thorough taste of "literate programming" before I dared to inflict such ideas on others [20]. I wanted to produce truly portable software that would have a chance to serve for many years as a reliable component of larger systems. I wanted TEX82 to justify the confidence that people were placing in TEX78, which was getting more praise than it deserved.

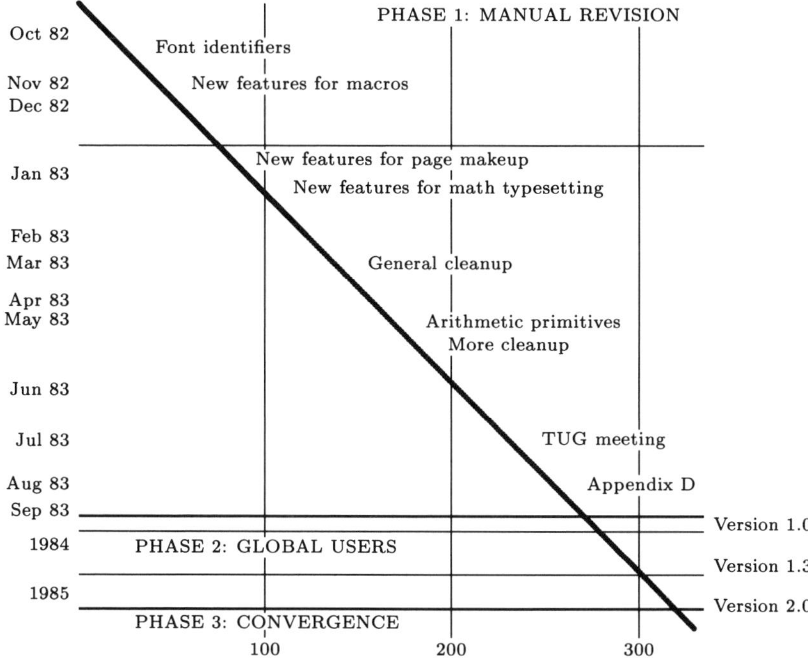

Figure 3. The errors of TeX82.

Figure 3 shows the development of TeX82, starting at the moment I decided that it was essentially bug-free; this illustration uses the same time-warp strategy as Figure 2. From the beginning there were hundreds of users, so TeX82's Phase 1 was analogous to TeX78's Phase 2. But now there was yet a new dimension: Several dozen people were also reading the code and making well-informed comments on how to improve it. Furthermore I had regular meetings with volunteer helpers who represented many different points of view. So I had a golden opportunity to hone the ideas to a new state of perfection.

Two major changes were installed very early in TeX82's history. One was to the way fonts are selected in a document (change #545), and the other was to the treatment of conditional parts of macros (change #564). Both of these changes impinged on many of the fundamental assumptions I had made when writing the code; these were definitely the most traumatic moments in TeX's medical history. I was glad to see that WEB's documentation facilities helped greatly to make such drastic revisions possible.

Phase 1 of TEX82 ended about a year after it began, when I completed writing *The TEXbook*. The log reveals that most of the changes made to TEX during 1983 relate to the chapters of the manual that I was writing at the time. This was the period when TEX really grew up. As I said above, manual writing provides an ideal incentive for system improvements, because you discover and remove glitches that you can't justify in print. When you're writing a user manual, you also have your last chance to make any enhancements that you've thought about before; if certain enhancements aren't made then, you know that you will forever wish you'd taken time to add them.

As with TEX78, the error log of enhancements to TEX82 shows a significant trend toward greater user control. More and more things that were originally hardwired in the system became parametric instead of automatic.

Phase 2 of TEX82 began with the paperback publication of *The TEXbook* and ended with the publication of the hardcover edition. During this phase (which lasted from October 1983 to May 1986) I was mostly working on METAFONT and Computer Modern, so TEX changed primarily in ways that would blend better with those systems. The log entries of Phase 2, #790 to #840, also show that a number of ever-more subtle bugs were detected by ever-more sophisticated users during this time. There was also a completely unsubtle bug, #808, which somehow had snuck through all my tests and caused no apparent harm for an amazingly long time.

Now TEX82 is in its third and final phase. It has grown from the original 4600 statements in SAIL to 1376 modules in WEB, representing about 14,000 statements in Pascal. Five volumes describing the complete systems for TEX, METAFONT, and Computer Modern have been published. No more changes will be made except to correct any bugs that still might lurk in the code (or perhaps to improve the efficiency or portability, when it's easy to do so while correcting a real bug). I hope TEX82 will remain stable at least until I finish Volume 7 of *The Art of Computer Programming.*

Test Programs

Since 1960 I have had extremely good luck with a method of testing that may deserve to be better known: Instead of using a normal, large application to test a software system, I generally get best results by writing a test program that no sane user would ever think of writing. My test programs are intended to break the system, to push it to its extreme limits, to pile complication on complication, in ways that the system programmer never consciously anticipated. To prepare such test data, I get into the meanest, nastiest frame of mind that I can manage, and I write the cruelest code I can think of; then I turn around and embed that in even nastier constructions that are almost obscene. The resulting test program is so crazy that I couldn't possibly explain to anybody else what it is supposed to do; nobody else would care! But such a program proves to be an admirable way to flush the bugs out of software.

In one of my early experiments, I wrote a small compiler for Burroughs Corporation, using an interpretive language specially devised for the occasion. I rigged the interpreter so that it would count how often each instruction was interpreted; then I tested the new system by compiling a large user application. To my surprise, this big test case didn't really test much; it left more than half of the frequency counts sitting at zero! Most of my code could have been completely messed up, yet this application would have worked fine. So I wrote a nasty, artificially contrived program as described above, and of course I detected numerous new bugs while doing so. Still, I discovered that 10% of the code had not been exercised by the new test. I looked at the remaining zeros and said, Shucks, my source code wasn't nasty enough, it overlooked some special cases I had forgotten about. It was easy to add a few more statements, until eventually I had constructed a test routine that invoked all but one of the instructions in the compiler. (And I proved that the remaining instruction would *never* be executed in *any* circumstances, so I took it out.)

I used such "torture tests" to debug three compilers during the 60s. In each case very few bugs were ever discovered after the tests had been passed, so the methodology was quite effective. But when I debugged TEX78, my test program was quite tame by comparison—except when I was first testing the mathematics routines (March 20–23). I guess I wasn't trying as hard as usual to make TEX a bulletproof system, because I was still thinking of myself as TEX's main user. My original test program for TEX78 was written with an "I hope it works" attitude, rather than "I bet I can make it fail." I suppose I would have found several dozen of the bugs that showed up later (like #240 and #263) if I had stuck to the torture-test methodology. Still, considering my mood at the time, I suppose it was a good idea to have a test program that would look like real typography; I didn't know what TEX should do until I could judge the æsthetic quality of its output.

At any rate, my first test program was based on a sampling of material from Volume 2. I went through that book and boiled it down to five pages that illustrated just about every kind of typographic difficulty to be found in the entire volume. (The output of this test program can be seen in another paper [6], where David Fuchs and I used the same test data to study some algorithms for font management.)

Years later, when TEX82 was ready to be debugged, I understood pretty clearly what the program was supposed to do, so I could then apply the superior torture-test methodology. My test program was called TRIP; I spent about five days preparing the first draft of TRIP in July, 1982. Here, for example, is a relatively mild portion of the original TRIP code:

```
\def\gobble#1{} \floatingpenalty 100
\everypar{A\insert200{\baselineskip400pt\splittopskip
  \count15pt\hbox{\vadjust{\penalty999}}\hbox to-10pt{}}%
  \showthe\pagetotal\showthe\pagegoal\advance\count15by1
  \mark{\the\count15}\splitmaxdepth-1pt
  \paR\gobble} % abort every paragraph abruptly
\def\weird#1{\csname\expandafter\gobble\string#1
  \string\csname\endcsname}
\message{\the\output\weird\one}
```

(Please don't ask me what it means.) Since then I've probably spent at least 200 hours modifying and maintaining TRIP, but I consider that time well spent, and I think TRIP is one of the most significant products of the TEX project [19]. The reason is that the TRIP test has detected extremely subtle bugs in hundreds of implementations of TEX, bugs that would have been almost impossible to track down in any other way. TEX82, with its TRIP test, has proved to be much more reliable than any of the Pascal compilers it has been compiled with. In fact, I believe it's fair to say that TEX82 has helped to flush out at least one previously unknown compiler bug whenever it has been ported to a new machine or tried on a compiler that has not seen TEX before! These compiler errors were detectable because of the TRIP test. Later I developed a similar test program for METAFONT, called TRAP [22], and it too has helped to exorcise dozens of compiler bugs.

A single test program cannot detect all possible mistakes. For example, TEX might terminate with a "fatal error" in several ways, only one of which can happen on any particular run. Furthermore, TRIP runs almost automatically, so it does not test all of TEX's capability for online interaction. But TRIP does exercise almost all of TEX's code, and it does so in tricky combinations that tend to fail if any part of TEX is damaged. Therefore it has proved to be a great time-saver: Whenever I modify TEX, I simply check that the results of the TRIP test have changed appropriately.

The only difficulty with the TRIP methodology is that I must check the output myself to see if it's correct. Sometimes I need to spend several hours before I've determined the appropriate output; and I'm fallible. So TEX might give the wrong answer without my being aware of it. This happened in bugs #543 and #722, when I learned to my surprise that TEX had never before done the correct thing with TRIP. A system utility for comparing files suffices now to convince me that incremental changes to TEX or TRIP cause the correct incremental changes to the TRIP test output; but when I began debugging, I needed to verify by hand that thousands of lines of output were accurate.

I should mention that I also believe in the merit of formal and informal correctness proofs. I generally try to prove my programs correct, informally, by stating appropriate invariants in my documentation and checking at my desk that those relations are preserved. But I can make mistakes in proofs and in specifying the conditions for correctness, just as I make mistakes in programming; therefore I don't rely entirely on correctness proofs, nor do I rely entirely on empirical test routines like TRIP.

Location and Type of Errors

Let me review again the fifteen classes of errors that are listed in my error log:

A — Algorithm	F — Forgotten	P — Portability
B — Blunder	G — Generalization	Q — Quality
C — Cleanup	I — Interaction	R — Robustness
D — Data	L — Language	S — Surprise
E — Efficiency	M — Mismatch	T — Typo

I mentioned before that each of the errors listed in the appendix refers where possible to its approximate location in the program listing of TEX82. It's natural to wonder whether the errors are uniformly interspersed throughout the code, or if certain parts were particularly vulnerable. Figure 4 shows the actual distribution. No part of the program has come through unscathed—or, shall we rather say, unimproved—but some parts have seen significantly more action. The boxes to the left of

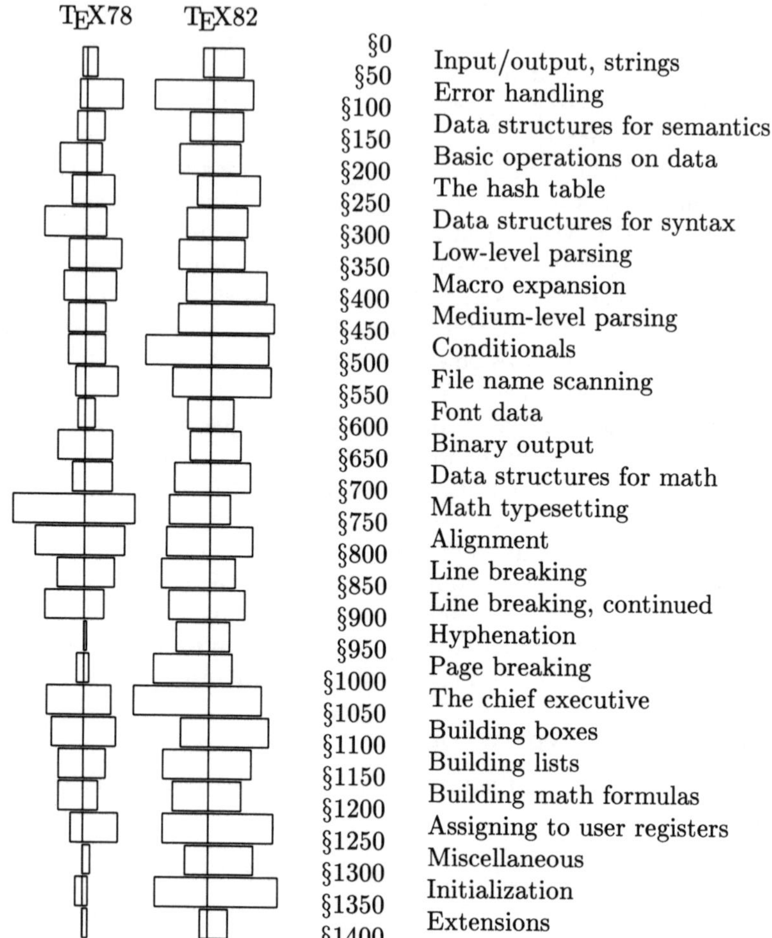

Figure 4. Distribution of [bugs | enhancements] by program location.

the vertical lines in Figure 4 represent "bugs" (A, B, D, F, L, M, R, S, T), while the boxes to the right represent "enhancements" (C, E, G, I, P, Q). The most unstable parts of TEX78 were the parts I understood least when I began to write the code, namely mathematical formatting and alignment. The most unstable parts of TEX82 were the parts that differed most from TEX78 (the conditional instructions and other aspects of macro expansion; also the increased user access to registers and internal quantities used in TEX's decision-making).

I should mention why hyphenation is almost never mentioned in the log of TEX78. Although I said earlier that TEX78 was entirely written before any of it was tested, that's not quite true. The hyphenation algorithm was quite independent of everything else and easily isolated from the code, so I had written and debugged it separately during three days in October, 1977. (There's obviously no advantage to testing independent programs simultaneously; that leads only to confusion. But the rest of TEX was highly interdependent, and it could not easily be run when any of the parts were absent, except for the routines that produced the final output.) The hyphenation algorithm of TEX78 was English-specific; Frank Liang, who had helped me with this part of TEX78, developed a much better approach in his thesis, and I ultimately incorporated his algorithm in TEX82 [see Chapter 8].

Figure 5 shows the accumulated number of errors of each type in TEX78, with bugs at the bottom and enhancements at the top. Initially the log entries are mostly bugs, with occasional enhancements of type I; at the end, however, enhancements C, G, and Q predominate. Figure 6 is a similar diagram for TEX82. The pattern is much the same; evidently an additional four years of experience did not teach me to make fewer mistakes.

Some Noteworthy Bugs

The gestalt of TEX's evolution can best be perceived by scanning through the log book, item by item. But I would like to single out several errors that were particularly instructive or otherwise memorable.

A, Algorithmic Anomalies.

I decided from the beginning that the algorithms of TEX would be in the public domain. But if I were to change my mind and charge a fee for my services in inventing them, I would probably request the highest price for a comparatively innocuous-looking group of statements now found in §851 and §854 of the program. This precise sequence of logical tests, used to control when a line break is being forced because there is no "feasible" alternative, has the essential form

if $\alpha_1 \vee \alpha_2$ **then**
  if $\alpha_3 \wedge \alpha_4 \wedge \alpha_5 \wedge \alpha_6$ **then** σ_1
  else if α_7 **then** σ_2 **else** σ_3
else σ_4

and most of the appropriate boolean conditions α_i were discovered only

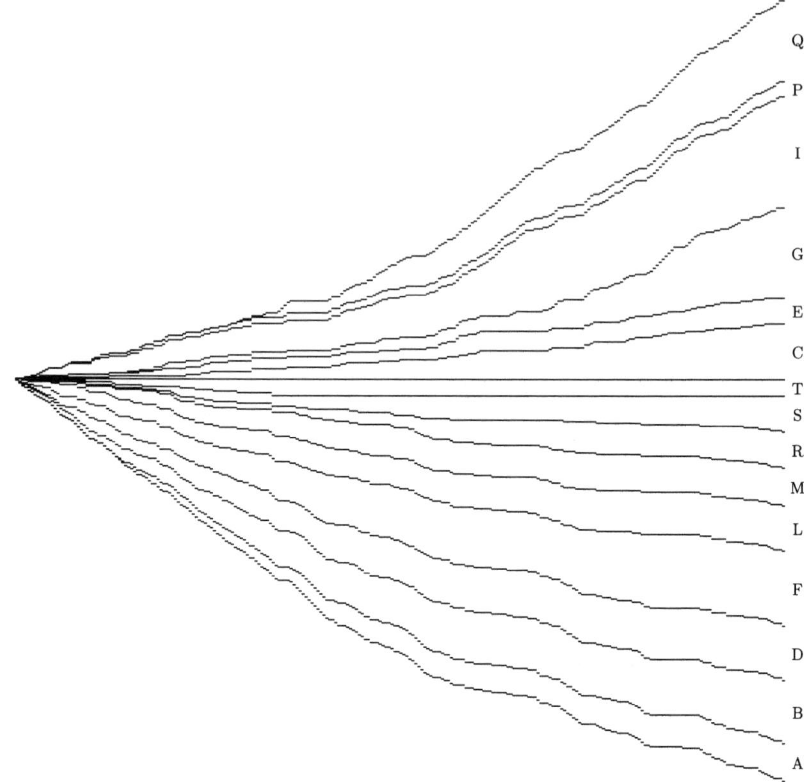

Figure 5. Accumulated errors of TEX78, divided into 15 categories.

with great difficulty. The program now warns any readers who seek to improve TEX to "think thrice before daring to make any changes here." Some indications of my struggles with this particular logic appear in errors #75, #93, and #506.

TEX's line-breaking algorithm determines the optimum sequence of breaks for each paragraph, in the sense that the total "demerits" are minimized over all feasible sequences of breaks. The original algorithm was fairly simple, but it continued to evolve as I fiddled with the formula used to calculate demerits. Demerits are based on the "badness" b of the line (which measures how loose or tight the spacing is) and the "penalty" p for the break (which may be at a hyphen or within a math formula). A penalty might be negative to indicate a good break. The original formula for demerits in TEX78 was

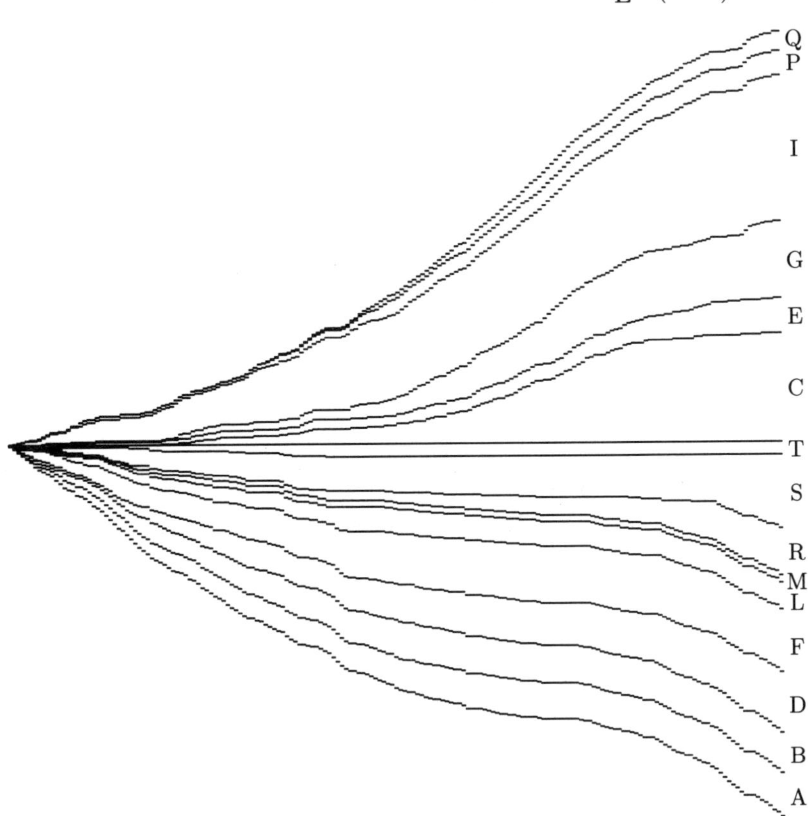

Figure 6. Accumulated errors of TEX82.

$$D = \max(b + p, 0)^2\,;$$

error #76 replaced this by

$$D = \begin{cases} (1 + b + p)^2, & \text{if } p \geq 0; \\ (1 + b)^2 - p^2, & \text{if } p < 0. \end{cases}$$

The extra constant 1 was used to encourage paragraphs with fewer lines; the subtraction of p^2 when $p < 0$ gave fewer demerits to good breaks. This improved formula was published on page 1128 of the article on line-breaking by Knuth and Plass [16]. The first draft of TEX82 added an obvious generalization to the improved formula by introducing a

`\linepenalty` parameter, l, to replace the constant 1. A further improvement was made in change #554, when I realized that better results would be obtained by computing demerits as follows:

$$D = \begin{cases} (l+b)^2 + p^2, & \text{if } p \geq 0; \\ (l+b)^2 - p^2, & \text{if } p < 0. \end{cases}$$

Otherwise, a line with, say, $(b,p) = (50,100)$, followed by a line with $(b,p) = (0,0)$, would be considered inferior to a pair of lines with $(b,p) = (0,100)$ and $(100,0)$, although the second pair of lines would actually look much worse.

B, Blunders.

A typical blunder, among the 50 or so errors of class B in the appendix, is illustrated by errors #7 and #92. I had declared two symbolic constants in my program, *new_line* (for one of the three states of TEX's lexical scanner) and *next_line* (for the sequence of ASCII codes *carriage_return* and *line_feed*, needed in SAIL output conventions). Although the meanings were quite dissimilar, the names were quite similar; therefore I confused them in my mind. The compiler didn't detect any syntax error, because both were legal in an output statement, so I had to detect and correct the bugs myself. I could have avoided these errors by using a name like *cr_lf* instead of *next_line*; but that sounds too jargony. A better alternative would have been *new_line_state* instead of *new_line*.

D, Data disasters.

My most striking error in data-structure updating was #630, which crept in when I made change #625. The error needs a bit of background information before I can explain it: Using an idea of Luis Trabb Pardo, I was able to save one bit in each node of TEX's main data structures by putting the nodes in which the bit would be 0—the so-called charnodes—into the upper part of the *mem* array, all other nodes into the lower part. (It was very important to save this bit, because I needed at least 32 additional bits in every charnode.) One of the aspects of change #625 was to optimize my data structure for representing mathematical subformulas that consist of a single letter. I could recognize and simplify such a subformula by looking for a list that consisted of precisely two elements, namely a charnode followed by a "kern node" (for an "italic correction"). A kern node is identified by (a) not being a charnode, i.e., not having a high memory address, and (b) having the subfield *type* $= 11$.

I forgot to test condition (a). But my program still worked in almost every case, because unsuitable lists of length 2 are rare as subformulas, and because the *type* subfield of a charnode records a font number. Amazingly, however, within one week of my installing change #625, some user happened to create a math list of length 2 in which the second element was a character from font number 11!

This example demonstrates that I was lucky to have a wide variety of users. Still, such a bug might survive for years before it would cause trouble for anybody.

F, Forgetfulness.

As I'm writing this paper, I'm trying to remember all the points I wanted to explain about TEX's evolution. Probably I'll forget something, as I did when I was writing the program for TEX.

Usually a bug of class F was easily noticed when I first looked at the corresponding part of the code, with my walk-through-in-execution-order method of debugging. But I'd like to mention two of the F errors that were among the most difficult to find. Both of them occurred in routines that had worked correctly the first few times they were exercised; indeed, these routines had been called hundreds of times, with perfect results, so I no longer suspected that they could be the source of any trouble.

Error #91 occurred in the memory allocation subroutine, the first time I ran out of memory. That subroutine had the general form

```
begin ⟨Get ready to search⟩;
repeat ⟨Look at an available slot⟩;
    if ⟨big enough⟩ then goto found;
    ⟨Move to next slot⟩;
until ⟨back at the beginning⟩;
found: ⟨Allocate and return, unless the available list
    becomes exhausted⟩;
ovfl: ⟨Give an overflow message⟩;
end
```

The bug is obvious: I forgot to say '**goto** *ovfl*' just before the label '*found*:'. And it's also obvious why this bug was hard to find: I had lost my suspicions that this subroutine could fail, but when it did fail it allocated one node right in the middle of another. My linked data structure was therefore destroyed, but its defective fields did not cause trouble until several hundred additional operations had been performed by the parts of the program where I was still looking for bugs.

Error #203 was even more difficult to find; it lurked in TEX's *get_next* routine, the subroutine that is executed far more than any other. Whenever TEX is ready to see another token of input, *get_next* comes into action. Therefore, by the time I had corrected 200 errors, *get_next* had probably gotten the correct next token more than 100,000 times; I considered it rock-solid reliable.

Since *get_next* is part of TEX's "inner loop," I had wanted it to be efficient. Indeed, I learned later that the very first statement of *get_next*, '$cur\_cs \leftarrow 0$', is performed more often than any other single statement of TEX82. (Empirical tests covering a period of more than a year show that '$cur\_cs \leftarrow 0$' was performed more than 1.4 billion times on Stanford's SUAI computer. The *get_avail* routine, which is next in importance, was invoked only about 438 million times.) Knowing that *get_next* was critical, I had tried to avoid performing '$cur\_cs \leftarrow 0$' in my first implementations, in cases where I knew that the value of *cur_cs* would not be examined by the consumers of *get_next*'s tokens. In fact, I knew that *cur_cs* would be irrelevant in the vast majority of cases. (But I also knew, and forgot, Hoare's dictum that premature optimization is the root of all evil in programming.)

Well, you can almost guess the rest. When I corrected my serious misunderstanding of alignments, errors #108 and #110, I introduced a new case in *get_next*, and that new case filled my thoughts so much that I forgot to worry about the '$cur\_cs \leftarrow 0$' operation. Still, no harm was done unless *cur_cs* was actually being looked at; TEX wouldn't fail unless `\cr` occurred in an alignment having a special sort of template that required backup in the parser. As before, the effect of this error was buried in a data structure, where it remained hidden until much later. I found the bug only by temporarily inserting new code that continually monitored the integrity of the data structures. (Such code later became a standard diagnostic feature of TEX82; it can be seen for example in §167.)

L, Language lossage.

Some of my errors (#98, #295, #296, #480) were due to the fact that algorithms involving floating-point numbers sometimes fail because of roundoff errors. (I have assigned these errors to class L instead of class A, although it was a close call.) TEX82 was designed to be portable so that it gives essentially identical results on all computers; therefore I avoided floating-point calculations in critical parts of the new program.

Two other errors in my log belong unambiguously to class L: In #63 and #827, I failed to insert parentheses into a macro definition. As a result, when I used the macro with text replacement, any frequent user of macros can guess what happened. (Namely, in #827, I had declared the macro

$$hi\_mem\_stat\_min \equiv mem\_top - 13$$

and used it in the statement

$$dyn\_used \leftarrow mem\_top + 1 - hi\_mem\_stat\_min;$$

this gave a minus where I wanted a plus.)

M, Mismatches.

When I write a program I tend to forget the exact specifications of its subroutines. One of my frequent flubs is to blur the distinction between an object and a pointer to that object. In TEX78, for example, I noticed when I got to error #79 that I had called *vpackage*$(p, \ldots)$ where p pointed to the first node of a vlist, while in the declaration of *vpackage* I had assumed parameters of the form $(h, \ldots)$ where h points to a list header; thus, $link(h)$, not h itself, was assumed to point to the first list item. The compiler didn't catch the error because both h and $link(h)$ were of type *pointer*.

While fixing this bug it occurred to me that *vpackage* was an oft-used subroutine and that I might have made the same mistake more than once. So I looked closely at each of the 26 places I had called *vpackage*, and the results proved that I was remarkably inconsistent: I had specified a list head 14 times, and a direct pointer 12 times! (Fortunately there wasn't a 13–13 split; that would have been unlucky.)

This error reminded me that I should always check the entire program whenever I notice a mistake; *failures tend to recur.* In fact, several errors of TEX82 (#803, #813, #815, #837) were first noticed when I was debugging similar portions of METAFONT.

R, Robustness.

Most of the changes of type R were introduced to keep TEX from crashing when users supply input that doesn't obey the rules. But some of the R's in the log are intended to keep TEX alive even when other parts of TEX are failing, because of my programming errors or because somebody else is trying to produce a new modification of TEX.

Thus, for example, in #99 and #123, I redesigned two of my procedures so that they would produce a symbolic printout of given data structures in memory even when those data structures were malformed. I made it possible to get meaningful output from arbitrary bit configurations in memory, so that while debugging TEX I could look interactively at garbage and guess how it might have arisen.

One of the most recent changes to TEX, #846, has the same flavor: The parameter to *show_node_list* was redeclared to be of type *integer* instead of type *pointer*, because buggy calls on *show_node_list* might not supply a valid pointer.

S, Surprises.

The most serious errors were those due to my global misunderstandings of how the system fits together. The final error in TEX78 was of type S, and I suppose the final error of TEX82 will be yet another surprise.

Let me mention just two of these. The first is extremely embarrassing, but it makes a good story. TEX produces `DVI` files as output, where `DVI` stands for DeVice Independent. The `DVI` language is like a machine language, consisting of 8-bit instruction codes followed in certain cases by arguments to the instructions. Two of the simplest instructions of `DVI` language are *push* (code 141) and *pop* (code 142). It turns out that TEX might output *push* followed immediately by *pop* in various circumstances, and this needlessly clutters up the `DVI` file; so I decided to optimize things a bit by checking to see whether the final byte in my output buffer was *push* before TEX would output a *pop*. If so, I could cancel both instructions. This technique even made it possible to detect and cancel long redundant sequences like *push push pop push push pop pop pop*. Naturally, I checked to see that the buffer hadn't been entirely cancelled out when I tested for such an optimization. (I wasn't 100% stupid.) But I failed to realize that the byte just preceding *pop* might just happen to be 141 (the binary code for *push*) when it was the final *operand* byte of some *other* instruction. Ouch!

The other S bug I want to discuss is truly an example of global misunderstanding, because it arose in connection with my misperceptions about `\global` definitions in TEX documents. Users can define control sequences like `\abc` inside a TEX "group," which is essentially a "block" in the sense of Algol scope rules. At the end of a group, local definitions are rescinded and control sequences revert to the meanings they had at the beginning of the group. In my first implementation of TEX78 I went even further: If `\abc` was defined inside a group but not before the group had begun, I actually removed `\abc` from the hash table when the group ended.

There is one exception, however, to TEX's local scope rules (and it's usually the exceptions that lead to surprises). Users can state that a definition is `\global`; this means that the new definition will survive at the end of the current group, unless it has been globally redefined again. Therefore my implementation removed control sequences from the hash table at group endings only when they had not been globally defined.

That caused bug #422, which was identical to one of the first serious bugs I had ever encountered when learning to program in the 50s: Deletions from an "open" hash table might make other keys inaccessible, unless the deletions occur in FIFO order, or unless the deletion algorithm takes special precautions to relocate keys in the table. (See my book *Sorting and Searching* [11], pages 526–527, where I say—in italics—"*The obvious way to delete records from a scatter table doesn't work.*") Alas, I had deleted the control-sequence records in the "obvious way" in TEX78, not realizing that global definitions destroyed the FIFO order.

To fix bug #422, I couldn't patch the definition procedure by using Algorithm 6.4R from my book [11], because the organization of TEX did not allow for relocation of keys. So I needed to change the hash table algorithm from linear probing to chaining, which supports arbitrary deletions. This change was not as painful as it might have been at this late date (August 1979), because I had needed an excuse anyway to overcome my initial hash table design. In order to keep the original implementation simple, I had decided to require that control sequence names be essentially unique when restricted to their first six letters. Such a restriction was quite reasonable when I was to be the only user of TEX; but it was becoming intolerable when the number of users began to grow into the thousands. Therefore change #422 not only altered the hash discipline, it also changed the entire representation mechanism so that identifiers of arbitrary length could be accommodated.

And that wasn't the end of the story. Another year and a half went by before I realized (in #493) that TEX allows declarations like

```
\def\abc{...}
\global\def\xyz{...\abc...}
```

within a group. In such cases I could not eliminate `\abc` from the hash table at the end of the group, because a reference to `\abc` still survived within `\xyz`. I finally decided not to delete *anything* from the hash table (although I did provide a mechanism to prevent unwanted keys from ever getting in; see #294 and #769).

How did such serious bugs remain undetected for so long? They lay dormant because normal usage of TEX does not require complicated interactions between local and global definitions in groups. Most formatting is simpler than this; even complex books such as *The Art of Computer Programming* and the TEX manual itself do not need such generality. But if I had used the TRIP test methodology in the early days, I would have found and corrected the local/global problems right at the start. This experience suggests that all software systems be subjected to the meanest, nastiest torture tests imaginable; otherwise they will almost certainly continue to exhibit bugs for years after they have begun to produce satisfactory results in large applications.

T, Typographic trivia.

The typographic errors of TeX weren't especially significant, but I'll mention two of them (#69 and #86), where my original SAIL code looked like this:

```
glueshrink(q)←glueshrink(q)←glueshrink(t);
x←x←width(q).
```

SAIL was written for the extended ASCII character set that once was widely used at Stanford, MIT, CMU and a few other places; one of the important characters was '←', for Algol's ':='. The language allowed multiple assignment, hence both of these statements were syntactically correct (although rather silly).

A language designer straddles a narrow line between restrictiveness and permissiveness. If almost every sequence of characters is syntactically correct, the inevitable typographic errors will almost never be detected. But if almost no sequences of characters are syntactically correct, typing becomes a real pain.

In TeX78 I made a terrible decision (#402) to allow users to type a letter like 'A' whenever TeX was expecting to see a number; the meaning was to use the ASCII code of A (97) as the number. This extended the language for certain hacker-type applications; but it caused all sorts of grief to ordinary users, because their typographical errors were being treated as perfectly meaningful TeX input, and they couldn't figure out what was going wrong. (I compounded the error in #507; see also #511. This is a sorry part of the record.) TeX82 resolved the problem by using a special character to introduce ASCII constants.

Some Noteworthy Enhancements

Let's turn now to the other six kinds of errors in the log.

C, Cleanups.

The stickiest issue in TeX has always been the treatment of blank spaces. Users tend to insert spaces in their computer files so that the files look nice, but document processors must also treat spaces as objects that appear in the final output. Therefore, when you see documents nowadays that have been prepared by systems other than TEX, you often find cases where double spaces appear incorrectly between words; and when you see documents prepared with TEX, you run into cases where a necessary space between words has disappeared. I kept searching for rules that would be simple enough to be easily learned, yet natural enough that they could be applied almost unconsciously. I finally concluded that no such rules existed, and I opted for the best compromise I could find.

Several of the log entries refer to the question of optional spaces after a macro definition. In #133, I decided to ignore a space that appears there; this was prompted by experiences recorded in my comments following #115 and #119. But #133 caused a timing problem in #560, because the macro definition hadn't been fully processed when TEX wanted to check for the optional space; if the user invoked the macro immediately, instead of putting a space there, TEX wasn't ready to respond. Finally in #606 I came to the conclusion that TEX users will best be able to keep their sanity if I do not ignore spaces after definitions; then dozens of similar-appearing cases all have consistent rules.

(See also #220, for space after '$$'; #361, #708, #720, and #723, for space after constants; #440, for space after active characters; and #632, for space after '\\'.)

G, Generalizations.

TEX continued to grow new capabilities as people would present me with new applications. When I couldn't handle the new problem nicely with the existing TEX, I usually would end up changing the system. (But I kept the changes minimal, because I always wanted to finish and get on with other things. More about that later.)

Such generalizations were often built incrementally on the shoulders of their predecessors. For example, the original TEX78 had `\output` and `\mark` and macro definitions, which scanned and remembered lists of tokens, but there was no good way to assign a list of tokens to a "token list variable" without causing macro expansion. Then TEX82 added a feature called `\everypar`, which Arthur Keller had long been lobbying for. One day I noticed that I could solve a user's problem in a tricky way by temporarily using `\everypar` to store a list of tokens. This was quite different from the intended use of `\everypar`, of course; so I introduced a new primitive operation called `\tokens` for such purposes (#559). Later, `\everypar` spawned several descendants called `\everymath` and `\everydisplay` (#568), `\everyhbox` and `\everyvbox` (#649), `\everyjob` (#657), `\everycr` (#688). I eventually found applications where `\tokens` wasn't enough by itself and I needed to borrow one of the `\every` features temporarily to do some nonstandard hackery. So I finally replaced `\tokens` by an array of 256 registers called `\toks` (#713), analogous to TEX's existing arrays of registers for integers, dimensions, boxes, and glue. TEX82 also acquired the ability to make assignments between different kinds of *token_list* variables (#746). In such ways I tried to keep the design "orthogonal" as the language grew.

Of course every language designer likes to keep a language simple by applying Occam's razor. I was pleased to discover early in 1977 that simple primitive operations involving boxes, glue, and penalties could account for many of the fundamental operations of typesetting. This was a real unification of basic principles, and it turned out to be even better when I realized that the concepts of ordinary line-breaking applied also to tasks that seemed much harder [16]. But I also fooled myself into thinking that TEX had fewer primitives than it really did, by "overloading" operations that were essentially independent and calling them single features.

For example, my original design of TEX78 would break paragraphs into lines by ignoring all lines whose badness exceeded 200. Later (#104) I made this threshold value user-settable by introducing a new primitive called `\jpar`. Setting `\jpar=2` was something like setting `\tolerance=200` in TEX82; but I also included a peculiar new convention: If `\jpar` was odd, the paragraphs would be set with ragged right margins, otherwise they would be justified to the full width!

Thus, in my attempt to minimize primitives, I had loaded two independent ideas onto a single parameter. I also had packed a half-dozen different kinds of diagnostic output into a single number called `\tracing` (see #199), whose binary digits were examined individually when TEX was deciding whether to trace parts of its operations.

Then I began to see the need for more user-settable numbers, and I shuddered to think at the resultant multiplicity of new primitives. So I replaced both `\jpar` and `\tracing` by a *single* primitive called `\chpar` (#244); one could now say, for example, `\chpar1=2` instead of `\jpar=2`. This change gave me the courage to add new parameters for hyphen penalties, etc., and I even added a new parameter to control the raggedness of right margins (#334). Now the parity of `\jpar` was irrelevant; henceforth, the right margins could be either straight or ragged, or they could be produced using some smoothly varying compromise between those extremes—"one third of the way to full raggedness."

My decision to introduce `\chpar` in TEX78 wasn't too bad, because TEX is a macro language and I immediately could define `\jpar` and

\tracing as abbreviations for \chpar1 and \chpar2. But still, those arbitrary numeric codes were inelegant. TeX82 now has fifty different primitive operations that denote integer-valued parameters, each with standard (but user-changeable) names. The old \jpar has become \tolerance and \pretolerance. The old \tracing has been unbundled into \tracingparagraphs, \tracingpages, \tracingmacros, and a half-dozen more, with separate parameters like \showboxdepth to govern the amount of display.

I, Interactions.

About 15% of the errors in the TeX log have been classified type I. The main issue in such cases is to help users identify and recover from errors in their source programs, and this is always problematical because there are so many ways to make mistakes. "When your error is due to misunderstanding rather than mistyping, ... TeX can only explain what looks wrong from its own viewpoint; such an explanation is bound to be mysterious unless you understand the machine's attitude." [21] Which you don't.

Still, I kept trying to make TeX respond more productively, and every such change was logged as an "error" in my original design. The most memorable error of this type was probably #213, when I first realized how nice it would be if I could insert a token or two that TeX could read immediately, instead of aborting a run and starting from scratch. (This was soon followed by #242, when deletion of tokens was also allowed in response to an error message.) I would never have thought of these improvements if I hadn't participated in the implementation and testing of TeX, and I have often wished for similar features in other software I've used since. This one feature must have saved me hundreds of hours as a TeX user during recent years.

Another improvement in interaction didn't occur to me until several months and several hundred pages of output later. Error #338 records the blessed day when I gave TeX the ability to track "runaways," parts of the program that were being processed in the wrong mode because of missing right delimiters. (Further refinements to that change were logged as entries #344, #426, and #793.) Without such provisions, errors that TeX could not have detected until long after their appearance would have been much harder to track down.

There was another significant improvement in interaction that never made it into my error log, because I included it in the original TeX82 without ever putting it into TeX78. This is the *short_display* procedure, for showing the contents of "overfull boxes" and such things in an abbreviated form easily understood by novice users. The *short_display* idea was invented by Ralph Stromquist, who installed it in his early version of TEX at the University of Wisconsin.

P, Portability.

The first changes of type P were simply enhancements to the comments in my SAIL program, but the advent of WEB made it possible for TEX to become truly independent of the machine and operating system it was being run on.

Change #633 is perhaps the most instructive class-P modification: I decided to guarantee compatibility between DEC-like systems (which break the source file into lines according to the appearance of ASCII *carriage_return* characters) and IBM-like systems (which have fixed-length source lines reminiscent of 80-column cards),[2] in the following way: Whenever TEX reads a line of input, on any system, it automatically removes all blank spaces that appear at the right end. The presence or absence of such blanks therefore cannot influence the behavior of TEX in any way. An ASCII file whose lines are at most 80 characters long (as defined by carriage returns, with or without blanks in front of those carriage returns) can be converted to a file of 80-character records that will produce identical results with TEX, simply by padding each line with blanks.

Change #791 carried #633 to its logical conclusion.

Q, Quality.

From the beginning, I wanted TEX to produce documents of the highest possible typographic quality. The time had come when computer-produced output no longer needed to settle for being only "pretty good"; I wanted to equal or exceed the quality of the best books ever printed by photographic methods.

As Kernighan and Cherry have said, "The main difficulty is in finding the right numbers to use for esthetically pleasing positioning. ... Much of this time has gone into two things—fine-tuning (what is the most esthetically pleasing space to use between the numerator and denominator of a fraction?), and changing things found deficient by our users (shouldn't a tilde be a delimiter?)." [8]

---

[2] Paradoxically, DEC has also introduced the VMS operating system, which has fixed-length lines that can include troublesome carriage-returns. But that's another story.

I too had trouble with numerators and denominators: Change #229 increased the amount of space surrounding the bar line in displayed fractions, and I should have made a similar change to fractions in text. (Page 68 of the new Volume 2 turned out to be extremely ugly because of badly spaced fractions.) TEX82 was able to improve the situation because of my experiences with TEX78, but even today I must take special precautions in my TEX documents to get certain fractions and square roots to look right.

The Evolution Process as a Whole

Looking now at the entire log of errors, I'm struck by the fact that my attitude during those years was clearly far from ideal: My overriding goal was always to finish, to finish, to get this long-overdue project done so that I could resume work on other long-overdue projects. I never wanted to spend extra time studying alternatives for the best possible typesetting language; only rarely was I in a mood to consider any changes to TEX whatsoever. I wanted TEX to produce the highest quality, sure, but I wanted to achieve that with the minimum amount of work on my part.

At the end of almost every day between March 29, 1978, and March 29, 1980, I felt that TEX78 was a complete system, containing no bugs and needing no further enhancements. At the end of almost every day since September 9, 1982, I have felt that TEX82 was a complete system, containing no bugs and needing no further enhancements. Each of the subsequent steps in the evolution of TEX has been viewed not as an evolutionary step towards a vague distant goal, but rather as the final evolutionary step towards the finally reached goal! Yet, over time, TEX has changed dramatically as a result of many such "final steps."

Was this horizon-limiting attitude harmful, or was it somehow a blessing in disguise? I'm pleased to see that TEX actually kept getting simpler as it kept growing, because the new features blended with the old ones. I was constantly bombarded by ideas for extensions, and I was constantly turning a deaf ear to everything that didn't fit well with TEX as I conceived it at the time. Thus TEX converged, rather than diverged, to its final form. By acting as an extremely conservative filter, and by believing that the system was always complete, I was perhaps able to save TEX from the "creeping featurism" [24] that destroys systems whose users are allowed to introduce a patchwork of loosely connected ideas.

If I had time to spend another ten years developing a system with the same aims as TEX—if I were to start all over again from scratch, without any considerations of compatibility with existing systems—I could no doubt come up with something that is marginally better. But at the moment I can't think of any big improvements. The best such system I can envision today would still look very much like TeX82; so I think this particular case study in program evolution has proved to be successful.

Of course I don't mean to imply that all problems of computational typography have been solved. Far from it! There still are countless important issues to be studied, relating especially to the many classes of documents that go far beyond what I ever intended TeX to handle.

Conclusions

My purpose in this paper has been to describe what I think are the most significant aspects of the experiences I had while developing TeX, basing this on a study of more than 800 errors that I noted down in log books over the years. I've tried to interpret many specific facts and observations in a sufficiently general way that readers may understand how to apply similar concepts to other software developments.

In Volume 1 of *The Art of Computer Programming* [9], I wrote:

> Debugging is an art that needs much further study ... The most effective debugging techniques seem to be those which are designed and built into the program itself ... Another good debugging practice is to keep a record of every mistake that is made. Even though this will probably be quite embarrassing, such information is invaluable to anyone doing research on the debugging problem, and it will also help you learn how to reduce the number of future errors.

Well, I hope that my error log in the appendix below, especially the first 237 items (which relate specifically to debugging), will be useful somehow to people who study the debugging process.

But if you ask whether keeping such a log has helped me learn how to reduce the number of future errors, my answer has to be No. I kept a similar log for errors in METAFONT, and there was no perceivable reduction. I continue to make the same kinds of mistakes.

What have I really learned, then? I think I've learned, primarily, to have a better sense of balance and proportion. I now understand the complexities of a medium-size software system, and the ways in which it can be expected to evolve. I now understand that there are so many kinds of errors, we cannot stamp them out by systematically eliminating everything that might be "considered harmful." I now understand enough about my propensity to err that I can accept it as an act of life; I now can be convinced more easily of my fallacy when I have made a mistake. Indeed, I now strive energetically to find faults in my own work, even though it would be much easier to look for assurances that everything is OK. I now look forward to making (and correcting) hundreds of future errors as I write Volume 4 of *The Art of Computer Programming*.

Addendum: Fifteen Months More

As mentioned above, I began to write this paper in May of 1987, but I decided to wait before publication until more time had gone by. Then I could present a "complete" and "final" record of TEX's errors.

Now it's September, 1988, and I've decided to bring this paper to a possibly premature conclusion, because I'm scheduled to present it at a conference [4]. TEX still hasn't shown encouraging signs of becoming quiescent; indeed, sixteen more entries have entered the error log since May, 1987, including three as recent as June, 1988. Therefore it still isn't the right moment to manufacture TEX on a chip!

All errors known to me as of September 1, 1988, are now included in the appendix to this paper; the total has now reached 865.[3]

I plan to publish a brief note ten years from now, bringing the list to its absolutely final form.

I have been paying a reward to everyone who discovers new bugs in TEX, and doubling the amount every year. Last December I made two payments of $40.96 each, and my checkbook has been hit for five $81.92 payments in recent months. I'm desperately hoping that this incentive to discover the final bugs will produce them before I am unable to pay the promised amount. (Surely in 1998 I won't be writing checks for $83,886.08?)

As I expected, half of the most recent errors have fallen into the surprise (S) category—even though surprises, by definition, are unexpected. But one of the others (error #854) was perhaps the most surprising of all, because it was the result of a terrible algorithm by a person who certainly should have known better (me). I wanted to multiply the two's-complement fixed-point number

$$A = -16 + a_1 \cdot 2^{-4} + a_2 \cdot 2^{-12} + a_3 \cdot 2^{-20}\,, \qquad 0 \le a_i < 256\,,$$

by the positive quantity $z/2^{16}$, where z is an integer, $2^{26} \le z < 2^{27}$, obtaining an answer of the form $P/2^{16}$ where P is an integer, $|P| < 2^{31}$;

[3] (Footnote added September 1991) In fact we are now up to 916, primarily because of major changes in 1989 that can be said to have inaugurated "Phase 4" of TEX82.

all intermediate quantities in the calculation were required to be less than 2^{31} in absolute value. My program did this by computing

$$C \leftarrow 16 * Z;$$
$$Z \leftarrow Z \;\mathbf{div}\; 16;$$
$$P \leftarrow \big((a_3 * Z) \;\mathbf{div}\; 256 + a_2 * Z\big) \;\mathbf{div}\; 256 + a_1 * Z - C;$$

I should rather have computed

$$Z \leftarrow Z \;\mathbf{div}\; 16;$$
$$P \leftarrow \big((a_3 * Z) \;\mathbf{div}\; 256 + a_2 * Z\big) \;\mathbf{div}\; 256 + (a_1 - 256) * Z.$$

(Consider, for example, the case $Z = 2^{26} + 15$ and $a_1 = a_2 = a_3 = 255$, so that $A = -2^{-20}$. The first method gives $P = -304$; the second method gives the correct answer, $P = -64$.)

Let me close by discussing one more recent error, #864. This change yields only a slight gain in efficiency, so I needn't have made it; but it was easy to correct one more statement while I was fixing #863. It's an instructive example of how a design methodology based on invariants might not lead to the best algorithm unless we think a bit harder about what is going on.

Here's the idea: Each run of TEX determines a threshold value θ above which the (one-word) charnodes will reside, below which all other (variable-size) nodes will be stored. Actually there are two values, θ_0 and θ_1; memory positions between θ_0 and θ_1 are unused. (In the program, θ_0 is actually called *lo_mem_max*, and θ_1 is called *hi_mem_min*.) TEX changes θ_0 and θ_1 conservatively as it runs, so that they will converge to values appropriate to particular applications. The boundary value θ was originally fixed at compile time; this transition to "late binding" was change #819.

When TEX needs more space for charnodes, it usually sets $\theta_1 \leftarrow \theta_1 - 1$; when TEX needs more space for variable-size nodes, it usually sets $\theta_0 \leftarrow \theta_0 + 1000$. But we need to have $\theta_0 < \theta_1$. Therefore, instead of setting $\theta_0 \leftarrow \theta_0 + 1000$, my original code said

if $\theta_1 - \theta_0 > 1000$ **then** $\theta_0 \leftarrow \theta_0 + 1000$
else if $\theta_1 - \theta_0 > 2$ **then** $\theta_0 \leftarrow (\theta_0 + \theta_1 + 2)$ **div** 2
else ⟨Report memory overflow⟩.

(The variable θ_0 had to increase by at least 2.) Chris Thompson of Cambridge University pointed out that this strategy, while preserving the necessary invariants, is discontinuous. If $\theta_1 - \theta_0 = 1001$, the algorithm gobbles up all the discretionary space that's left. Therefore change #864 substituted better logic:

if $\theta_1 - \theta_0 \geq 1998$ **then** $\theta_0 \leftarrow \theta_0 + 1000$
else if $\theta_1 - \theta_2 > 2$ **then** $\theta_0 \leftarrow \theta_0 + 1 + (\theta_1 - \theta_0)$ **div** 2
else ⟨Report memory overflow⟩.

The new version also avoids problems on certain computers when θ_0 and θ_1 are negative; that was error #863. (Of course, when TEX is this close to running out of memory, it probably won't survive much longer anyway. I'm grasping at straws. But I might as well grasp intelligently.)

Acknowledgments

I've already mentioned that the TEX project has had hundreds of volunteers who helped to guide me through all these developments. Their names can be found in the rosters of the TEX Users Group; I couldn't possibly list them all here. Luis Trabb Pardo and David R. Fuchs were my "right-hand men" for TEX78 and TEX82, respectively. The project received generous financial backing from several independent sources, notably the System Development Foundation, the National Science Foundation, and the Office of Naval Research. The material on which this report has been based is now housed in the Stanford University Archives; I wish to thank the archivist, Roxanne L. Nilan, for her friendly cooperation. Thanks are due to the referee who helped me to remove errors not from TEX but from this paper. And above all, I want to thank my wife, Jill, for ten years of exceptional tolerance; software development is much more demanding than the other things I usually do. Jill also helped me to design the format for the appendix that follows.

References

[1] Victor R. Basili and Barry T. Perricone, "Software errors and complexity: An empirical investigation," *Communications of the ACM* **27** (1984), 42–52.

[2] Beeton, Barbara [Ed.], *TEX and METAFONT: Errata and Changes, 09 September 1983*, distributed with *TUGboat* **4** (1983).

[3] L. A. Belady and M. M. Lehman, "A model of large program development," *IBM Systems Journal* **15** (1976), 225–252.

[4] Reinhard Budde, Christiane Floyd, Reinhard Keil-Slawik, and Heinz Züllighoven [Eds.], *Software Development and Reality Construction* (Berlin: Springer, 1991), in press.

[5] A. Endres, "An analysis of errors and their causes in system programs," *Proceedings of an International Conference on Software Engineering* (1975), 327–336.

[6] David R. Fuchs and Donald E. Knuth, "Optimal prepaging and font caching," *ACM Transactions on Programming Languages and Systems* **7** (1985), 62–79.

[7] Piet Hein, *Grooks* (Cambridge, Massachusetts: MIT Press, 1966).

[8] Brian W. Kernighan and Lorinda L. Cherry, "A system for typesetting mathematics," *Communications of the ACM* **18** (1975), 151–157.

[9] Donald E. Knuth, Fundamental algorithms: *The Art of Computer Programming* **1** (Reading, Massachusetts: Addison-Wesley, 1968), xxii + 634 pp. Second edition, 1973.

[10] Donald E. Knuth, Seminumerical Algorithms: *The Art of Computer Programming* **2** (Reading, Massachusetts: Addison-Wesley, 1969), xii + 624 pp. Second edition, 1981, xiv + 689 pp.

[11] Donald E. Knuth, Sorting and Searching: *The Art of Computer Programming* **3** (Reading, Massachusetts: Addison-Wesley, 1973), xii + 722 pp.

[12] Donald E. Knuth, "Mathematical typography," *Bulletin of the American Mathematical Society* (new series) **1** (1979), 337–372.

[13] Donald E. Knuth, *TEX, a System for Technical Text* (Providence, Rhode Island: American Mathematical Society, 1979), 198 pp.

[14] Donald E. Knuth, *TEX and METAFONT: New Directions in Typesetting* (Bedford, Massachusetts, Digital Press, 1979), xi + 45 + 201 + 105 pp.

[15] Donald E. Knuth, "The letter S," *The Mathematical Intelligencer* **2** (1980), 114–122.

[16] Donald E. Knuth and Michael F. Plass, "Breaking paragraphs into lines," *Software—Practice & Experience* **11** (1981), 1119–1184.

[17] Donald E. Knuth, "The concept of a meta-font," *Visible Language* **16** (1982), 3–27.

[18] Donald E. Knuth, *The WEB System of Structured Documentation*, Computer Science Department Report STAN-CS-83-980, Stanford University, Stanford, CA (September 1983), 206 pp.

[19] Donald E. Knuth, *A torture test for TEX*, Computer Science Department Report STAN-CS-84-1027, Stanford University, Stanford, CA (November 1984), 142 pp.

[20] Donald E. Knuth, "Literate programming," *The Computer Journal* **27** (1984), 97–111.

[21] Donald E. Knuth, *The TEXbook* (Reading, Massachusetts: Addison-Wesley, 1984), 483 pp.

[22] Donald E. Knuth, *A torture test for METAFONT*, Computer Science Department Report STAN-CS-86-1095, Stanford University, Stanford, CA (January 1986), 78 pp.

[23] Donald E. Knuth, TEX: The Program: *Computers & Typesetting* **B** (Reading, Massachusetts: Addison-Wesley, 1986) xvi + 594 pp.

[24] Guy L. Steele Jr., Donald R. Woods, Raphael A. Finkel, Mark R. Crispin, Richard M. Stallman, and Geoffrey S. Goodfellow, *Hacker's Dictionary: A Guide to the World of Wizards* (New York: Harper and Row, 1983).

[25] C. Széchy, *Foundation Failures* (London: Concrete Publications, 1961).

[26] Patrick Winston, *Artificial Intelligence: An MIT Perspective* (Cambridge, Massachusetts: MIT Press, 1979).

Chapter 11

The Error Log of TeX (1978–1991)

[This chapter is essentially an appendix to the paper in Chapter 10. It is more extensive than the appendix originally published in Software—Practice & Experience, because it includes recently discovered records of the debugging of TeX82; it also brings the log forward until September 1991, when the historic final (?) bug in TeX82 was discovered.]

Each entry in the following list is numbered and cross-referenced (where possible) to other entries and to the TeX program, as explained in the text above [Chapter 10]. Sometimes I have given credit to the person who detected the error or suggested the change, but (alas) I didn't always remember to note such information down. Here are the initials of people who made so many contributions that I've abbreviated their names in the log entries:

ARK	Arthur Keller	JS	Jim Sterken
CET	Chris Thompson	LL	Leslie Lamport
DRF	David Fuchs	MVL	Marc van Leeuwen
FM	Frank Mittelbach	MDS	Michael Spivak
FY	Frank Yellin	PB	Peter Breitenlohner
HWT	Howard Trickey	WGS	Wayne G. Sullivan

10 Mar 1978

1 Rename a few external variables to make their first six letters unique. L

2 Initialize *escape_char* to -1, not 0 [it will be set to the first character input]. §240 D

3 Fix bug: The test 'id < '*200*' was supposed to distinguish one-letter identifiers from longer (packed) ones, but negative values of *id* also pass this test. §356 L

4 Fix bug: I wrote '**while** $\alpha \wedge (\beta \vee \gamma)$' when I meant '**while** $(\alpha \wedge \beta) \vee \gamma$'. §259 B

5 Initialize the input routines in `INITEX` [at this time a short, separate program not under user control], in case errors occur. §1337 R

6 Don't initialize *mem* in `INITEX`, it wastes time. §164 E

7 Change '*new_line*' [which denotes a lexical scanning state] to '*next_line*' [which denotes *carriage_return* and *line_feed*] in print commands. B

8 Include additional test '$mem[p] \neq 0 \wedge$' in *check_mem*. §168 F

9 Fix inconsistency between the *eq_level* conventions of *macro_def* and *eq_define*. §277 M

• *About six hours of METAFONT debugging time today.*

• ***INITEX*** *appears to work, and the test routine got through start_input, chcode [the TEX78 command for assigning a cat_code], get_next, and back_input the first time.*

11 Mar 1978

10 Insert space before '(' on terminal when opening a new file. §537 I

11 Put '$p \leftarrow link(p)$' into the loop of *show_token_list*, so that it doesn't loop forever. §292 F

12 Shift the last item found by *scan_toks* into the *info* field. [With SAIL all packing of fields was done by arithmetic operations, not by the compiler.] §474 L

12 ↦ **13** Fix the previous bugfix: I shifted by the wrong amount. §474 B

14 Add a feature that prints a warning when the end of a file page occurs within a macro definition or call. [System dependent.] §336 I

• *Unintended bugs in my test routine [a format intended eventually to typeset The Art of Computer Programming] helped check out the error recovery mechanisms. For example, I had '`\lft{#}`' instead of '`\lft{##}`' inside a macro, and three cases of improper { and } nesting.*

15 Add the forgotten case '*set_font*:' to *eq_destroy*. §275 F

16 Change `\require` to `\input`. §376 C

17 Add code for the case $cur\_cmd = 0$ [later known as the case '$t \geq cs\_token\_flag$'] when scanning a tokenlist. §357 F

• *That's the first "big" error I've spotted so far.*

18 Introduce a '`d`' option in the error routine, to facilitate debugging. §84 I

19 Assign a floating-point constant *ignore_depth* to *prev_depth*, instead of assigning the integer constant *flag* [since *prev_depth* is type *real* in TEX78]. §215 L

20 Improve the readability and spacing of *show_node_list* output. §182, 187 I

21 Set the variable *v* before using the **case** construction in *show_node_list*, because there's one case where *v* didn't receive a value [as part of the field unpacking]. §182 F

• *About seven hours today.*

12 Mar 1978

• *One hour to enter yesterday's corrections and recompile.*

• *At this point TEX correctly located further unintended syntax errors in* `acphdr` *[the test file].*

22 Insert *debug_help* into *succumb*, giving a chance to look at memory before the system dies. §93 I

23 Use *eq_destroy* wherever necessary in *unsave*. §283 D

24 Change '$t \leftarrow (t-1) \bmod 8$' to '$t \leftarrow (t-1)$ land 7' in *id_name*, since SAIL has $-1 \bmod 8 = -1$. [At this time, *id_name* is a routine that unpacks control sequence names, according to a scheme that will become obsolete after change #422.] L

25 Remove the space that appears at end of paragraph. (I hadn't anticipated that.) §816 S

26 Throw away unwanted *line_feed* after getting a *carriage_return* in response to *in_chr_w* [a system routine for input from the terminal]. §83 L

27 Delete spurious call to *flush_list* in *end_token_list*. §324 B

• *Why did I make such a silly mistake?*

28 Fix bug in *get_x_token*: I forgot to say '*macro_call*' (which is the main point of that routine)! §380 F

• *While tracking that bug down, I found out incidentally that kerning is okay.*

• *Also TEX correctly caught an error* `0p` *for* `0pt`.

29 Fix bug in *scan_spec* (**while** instead of **repeat**). §404 L

30 Make the table entries for `\hfill` and `\hskip` consistent with the program conventions. §1058 M

31 Disable unforeseen coercion: When *scan_spec* put *hsize* on *save_stack*, the value changed from *real* to *integer*. §645 L

32 Use '`*`' instead of '`-1.0`' for running dimensions of rules in *show_node_list*. §176 I

33 Clear *mem*[*head*] to null in *push_nest* [in TEX82, this will be done by *get_avail*]. §216 D

- *A vrule link got clobbered because I forgot to do this.*

34 Translate ASCII control codes to special form when displaying them. §48, 68 I

- *Ligatures work, but show_node_list showed them funny.*

35 Remember to clear parameters off *save_stack* in *package* routine. §1086 F

- *About eight hours today.*

13 Mar 1978

36 Introduce a new variable *hang_first* [later the sign of *hang_after*]. §849 D

36 ↦ **37** Simplify the new code, realizing that if *hang_indent* = 0 then *hang_first* is irrelevant. §848 E

- *Time sharing is very slow today, so I'm mostly reading technical reports while waiting* **three hours** *for compiler, editor, and loading routine.*
- *I'm not counting this as debugging time!*
- *(Came back in the evening.)*

38 Spruce up the comments in the *line_break* routine, which appears to be almost working. §813 P

39 Rethink the setting of *best_line*; it's 1 too high in many cases. [The final line of a paragraph was handled in a treacherous way.] §874 D

40 Compute proper initialization for *prev_depth* when beginning an `\hbox` with a paragraph inside. [This refers to a special 'paragraph box' construction, used when an hbox of specified size becomes overfull; TEX78 doesn't have the concept of internal vertical mode.] §1083 D

41 Also initialize *tail* in that case. §1083 D

42 Also put the result of line-breaking into the correct list. M

43 Fix a typo in the *free_node* routine ('*link*' not '*llink*'); by strange chance it had been harmless until today. §130 T

44 Fix bug: *post_line_break* forgot to set *adjust_tail*. §889 F

45 Update *act_width* properly when looking for end of word while line breaking. §866 D

46 Repair the "tricky" part of *get_node*: I used the *info* field when I meant to say *llink*. §127 B

- *Now the* `\corners` *macro of* `acphdr` *works! [See* `\setcornerrules` *in The TEXbook, page 417.]*

47 Reset *contrib_tail* properly in *build_page*. §995 D

48 Fix typo (`-` for `+`) in computation of *page_total*. §1004 T

49 Change the page-breaking logic: TEX reached *fire_up* with *best_page_break* = *null* in one case, since the badness was too bad. §1005 S

50 Perform the operation *delete_token_ref*(*top_mark*) only when *top_mark* $\neq 0$. §1012 M

51 Make *scan_toks* omit the initial `{` of an `\output` routine. §473 F

52 Insert a comma to make memory usage statistics look better. §639 I

- *About seven good hours of debugging today.*
- *Tomorrow will be first-output day (I hope).*

14 Mar 1978

- *(Came in evening after sleeping most of day, to get computer at better time.)*
- *(Some day we will have personal computers and will live more normally.)*
- *8:30pm, began to enter corrections to yesterday's problems.*

53 Issue an error message for non-character in filename or in font name. §771 I

54 Display '`...`' for omitted stuff in *show_context* routine. §643 I

55 Watch out for the SAIL syntax '$\alpha + \beta \operatorname{lsh} \gamma$'; it doesn't shift $\alpha + \beta$ left (only β). §464 L

- *That error was very hard to track down; it created a spurious link field and sent hash*[0] = `\beta` *to the scanner!*
- *I could have found this bug an hour sooner if I had looked at the correct stack entries for name and token_type.*

56 Show the correct page number when tracing pages before output is shipped. §638 D

57 Remember to nullify a box after using it. §1079 F

58 Issue an error message if `\box255` isn't consumed by the output routine. §1015 I

- *I'm having trouble with the* `BAIL` *debugger; it makes an illegal memory reference and dies, when single-stepping past the entry to recursive procedures hlist_out and vlist_out. So I have to reload and be careful to go thru these procedures at high speed.*

59 Fix bug in comment (memory parameter description said $\geq$ not $\leq$). §11 P

60 Fix typo in definition of rule output (said x, y not $x0, y0$). [This part of the code went away when `DVI` files were introduced.] B

61 Correct the embarrassing bug in shellsort, where I said '$\leq str[k]$' not '$\leq t$'. [The first TEX had to sort all output by vertical position on page.] B

62 Make *start_input* set up *job_name* in the form needed by *shipout*; it uses obsolete conventions. §532, 537 M

63 Insert `(` and `)` into the SAIL macro definition of *new_string*. [This macro was for pre-`DVI` output.] L

64 Unscramble the parameters of *out_rule*: The declaration was $(x0, y0, x1, y1)$ while the call was $(x0, x1, y0, y1)$. M

- *4:30am, TEX's first page is successfully output!*
- *(It was '`\titlepage\setcpage1\corners\eject\end`'.)*

15 Mar 1978

- *10:30pm. Today I'm instrumenting the line-breaking routine and putting it through a bunch of tests.*
- *(The inserted instrumentation had bugs that won't be mentioned here.)*

65 Don't abort the job when *eq_destroy* redefines a TEX control sequence. §275 C

- *The first word of a paragraph won't be hyphenated ... so be it!*

66 Fix the typo in *line_break* that spoils the test for 'letters in the same font'. §896 T

- *The effect of that typo was to suppress all hyphenation attempts.*

25 ↦ **67** Replace the space at paragraph end by fillglue, not by zero. §816 B

68 Pack the hyphen character properly into its node. §582 L

69 Fix a typo ('←' for '+') in the computation of *break_width*. §838 T

70 Change the `\end` maneuver; the present code doesn't end the job, since I forgot that *back_input* uses *cur_tok*. §1054 M

71 Add a parameter to *try_break*, since the width is different at a discretionary hyphen. [This problem will be solved differently in TEX82, when discretionaries become much more general.] §840 A

72 Bypass kern nodes in pre-hyphenation. §896 F

73 Supply code for the forgotten case '$<$ `"a"`' in pre-hyphenation. [This case was later generalized to a test of *lc_code*.] §897 F

74 Change $mem[q]$ to $prev\_break(q)$ in the reverse-linking loop. §878 B

- *(Such blunders. Am I getting feeble-minded?)*

75 Introduce special logic for *eject_penalty*; I was wrong to think that forced ejection was exactly like an infinitely negative penalty. §851 A

76 Use $(1 + b)^2 - p^2$ when computing demerits with $p < 0$. §859 A

- *6:30am. The line-breaking algorithm appears to be working fine and efficiently. On small measures (about 20 characters per line), it gives overfull boxes instead of spaced out ones. Surprising but satisfactory.*

16 Mar 1978

- *9pm. The plan for tonight is to test page breaking and more paragraphing.*

77 Insert '`\topskip`' glue at beginning of page. §1001 G

78 Add '`\pausing`' feature. §363 I

79 Fix discrepancy: In *make_accent* I called *vpackage* with a pointer to the first list item, but *vpackage* itself assumes that the parameter is a pointer to that pointer. [The *vpackage* of TEX82 will be different.] §668 M

- *I checked for other lapses like that. Result: 14 calls OK, 12 NG.*

80 Create a new temporary list head location, *hold_head*, since there's a case where *vpackage* is improperly called with parameter *temp_head*. [At this time *vpackage* uses *temp_head* to make a list of all insertions found.] §1014 M

- *11:30pm. The machine is tied up again.*

81 Write code to handle charnodes in vlists; I forgot that I'd decided to allow them. [Later I prohibited them again!] §669 F

82 Combine the page lists before pruning off glue in *fire_up*; otherwise the pruning doesn't go far enough. §1017 F

25 ↦ **83** Fix typo where line-breaking starts: '*fill_glue*' should be '*new_glue(fill_glue)*'. §816 B

84 Add /q to **xspool** command (cosmetic change). [This changes a system command that causes TEX output to be printed on the Xerox Graphics Printer (XGP), the progenitor of future laser printers; the /q option says that the queue of printing requests should be displayed on the user's terminal.] §642 I

85 Don't write a form feed after the last page of output. §642 E

• *To fix this, I reorganized ship_out, and it became simpler.*

86 Correct a typo ('←' for '+') in the *vlist_node* case within *hlist_out*. [The output routines were quite different at this time, because output went directly to the XGP.] §622 T

87 Change the message '**completed page**' to '**Completed for page**'. §638 I

48 ↦ **88** Fix yet another typo in the computation of *page_total*: My original code said *stretch*(*p*) instead of *stretch*(*q*) (terrible). §1004 B

89 Document the dirty trick about *bot_mark*'s reference count. [That trick is, fortunately, no longer useful.] §1016 P

90 Rethink the algorithm for contributing an insertion: The original code tests for a page break after incrementing the totals but before the *contrib_list* is updated. [TEX78 handles insertions in a hardwired manner that will be greatly generalized in TEX82.] A

91 Fix *get_node* again: After the variable memory overflows, control falls through to *found* instead of going to the *overflow* call. §125 F

• *I spent several hours tracking down that data structure bug!*

92 Change *new_line* to *next_line* in yet another print command (see #7). B

75 ↦ **93** Amend the line-breaking algorithm: **\break** in paragraph doesn't work with really bad breaks. §851 A

• *A problem to be diagnosed tomorrow: Each time I run the test program, the amount of memory in use grows by 13 cells not returned.*

• *Seven hours tonight.*

17 Mar 1978

94 Introduce *dead_cycles* to keep **\end** active until *ship_out* occurs. §1054 G

95 Don't call *line_break* with an empty list. §1096 E

96 Take proper account of the (infinite) fillglue when computing the width of a paragraph line preceding a display. §1146 S

97 Add a new parameter to *hpack* so that *line_break* won't be called at the wrong time. [This is for the soon-to-be-obsolete feature described in #40.] M

98 Give a warning message if there's an **\hfill** in the middle of a paragraph; fillglue upsets the line breaker, because floating-point calculations don't have sufficient accuracy. §868 L

• *I spent an hour looking for another bug in TEX, but the following one was in METAFONT: The xgp_height data in fonts had been supplied wrong.*

• *It took two hours to recompile 32 fonts with proto-METAFONT.*

99 Make *show_node_list* and *show_token_list* more robust in the presence of software bugs. §182 R

97 ↦ **100** Do not remove nodes with *eject_penalty*, when the new parameter to *hpack* is *true*. D

97 ↦ **101** Put a fast exit into *hpack*; e.g., at glue nodes, test '**if** *paragraphing* ∧ ⟨current width is large⟩'. E

• *2am. I have to go to bed "early" tonight.*

18 Mar 1978

• *3:30pm. (Saturday)*

102 Add a parameter to *check_mem* (to suppress display unless needed). §167 I

103 Introduce a user-settable parameter **\maxdepth**, and pass it as a parameter to *vpackage*. §668 G

• *I realized the need for* **\maxdepth** *while fixing insertions (see #90).*

104 Introduce a user-settable parameter for *line_break*: The constant 2.0 in my original algorithm becomes **\jpar** [later **\tolerance**], to be set like **\tracing**. §828 G

105 Reclaim the *eject_penalty* nodes removed during line-breaking. §879 D

• *(Those were the 13 extra nodes reported on Thursday.)*

• *The init_align procedure worked right the first time!*

- *Also init_row, init_col. But then...*

106 Rethink the command codes: *endv* in a token list has too high a code for the assumptions of *get_next*. §207 S

107 Add a *prev_cmd* variable for processing delimited macro parameters; the original algorithm loses track of braces. [The rules will change slightly in TeX82, and *rbrace_ptr* will take on a similar function.] §400 A

108 Make the *get_next* routine intercept `&` and `\cr` tokens. §342 S

- *I'd thought I could just put* `&` *and* `\cr` *into big_switch [i.e., in the stomach of TeX, not the eyes]; that was a great big mistake.*

109 Make more error checks on *endv*; e.g., it must not occur in a macro definition or call. §780 R

108 ↦ **110** No, rethink alignments again; the new program still fails! §768 S

- *For the first time I can glimpse the hairiness of alignment in general (e.g., '*`\halign{\u#\v&...`*' when* `\u` *and* `\v` *are defined to include* `&`*'s and possible alignments themselves).*
- *I think there's a "simple" solution, by considering only whether an alignment is currently active [in §342].*
- *11:30pm. Went to bed.*

19 Mar 1978

- *Woke up with "better" idea on how to handle* `&` *and* `\cr`.
- *(Namely, to consider a special kind of* `\def` *whose parameters don't interrupt on* `&`*'s and* `\cr`*'s.)*
- *But replaced this by a much better idea (to introduce align_state).*
- *11pm. Began to use computer. Performed major surgery (inserting align_state and updating the associated routines and documentation).*

111 Pop the alignment stacks in *fin_align*. §800 D

110 ↦ **112** Fix a (newly inserted) typo in *show_context*. §314 T

110 ↦ **113** Set *align_state* false when a live `&` or `\cr` is found. [Originally *align_state* was of type *boolean*.] §789 D

114 Insert `\cr` when '`}`' occurs prematurely in an alignment. §1132 I

115 Remember to record *glue_stretch* when packaging an unset node. §796 M

- *I had a mistake in* `acphdr` *definition of* `\quoteformat`*; also extra spaces.*
- *My first test programs, used before today, were contrived to test macro expansion, line-breaking, and page layout.*
- *Next I'm using a test program based on Volume 2.*

116 Make carriage-return, space, and tab equivalent for macro matching. §348 C

117 Omit the reference count node when displaying a mark. §176 F

118 Correct a silly slip: I wrote '*type_displacement*' instead of '*value_displacement*' when packing data in a penalty node. §158 B

119 Don't go to *build_page* after seeing `\noindent`; TeX isn't ready for that. [In the original program, this was an instance of a bad **goto**.] §1091 M

- *I had undesired spaces coming thru the scanner in my macro definitions of* `\tenpoint` *[see The TeXbook, page 414].*
- *4am. TeX now knows enough to typeset page 1 of Volume 2!*
- *Also it did its first "math formula" (namely '*`$X$`*') without crucial error.*
- *(Except that the italic correction was missing for some reason.)*

120 Remember to decrement *cur_level* in *fin_align*. [The routines will eventually become more general and use *unsave* here.] §800 D

121 Remember to increment *cur_level* in error corrections by *handle_right_brace*. [A better procedure will be adopted later.] §1069 D

122 Fix a typo: ('`{`' instead of '`}`') in error message for *mmode* + *math_shift*. §1065 T

99 ↦ **123** Make *show_noad_list* more robust and more like the new *show_node_list*. [The routines will be combined in TeX82.] §690 R

124 Fix a typo in *char_box*: should say *font_info_real*. [In TeX78 a single array is used for both *real* and *integer*; in TeX82 things will be *scaled*.] §554 L

125 Fix typos in the definitions of *default_rule_thickness* and *big_op_spacing*; they shouldn't start at *mathex*(7). §701 B

126 Reverse the *before* and *after* conventions in math nodes. §1196 B

• *I had them backwards; this turned hyphenation on just before math, and off just after it!*

• *Seven and a half hours debugging today. Got through the test program a little more. But TeX blew up on '*`$Y+1$`*'; tomorrow I hope to find out why.*

20 Mar 1978

• *8pm. I decided to work next on a super-hairy formula.*

127 Change '`\ascii`' to '`\cc`' (character code). [This name will change again later, to '`\char`'.] §265 C

128 Don't bother to store a penalty node at the beginning of `$$` when the paragraph-so-far fits on a single line, since such a penalty has already been stored. [These conventions will change later, and the `\predisplaypenalty` will always be stored.] §1203 E

129 Avoid reference to *tail* in *build_page*, if *nest_ptr* > 0. §995 S

130 Correct a silly slip in *math_comp* (the exact opposite of what I did in #118). §1158 B

131 Rectify my mental lapse in *make_fraction*; I said *nucleus* instead of *thickness*. §743 B

132 Mask off the math class when scanning delimiters. §1160 F

133 Allow an optional space after `\def{...}`. [This decision will be retracted later.] §473 C

• *My test example is so complicated it causes the semantic stacks to overflow!*

134 Don't test for no pages output by looking at the channel status. §642 L

135 Fix typo in definition of `\mathop` (*open_noad* not *op_noad*). §1156 T

136 Rewrite *fin_mlist*, because '`\left(...\above...\right)`' doesn't parse correctly; the `\left` goes into the numerator, the `\right` into the denominator. §1184 A

137 Correct the use of *depth_threshold* in *print_subsidiary_data*: Simple fields get shown while others look empty. §692 B

78 ↦ **138** Return the carriage before showing the first line of a new file when pausing. §538 I

139 Fix bug: The call *show_noad_list*(*mem*[..]) should be *show_noad_list*(..), in the *incompleat_noad* case of *show_activities*. §219 M

• *3am. The whole messy formula has been parsed correctly into a tree.*

• *The easy part is done, now comes the harder part.*

140 Don't shift single characters down in *make_op*. §749 F

141 Make *clean_box* return a box (as its name implies), not an hlist. §720 D

• *Font info still isn't quite right, it has the wrong value of quad.*

142 Retain the italic correction when doing *rebox*; can make *glue_set* $\neq 0$ a flag for this. [A better solution will be adopted later.] §715 A

143 Fix the bug that makes *rebox* bomb out: *value*(p) should be *value*(*mem*[p]). §715 B

• *6am; ten hours today. TeX didn't do* `$\pi\over2$` *correctly, but was close.*

• *I found that the rebox problem (#142) went away when I fixed the clean_box problem (#141); but I will leave the extra stuff about glue_set* $\neq 0$ *in the program anyway, just for weird cases.*

144 Omit extra levels of boxing when possible in *clean_box*. §721 E

• *(To do this, I need to face the rebox problem anyway.)*

21 Mar 1978

• *10pm. The computer is rather heavily loaded tonight.*

145 Don't forget *thickness* when making a square-root sign (see #131). [The rule thickness will later be derived from the character height.] §737 F

146 Define p local to the *make_fraction* routine. §743 L

• *Unwittingly using the global p was a disaster.*

147 Don't show the amount of *glue_set* when it's zero. §186 I

142 ↦ **148** Make *glue_set* nonzero in the result of *var_delimiter*. §706 D

149 Fix bug: The *math_glue* function didn't return any result. §716 F

150 Fix typo in *char_box* (c not w); this caused a subscripted P to come out the same width as an unsubscripted P. [Later changes in the rules will move this computation to §755.] §709 T

144 ↦ **151** Revise *clean_box* to do operations that are needed often because of the *rebox* change. §720 P

152 Use the new *clean_box* to avoid a bug in `\sqrt{\raise...}`. §737 D

153 Change the definition of `\not` so that it's a relation (which will butt against the following relation). [All math symbols and Greek letters are defined in `INITEX` at this time, not in a changeable format definition.] Q

154 Give error message '`Large delimiter must be in mathex font`', instead of calling *confusion*, since the error can occur. [This particular error is impossible in TeX82.] §706 I

155 Change the use of p in *var_delimiter*; it isn't always set when I say **goto** *found*. §706 F

- *Another font problem now surfaced: The mathex meta-font didn't compute TeX info in a machine-independent way. (It took two hours to correct this.)*

156 Don't forget to set *type*(*b*) in all relevant cases of *var_delimiter*. §708 D

157 Use the correct sign convention for *shift_amount* in *hpackage*. §653 B

158 Always kern by *delta* when there's no superscript. §755 F

159 Declare *space_table* to be [0 . . 6, 0 . . 6] not [0 . . 7, 0 . . 7]; otherwise its entries are preloaded into the wrong positions. [The *space_table* in TeX78 is 7×7; it will become 8×8 in TeX82, represented as a string called *math_spacing*.] §764 M

160 Use a negative value, not zero, to represent a null delimiter. [Actually zero will come back again later.] §685 C

127 ↦ **161** Change `\cc` to `\char`. §265 C

162 Don't use tricky subtraction on packed data when changing q to an *ord_noad* in *mlist_to_hlist*; subtraction isn't always safe. §729 L

163 Fix two typos in the *space_table* (`*` for `0`). §764 B

164 Initialize *cur_size* everywhere (I forgot it in two places). §703 F

165 Reset *op_noad* before resetting *bin_noad*. §728 A

166 Treat *display_style* + *cramped* the same as *display_style* inside *make_op*. §749 F

167 Shift the character correctly in the non-`\displaystyle` case of *make_op*. §749 B

- *Still another font problem: The italic corrections are wrong because the corresponding array was declared real in proto-METAFONT (and italic corrections were used in nonstandard way in* `mathex`*).*

168 Use *depth* instead of *height* in *var_delimiter*. [Later, both were used.] §714 B

169 Skew the accents according to the font *slant*. [Soon retracted.] §741 Q

- *At this point I think nearly all the math routines have been exercised.*
- *Tomorrow they should work!*
- *Eight hours debugging today.*

22 Mar 1978

- *(Wednesday, but actually Thursday: I began at midnight because I was proofreading a paper.)*
- *I checked out the font access tables, slowly (i.e., all the* `\mathcode` *and special-character name entries were catalogued).*

169 ↦ **170** Do **not** consider slants after all in the math accent routine, since slanted math letters are put differently into fonts. §741 Q

171 Don't use q for two different things simultaneously in *make_math_accent*. §738 B

172 Fix bug in *compact_list* (I forgot to advance the loop variable). [This procedure became unnecessary in TeX82.] F

173 Avoid conflict between *var_delimiter* and *mlist_to_hlist*, which want to use *temp_head* simultaneously. §713 M

174 Fix bad typo in *overbar* routine (b for p). §705 T

- *Finally TeX got to after_math after dealing with that hairy formula . . .*

175 Fix another bad typo: p for b this time. §1199 T

176 Insert more parentheses (twice) because of '`lsh`' precedence in SAIL. §1199 L

36 ↦ **177** Use the new hanging-indentation conventions when formatting displayed equations. §1199 M

178 Recompute penalties so that break is allowed after *punct_noad*s. §761 Q

179 Center the large delimiters vertically. §749 F

180 Round all rule sizes (up) before drawing them. §589 Q

181 Provide more space over x in $\sqrt{x}$, and more space atop vincula. §705, 737 Q

182 Make large delimiters large enough to cover formula height (important for subscripts, superscripts). §762 Q

183 Insert /ntn=33 on XGP prompt message so that complex math won't blow the device driver. [See #84.] I

161 ↦ **184** Update the comment about the meaning of \char, since it can be used in math mode. §208 P

- *Six hours today.*

23 Mar 1978

- *11pm, Maundy Thursday.*

104 ↦ **185** Make \tracing and \jpar follow block structure. §283 C

- *It took me two hours to enter yesterday's corrections, because the changes were so numerous.*

186 Fix bad call on *begin_token_list* when marks are to be scanned. §396 M

- *Now the formula looks like it should, modulo problems in fonts.*

187 Prevent an exponent from going below baseline + xheight/4. §758 Q

188 Change *quad* to *math_quad* when finishing a display (several places). §1199 B

189 Don't use *append_to_vlist* when putting an \eqno box on a separate line, because the page shouldn't break at glue there. [Later, the *append* will be used but preceded by an infinite penalty.] §1205 A

190 Increase the input *stack_size*; TEX may need to back up a lot. §11 S

191 Don't assume that p always points to a glue node when a page is broken. §1017 A

192 Use *epsilon* in *scan_spec* (I had used a different small constant). [This was a kludge to avoid the extra parameter later called *exactly* or *additional*.] §645 A

193 Introduce a new procedure *scan_positive_length*, to prevent negative or zero lengths in *scan_rule_spec*. [This restrictive rule will be "overruled" later.] §463 R

194 Fix ridiculous bug in the leaders routine of *vlist_out*: I had the initialization *inside* the loop! §635 B

195 Eliminate confusion between the two temp variables named h; one is *real* and the other is *integer*. §629 L

196 Include forgotten case (*leader_node*) in *hlist_out*. [Type *leader_node* will be absorbed into *glue_node* in TEX82.] §622 F

197 Don't forget to compute *x0* in variable horizontal rules. §624 F

- *Seven and a half hours today.*
- *TEX seems to be ready to tackle my test file based on Volume 2.*

198 Calculate *y00* in horizontal rules as an integer number of pixels from the baseline, so that the baseline doesn't jump. §589 S

25 Mar 1978

- *2am Saturday. (Might as well drop Friday.)*

185 ↦ **199** Make *def_code* consistent with the new \tracing conventions. [Many tracing options are packed into a single parameter called \tracing.] §1233 D

185 ↦ **200** Don't allow users to change nonexistent things like \catcode1000. §1232 R

110 ↦ **201** Reset *align_state* at beginning of *init_align*. §774 F

202 Don't forget *scan_left_brace* after \noalign. §785 F

110 ↦ **203** Set *cur_cs* ← 0 in *get_next*, after \cr causes a switch to the $\langle v_j\rangle$ template. §342 F

- *Ouch, that was a big bad bug, which took me three hours to find (since I thought TEX's low-level scanning mechanism was working).*
- *Note to myself: I* **knew** *it would be cleaner to define get_next so that it sets cur_cs to zero every time it begins [i.e., in §341, where this change will in fact be made in TEX82]. But I had avoided this on grounds of efficiency in the inner loop. Well, now I have earned this tiny bit of efficiency.*

204 Prohibit the first word of an unavailable node from becoming negative. [The storage allocator of TEX78 uses a negative value to signify a node that is available, just as '*link* = *max_halfword*' will signal availability in TEX82.] §124 D

- *That was another bad one, it's not my night.*
- *At least I'm developing more subtle diagnostic techniques.*

205 Remember to un-negate the top *save_stack* entry when *handle_right_brace* finishes an *insert_group*. [This routine was completely revised in TEX82.] §1100 M

185 ↦ **206** Initialize \jpar [i.e., \tolerance]. §240 F

207 Correct the display of insertion nodes by *show_node_list*. §188 B

208 Prevent *show_token_list* from generating really long strings when in a loop. §292 R

209 Increase the reference count of *bot_mark* when *vpackage* finds it. [This was later the job of *fire_up*.] §1016 D
210 Remember that the tokenlist for a mark ends with a `}`. §1101 M
211 Don't let *vpackage* lose the top insert. (It fails when the very first item is a `\topinsert`.) §1014 D
212 And when that stupid code is corrected, make it handle insertions first-in-first-out. §1018 A
- *Seven hours today.*

26 Mar 1978

- *Easter Sunday, will work till sunrise.*

213 Add an '`i`' feature to the *error* recovery routine. §87 I
214 Include a prompt. §87 I
215 Ignore space after `\noalign{...}`. §1133 C
- *Otherwise, things are going well tonight; I'm finding more bugs in my test program than in TEX.*
- *The '`i`' feature is proving to be very helpful.*
- *I increased the size of mem (now $lo\_mem\_max = 3500$, $mem\_max = 10000$).*
- *In fact I just needed to increase it again (now $lo\_mem\_max = 4500$, $mem\_max = 11000$).*

216 Make **INITEX** output *mem_top* for consistency checking. §1307 R
217 Calculate the size of delimiters by considering the enclosed formula's distance from the axis, not from the baseline. §762 A
- *I'm having trouble with a SAIL compiler bug; I must rearrange the program, more or less at random, until it compiles correctly. I hope the bug isn't more severe than it appears.*

210 ↦ **218** Don't put a new group on *save_stack* if a null mark is expanded. [TEX82 will remove the '`}`' from the mark text.] §386 D
- *I had to redo the typewriter-style font since its width tables were wrong.*
- *And I increased low-memory size again to 5500, then 6500.*
- *Finally the entire test program was TEXed. Happy Easter! Six hours today.*

27 Mar 1978

- *Beginning at 2:30am.*

219 Move `\vcenter` processing to the first pass of *mlist_to_hlist*; otherwise the height, depth, subscripts, etc., are way off. §733 A
220 Omit space after closing `$$`. §1200 C
- *Spacing is wrong in the formula $Y_1 + \cdots + Y_k$; I have to rethink the use of three dots.*

221 Make conditional thin space available to user as `\≤`. [Later will retract this.] §226 G
222 Introduce `\dispaskip` and `\dispbskip` [later called `\abovedisplayshortskip` and `\belowdisplayshortskip`]. §226 Q
- *Reminder: I need to test line-breaking with embedded math formulas.*

223 Make sure that $interaction \neq error\_stop\_mode$ in the '`Whoa`' error [*fatal_error*]. §93 I
224 Fix a big mistake in the *style_node* routine (which points to a glue spec, not to glue itself); somehow this didn't cause trouble yesterday. [In TEX78, style nodes double as placeholders for math glue like thin spaces.] §732 B
225 Make `\fntfam` obey group structure. [TEX78's `\fntfam` operation is a combination of TEX82's `\textfont`, `\scriptfont`, and `\scriptscriptfont`.] §1234 C
- *At this point the test routine for Volume 2 works perfectly.*
- *But I will change the page width in order to check harder cases.*

178 ↦ **226** Disable automatic line breaks after punctuation in math (e.g., consider $f(x, y)$). §761 Q
227 Represent italic corrections as boxes, not glue, so that they won't be broken. [The `\kern` command doesn't exist yet.] §1113 S
- *Eight hours today.*

228 Fix a bug that just clobbered the memory: Call *free_avail*, not *free_node*, in the *ins_node* case of *vpackage*. [This logic will change completely in TEX82.] §1019 B

29 Mar 1978

- *(Wednesday) Again beginning at 2:30am.*

229 Put still more space above and below fraction lines in displayed formulas. §746 Q

189 ↦ **230** Install an infinite penalty feature, which positively suppresses breaks; use it in displayed formulas whose `\eqno` doesn't fit. §1205 G

231 Call *build_page* after finishing a display; and don't go to the `\noindent` routine because of the next remark. §1200 F

232 Put `\parskip` glue just before a paragraph, not just after (since it interferes with a penalty after). §1091 S

- *Although the test program gives correct output, it generates 46 locations of variable-size memory and 280 of one-word memory that are not freed.*

233 Recycle the ulists and vlists in *fin_align*. §801 F

25 ↦ **234** Fix bug when deleting space at end of paragraph: *delete_glue_ref*(*cur_node*) not *delete_glue_ref*(*value*(*cur_node*)). §816 M

- *There's also a more mysterious type of uncollected garbage, a fraction_noad corresponding to* `$p\choose$`, *an incompleat_noad not completed.*
- *Couldn't find that one, so I recompiled with #233 and #234 corrected.*
- *Now it gains just 10 locations of variable-size memory and 7 of the other kind.*

235 Extend *search_mem* to search *eqtb* also. §255 I

143 ↦ **236** Fix bug in *rebox* when *list_ptr*(b) = 0. §715 D

- *The seven one-word nodes were generated by this bug; rebox put them onto a linked list starting with mem[0], growing at the far end!*

237 Remember to complete each *incompleat_noad*. §1184 D

- *This solved the other mystery. I had never noticed that my test output was actually wrong:* `$p\choose k$` *came out as 'k'.*
- *After these corrections, the test routine worked... I feel that TEX is now pretty well debugged (except perhaps for error recovery)—it's time to celebrate!*

1 Apr 1978

238 Don't quit after file lookup fails. §530 I

2 Apr 1978

239 Add *TEX_font_area*, so that it's easier to change the default library area associated with a device. §514 P

3 Apr 1978

240 Insert parentheses again, to cope with the precedence of `lsh` when packing data. (See #55 and #176.) §1114 L

- *I had never tried hmode + discretionary before!*

241 Remember that *back_error* requires *cur_tok* to be set. (Problem can arise during error recovery on parameter `#`n with n out of range.) §476 M

4 Apr 1978

242 Add a deletion feature to the *error* routine. §88 I

5 Apr 1978

243 Reset *space_factor* after `\/` [this was later rescinded] and after math in text. §1196 Q

10 Apr 1978

104 ↦ **244** Replace `\jpar` and `\tracing` by a new primitive `\chpar` for parameters. It allows a user to change those quantities as well as the penalties for hyphens, relations, binary ops, widows. §209 G

14 May 1978

- *Beginning to typeset a real book (Volume 2, second edition), not just a test.*

245 Make math in text end with spacing as if it were followed by punctuation. [This rule will soon be rescinded.] §760 Q

246 Insert `\times` into the hash table; I left it out by mistake. [It will eventually move into `plain.tex`.] F

247 Change the names of Scandinavian accents from `\o`, `\oslash`, `\Oslash` to `\a`, `\o`, `\O`. [This will also move to `plain`.] C

17 May 1978

248 Fix a silly bug that hasn't been tweaked until today: '`\halign to size`' [obsolete in TEX82] used *vsize* instead of *hsize*. §645 B

19 May 1978

249 Add a `\topbaseline` feature [later called `\topskip`]. §1001 G

245 ↦ **250** Subtract the math spacing change of May 14. §760 Q

251 Skip past blanks in the *scan_math* procedure. [This blank-skipping will eventually go into *scan_left_brace*.] §403 A

252 Introduce a *missing_brace* routine [later generalized] to improve error recovery in *mmode* + *math_shift*, when the top of *save_stack* isn't a *math_shift_group*. §1065 I

253 Adjust the math spacing between closing parentheses and Ord, Op, Open, Punct. §764 Q

254 Make the underline go further under. §735 Q

96 ↦ **255** Compute the proper natural width when a displayed equation follows a paragraph whose fillglue has been deleted by *line_break*. §1146 S

20 May 1978

256 Fix the spurious value of *prev_depth* inside alignments. §775 A

257 Consider (and defeat) the following scenario: The u and v lists are built in *init_align* using *temp_head*; then while scanning '`\tabskip 2pt\rt{...}`' the macro `\rt` is expanded, clobbering *temp_head*. §779 S

- *That bug was more subtle than usual.*

258 Add the parameter *num3*, so that the positioning of `\atop` can be different from that for fractions. §700 Q

259 Add new parameters *delim1* and *delim2*, so that `\comb` can use fixed size delimiters, not computed as with `\left`. §748 Q

22 May 1978

221 ↦ **260** Change `\≤` to `\≥` and introduce `\≤` as the negative of `\≥`. [Later obsolete.] §226 C

261 Fix the display of negative penalty nodes; *show_node_list* is confused when a negative value has been packed into the middle of a word. §194 L

- *Memory overflow just occurred with lo_mem_max* = 7500 *and mem_max* = 16384. *So I have to go to 15-bit pointers. (A problem on 32-bit machines?)*

23 May 1978

262 Add a new parameter *big_op_spacing5*, for extra space above and below limits of big displayed operators. §751 Q

263 Initialize *incompleat_noad* in `$$\halign{...}$$`. §775 F

- *That was another heretofore-untested operation. How much of the code has not yet been exercised?*

238 ↦ **264** Close the file when doing lookup-failure recovery. §27 F

265 Improve the error recovery for '`Extra &`'. §792 I

266 The top piece must be calculated mod 128 in *var_delimiter*, to guarantee a valid subscript range. [Obsolete in TeX82.] §546 R

252 ↦ **267** Fix a blunder in new *missing_brace* code. §1065 B

262 ↦ **268** Fix a blunder in new code for limits on display operators. §751 B

26 May 1978

269 Don't insert a new penalty after an explicit penalty in math mode. §767 Q

- *The hash table overflowed; I ought to make it much bigger.*

110 ↦ **270** Avoid possible bad memory references in alignment when there is erroneous input after `\cr`. [Instead of *extra_info*, the value of *cur_align* in TeX78 is negated, because we need only distinguish `\cr` from `&`.] §789 R

271 Make the dimension parameters like `\hsize` all global, so that they can be set in the `\output` routine. §279 S

- *This led to major simplifications, also to major surgery.*
- *[But it was a kludgy decision, overruled in TeX82.]*

94 ↦ **272** Don't forget to set the type of the new null box in the `\end` routine. §1054 D

27 May 1978

- *The data overflowed memory again, both low and high, doing Section 3.3.2.*

184 ↦ **273** Mask off extra bits of `\char` in math mode, to avoid bad memory references. §1151 R

274 Zero out the negative `\medmuskip` in script styles. §732 B

29 May 1978

275 Be prepared to handle an undefined control sequence during *get_x_token*. (Can fix this by brute force, using *get_token* instead of *get_next*.) §380 S

276 Correct the superscript shift when a single character is raised. §758 D

184 ↦ **277** Mask off all but 7 bits in `\char` routine, to avoid space-factor index out of range. §435 R

• *More memory capacity overflows.*

22 ↦ **278** Fix TeX's overflow stop so that I don't have to wait for loading of the `BAIL` debug routines. [System dependent.] §93 E

279 Remember to adjust the page number when a file page ends in mid-macro. [System dependent.] §306 F

5 Jun 1978

280 Make sure that the arguments of positioning commands don't overflow their field size. §610 R

281 Report the excess amount when giving an overfull box warning. §666, 677 I

7 Jun 1978

282 Use $\geq$ instead of $>$ as termination criterion in *var_delimiter*. §714 Q

283 Disallow `\eject` in math mode. [In TeX78, `\eject` is distinct from `\break`; in horizontal mode it includes TeX82's '`\vadjust{\break}`'.] §1102 R

284 Don't put too much clearance above `\sqrt` in text style. §737 Q

9 Jun 1978

110 ↦ **285** Make *align_state* an integer variable, not *boolean*, so that `\eqalign` can be within another `\eqalign`. §309 G

286 A `\mark` should expand its input. §1101 C

10 Jun 1978

287 Provide for preloading of fonts. §1320 E

288 Close the output file before switching to edit the input file with the '`e`' option. §84 L

289 Return adjustments found by *hpack* to free storage if they're not used. [Later, *hpack* will detach them only when they're used.] §655 E

290 Strive for consistency between *make_under* and *make_over*. §735 Q

18 Jun 1978

236 ↦ **291** Fix a serious error in *rebox* ('*b*' instead of '*list_ptr*(*b*)'). §715 B

• *Strange that such a bug would now surface for the first time!*

292 Remove `\deg` from `INITEX`, since macros suffice. C

293 Add an extra hyphenation penalty for two hyphenated lines in a row. §859 Q

19 Jun 1978

294 Introduce the '*no_new_control_sequence*' switch. Among other things, this will prevent an undefined control sequence following *scan_math* from clobbering the save stack. §259 S

20 Jun 1978

295 Change the badness test '*glue* $\leq$ 0.0' to '*glue* $\leq$ 0.0001'. [TeX82 will avoid such problems by calculating badness without floating point arithmetic.] §99 L

296 Force *badness* to be at most 10^{19}. §108 R

297 Add *end_template* for better error recovery in alignments. §375 I

287 ↦ **298** Make `INITEX` more like the real TeX; my simple scheme for font preloading was no good because it left thousands of 'dead' words in memory. §8 E

299 Economize disk space by using internal arrays in load modules that aren't being reinitialized. [System dependent.] E

300 Move the declaration of *mem* to the semantics module, so that the object code will be more efficient. [System dependent. The code of TeX78 was divided into separately compiled modules for syntax, semantics, output, extensions, and general organization.] E

21 Jun 1978

• *Today I'm working on the user manual.*

301 Disallow `\input` except in vertical mode. [I will change this in TeX82, treating `\input` as a case of expansion.] §378 C

302 Add error recovery for *endv* and *par_end* occurring in math mode. §1047 I
303 Generalize `\ifT` to `\if T`. §506 G

22 Jun 1978

304 Preload the `\bullet` [later done by `plain.tex`]. F
256 ↦ **305** Get the correct *prev_depth* at the beginning of an alignment. §775 D
306 Change `\eject` so that it ejects only once. §1000 C

14 Jul 1978

307 Look in standard area if a file isn't found in the user's area. §537 I
308 Echo all online inputs in the transcript file. §71 I

19 Jul 1978

309 Equalize spacing when only one of numerator/denominator is big. §745 Q
310 Prevent subscript from getting too high above baseline. §757 Q
311 Avoid infinite loop when stack overflows: *push_input* should say '**if** $input\_ptr \ge stack\_size \wedge interaction = error\_stop\_mode$'. §321 R

22 Jul 1978

312 Make `\quad` meaningful outside math mode. (All fonts must be generated again!) §558 C
313 Show the nesting level at the end of *show_activities*. [But I decided not to do this in TEX82.] §218 I
314 Put in `\>` [namely, `\mskip\medmuskip`; TEX78 already has `\≥`, for conditional `\thinmuskip`, as well as the negative amounts `\<`, `\≤`]. Change the name of vector accent from `\>` to `\b`. [Math spacing operators will become much more general in TEX82.] §716 C

25 Jul 1978

94 ↦ **315** Give the correct `\hsize` and `\vsize` to the null boxes created at `\end`. §1054 Q
94 ↦ **316** And don't "append" them. [Later this was changed, so that it would work better with generalized output routines.] §1054 A
297 ↦ **317** Remove the control sequence `\endv`, since error recovery is now better. §375 I
318 Define another mode of tracing: It says '`OK`' and stops after `\showlists`. §1298 I
244 ↦ **319** Give better defaults to parameters. [Later done by `plain.tex`.] §209 Q
320 Allow more bits in the packed representation of `\showboxdepth`. §238 I
321 Scan past delimiters and/or dimensions when recovering from ambiguous fractions. §1183 I
322 Reduce accent numbers modulo 128 or 512, depending on the mode. §1165 R
323 Include a warning, '`(\end occurred on level ...)`'. §1335 I

28 Jul 1978

• *(I'm writing Chapter 27 of the manual: 'Recovery From Errors'.)*
324 Improve the error message in *scan_digit*. [This procedure will change its name to *scan_eight_bit_int*, when the number of registers increases from 10 to 256.] §433 I
325 Don't report overfull boxes if they're less than .1 point over. §666, 677 I
326 Give the user extra chances to define the font, if *read_font_info* is unsuccessful. §560 I
327 Change default recovery for bad parameter number from `#1` to `##`, since `#1` won't always work and since `##` is probably intended. §479 I
328 Omit the `"Negative?"` message on things like *scan_char_num*. §435 I
329 Improve error recovery when a large delimiter isn't in family 3. [Obsolete.] I
330 Give a more appropriate error message when the input is '`$\right`'. §1192 I
• *Currently TEX says '`Missing $`'!*
331 Call *back_input* before the error message in *back_error*, not afterwards. §327 I

1 Aug 1978

332 Give an appropriate warning when there's no input file and the user types '`e`'. §84 I
333 Increase the system pushdownlist size so that the manual will compile. [Procedures *hlist_out* and *vlist_out* can recurse deeply.] L
• *Yesterday I distributed 45 preliminary copies of the manual; today I took out the "debugging hooks" and put TEX up as a system program.*

2 Aug 1978

• *I'm typing Volume 2 again (currently in Section 4.2.2). Culture shock!*

334 Introduce a `\ragged` parameter, to indicate a degree of raggedness. [Previously, ragged-right setting was performed when the `\tolerance`/100 was odd! Eventually a better approach, with `\rightskip` and such things, will be discovered.] §886 G

335 Omit the 'widow penalty' in one-line paragraphs. §890 Q

5 Aug 1978

336 Generalize `\pageno` to `\count`⟨digit⟩. §236 G

285 ↦ **337** Update *align_state* when recovering from '`Missing {`' and '`Extra }`' errors. §1069, 1127 D

338 Show "runaway" tokens, making it easier to pinpoint an error. §306 I

22 Aug 1978

339 Add `\predisplaypenalty`. §1203 G

340 Clarify error messages; they should indicate when something has been inserted, etc. §1064 I

23 Aug 1978

114 ↦ **341** Substitute '`Extra }`' for the losing '`Missing \cr`' error message. §1069 I

213 ↦ **342** Go past online insertions in *show_context*. §311 I

343 Exact no penalty for breaking one line before a display. §1145 Q

338 ↦ **344** Check for runaways at end of file. §362 I

345 Give error message when a macro argument begins with `}`. §395 I

24 Aug 1978

213 ↦ **346** Remove extra line-feed in *show_context* after printing insertions. [System dependent.] §318 L

25 Aug 1978

347 Leave no glue at top of page, even after `\eject`. §997 Q

27 Aug 1978

348 Adopt Guy Steele's new version of the TeX source files. [He has recently made a copy and modified it by introducing compile-time switches for MIT conventions as an alternative to SUAI. This is the first time that TeX is being ported to another site; additional switches for PARC, TENEX, TOPS10, and TOPS20 will be added later, using the Steele style.] P

1 Sep 1978

349 Don't pass over leader nodes in the *try_break* background computation. [At this time, leaders have not yet been unified with glue.] §837 Q

82 ↦ **350** Prune away all penalties at the top of a page. §997 Q

4 Sep 1978

338 ↦ **351** Include '`\`' in error message about a runaway argument. §306 I

8 Sep 1978

• *I just remade all the fonts, with increased ligature field size.*

350 ↦ **352** Insert a necessary **goto** statement in the first branch of the new penalty routine within *build_page*. §997 B

30 Sep 1978

338 ↦ **353** Make the token list for runaway arguments meaningful outside of *macro_call*. (I just had a runaway argument ending with '`\lcm`', which turned out to be the control sequence in hashtable location 0.) §371 M

354 Avoid infinite loop when recovering from **$$** in restricted horizontal mode. §1138 R

355 Fix two hyphenation bugs related to `-ages`, `-ers`. [A completely new algorithm for hyphenation will go into TeX82.] L

356 Add `-est` to hyphenation routine; also disable `puz-zled` and `rat-tled`, etc. Q

4 Oct 1978

357 Add new primitive `\vtop`. §1087 G

358 Treat implicit kerns properly after discretionary hyphens have been inserted. §914 Q

4 Nov 1978

359 Forget the half quad originally required at left and right when centering displayed equations without equation numbers. §1202 Q

11 Nov 1978

360 Don't let the postamble come out empty. [This could occur if no fonts were selected.] §642 R

15 Nov 1978

361 Allow optional space after digit in *scan_int* routine. §444 C

17 Nov 1978

362 Make the *check_mem* procedure slightly more robust. §167 R

20 Nov 1978

363 Make the `\par` in a `\def` match the `\par` that comes automatically with a blank line. (Suggested by Terry Winograd.) §351 C

364 Add new parameter `\mathsurround` for spacing before and after math in text. §1196 G

365 Extend `\advance` to allow increase by other than unity. [At this time it applies only to the ten `\count` registers, and it is called `\advcount`.] §1238 G

25 Nov 1978

366 Add a new primitive: `\unskip`. §1105 G

367 Add new primitives `\uppercase` and `\lowercase`. §1288 G

28 Nov 1978

338 ↦ **368** Don't let `\mark` and *macro_call* interfere with each other's *scanner_status*. §306 M

369 Omit extra `}` after *show_node_list* shows a `\mark`, since the right brace is already there. (See #210.) §176 M

370 Add a new primitive suggested by Terry Winograd: `\xdef`. §1218 G

29 Nov 1978

371 Delete a space following `\else{...}` also in the false case. [TeX78 uses braces, not `\fi`, for conditionals.] S

320 ↦ **372** Make `\tracing` set `\showboxbreadth` as advertised. §198 D

373 Account properly for kerns in width calculations of *line_break*. §866 F

364 ↦ **374** Delete a *math_node* at the beginning of a line. §148 Q

339 ↦ **375** Guarantee that `\predisplaypenalty=10000` will suppress page breaking before a display. §1005 A

6 Dec 1978

376 Change the file opening statement to allow lines up to 150 characters long. [System dependent.] L

16 Jan 1979

365 ↦ **377** Initialize *negative* properly in the `\advance` routine with a `\count` as argument. §440 F

20 Jan 1979

378 Try to keep complex, buggy preambles of alignments from crashing the program. §789 R

17 Feb 1979

376 ↦ **379** Give more detailed information when warning about a long line being broken. [System dependent; the buffer size in TeX78 is very limited.] I

380 Declare *p* local to *try_break*, for the "rare" case code. [My original program included the following comment: "This case can arise only in weird circumstances due to changing line lengths, and the code may in fact never be executed." Later Michael Plass will discover that variable line lengths require an entirely different algorithm, using *last_special_line*.] §847 L

334 ↦ **381** Don't omit the raggedness correction when the last line of paragraph has to shrink. [Obsolete in TeX82.] F

22 Feb 1979

363 ↦ **382** Don't forget to return from *get_x_token* after finding `\par`. §351 F

383 Add a new parameter: `\lineskiplimit`. §679 Q

384 Change the syntactic sugar: '`\hbox par`' replaces '`\hjust to ...{overfull}`'. [This vastly improves on the old idea (see #40), but there still is no internal vertical mode.] C

385 Introduce new names `\hbox` and `\vbox` for `\hjust` and `\vjust`. §1071 C

386 Add a new condition: `\ifpos`. [It will later be generalized to `\ifnum` and `\ifdim`.] §513 G

387 Add `vu` and `\varunit`. [TEX82 will eventually allow arbitrary internal dimensions as units of measure.] §453 G

312 ↦ **388** Add an `em` unit. §455 G

389 Legalize `\hbox spread` ⟨negative dimension⟩ [since *scan_spec* no longer uses the sign as a flag]. §645 C

10 Mar 1979

370 ↦ **390** Make *scan_toks* expand `\count` during `\xdef`. [This will change later when `\the` and `\number` are introduced.] §367 C

23 Mar 1979

391 Put only 100000 pt stretch at the end of a paragraph instead of 10000000000 pt. [In TEX78, "infinite" glue is actually finite but large; in the language of TEX82 we would say that `\parfillskip`, which is not yet user-settable, is being changed to be like `\hfil` instead of like `\hfill`.] §816 Q

392 Treat the last line of a paragraph more consistently with the other lines (e.g., when `\hfil` appears in mid-paragraph), by effectively inserting *inf_penalty* at the end. §816 Q

31 Mar 1979

393 Ensure that penalty nodes aren't wiped out, in weird cases where breaks occur at penalties that normally disappear. §879 S

27 Apr 1979

394 Correct the page number count when files begin with an empty page. [System dependent.] A

395 Allow the *math_code* table to be changeable via `\chcode`. [In TEX82, `\chcode` will split into `\mathcode` and `\catcode`.] §1232 G

332 ↦ **396** Don't accept '`e`' after an error message if not inputting from a file. §84 I

29 May 1979

397 Don't call *end_file_reading* if you haven't already invoked *begin_file_reading*; this could happen when trying to recover from an error in *start_input*. §537 F

7 Jun 1979

306 ↦ **398** Be sure to eject two pages, when `\eject` comes just at the time another break is preferable (e.g., when the page has just become too full). §1005 A

27 Jun 1979

354 ↦ **399** Don't say '`You can't do that in math mode`' when the user says '`$$`' in restricted horizontal mode! §1138 I

30 Jun 1979

400 Add `wd`, `dp`, `ht` dimension units. §455 G

307 ↦ **401** Don't try the system area for file names whose area is explicitly indicated. §537 I

1 Jul 1979

402 Allow letters as (ASCII) numbers [without the ` marker introduced later]. §442 G

2 Jul 1979

403 Fix a `\gdef` bug: If the control sequence was never defined before [this later became the *restore_zero* option], don't remove it at group end. §282 F

16 Jul 1979

320 ↦ **404** Update *show_noad_list* to be like *show_node_list*. [The two routines, originally separate, will be merged in TEX82.] §238 I

18 Jul 1979

405 Extend capacity from 32 fonts to 64 fonts if desired. §134 G

406 Add new *extra_space* parameter to all text fonts (requested by Frances Yao). §558 Q

407 Make each *node_noad* print properly in *show_noad_list*. §183 F

408 Make \jpar allow any break if it is 1000000 or more. [In TeX82, a \tolerance of 10000 or more allows any break.] §851 Q

23 Jul 1979

409 Introduce new primitives \hfil, vfil, \hfilneg, \vfilneg. §1058 E

410 Add \ifmmode. §501 G

411 Add \firstmark. §1012, 1016 G

412 Allow break at leaders (horizontal mode only). §149 C

25 Jul 1979

213 ↦ **413** Revise *error* so that online insertions work properly after end-of-file errors. §336 I

411 ↦ **414** Change '**if** *first_mark* $\neq 0$' to '**if** *first_mark* ≥ 0' [because -1 is used to indicate 'not yet given a value']. §1012 B

28 Jul 1979

370 ↦ **415** Stop \xdef from expanding control sequences after \def's. [This decision will be rescinded later, after several more years of experience with macro expansion will suggest better ways to cure the problem.] §366 C

416 Change symbolic printout for control symbols. [System dependent.] §49 I

308 ↦ **417** Avoid linefeeds in the transcript file. [System dependent.] L

370 ↦ **418** Expand topmark, etc., in \xdef. §366 C

4 Aug 1979

413 ↦ **419** Fix an error introduced recently: \par was suddenly omitted at end of page. [System dependent.] B

11 Aug 1979

420 Change error messages that use SAIL characters not in standard ASCII. §360 P

28 Aug 1979

411 ↦ **421** Move the command '*first_mark* ← −1' from *vpackage* to *fire_up*. §1012 D

403 ↦ **422** Correct a serious \gdef bug: Control sequences don't obey a last-in-first-out discipline, so TeX loses things from the hash table when deleting a control sequence. §259 S

- *To fix this, I either need to restrict TeX (so that* \gdef *can be used inside a group only for control sequences already defined on the outer level) or need to change the hash table algorithm. Although all applications of TeX known to me will agree to the former restriction, I've chosen the latter alternative, because it gives me a chance to improve the language: Control sequences of arbitrary length will now be recognized.*

423 Make sure that *unsave* cannot call *eq_destroy* with a value from the upper part of *eqtb*. §282 D

- *I noticed this long-standing bug while fixing #422. It had very low probability of causing damage (e.g., it required a certain field of a floating-point number to have a certain value), but it would have been devastating on the day it first showed up!*

29 Aug 1979

424 Call *eq_destroy* when a control sequence is \gdef'ed after being \def'ed. §283 F

418 ↦ **425** Treat the first token consistently when \topmark and its cousins are expanded in *scan_toks*. §477 F

- *Now I've checked things pretty carefully and I think TeX is "fully debugged."*

25 Jan 1980

338 ↦ **426** Display runaway alignment preambles. §306 I

427 Introduce active characters (one-stroke control sequences). [I don't yet go all the way: The meanings of 'x' and '\x' have to be identical.] §344 G

7 Feb 1980

314 ↦ **428** Fix a glaring omission: Op space \> was never implemented in math mode! §716 F

25 Feb 1980

429 Add a new dimension 'ex' (for units of xheight). §455 G

3 Mar 1980

427 ↦ **430** Allow the control sequence `\:` to be redefined [it was the 'select font' operator]; this allows the character `:` to be active. [Obsolete.] C

23 Mar 1980

• *An extend-TeX-for-the-eighties party:*

431 Add a new `\copy` feature. §204 G

432 Add a new `\unbox` feature. §1110 G

433 Add a new `\open` feature [later `\openout`]. §1351 G

434 Add a new `\send` feature [later `\write`]. §1352. G

435 Add a new `\leqno` feature, requested by MDS. §1204 G

436 Add a new `\ifdimen` feature [later `\ifdim`]. §513 G

437 Make \⟨space⟩ in vertical mode begin a paragraph. §1090 C

438 Add a new `\font` feature [replacing the silly previous convention that a font must be defined when it is first selected]. §1256 G

439 Add new `\parval` and `\codeval` features [later `\the` ⟨whatever⟩]. §413 G

427 ↦ **440** Don't let active characters gobble the following space. §344 C

208 ↦ **441** Add a new parameter to govern amount of token list dumped. [Obsolete.] §295 G

442 Add a new `\linebreak` feature [later replaced by `\break`]. §831 G

25 Mar 1980

• *(Still working on the above, also thought of more.)*

443 Add a new `\mskip` feature. §716 G

444 Add a new `\newname` feature (soon changed to `\let`). §1221 G

430 ↦ **445** Allow any control sequence to be redefined. §275 G

446 Send the output to the user's current file area, even when input comes from elsewhere. §532 I

27 Mar 1980

447 Compute the xheight for accents in math mode from family 1, not family 3. [Obsolete.] Q

28 Mar 1980

448 Increase minimum clearance between subscript and superscript. §759 Q

29 Mar 1980

222 ↦ **449** When a display follows a display, the second should have the 'shortskip' glue. §1146 Q

4 Apr 1980

445 ↦ **450** Look at current token meanings when trying to recognize `\tabskip` in alignment preambles. §782 A

23 Apr 1980

451 Estimate the length of printed output, for the new priority feature on our XGP device driver. [System dependent.] I

434 ↦ **452** Break long `\send` lines into pieces so that the file can be read in again. [System dependent.] C

19 May 1980

182 ↦ **453** Don't make `\left` and `\right` delimiters too large; they need to be only 90% of the enclosed size. [This eventually became `\delimiterfactor`.] §762 Q

21 May 1980

454 Add a new `\pagebreak` feature [later `\vadjust{\break}`]. §655 G

13 Jun 1980

• *Today I'm beginning to overhaul the line-breaking routine, and I'll also install miscellaneous goodies.*

455 Allow a radical sign to be in different font positions. §737 G

456 Clear empty tokenlists off input stacks to allow deeper recursions (suggested by Jim Boyce's macros for chess positions). §325 E

457 Make `\spaceskip` and `\parfillskip` changeable. §1228 G

458 Add a new parameter `\rfudge` (per request of Zippel) [later `\mag`]. §288 G

459 Add a new parameter `\loose` [later `\looseness`]; now parameters are allowed to take negative values. §875 G

460 Remove the variable *just_par*. [Obsolete; it was the *real* equivalent of an *integer*]. E

14 Jun 1980

461 Install new line-breaking routines, including `\parshape`. (These major changes are introduced as Michael Plass and I write our article.) §813 Q

462 Add a new parameter `\exhyf` [later `\exhyphenpenalty`]. §869 G

16 Jun 1980

444 ↦ **463** Change conventions in *eqtb* so that glue is distinguishable from other equivalents. §275 S

444 ↦ **464** Don't expand `\b` in `\xdef{\d\b{...}}` after `\let\d=\def`. [Obsolete.] A

444 ↦ **465** Avoid creating dead storage when doing *unsave* in certain regions. §275 D

17 Jun 1980

466 Allow negative dimensions in rules. §138 C

19 Jun 1980

463 ↦ **467** Make the new test for glue at the outer level of *show_eqtb*. §252 B

27 Jun 1980

453 ↦ **468** Don't let `\left` and `\right` become too small for big matrices. [This eventually became `\delimitershortfall`.] §762 Q

3 Aug 1980

469 Don't move extra-wide, numbered equations flush left unless they begin with glue. §1202 Q

15 Sep 1980

461 ↦ **470** Say '$\geq fz$' instead of '$> fz$' in the pre-hyphenation routine; I'd forgotten my definition of *fz* [a variable used to test for a sequence of lowercase letters in the same font]. §897 M

395 ↦ **471** Check the range of the index in `\chcode` before saving the old value. §1232 R

18 Sep 1980

457 ↦ **472** Don't forget to increase the reference count to `\parfillskip`, or it will mysteriously vanish. §816 D

19 Sep 1980

412 ↦ **473** Make leaders break like glue in both horizontal and vertical modes. §149 C

364 ↦ **474** Make `\mathsurround` break properly at left and right end of lines. §879 Q

13 Oct 1980

461 ↦ **475** Remove spurious overfull boxes generated when the looseness criterion fails. [Obsolete.] I

461 ↦ **476** Redesign the iteration for looseness; breakpoints were not chosen optimally. §875 A

461 ↦ **477** Avoid storing a lot of breakpoints when they are dominated by others. §836 E

366 ↦ **478** Don't say '*cur_node*' when you mean '*mem*[*cur_node*]'. §1105 B

461 ↦ **479** Prefer the oldest break to the youngest break when two break nodes have the same total demerits. §836 Q

461 ↦ **480** Don't make badness too big for floating-point calculations, when forced to make an overfull box. [Obsolete.] L

10 Dec 1980

481 Make it impossible to get unmatched '}' in a delimited macro argument. §392 R

482 Add new `\topsep` and `\botsep` features. [These are TeX78's way to put space at the edge of inserts, replaced in TeX82 by the `\skip` register corresponding to an `\insert` class.] §1009 G

6 Jan 1981

483 Install new routines for reading the font metrics, using Ramshaw's `TFM` files instead of `TFX` files. §539 P

484 Abort after reporting 100 errors, if not pausing on errors. §82 I

485 Add new `\spacefactor` and `\specskip` and `\skip` primitives. [At this time we write '`\specskip3=10pt`' and '`\skip3`' for what will become '`\skip3=10pt`' and '`\hskip\skip3`' in TeX82.] §1060 G

366 ↦ **486** `\unskip` is now allowed in internal vertical mode. §1105 G

26 Jan 1981

482 ↦ **487** Don't say '*mem*[*q*]' when you mean '*q*'. (See #143 and #478.) §1009 B

27 Feb 1981

417 ↦ **488** Put some linefeeds back into the transcript file, in order to prevent overprinting in listings. [System dependent.] I

489 Add a new `\dpenalty` feature [later `\postdisplaypenalty`]. §1205 G

490 Add the dimension `cc` for European users. §458 G

491 Make *scan_keyword* match uppercase letters as alternatives to lowercase ones (suggested by Barbara Beeton's experiments with `\uppercase`). §407 C

492 Add nonstop mode so that overnight batch processing is possible. §73 I

2 Mar 1981

422 ↦ **493** Fix a still more serious `\gdef` bug: The generality of `\gdef` almost makes it a crime to forget *any* control sequence names, ever! (The previous bug was only the tip of an iceberg.) §259 S

494 Issue warning message at the end of a file page if nesting level isn't zero. [System dependent.] I

5 Mar 1981

495 Keep track of maximum memory usage, for statistical reporting. [Obsolete.] §125 I

350 ↦ **496** Prune away glue and penalties at top of page after marks, sends, inserts. §1000 Q

497 Allow `\mark` in horizontal mode. [Later it will be `\vadjust{\mark...}`.] §655 G

498 Allow optional space before a required left brace, e.g., `\if AA {...}`. [See #251.] §403 C

499 Issue an incomplete `\if` error, to help catch a bad `\if`. §336 I

17 Mar 1981

494 ↦ **500** Omit the warning message at end of a file page unless the nesting level has changed on that page. [System dependent.] I

310 ↦ **501** Fix the spacing when there is a very tall subscript with a superscript. §759 Q

20 Mar 1981

371 ↦ **502** Make space-eating after `\else` fully consistent between the true and false cases. [Obsolete.] S

24 Mar 1981

496 ↦ **503** Change *glue_spec_size* to *ins_spec_size* in *vpackage* [where insertions are done]. [Obsolete.] B

5 Apr 1981

501 ↦ **504** Fix a typo ('+' instead of '-') in the new subscript code; this shifted certain subscripts down instead of up. §759 B

18 Apr 1981

505 Make leaders with rules of specified size act like variable rules. §626, 635 G

29 Apr 1981

461 ↦ **506** Don't consider *badness* > *threshold* at a line `\break` except in an emergency. §854 A

13 Jul 1981

402 ↦ **507** Allow other characters as numbers. §442 C

294 ↦ **508** Avoid dead storage if a *no_new_control_sequence* error occurs. [Obsolete.] §259 R

509 Add a new `\ifx` feature. §507 G

510 Add new features `\xleaders` and `\cleaders`. §626, 635 G

14 Jul 1981

507 ↦ **511** Amend the new code for constants; the '`.`' in '`.5`' is thought to mean *'056*! §442 S

507 ↦ **512** And fix an egregious blunder in that code: New commands at the end of a procedure are ignored when earlier statements exit via **return**. §442 L

4 Aug 1981

513 Accept alphabetic codes for all online error recovery options, instead of insisting on control codes like line feed or form feed. [The original error-recovery codes were suggested by the conventions of the SAIL compiler.] §84 P

514 Add a new `\thebox` feature [later `\lastbox`]. §1079 G

7 Aug 1981

515 Add `fil`, `fill`, and `filll` as units for glue stretching or shrinking. §454 G

516 Suppress the overfull box error when shrinkage amount is negative. §664 I

9 Aug 1981

517 Let unset boxes inherit the size of their parent in alignments. §810 Q

12 Apr 1982

518 Make `INITEX` dump out the *font_dsize* array needed by the new `DVI` output module. §1322 F

1 May 1982

151 ↦ **519** Fix *clean_box* so that *mlist_to_hlist* cannot make $link(q) = 0$ and $type(q) = glue\_node$. §720 S

• *[That was the historic final change to TEX78. All subsequent entries in this log refer to TEX82.]*

15 Jul 1982

• *Finished draft of test program and began debugging about 1430 [2:30 pm]. Taking my time.*

X1 Change *eqtb*[*cur_font*] to *eqtb*[*cur_font_loc*]. §232 B

• *Not logging changes to the exposition.*

• *Compile time is about 2 minutes CPU, times 5 for time sharing; add another half minute for linking and loading.*

• *Hash table and get_next seem to be working, with no changes needed!*

• *Time out 1630–1815 for Jill's birthday party.*

X2 Insert **begin** ... **end** around *dump_int* macro. §1305 L

X3 Print two blank spaces before date in *open_log_file*. §536 I

X4 Update x and *var_used* outside the **for** loop. §1311 A

X5 Change **if** = to **if** ≠ as loop exit condition. §1315, 1316 B

• *The `TRIP` test should preload more fonts.*

X6 Insert **begin** ... **end** around statistics output. §1334 L

X7 Must *get_x_token* when scanning a number. §445 F

X8 Interactive *debug_help* needs to print a newline. §1338 I

X9 Include *ignore_spaces* and *math_accent* in *print_cmd_char* cases. §266 F

X10 Don't call *confusion* when *print_cmd_char* sees unknown code. §298 I

• *Compiler bug causes stack overflow. Retiring for the night at 2145.*

16 Jul 1982

• *Starting at 0700; DRF has fixed the compiler.*

X11 Allow arbitrary integer parameters in diagnostic print routines. §237, 699 R

X12 Say *cur_tok*, not *cur_val*, when you mean *cur_tok*. §440 T

X13 Make **\pause** effective also on first line of a file. §538 F

X14 Show context after online deletion. §88 F

X15 Bypass reference count when *debug_help* shows a token list. §1339 I

X16 Change '**case** p' to '**case** $type(p)$'. §1000 B

X17 Fix timing of *print_ln* when scrolling help messages. §90 F

X18 Make *other_char* the default category for ASCII control codes too. §232 P

X19 Use special scanning method for font number in *new_font*. §1257 A

• *Eating lunch, 1020–1035, while the machine slowly recompiles everything.*

X20 Don't forget to increase k in the **while** loop. §355 F

X21 Adjust *limit* properly after line changed when pausing. §363 D

X22 Remember to return a value in *new_spec* and *new_penalty*. §151, 158 F

• *Now stepping through line_break in simple case.*

X23 Don't prune unwanted nodes if $cur\_p = null$. §877 A

X24 Print a closing parenthesis when displaying glue nodes. §189 F

X25 Use *last*, not *limit*, in *term_input*; else error prompt causes trouble when $state = token\_list$. §71, 87 S

X26 Set $first \leftarrow limit + 1$ after *init_terminal*. §331 D

X27 Make sure *set_trick_count* is always performed. §317 D

17 Jul 1982

X28 Add new diagnostic feature `\tracingcommands`. §299, 1031 I
- *Debugging of system-dependent code not shown in this log.*
- *Tangling TEX now takes 1.75 minutes; about 75K bytes, 108K tokens.*
- *Redundant semicolon sends Pascal compiler into infinite loop!*

X29 Initialize *passive* ← *null*. §864 F
X30 Fix pseudoprinting when the line is empty. §318 A
X31 Merge adjacent free areas of dynamic memory before dumping. §131 E
X32 Print the word `mode` in *print_mode*. §211 F
X33 Improve message and help in case of weird error. §415 I
X34 Allow optional space after `\def` and similar constructions. §473 G
X35 Declare *alpha* to be integer in *read_font_info*. §560 M
X36 Fix timing of *back_input* in *scan_dimen*. §448 A
X37 Back up after missing number error. §446 I
X38 Show the '`at`' size that is considered improper. §1259 I
X39 Streamline the dialog in *debug_help*. §1338 I
X40 Take output of *the_toks* from the advertised place. §467, 1297 M
X41 Say *trie_fix*(q), not *trie_fix*(p). §959 T
X42 Decrease low limit of *error_count* to -1. §76 S

18 Jul 1982

X43 Clear initial reference count of macro definitions. §473 F
X44 Fix timing of *back_input* in *scan_glue*. §461 A
X45 Use *cur_val_level*, not *cur_val*, when checking levels. §461 B
X46 Multiply `fil` units by 2^{16} for correct scaling. §454 B
X47 Don't confuse *glue_base* with *skip_base*. §1237 B
X48 Fix *print_scaled* so that 0.01 doesn't come out `0.1`. §103 A
X28 ↦ **X49** Show mode changes when tracing commands. §299 I
X50 Don't say **if** $(n = 0) \lor (\ldots$ **div** $n)$ in Pascal. §105 L
X51 Don't confuse *box_flag* with *box_code*. §1075 B
X52 Reset *offset* on *print_ln* even in *no_print* mode. §57 S
X53 Fix restarting of interrupts after *big_switch*. §1031 S
X54 Don't loop **for** $k \leftarrow a$ **to** $b - 1$ when $b = 0$ if k is declared nonnegative. L
X55 Put '`=`' sign into the *format_ident*. §1328 I
X56 Allow r to be any integer in *get_node*. §125 S
X57 Don't put the output of *print_file_name* in quotes. §518 I
X58 Say '`dumped`' after dumping. §1311 I
X59 Eliminate unnecessary initialization code. §1332 E
X60 Get the file reading started right when beginning to undump. §1308 L
X61 Give forlorn message if format file can't be loaded. §1303 I
X62 Assign value to *cur_val* after glue arithmetic. §1239, 1240 F

19 Jul 1982

X63 Don't say **if** $p > max \lor free[p]$ in Pascal. §169 L
X64 Fix memory-undump logic; loops are out of phase with input. §1312 A
X65 Undump *hyph_word*[j], not *hyph_word*[k]. §1325 B
- *At last* `trip.fmt` *loads without bombing out.*

X66 Remove assignment of array to array, not allowed by IBM Pascal (Susan Plass). §167 P
X67 Simplify an expression that's too big for IBM Pascal (Susan Plass). §1009 P
X68 Go to *contribute*, not *done*, after insertions. §1000 A
X69 Decrease *depth_threshold* if there's not enough string space. §198 I
X70 Show rules as '`|`' in short displays. §175 I
X71 Don't show null glue in short displays. §175 I
X72 Set *job_name* ← 0 as part of output initialization. §528 S
X73 Don't complain of infinite shrinkage on `0pt minus 0fil`. §825, 976, 1009 S
X74 Use different prompt at beginning when accepting a file name. §37 I
X75 Reset *last_glue* on nonglue nodes. §996 F
X76 Remember to call *error* after printing `OK`. §1293 B
X77 Insert **begin** ... **end** around program text of section. §1025 L
X78 Define the `\shipout` primitive. §1071, 1073 F

X79 Introduce *write_loc* analogous to *par_loc*. §1344, 1371 A

X80 Dump and undump *par_loc* and *write_loc*. §1313, 1314 F

X81 Allow *the* in *scan_the* [later *scan_something_internal*]. §413 F

X82 Interchange command codes *the* :=: *number* [later *convert*]. §210 E

X83 Don't confuse *breadth* with *depth*. §236 B

X84 Add string printing feature to *debug_help*. §1339 I

X85 Set *state* ← *mid_line* in *begin_file_reading*. §328 F

• *Time out 2105–2200 to pick up Jenny from driving lesson.*

X86 Keep $c \le 127$ when deleting 99 tokens. §88 L

X87 Don't check for *str_room* error when *selector* = *new_string*. §1328 S

21 Jul 1982

X88 Gather more statistics: String usage, font info, hyphen exceptions, stacks. §1334 I

X79 ↦ **X89** Initialize *write_loc* from *cur_val*, not from *cs_ptr*. §1344 D

X90 Remember to pack file name for `\open`. §1374 F

X34 ↦ **X91** Defuse `\outer` test before scanning optional space after '`}`'. §473 S

X92 Don't allow *prepare_mag* to cause errors after *jump_out*. §84 S

• *The first page of* `DVI` *output is perfect! Pause to play piano.*

X93 Don't confuse *dimen_base* with *scaled_base*. §1237 B

X94 Initialize *link*(*page_head*) ← *null* when beginning a page. §991 D

X95 Correct *cur_height* more often, since *max_depth* might be negative. §972, 973 S

X96 Calculate page dimensions properly after vertical kerns. §973 A

X97 Install new *page_contents* logic to handle interaction between insertions and `\topskip`. §987, 1008 S

X98 Allow *top_skip* glue to be a valid breakpoint. §1001 S

X99 Don't forget to count *dyn_used* in inner loop [erroneous analysis retracted later]. §1034 F

X100 Set $p \leftarrow q$ after migration step. §655 F

X101 Clear *prev_graf* to zero at start of paragraph. §1091 F

X102 Put parens into negated *leader_flag* macro. §1078 L

• *Time out 1720–1920 for John's birthday dinner.*

X103 Scale *best_height* when adjusting *page_goal*. §1010 D

X104 Simplify logic of split insertions; three states become two. §981, 1019, 1020 A

X105 Don't omit first character when showing a macro argument. §400 M

X106 Prevent clobberage if macros have too many parameters. §390 R

22 Jul 1982

X107 Tell how many `DVI` bytes were output. §642 I

X88 ↦ **X108** Adjust for singular or plural statistics. §1320, 1334 I

X98 ↦ **X109** Consider *page_head* a glue node, to inhibit unwanted break. §988 S

X110 Introduce *new_skip_param* to keep reference counts updated. §679, 969, 1001 D

X111 Record the correct size of new insertion after it's split. §1010 D

X112 Use *free_node*, not *flush_node_list*, when recycling insertion nodes. §1022 D

X113 Make online insertions work after *get_next* is interrupted. §87, 324, 343 S

X114 Print newline on interruption stop. §98 B

X34 ↦ **X115** Put space before *end_write_token*. §1371 S

X116 Don't confuse *glue_order* with *stretch_order*. §838 B

X117 Set *max_dimen* ← *'7777777777*, not *'777777777*. §421 T

X118 Make `\global\textfont` legal. §1211 M

X119 Fetch `\the\textfont` with *equiv*, not *fam_font*. §415 B

X120 Call *new_ligature*$(f, l, \ldots)$ not $(f, c, \ldots)$. §1035 B

X121 Make *show_box* work on random garbage. §174, 177 R

X122 Count reference to *zero_glue* from *cond_math_glue*. §1171 D

23 Jul 1982

X123 Allow *avail* = *null* when undumping. §1312 R

X110 ↦ **X124** Set *width*(*glue_ptr*(*p*)), not *width*(*p*). §679 B

X125 Put *begin_file_reading* inside the *start_input* loop. §537 A

X116 ↦ **X126** Don't confuse *glue_stretch* with *stretch_order* [the previous fix went only half-way]. §838 B

X127 Negate x when calculating badness of shrinkage. §667, 678 B

X121 $\mapsto$ **X128** Remove dangling **else** that parses wrong. §174 L

X28 $\mapsto$ **X129** Print newline before `{`, not after `}`, when tracing commands. §299 I

X130 Remove colon from overfull box messages. §663, 675 I

X97 $\mapsto$ **X131** Compute *page_goal* properly when the first box arrives after inserts. §1001 D

X132 Don't confuse *page_size* [now *page_goal*] with *best_size*. §1017 B

X133 Put heldover insertions at front of contribution list. §1023 A

X88 $\mapsto$ **X134** Output stats before closing `DVI` file, since the latter decreases *font_ptr*. §1333 S

X135 Don't call a `\vbox` an `\hbox`. §674 T

X136 Fix misplaced **end** caused by editing error. §675 T

24 Jul 1982

X137 Don't *eq_destroy* any paragraph shape when *par_shape* is null. §275 D

X138 Omit blank before `\message` at the beginning of a line. §1280 I

X104 $\mapsto$ **X139** Don't try to split an insertion when *best_node* isn't the split one. §1021 A

X140 Correct another case of '**if** $x \wedge y$' misunderstood by Pascal. §1021 L

X141 Provide diagnostic info about insertions via `\showlists`. §986 I

X142 Add '`inside a group`' to clarify a warning message. §1335 I

X143 Report *prev_depth* on a separate line in `\showlists`. §219 I

X144 Back up input to avoid unexpected clobberage of *cur_tok*. §1090 S

- *Wow what a bug: new_graf calls build_page, which invokes the output routine, after which '**goto** reswitch' is a disaster.*

X145 Add insertion glue to *page_so_far* instead of subtracting it from the goal. §1009 D

X146 Put extra blank line before overfull box warning. §660 I

X147 Define break at kern consistently between horizontal and vertical lists. §973, 1000 C

X148 Renumber so that math nodes are nondiscardable. §147 D

X149 Correct the *char_kern* macro: `#`, not f. §557 T

X150 Decrease l after reconstituting discretionary break. §916 F

X151 Simplify the hyphen routine, knowing that $link(s) = null$. §918 E

X152 Initialize $r \leftarrow q$ in discretionary destruction routine. §883 F

25 Jul 1982

X153 Don't add interline penalty after last line of paragraph. §890 A

X154 Adjust spacing in diagnostic messages. §245 I

X155 Avoid simultaneous use of *temp_head* by *prune_page_top* and the page builder. §1017 D

X156 Clear the *post_break* field of simple discretionaries. §916 F

X157 Split *offset* into independent variables *term_offset*, *file_offset*. §54, 57, 58 A

- *Am freezing current program as version −0.25; a week of TUG lectures begins tomorrow.*

5 Aug 1982

X158 The '`.err`' file should be '`.log`' instead. §534 I

X159 Allow `\special` strings to contain more than 256 bytes. §585, 1368 G

X99 $\mapsto$ **X160** Undo "correction" to a non-bug. §1034 M

X161 Suggest `\&` in help message for unexpected `&`. §1128 I

X162 Make '`E`' a standard option for exiting. §84 G

X163 Restore the use of dead cycles à la TEX78. §1024, 1054 G

- *The previous six changes were suggested during discussions with TEX82 class.*

X164 Fix global variable conflict between *open_log_file* and *new_font*. §1257 S

X165 Allow optional '`=`' when assign to font parameter. §1253 C

X166 Set *cur_val* after increasing the number of font parameters. §580 F

X167 Set *hash_brace* when matching '`{`'. §476 D

X88 $\mapsto$ **X168** Clarify meaning of statistics printed. §1334 I

X169 Change `DVI` format to include design size. §602, 1260 G

X170 Introduce *def_ref* for *runaway* messages. §306 D

X171 Restore *cur_cs* before calling *scan_toks*. §1226 M

X157 $\mapsto$ **X172** Update *print_nl* to dual offset conventions. §62 A

X163 $\mapsto$ **X173** Move endgame logic inside *main_control*, because the output routine becomes active. §1054 A

6 Aug 1982

X174 Allow `INITEX` to load format files. §1337 C

X175 Conserve input stack space by deleting finished token lists. §325 E

X74 ↦ **X176** Print the opening '`**`' in the transcript file. §534 I

• *Now ready to try breaking new ground in* `TRIP`.

X177 Preserve *align_state* from tokens deleted online. §88 S

X178 Set t in all branches of *scan_toks*. §473 D

X179 Change '*cur_cmd* $\le$ *right_brace*' to '*cur_tok* $\le$ *right_brace_limit*'; otherwise `\relax` gets through. §477 S

X180 Allow optional `=` when setting `\spacefactor`; disallow zero. §1243 C

X181 Change *vpackage*(*head*) to *vpackage*(*link*(*head*)). §796 B

• *Shades of 1978!*

X182 Insert missing **begin** ... **end**. §798 L

7 Aug 1982

X183 Keep *trie_max* declared in non-`INITEX` [later rescinded]. §950 L

X184 Watch out for empty token list when copying. §466 D

X185 Free unused reference count slot when defining `\everypar`. §1226 D

X163 ↦ **X186** Introduce `\maxdeadcycles`. §1012 G

• *I believe the line_break routine has passed its test perfectly.*

X187 Don't put discretionary after `-` inside a discretionary. §1039 S

X188 Change '`\minus`' to '`\minusthe`' [this feature retracted later]. §413 C

X189 Change *cur_p* to r (three places). §875 B

X190 Increase range of *hc* to *halfword*; otherwise end-of-word mark might match a vacant entry in the trie. §892 A

X191 Initialize b in *shift_case* routine. §1288 F

X192 Don't back up if a space follows a decimal fraction. §452 E

X193 Don't confuse *glue_base* with *dimen_base*. §1145 B

X194 Guard against anomalous floating-point values in glue display. §186 L

8 Aug 1982

X195 Avoid infinite loop when `\outer` leads to runaways. §339 S

• *I worked on that problem about two hours before fixing it.*

X196 Move final *debug_help* to *succumb*, except in batch mode. §93 I

X197 Insert kern after spanned box, to defeat access to floating point. §808 R

9 Aug 1982

X198 Include `\leftskip` and `\rightskip` in displayed equations [rescinded later]. §1199 C

X199 Trace line-break computations if *tracing_stats* > 2. §846, 856 I

X200 Keep *prev_p* up to date when passing a string. §867 D

• *Now stepping through math stuff; a lot is working.*

X201 Set *link*(p) $\leftarrow z$ when making a fraction. §747 D

X202 Don't reset space factor when beginning `\valign`. §775 C

X203 Don't show glue setting if *glue_sign* $=$ *normal*. §186 I

X204 Clear *glue_stretch* and *glue_shrink* when creating an unset box. §801 D

X205 Do *vpack* in hmode and vice versa when aligning. §804 B

X206 Remove fallacious call to *confusion* after alignment in display. §1206 A

X207 Don't test *mode* $=$ *vmode* in display, test *nest_ptr* $= 1$. §1145 A

X208 Show an *inner_noad* as well as the other types. §690, 696 F

X209 Renumber *mu_glue* and *cond_math_glue* so that the glue display logic works. §149 D

X210 Don't confuse *cur_size* with *cur_style*. §703 B

X211 Advance $p \leftarrow q$ during second pass over mlist. §761 F

X212 Add helpful hint about `\tracingonline=1`. §1293 I

X213 Delete spurious statement left from sloppy editing. §710 T

X214 Change the subtype when *mskip* becomes *hskip*. §732 D

X215 Don't forget to use the remainder when computing math glue. §716 F

X199 ↦ **X216** Improve paragraph diagnostics using *short_display*. §857 I

X199 ↦ **X217** Introduce *artificial_badness* for better diagnostics. §854, 856 I

11 Aug 1982

X218 Introduce *char_box* subroutine so that *var_delimiter* adds italic correction. §709 A

X219 Save font and char in local variables of *make_math_accent*, since it can be recursive. §738 S

X220 Call *error* after decrying an invalid character. §346 F

12 Aug 1982

X199 ↦ **X221** Install new format for showing break nodes. §846 I

• *I have been testing line_break and I think it's working fine.*

X222 Change q to p, in order to catch empty alignments. §812, 1206 B

X223 Disallow third part of discretionary in math mode. §1120 S

X224 Don't change *tail* if discretionary third part is empty. §1120 D

X225 Say `nonscript`, not `non_script`. §189 I

X226 Inhibit math if `\scriptfont3` is improper. §1195 S

X199 ↦ **X227** Introduce `@firstpass` and `@secondpass` comments. §863 I

X228 Change p to r when you mean r. §1204 T

X108 ↦ **X229** Say `page`, not `pages`, if there's only `1`. §642 I

X230 Insert space before `[]` on truncated `\showlists`. §182 I

28 Aug 1982

• *Back from vacation after having looked at hardcopy listing of* `TRIP` *test.*

X231 Allow `dm` as a unit [later `.5dm1` will be `.5\dimen1`]. §455 G

X108 ↦ **X232** Singularize `prevgraf 1 lines`. §219 I

X233 Omit trailing zero count registers when showing completed page numbers. §638 I

X234 Avoid clobbering a by introducing a new local variable t. §986 L

X216 ↦ **X235** Fix diagnostic printing of discretionaries. §858 D

X236 Don't show unset stretch/shrink that's zero. §185 I

X198 ↦ **X237** Make `\halign` in displays consistent with other displays. (Namely, ignore `\leftskip` and `\rightskip` in nonaligned displays; respect the paragraph shape in aligned displays.) §800, 1199 C

X238 Parenthesize '`If you're confused ...`'. §403 I

X239 Say '`\fraction`', not '`\xabovex`'. §697 I

X240 Remember to **return** when you should. §1153 F

X241 Use absolute value to make sure **div** is unambiguous. §737 P

X218 ↦ **X242** Don't confuse depth with height. §709 B

X243 Use $delta - height$, not $height - delta$. §736 B

X244 Increase *shift_down* to increase the clearance. §745 B

X245 Don't back up after improper use of `\the`. §428 I

X246 Don't give `0pt` as the default result when looking for *tok_val*. §428 I

X247 Initialize *second_indent* in the easy case. §848 F

X248 Package the equation number. §1204 F

X249 Don't resort to $v \leftarrow max\_dimen$ when glue doesn't stretch or shrink. §1148 Q

X250 Insert newline before showing current `\botmark`. I

X251 Call *error* after giving error message. §784 F

X252 Change implementation of `\number`; it should *scan_int*, not something internal. §471 A

X253 Introduce symbolic constants like *format_area_length*. §524 P

X254 Change *quit* to *jump_out*, since some compilers treat *quit* as a reserved word. §81 P

X255 Add more parentheses to get proper parsing. §1260 L

X256 Say `please` in order to be friendly (or at least polite). §360 I

X257 Don't confuse *cur_vcmd* with *cur_chr*. §508 B

X258 Use `&` instead of `!` to specify a preloaded format. §1337 I

X177 ↦ **X259** Correct `s3` to `s4`. §88 T

X260 Introduce new primitive `\mathchardef`, to save space and time. §1224 G

X261 Use the `[]` convention for noads as well as nodes. §692 C

X262 Correct spelling in call to *primitive*: `\xatopx` should be `\xoverx` [later renamed, thank goodness]. §1178 T

30 Aug 1982

X263 Don't fetch *link*(*null*) in malformed list. §175 R

X264 Initialize *align_state* at a better time so that *align_peek* doesn't see `&` or `\span`. §785, 791 S

X265 Outlaw preamble interfering with *align_state* $= 0$. §789 S

X266 Add level of grouping to alignment to tabskip locality. §774 C

X267 Check *align_state* when scanning $\langle u_j \rangle$. §783 F

X268 Move '*unsave*; *new_save_level*' from *main_control* into *fin_col*. §791, 1131 A

X180 ↦ **X269** Remember *cur_chr* when you're looking for optional '`=`'. §1243 S

X270 Change q to r [in code now obsolete]. §804 T

X271 Disable interrupts during *back_error* so that help messages aren't clobbered. §327 I

X272 Introduce *slow_print* for printing control sequences. §60 S

X273 Initialize *del_code*("`.`") ← 0 for error recovery. §240 I

X274 Call *end_file_reading* before calling *check_outer_validity*. §362 S

X275 Don't delete an extra '`}`' when `\par` will help find a runaway. §395 I

31 Aug 1982

X276 Don't confuse *thin_muskip* with *thin_muskip_code*. §413 B

X266 ↦ **X277** Recover from error if new *align_group* ends abnormally. §1132 F

X278 Recover from error if `\par` occurs when *align_state* < 0. §1094 I

X279 Make `\hskip\the\thinmuskip` and `\mskip\the\baselineskip` erroneous. §413 C

X280 Add `\muskip` and `\setmuskip` analogs to `skip` and `\setskip`. §413, 1228 G

X281 Don't output `pop` right after `push`. §601 E

- *The `TRIP` test looks right; now to test for wasted memory.*
- *When memory should be empty I find dyn_used* $= 18$, *var_used* $= 267$.

1 Sep 1982

- *Made special `MEMTEX` program, designed to track all memory allocation.*

X282 Delete reference to *last_glue* when a page is packaged. §1017 D

X283 Include *save_stack* in the *search_mem* debugging routine. §285 I

X284 Disallow `\vfill` in restricted horizontal mode. §1095 C

- *Most of the memory locations I thought were wasted were actually in good use.*
- *Total 192 hours (approx) debugging time so far since July 15.*

2 Sep 1982

- *Now looking at all zero counts in profile and extending `TRIP`.*

X285 Simplify the creation of `vtop` boxes. §1087 E

X286 Set *space_factor* ← 1000 after `\hbox`. §1076 C

X287 Introduce preamble into `DVI` format. §617 P

X288 Give special *chr_code* to `\relax`. §265 S

X289 Don't show '`(null)`' when token list is null, just show nothing. §295 I

X290 Delete the procedure *write_name_string*, which is never used. E

X291 Rename `\xabovex` to `\abovewithdelims`; do the same for `\xatopx` and `\xoverx`. §1178 C

X292 Improve *clean_box* so that it recognizes cleanliness better. §720 Q

X293 Report a `Missing delimiter` more meaningfully. §1161 I

X294 Give *endv_token* a *chr* code of 128 so that it will end a file name. §289 R

X295 Test present of math fonts *after* parsing an mlist, not before. §1138, 1195 R

X296 Omit '`recent contributions`' and/or '`current page`' when they are empty. §218, 986 I

X297 Display what TeX has deleted after improper discretionary list has arisen. §1121 I

X298 Show what math character was undefined. §723 I

X299 Improve the `Incompatible magnification` error; break it into two lines. §288 I

X300 Put new cases into *flush_node_list*, to recycle mlist noads. §698 D

6 Sep 1982

X300 ↦ **X301** Insert a necessary '**goto** *done*' in that new material. §698 F

- *It took two hours to diagnose that* **goto** *problem.*

X295 ↦ **X302** Change '2' to '3' in help message for extension fonts. §1195 T

X303 Add a special note if material is being held over for the next output. §986 I

X304 Divide before multiplying in *make_left_right*, to avoid overflow. §762 R

X305 Introduce the *box_error* routine. §992 I

X306 Clear *arith_error* after overflow has been reported. §460 F

X249 ↦ **X307** Don't confuse *stretch* with *glue_stretch*. §1148 B

X308 Set *glue_sign* ← *normal* when packaging with glue ratio zero. §558, 664 D

X309 Test for overflow before attaching the sign. §448 A

- *That all worked! Now trying* **min_quarterword** *negative.*

X310 Take absolute value before applying **mod** in *new_trie_op*. §944 L
X311 Say *qi*(*c*), not *c*, when testing **TFM** flags [now obsolete]. §573 L
X312 Initialize *token_ref_count*(*def_ref*) to *null*, not zero. §473 L
X313 Change the type of *vsplit* parameter *n* from *quarterword* to *eight_bits*. §977 L
X314 Initialize *null-delimiter* different form *null_character*. §685 L
X315 Insert *qi* twice in *scan_delimiter*. §1160 L
X316 Insert *qi* in *scan_math*. §1151 F
X317 Insert *qo* in *fetch*. §722, 723 F
X318 Insert *qi* in *set_math_char*. §1155 F
X319 Insert *qi* in *math_ac*. §1165 F
X320 Insert *qo* in *mlist_to_hlist*. §755 F
X321 Use brackets around 8-bit characters in *print_ASCII*. §68 I
X322 Include *hyph_list* in the *search_mem* debugging routine. §933 I

- *Now compiling non-***INITEX** *to try an industrial-strength version.*

X323 Add **return** to *final_cleanup*, because some Pascal compilers insist that each label be used. §1335 L
X324 Compute *par_token* when undumping. §1314 D

11 Sep 1982

X325 Emit newline before file name, if near end of line. §537 I
X326 Define `\ifx` for arbitrary tokens. §507 C

12 Sep 1982

X327 Don't ask users to type `x` twice before exiting. §84 I
X328 Install new features `\openin`, `\read`, `\ifeof`, `\closein`; rename existing `\open`, `\send`, `\close` to be `\openout`, `\write`, `\closeout`. §209, 313, 1275 G
X329 Install new feature `\expandafter`. §368 G
X330 Change the default file area from '`<TeX>`' to '`TeXinputs:`'. §574 P

13 Sep 1982

X331 Install new feature `\string`. §472 G
X332 Remove spurious space printed by `sprint_cs`. §263 A

- *All tests passed now! But when I played with the system I found another bug (undetected by* **TRIP***):*

X333 Set $r \leftarrow s$ after matching macro parameter tokens. §397 F

16 Sep 1982

X199 ↦ **X334** Introduce serial numbers in line-break records, improving readability and independence. §846 I
X335 Don't abort when *file_name_size* is exceeded. §519 I

17 Sep 1982

X336 Remove unwanted period from font capacity message. §567 I

18 Sep 1982

X329 ↦ **X337** Make `\expandafter` more powerful by moving it from semantics to syntax [i.e., from stomach to mouth]. §368 G

19 Sep 1982

X338 Improve error recovery for '`Missing number`'. §415 I

22 Sep 1982

X339 Suppress italic correction between letters in math mode except in math fonts. §752 Q

24 Sep 1982

X340 Define *null* = *mem_bot*, not *min_halfword*, because there's a reference to *link*(*null*) in *try_break*. §115 P
X341 Initialize *str_start*[0] ← 0. §47 D
X342 Avoid blank space at beginning of line. §638 I
X343 Set type of new box in math mode to *ord_noad*, not *inner_noad*. §1076 D

28 Sep 1982

- *Here are the first changes made to the preliminary listing of TeX82 that was published by the TeX project earlier this month.*

520 Insert the missing cases *letter* and *other_char* after *x_token* looks ahead. §1038 F

521 Change '`\pause`' to '`\pausing`'. §236 C

522 Reset *overfull_rule* when determining tabskip glue. §804 D

523 Fix the logic for scanning `\ifcase` [in obsolete syntax—everything is still done with braces since '`\fi`' doesn't exist yet]. §509 A

30 Sep 1982

524 Change "`0.0`" to "`?.?`" (suggested by DRF). §186 I

2 Oct 1982

525 Use conditional thin spacing next to 'Inner' noads. §764 Q

526 Make thick spaces conditional. §766 Q

4 Oct 1982

527 Increase *trie_size* from 7000 to 8000, because of Frank Liang's improved (but longer) hyphenation patterns. §11 P

6 Oct 1982

X330 ↦ **528** Change the string lengths to match the new *TeX_format_default*. §520 F

- *Version 0 of TeX is being released today!*

8 Oct 1982

529 Fix a blunder: I decreased h mod a quarterword when it should have been decreased mod *trie_op_hash_size* (HWT). §944 B

9 Oct 1982

X258 ↦ **530** Fix a typo ('`!`' not '`&`') in the `WEB` documentation. §524 P

531 Remember to call *initialize* if a different format was preloaded (Max Díaz). §1337 F

- *Version 0.1 incorporates the above changes.*

12 Oct 1982

532 Add the '`\immediate`' feature, by popular request. §1375 G

- *Version 0.2 incorporates this (somewhat extensive) change.*

13 Oct 1982

533 Introduce new `WEB` macros so that *glue_ratio* is more easily changed. §109 P

- *I began writing The TeXbook today: edited the old preface and searched in the library for quotations.*

14 Oct 1982

534 Change the type of *hd* to *eight_bits*; it's not a *quarterword* (HWT). §649 B

X281 ↦ **535** Revise the optimization of `DVI` commands: It's not always safe to eliminate *pop* when the preceding byte is *push*, since `DVI` commands have variable length! (Embarrassing oversight caught by DRF.) §601 S

15 Oct 1982

536 Test '$prev\_depth > ignore\_depth$', not '$\neq$'. §679 C

- *Version 0.3 incorporates the above changes.*

16 Oct 1982

537 Omit definition of *align_size*; it's never used (Bill Scherlis). §11 P

538 Inhibit error messages when packaging box 255. §1017 I

21 Oct 1982

X145 ↦ **539** Subtract $width(q)$ from *page_goal*, don't add it to *page_so_far*[1]. §1009 A

- *Version 0.4 incorporates the above changes.*

22 Oct 1982

540 Increase the amount of lower (variable-size) memory from 12000 to 13000, since the TeX program listing now needs about 11500. [At this time there still is a fixed boundary between upper and lower memory.] §12 P

541 Add a new parameter `\boxmaxdepth`. §1086 G

- *Version 0.5 incorporates the above changes.*

26 Oct 1982

542 Fix an off-by-one error caught by Gabi Kuper and HWT. (I forgot '$+1$'). §1317 B

543 Fix the spacing of displayed control sequences: *print_cs* should base its decision on *cat_code*$(p - \mathit{single\_base})$, not *cat_code*$(p)$. §262 B

- *The `TRIP` test detected this bug, but I didn't notice.*

27 Oct 1982

544 Set *math_type* before saying *fetch*(*nucleus*(q)), since fetching can have a side effect. §752 S

28 Oct 1982

545 Install a major change: Fonts now have identifiers instead of code letters. Eliminate the '`\:`' primitive, and give corresponding new features to '`\the`'. §209 G

- *Actually I began making these changes on October 26, but I needed two days to debug them and to put Humpty Dumpty together again.*
- *At this time I'm also drafting macros for typesetting The TeXbook.*
- *The above changes have been incorporated into Version 0.6.*

30 Oct 1982

- *After years of searching, I've finally found a definitive definition of the printer's point; and (unfortunately) my previous conjecture was wrong. The truth is that* 83 pc = 35 cm, *exactly; so I am changing TeX to conform.*

546 Revise unit definitions for the 'real' printer's point. §458, 617 C

- *Version 0.7 incorporates the above.*

1 Nov 1982

- *Oops! Retract error #546, and retract TeX Version 0.7; the source of my information about points was flaky after all. My original suppositions were correct, as confirmed by NBS Circular 570.*

4 Nov 1982

547 Revise the definition of `dd`, conforming to the definitive value shown me by Chuck Bigelow. §458 C

545 ↦ **548** Introduce "frozen" copies of font identifiers, to be returned by `\the\font`, so that font manipulation is more robust. §1257 R

5 Nov 1982

549 Reset *looseness* and paragraph shape when beginning a `\vbox`. §1083 D

6 Nov 1982

550 De-update *align_state* when braces are in constants. §442 D

X294 ↦ **551** Improve error recovery for bad alignments. §1127 I

- *Today I wrapped up Chapters 4 and 5.*

8 Nov 1982

552 Give more power to `\let`: the right-hand side needn't be a control sequence. §1221 G

553 Amend *show_context* to say '(*base_ptr* = *input_ptr*) ∨ '; otherwise undefined control sequences can be invisible in unusual cases (John Hobby). §312 I

554 Compute demerits more suitably by adding a penalty squared, instead of adding penalties before squaring. §859 A

- *Previously a slightly loose hyphenated line followed by a decent line was considered worse than a decent hyphenated line followed by a quite loose line.*

10 Nov 1982

555 Save a bit of buffer space by declaring *pool_file* only in `INITEX`. §50 E

11 Nov 1982

556 Introduce a new context indicator to clarify TeX's scanning state: A special type called *backed_up* is distinguished from other kinds of *inserted* lists; it is called 'recently read' or 'to be read again', while others are called 'inserted'. §314 I

557 Append a comment, '`treated as zero`', to the missing-number message. §446 I

558 Ignore the settings of `\hfuzz` or `\vfuzz` if `\hbadness` or `\vbadness` is less than 100. §666, 677 I

13 Nov 1982

- *Major surgery on the program is planned for today, because of new ideas suggested by correspondence with MDS and other macro writers.*

559 Introduce a new `\tokens` register; this will be useful and easy to add, since TEX already can handle `\everypar` and `\output`. §1227 G

X34 ↦ **560** Change *get_x_token* to *get_token* when scanning an optional space; then a construction like `\def\foo{...}\foo` won't complain that `\foo` is undefined. §443 C

- *This change was retracted when it was being debugged, because it could cause endv to abort the job. Then it was re-established again when I found that endv needed to be more robust anyway. [But it was eventually rescinded again.]*

561 Make `\span` mean 'expand' in a preamble. §782 G

562 Use three separate **if** tests instead of '∧' in the inner loop of *get_next*, to gain efficiency. §342 E

563 Introduce *get_r_token* so that assignments have uniform error messages and so that frozen equivalents cannot be changed. §1215 R

- *I gave a few variables more mnemonic names as I made these changes.*

564 Move conditional statements from the semantics ('stomach') part of TEX to the syntax ('mouth') part, by introducing '`\fi`'. Also introduce `\csname` and `\endcsname`. §372, 489–500 C

- *This makes macros much more predictable and logical, but it is by far the most drastic change ever made to TEX. The program began to come back to life only after three days of solid hacking.*
- *Several other things were cleaned up as part of this change because it is now more natural to handle them differently. For example, a null control sequence has now become more logical.*
- *The result of all this is called Version 0.8.*

18 Nov 1982

- *Today I resumed writing Chapter 8. Tomorrow I'm 2^{14} days old!*

21 Nov 1982

565 Declare *c* as a local variable for hyphenation (DRF). §912 F

566 Omit the "first pass" and try hyphenations immediately, if `\pretolerance` is negative (suggested by DRF). §863 E

567 Don't ship out incredibly huge pages; they might foul up `DVI` files. §641 R

2 Dec 1982

568 Add new features `\everymath` and `\everydisplay`. §1139, 1145 G

569 Add a new feature `\futurelet`. §1221 G

- *The changes above have been incorporated into Version 0.9 of TeX.*

7 Dec 1982

570 Add a new `\endinput` primitive (suggested by FY). §362, 378 G

8 Dec 1982

571 Try *off_save*, if `\par` occurs in restricted horizontal mode. (This avoids embarrassment if TEX says 'type a command or say `\end`', then when you type `\end` it says you can't!) [However, I soon retracted this change.] §1094 I

21 Dec 1982

572 Redefine `\relax` so that its *chr* field exceeds 127. (This facilitates the test for end in *scan_file_name*.) §265 A

566 ↦ **573** Call *begin_diagnostic* when omitting the first pass of line breaking. §863 F

574 Fix the logic of glue scanning: In `\hskip-1pt plus2pt` the minus should apply only to the `1pt`. §461 A

23 Dec 1982

575 Renumber the decimal codes in paragraph statistics for loose and tight lines; they were ordered backwards. §817 I

576 Treat a paragraph that ends with leaders like a paragraph that ends with glue. §816 C

577 Allow commas as alternates to radix points, for Europeans. §438 C

578 Change \hangindent to a normal dimension parameter. [It had been a combination of \hangindent and \hangafter, with special syntax.] §247 C

579 Make \prevgraf accessible to users. §422, 1244 G

580 Split \clubpenalty off from \widowpenalty. §890 G

• *I'm typing Chapter 14 while making these changes.*

24 Dec 1982

581 Use *back_input* instead of **goto** *reswitch* when inserting \par, because \par may have changed. §1095 S

25 Dec 1982

• *It's 10pm after a very Merry Christmas!*

X328 ↦ **582** Don't prompt for a new file name if \openin doesn't find a file. §1275 I

583 Add a new \jobname primitive. §472 G

584 Give the user a way to delete the dollar sign, when TeX decides to insert one. §1047 I

585 Allow optional equals after \parshape, and implement \the\parshape. §423, 1248 C

26 Dec 1982

586 Add an *if_line_field* to the condition stack entries, so that more informative error messages can be given. §489 I

549 ↦ **587** Introduce a *normal_paragraph* procedure, since initialization is needed also within \insert, \vadjust, \valign, \output. §1070 D

27 Dec 1982

588 Give users access to \pagetotal and \pagegoal. (Analogous to #679 and #585, but simpler.) §1245 G

X199 ↦ **589** Introduce \tracingpages, allowing users to see page-optimization calculations. Also split \tracingparagraphs off from \tracingstats. §987, 1005, 1011 I

• *The changes above have been incorporated into Version 0.91 of TeX.*

31 Dec 1982

590 Break the *build_page* procedure into two parts, by extracting the section now called *fire_up*. [This is necessary because some Pascal compilers, notably for IBM mainframes, cannot deal with large procedures.] §1012 P

564 ↦ **591** Make \ifodd1\else legal by introducing *if_code*. §489 S

592 Improve alignments when columns don't occur: Don't append null boxes for columns missing before \cr, and zero out the tabskip glue after nonpresent columns. §802 Q

593 Make the error message about overfull alignment more intelligible. §801, 804 I

• *The changes above have been incorporated into Version 0.92 of TeX82, which was the last version of 1982, completed at 11:59pm on December 31.*

3 Jan 1983

• *Today I'm beginning to write Chapter 15, and planning the* \output *routine of* plain.tex.

X186 ↦ **594** Change the logic of *its_all_over*; use *max_dead_cycles* here too, instead of the fixed constant 100. §1054 C

X34 ↦ **595** Don't forget to *pop_nest* when an insert is empty. Also disallow optional space after \insert *n*{...}. §1100 F

4 Jan 1983

541 ↦ **596** Use the \boxmaxdepth that's declared inside a \vbox when packaging it. §1086 C

597 Rename \groupbegin and \groupend as \begingroup and \endgroup. §265 C

594 ↦ **598** Make \deadcycles accessible to users. §1246 G

599 Base the split insertions on natural height plus depth, not on *delta*. §1010 Q

• *The changes above have been incorporated into Version 0.93.*

6 Jan 1983

600 Add *push_math* to handle a case where I forgot to clear *incompleat_noad*. (This long-standing bug was unearthed today by Phyllis Winkler.) §1136 D

588 ↦ **601** Add \pageshrink, etc., too. §1245 G

602 Introduce new parameters \floatingpenalty, \insertpenalties. Also adopt a new internal representation of insertion nodes, so that \floatingpenalty, \splittopskip and \splitmaxdepth can be stored with each insertion. §140, 1008 G

7 Jan 1983

603 Improve the rules for entering *new_line*, in particular when the end-of-line character is active. §343 Q

9 Jan 1983

604 Distinguish between implicit and explicit kerns. §155, 896 Q

605 Change the name `\ignorespace` to `\ignorespaces`. §265 C

560 ↦ **606** Don't omit a blank space after `\def`, `\message`, `\mark`, etc.; the previous hodge-podge of rules is impossible to learn. §473 C

- *The above changes appear in Version 0.94.*

12 Jan 1983

- *Beginning to write the chapters on math today.*

607 Add a new feature: active characters in math mode. §1151 G

15 Jan 1983

608 Fix a surprise bug: '`$1-$`' treated the `-` as binary. §729 A

609 Initialize *space_factor* inside discretionaries. §1117 D

16 Jan 1983

610 Fix an incredibly embarrassing bug: I forgot to update *spotless* in the *error* routine! F

- *While fixing this, I decided to change spotless to a more general history variable, as suggested by IBMers who want a return code.* §76, 82, 1335

611 Replace two calls of *confusion* by attempts at error recovery, in places where '`This can't happen`' could actually happen. §1027, 1372 I

18 Jan 1983

612 Introduce the *normalize_selector* routine to protect against startup anomalies when the transcript file isn't open. Also make *open_log_file* terminate in some cases. §92, 535 R

591 ↦ **613** Insert `\relax`, not a blank space, to cure infinite loop like `\ifeof\fi` (LL). §510 R

614 Change the old `\limitswitch` to `\limits`, `\nolimits`, and `\displaylimits`. Incidentally, this fixes a bug in the former positioning of integral signs. §682, 749 G

615 Give a `\char` in math mode its inherited `\mathcode`. §1151 C

525 ↦ **616** Make underline, overline, radical, vcenter, accent noads and `{...}` all revert to type Ord instead of type Inner. Introduce a new primitive `\mathinner`. (This fixes the spacing, which got worse in some ways after change #525.) §761 Q

- *I'm working on Appendix G today.*

19 Jan 1983

617 Introduce a `\mathchoice` primitive. §1174 G

618 Move `\input` from the stomach to the mouth. §378 C

X260 ↦ **619** Introduce `\chardef`, analogous to `\mathchardef`. §1038, 1224 C

620 Change `\unbox` to `\unhbox` and `\unvbox`; also add `\unhcopy`. §1110 G

621 Consider `\spacefactor`, `\pagetotal`, etc., as part of *prefixed_command*, even though they are always global. §1211 C

20 Jan 1983

622 Switch modes when `\hrule` occurs in horizontal mode or `\vrule` in vertical. §1090, 1094 C

623 Add a new `\globaldefs` feature. §1211 G

21 Jan 1983

624 Optimize the code, in places where it's important (based on frequency counts of TeX usage accumulated during the past week): Introduce *fast_get_avail* and *fast_store_new_token*; reduce procedure-call overhead in *begin_token_list*, *end_token_list*, *back_input*, *flush_node_list*; change some tests from '**if** $a \land b$' to '**if** a **then if** b'. §122, 371 E

22 Jan 1983

625 Save space in math lists: Don't insert penalties within restricted horizontal mode; simplify trivial boxes. §721, 1196 E

626 Fix a surprising oversight in the *rebox* routine: Ensure that b isn't a vbox. §715 S

545 ↦ **627** Make `\nullfont` a primitive, so that *cur_font* always has a value. (This is a dramatic improvement over TeX78, where a missing font was a fatal error called '`Whoa`'!) §552 C

24 Jan 1983

586 ↦ **628** List all incomplete `\if`'s when the job ends. §1335 I

29 Jan 1983

552 ↦ **629** Change initialization of *align_state* so that `\halign\bgroup` works. §777 C

30 Jan 1983

625 ↦ **630** Be sure to test '*is_char_node*(*q*)' when checking for a trivial box. §721 D

- *By extraordinary coincidence, this bug was caught when somebody used font number 11 (= kern_node) in the second character of a list of length 2!*

X168 ↦ **631** Improve format for stats at end of run, as suggested by DRF. §1334 I

- *The changes above have been incorporated into Version 0.95.*

632 Don't ignore the space after a control symbol (except '`\ `'). §354 C

633 Remove all trailing spaces at the right of input lines, so that there's perfect compatibility with IBM systems that extend short lines with spaces. §31 P

3 Feb 1983

634 Assume that a *math_accent* was intended, after giving an error message in the case *mmode* + *accent*. §1165 I

635 Add new primitives `\iftrue` and `\iffalse`. §488 G

6 Feb 1983

X304 ↦ **636** Improve the accuracy of fixed-point arithmetic when calculating sizes for `\left` and `\right`. (I had started by dividing *delimiter_factor*, not *delta1*, by 500.) §762 A

12 Feb 1983

637 Change the name `\delimiterlimit` to `\delimitershortfall`. §248 C

638 Make `\abovewithdelims..` equivalent to `\above`; change the order of operands so that delimiters precede the dimension. §1182 C

607 ↦ **639** Remove the kludgy math codes introduced earlier; make `\fam` a normal integer parameter and allow `\mathcode` to equal 2^{15}. §1233 C

640 Don't let `\spacefactor` become more than 2^{15}. §1233, 1243 R

- *I finished drafting Chapter 17 today.*

14 Feb 1983

639 ↦ **641** Replace octal output (*print_octal*) by hexadecimal (*print_hex*) so that math codes are clearer. §67 I

619 ↦ **642** Don't forget *char_given* in the *math_accent* routine. §1124 F

17 Feb 1983

622 ↦ **643** Switch modes when `\halign` occurs in horizontal mode, or `\valign` in vertical mode. §1090, 1094 C

18 Feb 1983

644 Add a new feature `\tracingrestores`. This requires a new procedure called *show_eqtb*, whose code can be interspersed with the *eqtb* definitions. §252 I

25 Feb 1983

622 ↦ **645** Suggest using `\leaders` when the user tries a horizontal rule in restricted horizontal mode. §1095 I

27 Feb 1983

646 Specify the range of source lines, when giving warning messages for underfull or overfull boxes in alignments. §662, 675 I

- *Why did it take me all day to type the middle part of Chapter 18?*

4 Mar 1983

647 Introduce a new feature `\xcr` (suggested by LL). [Changed later to '`\crcr`'.] §785 G

631 ↦ **648** Subtract out TeX's own string requirements from the stats. §1334 I

6 Mar 1983

649 Add new features `\everyhbox` and `\everyvbox`. §1083, 1167 G

9 Mar 1983

X295 ↦ **650** Avoid accessing *math_quad* when the symbol fonts aren't known to be present. §1199 R

533 ↦ **651** Introduce *float* and *unfloat* macros to aid portability (HWT). §109 P

652 Introduce new names `\abovedisplayskip` and `\belowdisplayskip` for the old `\dispskip`; also `\abovedisplayshortskip` and `\belowdisplayshortskip` for the old `\dispaskip` and `\dispbskip`. §226 C

10 Mar 1983

653 Unbundle `\romannumeral` from `\number` (suggested by FY). §468 C

12 Mar 1983

654 Ignore leading spaces in *scan_keyword*. §407 C

14 Mar 1983

631 ↦ **655** Use *write* and *write_ln* directly when printing stats. §1334 E

16 Mar 1983

602 ↦ **656** Refine the page-break cost function (introducing '*deplorable*', which is not quite '*awful_bad*'), after suggestion by LL. §974, 1005 Q

- *The changes above have been incorporated into Version 0.96.*

18 Mar 1983

657 Add a new feature `\everyjob` suggested by FY. §1030 G

19 Mar 1983

658 Don't treat left braces specially when showing macros. §294 I

659 Ignore blanks that would otherwise become undelimited arguments. §393 C

21 Mar 1983

X280 ↦ **660** Make `\lastskip` handle *mu_glue* as well as ordinary glue. §424 F

561 ↦ **661** Expand only one level in a preamble `\span`. §782 C

22 Mar 1983

662 Let a single `#` suffice in `\tokens`, `\message`, etc. (The previous rule, in which `##` was always required as in macros, was a loser especially in `\write` where you had to say `####`!) §477 C

X328 ↦ **663** Require the keyword '`to`' in `\read`. (This will avoid the common error of an incomplete constant when no space appears before the `\cs`.) Also allow terminal I/O as a default when a stream number is out of range. §482, 1225, 1370 C

26 Mar 1983

664 Replace `\ifeven`⟨countnumber⟩ by `\ifodd`⟨number⟩, for better consistency of language. §504 C

564 ↦ **665** Introduce the *change_if_limit*, to overcome a big surprise bug relating to `\if\if aabc\fi`. §497 S

- *Such examples show that cur_if might not be current, in my original implementation.*

28 Mar 1983

X326 ↦ **666** Tolerate non-characters as arguments to `\if` and `\ifcat`. §506 G

667 Change '`absent`' to '`void`', a better word. §487 C

668 Clear the *shift_amount* in `\lastbox`, since I don't want to figure out what it means in all cases. §1081 C

29 Mar 1983

669 Wake up the terminal before giving an error message. (This means a special *print_err* procedure is introduced.) (Suggested by DRF.) §34, 73 I

1 Apr 1983

- *Today I finished Chapter 21 (boxes) and began to draft Chapter 22 (alignments).*

670 Allow periodic preambles in alignments. §793 G

671 Make `\leaders` line up according to the smallest enclosing box. §627, 636 C

672 Allow hyphenation after whatsits (e.g., after items for an index). §896 Q

2 Apr 1983

673 Call *build_page* when `\par` occurs in vertical mode. §1094 Q

674 Clear *aux* in *init_row*, for tidyness. §786 C

4 Apr 1983

675 Let digits switch families in math mode. §232 C

7 Apr 1983

602 ↦ **676** Refine the test for not splitting an insertion. §1008 Q

8 Apr 1983

647 ↦ **677** Rename `\xcr` as `\crcr`, at LL's request. §780 C

9 Apr 1983

- *Took a day off and had a chance to help print a sample page on a 150-year-old letterpress in Murphys, California.*

11 Apr 1983

678 Recover more sensibly after a runaway preamble. §339 I

12 Apr 1983

X328 ↦ **679** Make `\read` span several input lines, if necessary to get balanced braces. §482 C

14 Apr 1983

680 Fix a subtle bug found by JS: §882 can make q a *char_node*, so we need to test '**if** $\neg$*is_char_node*(q)'. [Actually I discovered much later that the real bug was to omit '**else**' at this point.] §881 S

15 Apr 1983

681 Make `\uppercase` and `\lowercase` apply to all characters, regardless of category. §1289 C

- *7:30am. After working all night, I completed a draft of the manual thru Chapter 22, for distribution to volunteer readers.*
- *5pm. The changes above have been incorporated into Version 0.97.*

17 Apr 1983

682 Change '*small_number*' to '0 . . 65' in the hyphenation routine (DRF). §901 R

683 Flush patterns in the input when the user tries `\patterns` outside of `INITEX` (suggested by DRF). §1252 I

- *Tomorrow I fly to England, where I'll lecture and write a paper about 'Literate Programming' [Comp. J.* **27** *(1984), 97–111] [Chapter 4 of the present book].*

14 May 1983

663 ↦ **684** Improve the behavior of `\read` from terminal (suggested by Todd Allen at Yale). [I'd forgotten to implement the extended stream numbers in #663. Also, the prompt is now omitted if $n < 0$.] §484 I

18 May 1983

685 Restrict `\write` n to the transcript file only, if $n < 0$. §1350 I

X188 ↦ **686** Unify the syntax for registers and internal quantities. (Remove primitives called '`\insthe`' and '`\minusthe`'; rename *scan_the* to *scan_something_internal*, and change its interface accordingly; clean up command codes generally.) §209, 413 C

687 Introduce new parameters `\hoffset`, `\voffset`. §617 G

24 May 1983

688 Introduce a new parameter `\everycr` (suggested by MDS). §774, 799 G

- *Many macro writers and preliminary-manual readers have been requesting new features; I'll try to keep the language as concise and consistent as possible.*

25 May 1983

689 Introduce `\countdef`, `\dimendef`, etc. (suggested by DRF long ago, easy now in view of #686). §1224 G

690 Introduce `\advance`, `\multiply`, `\divide` (suggested by FY). §1240 G

691 Introduce `\hyphenchar`; this requires a new command *assign_font_int*, plus minor changes to about 15 modules. §915 G

692 Introduce `\skewchar` (easy because of #691). §741 G

693 Introduce `\noexpand`. (I had difficulty thinking of how to implement this one!) §358, 369 G

694 Introduce `\meaning`. §296 G

X231 ↦ **695** Remove '`dm`' and '`vu`'; allow the more general '`.5\hsize`'. §455 G

696 Change '`\texinfo` f n' to '`\fontdimen` n f'. §578 C

27 May 1983

697 Add a new feature \afterassignment (suggested by ARK). §1269 G

619 ↦ **698** Adjust the timing so that commands like '\chardef\xx=5\xx' behave sensibly. §1224 C

28 May 1983

699 Ignore '\relax' as if it were a space, in math mode and in a few other places where \relax would otherwise be erroneous. §404 C

700 Improve \mathaccent spacing with respect to subscripts and superscripts (suggested by HWT). §742 Q

30 May 1983

598 ↦ **701** Terminate a job only when *dead_cycles* = 0. §1054 C

- *The changes above constitute Version 0.98.*

3 Jun 1983

- *I finished the draft of Chapter 23 (output routines) today.*

702 Allow \mark and \insert and \vadjust in restricted horizontal mode, and also in math mode. (This is a comparatively big change, triggered by the fact that \mark in a display presently causes TEX to crash with 'This can't happen'!) The global variable *adjust_tail* is introduced. §796, 888, 1085 G

6 Jun 1983

695 ↦ **703** Replace (and generalize) the previous uses of ht, wd, and dp in dimensions by introducing the new control sequences \ht, \wd, and \dp. §1247 G

704 Display sub-parts of noads with the symbols ^ and _ instead of (and [. §696 I

694 ↦ **705** Allow A..F in hex constants to be *other_char* as well as *letter*. §445 C

7 Jun 1983

654 ↦ **706** Remove an instance of ⟨Scan optional space⟩, since it's now redundant. §457 E

707 Legalize \mkern\thinmuskip and \mkern5\thinmuskip. §456 C

708 Clean up the treatment of optional spaces in numerical specifications. §455 C

- *A construction like* 2.5\space\space\dimen0 *was previously valid after* 'plus' *or* 'minus' *only!*
- *I'm obviously working on Chapter 24 today.*

545 ↦ **709** Allow '\font' as a ⟨font identifier⟩ for the current font. §577 C

623 ↦ **710** Don't make \gdef global when *global_defs* < 0. §1218 C

711 Produce *zero_glue* as the outcome of \advance\spaceskip by-\spaceskip. §1229 E

712 Make \show do something appropriate for every possible token. §1294 I

559 ↦ **713** Replace the (single) \tokens parameter by an array of 256 token registers. §230 G

714 Allow \indent in math mode; also make \valign in math mode produce the 'Missing $' error. §1046, 1093 C

715 Remove redundant code: There's no need to check *cur_group* or call *off_save* when starting alignments or equation numbers in displays. §1130, 1142 E

8 Jun 1983

716 Disallow \openout-1 and \closeout-1. §1350 C

717 Disallow \lastbox in math mode. §1080 C

9 Jun 1983

718 Call *back_error*, not *error*, when \leaders aren't followed by proper glue. §1078 I

719 Initialize for a possible paragraph, after \noalign in a \valign. §785 D

10 Jun 1983

708 ↦ **720** Expand the optional space after an ASCII constant. §442 C

12 Jun 1983

721 Set *space_factor* ← 1000 after a rule or a constructed accent. §1056, 1123 C

14 Jun 1983

722 Correct a serious blunder: Set *disc_width* ← 0 before testing if *s* is null (caught by JS). §869 D

- *This is a real bug that existed since the beginning! It showed up on page 37 of the Version 0* TRIP *manual, but I didn't notice the problem.*

708 ↦ **723** Make optional spaces after ⟨dimen⟩ like those after ⟨number⟩. §448 C

568 ↦ **724** Insert *every_display* before calling *build_page*. §1145 C

648 ↦ **725** Report TEX's capacity on overflow errors in a way that's fully consistent with other statistical reports. §42 I

17 Jun 1983

726 Make all `\tracing` decisions on the basis of ≥ versus <, not ≠ versus =. §581 C

- *Today I finished the draft of Chapter 27 (the last chapter)!*
- *The changes above were released as Version 0.99 on June 19, 1983.*

20 Jun 1983

727 Set `\catcode`\%=14` in `INITEX`. §232 C

587 ↦ **728** Call *normal_paragraph* when `\par` occurs in vertical mode. §1094 C

- *Once again I'm retiring about 8am and awaking about 4pm.*

21 Jun 1983

558 ↦ **729** Don't append an overfull rule solely because of `\hbadness`. §666 C

730 Don't allow the glue-ratio of shrinking to be less than −1. §810, 811 R

22 Jun 1983

653 ↦ **731** Declare the parameter to *print_roman_int* to be of type *integer*, instead of *nonnegative_integer* (found by Debby Clark). §69 B

690 ↦ **732** Make the keyword '`by`' optional (suggested by LL). §1236 C

24 Jun 1983

733 Say '`preloaded`' when announcing *format_ident*. §1328 I

25 Jun 1983

734 Add extra boxes and glue to the output of alignment. [This thwarts possible attempts at trickery by which system-dependent glue set values computed by `\span` could have gotten into TEX's registers by things like `\valign` and `\vsplit`. It also has the advantage of perfect accuracy in alignment of vertical rules.] §809 R

735 Make leaders affect the height or width of the enclosing boxes. §656, 671 C

- *Today I'm mainly installing a much-improved format for change files in* **`WEB`** *programs (suggested by DRF).*

28 Jun 1983

736 Permit `\unskip` in vertical mode when we know that it does nothing. §1106 C

1 Jul 1983

700 ↦ **737** Avoid redundant boxes when things like '`{\bf A}`' occur in math. §1186 E

738 Add a '`scaled`' feature to `\font` input. §1258 G

700 ↦ **739** Remember to correct *delta* when an accented box changes. §742 D

2 Jul 1983

740 Introduce *bypass_eoln*, to remove anomalous behavior on input files of length 1. (Suggested by DRF after the problem was discovered by LL). §31 R

4 Jul 1983

741 Allow codes like `^^b` as well as `^^B`. §352, 355 G

742 Introduce new parameters `\escapechar`, `\endlinechar`, `\defaulthyphenchar`, and `\defaultskewchar`, to make TEX less dependent on the character set. (This affects many modules, since a lot of error messages must be broken up so that they use *print_esc*.) G

7 Jul 1983

743 Use a system-dependent function *erstat* when opening or closing files (suggested by DRF). §27 P

11 Jul 1983

- *The computer is back up after more than 50 hours down time (due to air conditioning failure).*

744 Show total glue in the output of `\tracingpages`. §985 I

745 Guard against insertion into an hbox. §993 R

746 Legalize the assignment ⟨tokenvar⟩=⟨tokenvar⟩. §1227 C

747 Introduce a new parameter `\errhelp`. §1283 I

623 ↦ **748** Don't forget to check *global_defs* when `\tabskip` is changed. §782 F

12 Jul 1983

749 Allow an `\outer` macro to appear after `\string`, `\noexpand`, and `\meaning` (Todd Allen). §369, 471 C

750 Make '`\the`' an expandable control sequence (i.e., move it from the stomach to the throat); this cleans up several annoying glitches. §367 C

620 ↦ **751** Allow `\unhbox` and `\unhcopy` in math mode if the box is void. §1110 C

13 Jul 1983

- *I lectured for four hours at the TUG meeting today after very little sleep!*

16 Jul 1983

- *The following were suggested by TUG meeting discussions.*

752 Round the value of *default_rule* more properly: It should be 26215. §463 L

700 ↦ **753** Fix `\mathaccent` again; it's still not right! The final height should be the maximum of the height of accented letter without superscript and the height of unaccented letter with superscript. §742 Q

754 Add a new feature `\newlinechar`. §59 G

755 Allow boxes and rules in discretionaries (suggested by somebody from Hewlett-Packard). §1121 G

X28 ↦ **756** Show all token expansions, not just macros, when `\tracingcommands`. §367 I

757 Allow `\char` in a `\hyphenation` list. §935 C

758 Introduce a new feature `\aftergroup`; it can be implemented with *save_stack*. §326 G

759 Run the running dimensions to alignment boundaries (suggested by ARK). §806 C

17 Jul 1983

760 Zero out *hyf* values at the edges, so that weird pattern data cannot lead to Pascal range checks. §965 R

X190 ↦ **761** Decrease the `hc` codes for hyphenation, so that code 127 cannot possibly be matched. §937, 962 R

672 ↦ **762** Allow whatsits after hyphenatable words. §899 C

604 ↦ **763** Represent an italic correction as an explicit kern. §1113 C

18 Jul 1983

764 Allow lowercase letters in file names. §519 C

765 Change the message '`No output file`' to: '`No pages of output`'. §642 I

766 Confirm that a quiet mode is being entered, when error interaction ends with `Q`, `R`, or `S` (suggested by ARK). §86 I

- *Version 0.999 was finally installed today; a new program listing has been printed.*
- *From now on, I plan to keep all section numbers unchanged.*
- *I'm done writing Appendix H; beginning to revise Chapter 20.*

25 Jul 1983

663 ↦ **767** Allow space after '`to`' in the `\read` command (FY). §1215 C

- *To bed at 1pm today.*

27 Jul 1983

665 ↦ **768** Stack the current type of `\if`; this precaution is necessary in general (FY). §498 S

- *To bed at 2pm today.*

29 Jul 1983

769 Avoid putting a control sequence in the hash table when it occurs after `\ifx`. (Requested by Math Reviews people.) §507 E

- *Finished a version of The TEXbook lacking only Appendices D, E, and I, for distribution to interested readers.*
- *To bed at 10:30pm, planning to arise regularly at 6am for a change.*

31 Jul 1983

766 ↦ **770** Call *update_terminal* when going quiet (HWT). §86 I

1 Aug 1983

771 Don't put an empty line at the end of an `\input` file! (This simplifies the rules and the program, and also gets around a bug that occurred at the end of files with *end_line_char* < 0.) §362 C

- *The changes above went into Version 0.9999, which was widely distributed.*

16 Aug 1983

665 ↦ **772** Rectify a ridiculous gaffe: I initialized q every time the loop of *change_if_limit* was performed! (Found by FY.) §497 B

648 ↦ **773** Distinguish '`string`' from '`strings`' when reporting statistics. §1334 I

774 Introduce *lx*, to correct a bug in `\xleader` computations (found by FY). §627 A

20 Aug 1983

775 Don't forget to apply `\/` to ligatures. §1113 F

- *Today I began to read all previous issues of TUGboat, in preparation for Appendix D.*

27 Aug 1983

776 Add debugging hack number 16, to help catch subtle data structure bugs. §1339 I

777 Remove redundant setting and resetting of *name_in_progress*. §531 E

618 ↦ **778** Suppress `\input` during a font size spec; otherwise *cur_name* is clobbered (found by MDS). §1258 S

779 Introduce new conditionals `\ifhbox` and `\ifvbox`. §505 G

29 Aug 1983

750 ↦ **780** Test for an empty list, if emptiness will mess up the data structure. (Found by Todd Allen.) §478 D

624 ↦ **781** Use *fast_store_new_token* in another place for efficiency. §466 E

782 Say '`has only`' instead of '`has`'. §579 I

- *These changes yield Version 0.99999, used only at Stanford.*

30 Aug 1983

783 Make funny blank spaces showable. §298 C

31 Aug 1983

754 ↦ **784** Make `\newlinechar` affect *print_char*, not just *print*. §58 C

4 Sep 1983

785 Add new features `\lastkern`, `\lastpenalty`, `\unkern`, `\unpenalty`. §424, 996, 1105 G

- *OK, Appendix D is finished!!*
- *The above changes have been installed in Version 0.999999.*

17 Sep 1983

548 ↦ **786** Don't bother making duplicate font identifiers; that was overkill, not really needed. §1258 P

- *Will this be the historic last change to TeX?*

18 Sep 1983

787 Correct a minor inconsistency, '`display`' not '`displayed`'. §211 I

20 Sep 1983

604 ↦ **788** Treat the kerns inserted for accents as explicit kerns. §1125 C

26 Sep 1983

789 Change '`log`' to '`transcript`' in several messages. §535, 1335 I

- *The index was finished today; I mailed the entire TeXbook to Massachusetts for final proofreading before publication.*

1 Oct 1983

790 Prevent uninitialized trie positions in case of overflow (found by Bernd Schulze). §944 D

7 Oct 1983

- *Henceforth our weekly 'TeX lunch' meetings will be called 'METAFONT lunch'.*
- *DRF begins to produce The TeXbook on our APS phototypesetter.*

14 Oct 1983

633 ↦ **791** Ignore spaces at the ends of lines also in `TEX.POOL` (found by DRF). §52 P

610 ↦ **792** Initialize the *history* variable at *start_here* (DRF). §1332 D

18 Oct 1983

793 Extend *runaway* to catch runaway text (suggested by FY). §306 I

794 Reset *cur_cs* after *back_input*, not after scanning the '`=`' (found by FY). §1226 D

24 Oct 1983

638 ↦ **795** Change the error recovery for bad delimiters, in accordance with the changed syntax. (Found by Barry Smith.) §1183 I

9 Nov 1983

796 Optimize the code a bit more, based on empirical frequency data gathered during September and October: In §45, use the fact that the result is almost always true. In §380, delete '**while** *true* **do**' since many compilers implement that badly. Rewrite §852 to avoid calling *badness* in the most common case. §45, 380, 852 E

3 Dec 1983

797 Don't forget to call `error` after the message has been given (noticed by Gabi Kuper). §500 F

- *Version 1.0 released today incorporates all of the above.*

9 Dec 1983

- *Dinner party with 36 guests to celebrate TEX's coming of age.*

2 Feb 1984

786 ↦ **798** Reinstall `\font` precautions that I thought were unnecessary. I overlooked many problematic possibilities, like '`{\font\a=x \global\a} \the\font`' and '`\font\a=x \font\b=x \let\b=\undefined \the\a`', etc. (Found by Mike Urban.) The new remedy involves removal of the *font_ident* array and putting the identifiers into a frozen part of the hash table; so there's a sprinkling of corrections in lots of modules. But basically the change is quite conservative, so it shouldn't spawn any new bugs (it says here). §222, 267, 1257 S

9 Feb 1984

799 Remove the possibility of double interrupt, in a scenario found by Clint Cuzzo. §1031 S

12 Feb 1984

800 Improve spacing in a formula like `$(A,<)$`. §764 Q

13 Feb 1984

801 Avoid a bad **goto**, as diagnosed by Clint Cuzzo and George O'Connor. (Must not go directly to *switch*.) §346 A

802 Conserve string pool space by not storing file name in two guises (suggested by DRF). §537 E

26 Feb 1984

803 Make scaled output look cleaner by printing fewer decimals whenever this involves no loss of accuracy. (Suggested by METAFONT development.) §103 I

2 Mar 1984

804 Maintain 17-digit accuracy, not 16; now constants like '`.00000762939453126pt`' will round correctly. §452 R

16 Mar 1984

805 Plug a loophole that permitted recursion in *get_next*, by disallowing deletions in *check_outer_validity*. §336 R

24 Mar 1984

806 Open the terminal before trying to wake it up, when the program starts bad. §1332 I

27 Mar 1984

807 Check that $k < 63$, to avoid the `\patterns{xxx...xxxdxxxdxxx}` anomaly found by Jacques Désarménien. §962 R

11 Apr 1984

808 Supply code for the missing case *adjust_node* in *copy_node_list*. §206 F

- *Yoicks, how could serious bugs like that have escaped detection?*

11 Jun 1984

627 ↦ **809** Initialize *char_base*, etc., for *null_font*. (Found by Nick Briggs.) §552 D

810 Clear the *buffer* array initially (Briggs). §331 R

21 Jun 1984

811 Look ahead for ligature or kern after a `\chardef`'d item (Désarménien). §1038 C

4 Jul 1984

812 Make the quarterword constraint explicit with a new '*bad*' case (19). §111 R

7 Jul 1984

813 Optimize *firm_up_the_line* slightly, to be consistent with the METAFONT program. §363 E

8 Jul 1984

814 Give additional diagnostics when `\tracingmacros>1`. §323 I

- *The changes above were incorporated in Version 1.1, released July 9, 1984.*

27 Jul 1984

815 Say '`see the transcript file`' after handling offline `\show` commands. (Suggested by METAFONT.) §1298 I

20 Oct 1984

816 Allow '0' in response to error prompts. §84 I

- *Those two changes led to Version 1.2.*

25 Nov 1984

817 Don't forget to check for *null* before looking at subfields of a node. (This was "dirty Pascal," with two quarterword 0's read as a halfword.) §846 R

818 Ditto in another place! §939 R

819 Remove the fixed-at-compile-time partition between lower and upper memory. §116, 125, 162 E

- *This major change in memory management completes Version 1.3, which was published in preliminary looseleaf form as 'TEX: The Program'.*

20 Dec 1984

820 Keep the *node_size* field from overflowing if the lower part of memory is too large. §125 R

- *That was another bug in existence from the beginning!*

5 Jan 1985

821 Improve the missing-format-file error (DRF). §524 I

7 Jan 1985

822 Update the terminal right away so that the welcoming message will appear as soon as possible (DRF). §61 I

23 Jan 1985

823 Convey more uncertainty in the help message at times of *confusion*. §95 I

610 ↦ **824** Improve the *history* logic in the *warning_issued* case. §245 I

18 Feb 1985

810 ↦ **825** Stick to standard Pascal: Don't use *first* in a **for** loop. [Some procedures "threaten" it globally, according to British Standard 6192, section 6.8.3.9.] (Pointed out by CET.) §331 P

11 Apr 1985

826 Prevent nonexistent characters from being output by unusual combinations of ligatures and hyphenation. §915 S

15 Apr 1985

819 ↦ **827** Compute memory usage correctly in `INITEX`; the previous number was wrong because of a `WEB` text macro without parentheses (DRF). §164 L

16 Apr 1985

828 Speed up *flush_list* by not calling *free_avail* (DRF). §123 E

17 Apr 1985

788 ↦ **829** Introduce a special kind of kern for accent positioning; it must not disappear after a line break. §837, 879, 1125 A

18 Apr 1985

755 ↦ **830** Prevent `\lastbox` and `\unkern` from removing discretionary replacements. §1081, 1105 R

- *That completes Version 1.4.*

26 Apr 1985

831 Don't try *TEX_area* if a nonstandard file area has been specified (DRF). §537 C

• *That was #401 in TEX78; I never learn!*

30 Apr 1985

754 ↦ **832** Eliminate the limitation on `\write` length; the reason for it has disappeared (Nancy Tuma). §1370 C

8 May 1985

819 ↦ **833** Allocate two words for the head of the *active* list (CET). §162 D

11 May 1985

834 Change *wterm* to *wterm_ln* after a bad beginning (Bill Gropp). §1332 I

806 ↦ **835** Don't open the terminal twice (CET). §1332 E

22 May 1985

836 Test for *batch_mode* after trying to open the transcript file, not before (DRF). §92 R

837 Be prepared for string pool overflow while reading the command line! (This bug was first found in METAFONT, when it could occur more easily.) §525 R

7 Aug 1985

838 Fix a bug in `\edef\foo{\iffalse\fi\the\toks0}`: TEX should stay in the loop when expanding non-`\the`. (Found by Dan Brotsky.) §478 A

• *The above changes were incorporated in Version 1.5.*

27 Nov 1985

764 ↦ **839** Make '`plain`' a lowercase name, for consistency with the manual. §521 C

669 ↦ **840** Wake up the terminal for `\show` commands. §1294, 1297 I

• *The above changes were incorporated in Version 2.0, which was published as Volume B of the Computers & Typesetting series.*

15 Dec 1986

841 Punctuate the Poirot help message more carefully. §1283 I

28 Jan 1987

842 Make sure that *max_in_open* doesn't exceed 127 (DRF). §14 R

680 ↦ **843** Don't allow a `\kern` to be clobbered at the end of a pre-break list when a discretionary break is taken. (A missing '**else**' was the source of the error, diagnosed incorrectly before.) §881 D

844 Take account of discarded nodes when computing the background width after a discretionary. §840 D

• *That was the first really serious bug detected for more than 17 months! I found it while experimenting with right-to-left extensions.*

• *Version 2.1 was released on January 26, 1987.*

5 Feb 1987

845 Remove cases in *shorthand_def* that cannot occur (found by Pat Monardo). §1224 E

14 Apr 1987

846 Improve robustness of data structure display when debugging (Ronaldo Amá). §174, 182 R

21 Apr 1987

847 Make the storage allocation algorithm more elegant and efficient. §127 E

22 Apr 1987

742 ↦ **848** Calculate the empty-line condition properly when *end_line_char* is absent. §360 A

• *The previous three changes were found while I was teaching a class based on Volume B; they led to Version 2.2.*

28 Apr 1987

849 Avoid closing a file when TEX knows that it isn't open (JS). §560 E

3 Aug 1987

850 Clean up unfinished output if it's necessary to *jump_out* (Klaus Guntermann). §642 S

• *That makes Version 2.3; subsequent version numbers won't be logged here.*

19 Aug 1987

851 Indent rules properly in cases like `\hangindent=1pt$$\halign{...\cr\noalign{\hrule}}$$`. §806 A

20 Aug 1987

852 Introduce *co_backup* because of cases like `\hskip 0pt plus 1fil\ifdim` (Alan Guth). §366 S

9 Nov 1987

853 Change the calculation for number of leader boxes, so that it won't be too sensitive to roundoff error near exact multiples (M. F. Bridgland). §626 S

17 Nov 1987

854 Replace my stupid algorithm for fixed-point multiplication of negatives (WGS). §572 A

12 Dec 1987

855 Fix a typo in the initialization of hyphenation tables (PB). §952 B

- *That error was almost completely harmless, thus undetectable, except if some* `\lccode` *is 1 and no* `\patterns` *are given.*

23 Dec 1987

564 ↦ **856** Be more cautious when "relaxing" a previously undefined `\csname`; you might be inside a group (CET). §372 S

20 Apr 1988

857 Make sure *temp_head* is well-formed whenever it can be printed in a "runaway" message: Consider constructions like `\outer\def\a0{}\a\a` (Silvio Levy). §391 S

24 Apr 1988

618 ↦ **858** Avoid conflicting use of the string pool in constructions like `\def\\#1{}\input a\\\z` (Robert Messer). §260 S

10 May 1988

859 Amend the `\patterns` data structure when *trie_min* = 0 (PB). §951, 953 R

25 May 1988

860 Guarantee that *trie_pointer* cannot be out of range. §923 R

618 ↦ **861** Avoid additional bugs like #858 in constructions like `\input a\romannumeral1`, etc. §464, 465, 470 S

618 ↦ **862** Prevent similar string pool confusion that could occur during the processing of `**\input\romannumeral6`. §525 R

19 Jun 1988

819 ↦ **863** Prevent a negative dividend from rounding upward, causing a loop (CET). §126 S

819 ↦ **864** Adopt a smoother allocation strategy when memory is nearly gone (CET). §126 E

20 Jun 1988

852 ↦ **865** Initialize *cur_order*, now that it's being backed up (Tsunetoshi Hayashi). §439 D

6 Nov 1988

612 ↦ **866** Disable *fatal_error* in *prompt_input*, so that *open_log_file* can use it safely (Tim Morgan). §71 S

836 ↦ **867** Force terminal output whenever *open_log_file* fails. §535 S

14 Dec 1988

866 ↦ **868** Restore *fatal_error* in *prompt_input*, but don't let it be unsafe for *open_log_file*. §92, 534 P

23 Jan 1989

869 Give q a legal value when recovering from "infinite shrinkage" error. §976, 1004 D

17 Feb 1989

758 ↦ **870** Avoid spurious error message for `\aftergroup\relax\dump` by avoiding inaccessible `\aftergroup` tokens (FM and Rainer Schöpf). §280 D

20 Mar 1989

871 Don't refer to *link*(*null*) even when it "can't happen" (PB). §791 R

7 Jun 1989

872 Avoid confusion from `$$\begingroup\halign{#\cr}$$` (FM). §1130 S

20 Jun 1989

873 Put fraction digits into dynamic memory, not the global *dig* array, because of constructions like `.5\ifdim.6` (FM). §452 S

17 Jul 1989

874 Prevent embarrassing attempts to report errors before the string mechanism has been fully initialized, for example when the command line exceeds the buffer size (WGS). §31 S

16 Aug 1989

875 Allow integer products to be 31 bits long (FM). §105 M

31 Aug 1989

441 ↦ **876** Increase the number of tokens shown by *token_show* (J. Lavagnino). §295 C

877 Avoid confusion from `$$\begingroup\eqno$$` (FM). §1140 S

- *The recent TUG meeting turned out to be an extend-TEX-for-the-nineties party! I agreed that some extensions for non-English languages ought to be made while I still knew how to do them. (In other words, I broke my firm commitment to keeping TEX completely stable; but in this case nobody objected.) The following eleven changes were coded during the month of September.*

30 Sep 1989

878 Install major change allowing general 8-bit code input. §38, 352 G

879 Install major change allowing multiple hyphenation tables (M. Ferguson). §923 G

880 Introduce new parameters `\lefthyphenmin` and `\righthyphenmin`. §923 G

881 Introduce major new ligature capabilities including implicit boundary characters. §908, 1037 G

882 Install new `\inputlineno` feature suggested by MDS. §424 G

883 Install new `\holdinginserts` feature suggested by FM. §1014 G

884 Install new `\badness` feature. §424, 664 G

885 Install new `\emergencystretch` feature. §863 G

886 Install new `\errorcontextlines` feature suggested by FM. §311 G

887 Recover from anomaly when hyphenation `char_warning` clobbers `old_setting`. §863 S

888 Make it easier to change the format extension (Don Hosek). §520, 1328 P

16 Oct 1989

889 Avoid range check in null font with `bc=256` (PB). §565 R

22 Nov 1989

856 ↦ **890** Prevent *save_stack* conflicts in `{\hbox\expandafter{\csname\endcsname}}` and similar constructions (WGS). §645, 1117 S

858 ↦ **891** System-dependent parts of file names must be addressed relatively, not absolutely (FM and Rainer Schöpf). §516, 517 S

3 Dec 1989

880 ↦ **892** Allow different hyphenmins in the same paragraph (M. Ferguson). §1376 G

893 Distinguish `\par` from characters on `\if` tests. (MVL). §334 S

378 ↦ **894** Alignments need to be more robust against malicious attacks (MVL). §782 S

895 Don't let kerns in discretionaries disappear at breaks (MVL). §869 C

881 ↦ **896** Make the new hyphenation reconstruction procedure less cautious, so that it doesn't lose hyphens found by the old method. §914 Q

11 Dec 1989

879 ↦ **897** Make an undumped trie dumpable again (PB). §1325 D

18 Dec 1989

588 ↦ **898** Allow access to page totals in `\output` routines (FM and Chris Rowley). §421 G

22 Jan 1990

611 ↦ **899** Recognize more cases of unbalanced `\output` (CET). §1026 R

29 Jan 1990

758 ↦ **900** Make `\aftergroup` work properly after `\eqno` (Michael Downes). §1194 S

1 Feb 1990

878 ↦ **901** Fix one more case of *end_line_char_inactive* (WGS). §360 S

22 Feb 1990

902 Don't lose the last active node when total demerits are very high (FM). §836, 854 R

13 Mar 1990

903 Doublecheck math fonts after making equation number (MVL). §1194 D
904 Don't forget to rule out charnodes before testing *type* (MVL). §805, 1202 D

23 Mar 1990

881 ↦ **905** Don't change the font of punctuation preceding a hyphenated word (Scott C. Allendorf). §903 F
906 Balance the parentheses shown on the terminal during normal runs. §1335 I
907 Optimize `\ifx\p\q` after `\let\p=\q` (MVL). §508 E
908 Treat migration properly in displays (MVL). §1199, 1205 S
• *We're now up to Version 3.0; I sincerely hope all bugs have been found.*

11 May 1990

881 ↦ **909** Initialize `\nullfont` ligature parameters (Lance Carnes). §552 F

22 July 1990

579 ↦ **910** Treat `\prevgraf` as zero within `\write` (Bogusław Jackowski). §422 S

26 July 1990

911 Report '`l.1`' when first line of file overflows buffer (George Russell). §538 S

5 December 1990

878 ↦ **912** Translate unprintable characters in font identifiers (WGS). §63 S

28 December 1990

913 Avoid range check when there are 65536 or more pages (Eberhard Mattes). §642 R

20 September 1991

878 ↦ **914** Improve error message for `\mathchar` out of range. §436 I
878 ↦ **915** Retain unprintable internal strings in 8-bit form (FM). §59 S
881 ↦ **916** Retain right punctuation context for ligature reconstruction (problem found by Brian Hamilton Kelly). §903 S

Chapter 12

An Example of CWEB (1990)

[The following short program by Silvio Levy and D. E. Knuth illustrates the use of CWEB, an offshoot of WEB that substitutes C for Pascal as the underlying programming language. The CWEB conventions are supported by two freely available system programs called CTANGLE and CWEAVE, both written entirely in CWEB by Levy and Knuth. CWEB does not require special facilities for macro processing and string manipulation, because C already provides such features.]

---

1. Counting words. This example, based on a program by Klaus Guntermann and Joachim Schrod [*TUGboat* **7** (1986), 135–137], presents the "word count" program from UNIX, rewritten in CWEB to demonstrate literate programming in C. The level of detail in this document is intentionally high, for didactic purposes; many of the things spelled out here don't need to be explained in other programs.

The purpose of `wc` is to count lines, words, and/or characters in a list of files. The number of lines in a file is the number of newline characters it contains. The number of characters is the file length in bytes. A "word" is a maximal sequence of consecutive characters other than newline, space, or tab, containing at least one visible ASCII code. (We assume that the standard ASCII code is in use.)

2. Most CWEB programs share a common structure. It's probably a good idea to state the overall structure explicitly at the outset, even though the various parts could all be introduced in unnamed sections of the code if we wanted to add them piecemeal.

Here, then, is an overview of the file `wc.c` that is defined by this CWEB program `wc.w`:

⟨ Header files to include 3 ⟩
⟨ Global variables 4 ⟩
⟨ Functions 20 ⟩
⟨ The main program 5 ⟩

3. We must include the standard I/O definitions, since we want to send formatted output to *stdout* and *stderr*.

⟨ Header files to include 3 ⟩ ≡

```
#include <stdio.h>
```

This code is used in section 2.

4. The *status* variable will tell the operating system if the run was successful or not, and *prog_name* is used in case there's an error message to be printed.

```
#define OK 0    /* status code for successful run */
#define usage_error 1    /* status code for improper syntax */
#define cannot_open_file 2    /* status code for file access error */
```

⟨ Global variables 4 ⟩ ≡

```
  int status = OK;    /* exit status of command, initially OK */
  char *prog_name;    /* who we are */
```

See also section 14.

This code is used in section 2.

5. Now we come to the general layout of the *main* function.

⟨ The main program 5 ⟩ ≡

```
  main(argc, argv)
       int argc;
         /* the number of arguments on the UNIX command line */
       char **argv;
         /* the arguments themselves, an array of strings */
  {
     ⟨ Variables local to main 6 ⟩
     prog_name = argv[0];
     ⟨ Set up option selection 7 ⟩;
     ⟨ Process all the files 8 ⟩;
     ⟨ Print the grand totals if there were multiple files 19 ⟩;
     exit(status);
  }
```

This code is used in section 2.

6. If the first argument begins with a '-', the user is choosing the desired counts and specifying the order in which they should be displayed. Each selection is given by the initial character (lines, words, or characters). For example, '`-cl`' would cause just the number of characters and the number of lines to be printed, in that order.

We do not process this string now; we simply remember where it is. It will be used to control the formatting at output time.

```
⟨ Variables local to main 6 ⟩ ≡
  int file_count;    /* how many files there are */
  char *which;       /* which counts to print */
```

See also sections 9 and 12.

This code is used in section 5.

7. ⟨ Set up option selection 7 ⟩ ≡

```
  which = "lwc";    /* if no option is given, print all three values */
  if (argc > 1 ∧ *argv[1] ≡ '-') {
    which = argv[1] + 1;
    argc--;
    argv++;
  }
  file_count = argc − 1;
```

This code is used in section 5.

8. Now we scan the remaining arguments and try to open a file, if possible. The file is processed and its statistics are given. We use a **do** ... **while** loop because we should read from the standard input if no file name is given.

```
⟨ Process all the files 8 ⟩ ≡
  argc--;
  do {
    ⟨ If a file is given, try to open *(++argv); continue if
        unsuccessful 10 ⟩;
    ⟨ Initialize pointers and counters 13 ⟩;
    ⟨ Scan file 15 ⟩;
    ⟨ Write statistics for file 17 ⟩;
    ⟨ Close file 11 ⟩;
    ⟨ Update grand totals 18 ⟩;    /* even if there is only one file */
  } while (--argc > 0);
```

This code is used in section 5.

9. Here's the code to open the file. A special trick allows us to handle input from *stdin* when no name is given. Recall that the file descriptor to *stdin* is 0; that's what we use as the default initial value.

```
⟨ Variables local to main 6 ⟩ +≡
  int fd = 0;    /* file descriptor, initialized to stdin */
```

10. **#define** READ_ONLY 0
/* read access code for system *open* routine */

⟨ If a file is given, try to open *(++*argv*); **continue** if unsuccessful 10 ⟩ ≡

```
if (file_count > 0 ∧ (fd = open(*(++argv), READ_ONLY)) < 0) {
  fprintf(stderr, "%s:␣cannot␣open␣file␣%s\n", prog_name, *argv);
  status |= cannot_open_file;
  file_count--;
  continue;
}
```

This code is used in section 8.

11. ⟨ Close file 11 ⟩ ≡

```
close(fd);
```

This code is used in section 8.

12. We will do some homemade buffering in order to speed things up: Characters will be read into the *buffer* array before we process them. To do this we set up appropriate pointers and counters.

#define *buf_size* BUFSIZ
/* stdio.h's BUFSIZ is chosen for efficiency */

⟨ Variables local to *main* 6 ⟩ +≡

```
char buffer[buf_size];    /* we read the input into this array */
register char *ptr;
  /* the first unprocessed character in buffer */
register char *buf_end;    /* the first unused position in buffer */
register int c;
  /* current character, or number of characters just read */
int in_word;    /* are we within a word? */
long word_count, line_count, char_count;    /* number of words,
    lines, and characters found in the file so far */
```

13. ⟨ Initialize pointers and counters 13 ⟩ ≡

```
ptr = buf_end = buffer;
line_count = word_count = char_count = 0;
in_word = 0;
```

This code is used in section 8.

14. The grand totals must be initialized to zero at the beginning of the program. If we made these variables local to *main*, we would have to do this initialization explicitly; however, C's globals are automatically zeroed. (Or rather, "statically zeroed.") (Get it?)

⟨ Global variables 4 ⟩ +≡

```
long tot_word_count, tot_line_count, tot_char_count;
  /* total number of words, lines, and chars */
```

15. The present section, which does the counting that is wc's *raison d'être*, was actually one of the simplest to write. We look at each character and change state if it begins or ends a word.

```
⟨ Scan file 15 ⟩ ≡
  while (1) {
    ⟨ Fill buffer if it is empty; break at end of file 16 ⟩;
    c = *ptr++;
    if (c > '␣' ∧ c < '177) {      /* visible ASCII codes */
      if (¬in_word) {
        word_count++;
        in_word = 1;
      }
      continue;
    }
    if (c ≡ '\n') line_count++;
    else if (c ≠ '␣' ∧ c ≠ '\t') continue;
    in_word = 0;      /* c is newline, space, or tab */
  }
```

This code is used in section 8.

16. Buffered I/O allows us to count the number of characters almost for free.

```
⟨ Fill buffer if it is empty; break at end of file 16 ⟩ ≡
  if (ptr ≥ buf_end) {
    ptr = buffer;
    c = read(fd, ptr, buf_size);
    if (c ≤ 0) break;
    char_count += c;
    buf_end = buffer + c;
  }
```

This code is used in section 15.

17. It's convenient to output the statistics by defining a new function *wc_print*; then the same function can be used for the totals. Additionally we must decide here if we know the name of the file we have processed or if it was just *stdin*.

```
⟨ Write statistics for file 17 ⟩ ≡
  wc_print(which, char_count, word_count, line_count);
  if (file_count) printf("␣%s\n", *argv);      /* not stdin */
  else printf("\n");      /* stdin */
```

This code is used in section 8.

18. ⟨Update grand totals 18⟩ ≡

```
tot_line_count += line_count;
tot_word_count += word_count;
tot_char_count += char_count;
```

This code is used in section 8.

19. We might as well improve a bit on UNIX's `wc` by displaying the number of files too.

⟨Print the grand totals if there were multiple files 19⟩ ≡

```
if (file_count > 1) {
  wc_print(which, tot_char_count, tot_word_count, tot_line_count);
  printf(" total in %d files\n", file_count);
}
```

This code is used in section 5.

20. Here now is the function that prints the values according to the specified options. The calling routine is supposed to supply a newline. If an invalid option character is found we inform the user about proper usage of the command. Counts are printed in 8-digit fields so that they will line up in columns.

```
#define print_count(n) printf("%8ld", n)
```

⟨Functions 20⟩ ≡

```
wc_print(which, char_count, word_count, line_count)
    char *which;    /* which counts to print */
    long char_count, word_count, line_count;    /* given totals */
{
  while (*which)
    switch (*which++) {
    case 'l': print_count(line_count);
      break;
    case 'w': print_count(word_count);
      break;
    case 'c': print_count(char_count);
      break;
    default:
      if ((status & usage_error) == 0) {
        fprintf(stderr, "\nUsage: %s [-lwc] [filename ...]\n",
            prog_name);
        status |= usage_error;
      }
    }
}
```

This code is used in section 2.

21. Incidentally, a test of this program against the system `wc` command on a SPARCstation showed that the "official" `wc` was slightly slower. Furthermore, although that `wc` gave an appropriate error message for the options '`-abc`', it made no complaints about the options '`-labc`'! Dare we suggest that the system routine might have been better if its programmer had used a more literate approach?

---

22. Index. Here is a list of the identifiers used, and where they appear. Underlined entries indicate the place of definition. Error messages are also shown.

⟨ Process all the files 8 ⟩ Used in section 5.
⟨ Scan file 15 ⟩ Used in section 8.
⟨ Set up option selection 7 ⟩ Used in section 5.
⟨ The main program 5 ⟩ Used in section 2.
⟨ Update grand totals 18 ⟩ Used in section 8.
⟨ Variables local to *main* 6, 9, 12 ⟩ Used in section 5.
⟨ Write statistics for file 17 ⟩ Used in section 8.

Further Reading

E. W. van Ammers, "Literate programming with VAMP," *Informatie* **32** (1990), 380–388.

N. Anand, "Clarify function!" *ACM SIGPLAN Notices* **23**,6 (June 1988), 69–79.

Wolfgang Appelt and Karin Horn, "Multiple changefiles in WEB," *TUGboat* **7**,1 (March 1986), 20–21.

A. Avenarius, S. Oppermann, I. Peides, J. Stritzinger, *The FWEB System of Structured Documentation*, Report PI-R6/89, Institut für Praktische Informatik, Technische Hochschule Darmstadt (1989).

Adrian Avenarius and Siegfried Oppermann, "FWEB: A literate programming system for Fortran8x," *ACM SIGPLAN Notices* **25**,1 (January 1990), 52–58.

Ronald M. Baecker and Aaron Marcus, *Human Factors and Typography for More Readable Programs* (Reading, Massachusetts: Addison-Wesley, 1990), ISBN 0-20-110745-7, xx + 348 pp.

Kent Beck and Ward Cunningham, *The Literate Program Browser*, Technical Report CR-86-52, Computer Research Laboratory, Tektronix, Incorporated (1986).

Helmut Becker, "WEB system extensions," *TUGboat* **7**,2 (June 1986), 109.

Nelson H. F. Beebe, online bibliography of literate programming, available on the Internet for anonymous ftp from `math.utah.edu` as file `~ftp/pub/tex/bib/litprog.bib`.

Mordechai Ben-Ari, "Foreet: A tool for design and documentation of Fortran programs," *Software—Practice & Experience* **16**,10 (October 1986), 915–924.

Jon Bentley with David Gries, "Programming Pearls: Abstract data types," *Communications of the ACM* **30**,4 (April 1987), 284–289.

Jon Bentley with Donald E. Knuth, "Programming Pearls: Literate programming," *Communications of the ACM* **29**,5 (May 1986), 364–369. [Reprinted as Chapter 5 of the present book.]

Jon Bentley with Donald E. Knuth and M. D. McIlroy, "Programming Pearls: A literate program," *Communications of the ACM* **29**,6 (June 1986), 471–483. [Reprinted as Chapter 6 of the present book.]

Judy M. Bishop, "Computer programming—Is it computer science?" *South African Journal of Science* **87** (1991), 22–33.

Peter Breitenlohner, "Still another aspect of multiple change files: The PATCH processor," *TUGboat* **9**,1 (April 1988), 11–12.

Peter Brössler, Andreas Freiherr, T. Kampfmann, R.-D. Nausester, and Helmut Waldschmidt, *Modulare Programmierung in WEB*, Report TI-3/86, Institut für Theoretische Informatik, Technische Hochschule Darmstadt (June 1986), 15 pp. [A revised version was published by Guntermann and Waldschmidt, see below.]

Marcus E. Brown, *An Interactive Environment for Literate Programming*, Ph.D. dissertation, Department of Computer Science, Texas A&M University, College Station, TX (August 1988), 112 pp.

M. E. Brown, *The Literate Programming Tool*, Computer Science Department Report TR-88-012, Texas A&M University, College Station, TX (August 1988). [CWEB source code for a prototype Literate Programming Environment.]

Marcus Brown and Bart Childs, "An interactive tool for literate programming," *Third Workshop on Empirical Studies of Programmers*, unpublished proceedings, Austin, TX (April 1989), 9 pp.

Marcus Brown and Bart Childs, "An interactive environment for literate programming," *Structured Programming* **11** (1990), 11–25.

Marcus Brown and David Cordes, "Literate programming applied to conventional software design," *Structured Programming* **11** (1990), 85–98.

M. Brown and D. Cordes, "A literate programming design language," COMPEURO'90, *Proceedings of the 1990 IEEE International Conference on Computer Systems and Software Engineering*, Tel Aviv, Israel (8–10 May 1990), 548–549.

M. Brown and B. Czejdo, "A hypertext for literate programming," *Advances in Computing and Information*, Proceedings of International Conference ICCI'90, edited by Selim G. Akl et al., Niagara Falls, Ontario, Canada (23–26 May 1990), *Lecture Notes in Computer Science* **468** (1990), 250–259.

Carlos F. Bunge and Gerardo Cisneros, "Modular libraries and literate programming in software for *ab initio* atomic and molecular electronic structure calculations," *Computers & Chemistry* **12** (1988), 85–89.

Pehong Chen and Michael A. Harrison, "Index preparation and processing," *Software—Practice & Experience* **18**,9 (September 1988), 897–915.

Bart Childs, "`Ps_Quasi`," to appear as a technical report of the School of Mathematical Sciences, Australian National University, Canberra, Australia. [An `fweb` program for the solution of multipoint boundary value problems in ordinary differential equations. Available via anonymous ftp from `csseq.cs.tamu.edu` in directory `/usr/ftp/web/num`.]

Bart Childs and Timothy Jay McGuire, "Symbolic computing, automatic programming, and literate programming," *Computational Techniques and Applications*, Proceedings of CTAC-91, Adelaide, Australia (15–17 July 1991); to appear as a technical report of the School of Mathematical Sciences, Australian National University, Canberra, Australia.

David Cordes and Marcus Brown, "The literate-programming paradigm," *Computer* **24**,6 (June 1991), 52–61.

Ward Cunningham and Kent Beck, *Scroll Controller Explained, An Example of Literate Programming in Smalltalk*, Technical Report CR-86-53, Computer Research Laboratory, Tektronix, Incorporated (1986).

R. M. Damerell, "Error detecting changes to `TANGLE`," *TUGboat* **7**,1 (March 1986), 22–24.

Peter J. Denning, "Announcing Literate Programming," *Communications of the ACM* **30**,7 (July 1987), 593.

Christine Detig and Joachim Schrod, *MWEB, A WEB system for Modula-2*, Report PI-R10/88, Institut für Praktische Informatik, Technische Hochschule Darmstadt (March 1988), 17 pp. [The report and the system may be fetched by anonymous ftp from `ftp.th-darmstadt.de` on directory `~ftp/pub/tex/src-webware`.]

Jim Fox, "Webless literate programming," *TUGboat* **11**,4 (November 1990), 511–513.

Daniel Hill Greene, "Diminished tree search," in *Labelled Formal Languages and Their Uses*, Ph.D. dissertation, Computer Science Department report STAN-CS-83-982, Stanford University, Stanford, CA (June 1983), 88–94.

Daniel Hill Greene, "A general-purpose generator of combinatorial objects," in *Labelled Formal Languages and Their Uses*, Ph.D. dissertation, Computer Science Department report STAN-CS-83-982, Stanford University, Stanford, CA (June 1983), 95–138.

Daniel Hill Greene, "An example of Polya-Redfield enumeration," in *Labelled Formal Languages and Their Uses*, Ph.D. dissertation, Computer Science Department report STAN-CS-83-982, Stanford University, Stanford, CA (June 1983), 139–141.

K. M. Gregson and J. M. Bishop, *LIPED: literate program editor*, User manual, University of the Witwatersrand, Johannesburg (1988).

Klaus Guntermann and Wolfgang Rülling, "Another approach to multiple changefiles," *TUGboat* **7**,3 (October 1986), 134.

Klaus Guntermann and Joachim Schrod, "WEB adapted to C," *TUGboat* **7**,3 (October 1986), 134–137.

Klaus Guntermann and Helmut Waldschmidt, "Modular programming with WEB," *Electrosoft* **1**,1 (March 1990), 27–43.

Eric Hamilton, "Literate Programming: Expanding generalized regular expressions," *Communications of the ACM* **31**,12 (December 1988), 1377–1382; introduction by Christopher J. Van Wyk, 1376; review by Dan Colner, 1382–1385.

David R. Hanson, "Literate Programming: Printing common words," *Communications of the ACM* **30**,7 (July 1987), 594–598; introduction by Christopher J. Van Wyk, 594; review by John Gilbert, 598–599.

Michael Hines, *Literate Programming*, unpublished technical report, Department of Physiology, Duke University Medical Center, Durham, NC (5 June 1986). An electronic copy is available from `hines@neuro.duke.edu`.

Allen I. Holub, *Compiler Design in C* (Englewood Cliffs, New Jersey: Prentice-Hall, 1990), ISBN 0-13-155045-4, xviii + 924 pp.

Marco S. Hyman, "Literate `C++`," *Computer Language* **7**,7 (July 1990), 67–79.

Michael Jackson, "Literate Programming: Printing invoices," *Communications of the ACM* **30**,12 (December 1987), 1001–1008; introduction by Christopher J. Van Wyk, 1000–1001; review by David Wall, 1008–1010.

David Kennedy, "TEX adapted to `CWEB`," *TUGboat* **9**,2 (August 1988), 124–125.

Donald E. Knuth, "Fixed point glue setting—An example of `WEB`," *TUGboat* **3,1** (March 1982), 10–27. Errata, *TUGboat* **12**,2 (June 1991), 313.

Donald E. Knuth, *`WEB` User Manual: The `WEB` System of Structured Documentation*, Computer Science Department Report STAN-CS-83-980, Stanford University, Stanford, CA (September 1983), 206 pp. [The programs for `TANGLE` and `WEAVE`, which form the bulk of this report, have been reprinted in *Weaving a Program: Literate Programming in `WEB`* by Wayne Sewell (New York: Van Nostrand Reinhold, 1989), 271–434.]

Donald E. Knuth, "Literate programming," *The Computer Journal* **27**,2 (May 1984), 97–111. [Reprinted as Chapter 4 of the present book.] Japanese translation by Toshiaki Kurokawa in *bit* **17** (1985), 426–450; reprinted in *Kunusu Sensei no Program-Ron* [*Professor Knuth's Programming Discipline*], anthology edited by Makoto Arisawa (Tokyo: Kyoritsu-Shuppan, 1991), 82–128. Review by O. Lecarme in *Computing Reviews* **26**,1 (January 1985), 75.

Donald E. Knuth, "Dynamic Huffman coding," *Journal of Algorithms* **6** (1965), 163–180.

Donald E. Knuth, *TEX: The Program*, Volume B of *Computers & Typesetting* (Reading, Massachusetts: Addison-Wesley, 1986), ISBN 0-20-113437-3, xvi + 594 pp. Fourth printing, revised, xviii + 600 pp., 1991. [Excerpts reprinted in Chapter 8 of the present book.]

Donald E. Knuth, *METAFONT: The Program*, Volume D of *Computers & Typesetting* (Reading, Massachusetts: Addison-Wesley, 1986), ISBN 0-20-113438-1, xvi + 560 pp. Third printing, revised, xviii + 566 pp., 1991. [Excerpts reprinted in Chapter 8 of the present book.]

Donald E. Knuth and David R. Fuchs, *TEXware*, Computer Science Department Report STAN-CS-86-1097, Stanford University, Stanford, CA (April 1986), 10 + 30 + 53 + 53 pp. [Contains the WEB programs for POOLtype, TFtoPL, PLtoTF, and DVItype, four utility routines used with TEX.]

Donald E. Knuth, Tomas G. Rokicki, and Arthur L. Samuel, *METAFONTware*, Computer Science Department Report STAN-CS-89-1255, Stanford University, Stanford, CA (April 1989), 30 + 42 + 87 + 48 pp. [Contains the WEB programs for GFtype, GFtoPK, GFtoDVI, and MFT, four utility routines used with METAFONT.]

Donald E. Knuth, *The Stanford GraphBase: A Testbed for Combinatorial Algorithms*, book in preparation. [Includes approximately 30 CWEB programs for a wide variety of applications.]

Eduardo Kortright, CNEST and CSCOPE, available by anonymous ftp from utah.math.edu on directory ~ftp/pub/tex/pub/cscope. [Enhancements to CWEB, will show the environment of the current position or the scope of functions when using GNU Emacs.]

Heinz Kredel, "Software development for computer algebra; or, From ALDES/SAC–2 to WEB/Modula-2," in *Symbolic and Algebraic Computation*, Proceedings of International Symposium ISSAC'88, 4–8 July 1988, Rome, Italy, edited by P. Gianni, *Lecture Notes in Computer Science* **358** (1988), 447–455.

John Krommes, "FWEB (Krommes) vs. FWEB (Avenarius and Oppermann), TeXhax Digest **90**,19 (February 1990). [TeXhax Digest is an online service of the TEX Users Group; this issue is available by anonymous ftp from labrea.stanford.edu as file ~ftp/pub/tex/texhax/texhax90.019. The FWEB system of Krommes supports Fortran, Ratfor, and C.]

Christine Lafontaine, Yves Ledru, and Pierre-Yves Schobbens, "An experiment in formal software development: Using the **B** theorem prover on a VDM case study," *Communications of the ACM* **34**,5 (May 1991), 62–71, 87. [Page 70 notes that a WEB-like preprocessing tool was added to the theorem prover.]

Laura Marie Leventhal, "Experience of programming beauty: some patterns of programming aesthetics," *International Journal of Man-Machine Studies* **28** (1988), 525–550.

Silvio Levy, "`WEB` adapted to C—another approach," *TUGboat* **8**,1 (April 1987), 12–13.

Silvio Levy and Donald E. Knuth, *`CWEB` User Manual: The CWEB System of Structured Documentation*, Computer Science Department Report STAN-CS-90-1336, Stanford University, Stanford, CA (October 1990), 200 pp. Also published as research report GCG 23, University of Minnesota Geometry Center, Minneapolis, MN (October 1990), 200 pp. [Includes the `CWEB` programs for `CTANGLE` and `CWEAVE`.] Available on the Internet for anonymous ftp from `labrea.stanford.edu` on directory `~ftp/pub/cweb`.

Franklin Mark Liang, "`PAT`tern `GEN`eration program for the TEX82 hyphenator," in *Word Hy-phen-a-tion by Com-pu-ter*, Ph.D. dissertation, Computer Science Department report STAN-CS-83-977, Stanford University, Stanford, CA (June 1983), 45–73.

Donald Lindsay, "Literate Programming: A file difference program," *Communications of the ACM* **32**,6 (June 1989), 740–752; introduction by Christopher J. Van Wyk, 740; review by Harold Thimbleby, 752–755.

Chuck Lins, "A first look at literate programming," *Structured Programming* **10** (1989), 60–62.

Charles Lins, "An introduction to literate programming," *Structured Programming* **10** (1989), 107–112.

R. J. Mitchell, *Literate Programming*, Ph.D. dissertation, Computer Science Report TR-75, School of Information Sciences, Hatfield Polytechnic, College Lane, Hatfield, Herts AL10 9AB, UK (February 1988), 279 pp. [Uses both Modula-2 and the specification language OBJ as formal languages.]

Mark Bentley Motl, *A Literate Programming Environment Based on an Extensible Editor*, Ph.D. dissertation, Department of Computer Science, Texas A&M University, College Station, TX (December 1990), 118 pp.

K. Nilsen, "Garbage collection of strings and linked data structures in real time," *Software—Practice & Experience* **18**,7 (July 1988), 613–640.

Paul W. Oman and Curtis Cook, "Typographic style is more than cosmetic," *Communications of the ACM* **33**,5 (May 1990), 506–520.

T. L. (Frank) Pappas, "Literate programming for reusability: A queue package example," *Proceedings of the Eighth Annual Conference on Ada Technology*, Atlanta, GA (5–8 March 1990), 500–514.

David Lorge Parnas and Paul C. Clements, "A rational design process: How and why to fake it," *IEEE Transactions on Software Engineering* **SE–12**,2 (February 1986), 251–257.

P. J. Plauger, *The Standard C Library* (Englewood Cliffs, New Jersey: Prentice-Hall, 1992), ISBN 0-13-838012-0 (case) 0-13-131509-9 (paper), xviii + 924 pp.

Roy Rada, "Writing and reading hypertext—An overview," *Journal of the American Society for Information Science* **40**,3 (May 1989), 164–171.

J. D. Ramsdell, "SchemeTEX—Simple support for literate programming in Lisp," `TeXhax Digest` **88**,39 (23 April 1988). [`TeXhax Digest` is an online service of the TEX Users Group; this issue is available by anonymous ftp from `labrea.stanford.edu` as file `~ftp/pub/tex/texhax/texhax88.039`.]

N. Ramsey, *A Spider User's Guide*, Computer Science Department Report CS-TR-225-89, Princeton University, Princeton, NJ (August 1989), 33 pp.

N. Ramsey, *Spidery* `WEB` *User Manual: The Spidery* `WEB` *System of Structured Documentation*, Computer Science Department Report CS-TR-226-89, Princeton University, Princeton, NJ (August 1989), 12 pp.

Norman Ramsey, "Literate Programming: Weaving a language-independent `WEB`," *Communications of the ACM* **32**,9 (September 1989), 1051–1055. Introduction by Christopher J. Van Wyk, 1051.

Norman Ramsey and Carla Marceau, "Literate programming on a team project," *Software—Practice & Experience* **21**,7 (July 1991), 677–683.

Thomas J. Reid, "`TANGLE` modification causes problems in METAFONT and PK files," *TUGboat* **8**,3 (November 1987), 264–265.

Trygve Reenskaug and Anne Lise Skaar, "An environment for literate Smalltalk programming," OOPSLA89, *Proceedings of the Conference of Object-Oriented Programming Systems, Languages, and Applications*, New Orleans, LA, *ACM SIGPLAN Notices* **24**,10 (October 1989), 337–345.

Yves Roy, *TEX/WEB et le traitement de textes mathématiques* (Paris: Masson Editeur, 1984), ISBN 2-22-580249-1, vii + 102 pp.

Ben Ross Schneider Jr., "Programs as essays," *Datamation* **30**,7 (May 15, 1984), 162–168.

Joachim Schrod, *The CWEB System*, Report TI-2/90, Institut für Theoretische Informatik, Technische Hochschule Darmstadt (January 1990), 18 pp.

E. Wayne Sewell, "How to MANGLE your software: the WEB system for Modula-2," *TUGboat* **8**,2 (July 1987), 118–128.

Wayne Sewell, *Weaving a Program: Literate Programming in WEB* (New York: Van Nostrand Reinhold, 1989), ISBN 0-44-231946-0, xx+556 pp. Review by P. N. van den Bosch in *Computing Reviews* **31**,7 (July 1990), 343–344.

Lisa M. C. Smith and Mansur H. Samadzadeh, "An annotated bibliography of literate programming," *ACM SIGPLAN Notices* **26**,1 (January 1990), 14–20.

Lisa Min-yi Chen Smith, "Measuring complexity and stability of WEB programs," M.S. thesis, Department of Computer Science, Oklahoma State University, Stillwater, OK (August 1990), 137 pp.

Lisa M. C. Smith and Mansur H. Samadzadeh, "Complexity and stability of WEB programs," *Structured Programming* **13** (1992), to appear.

Thomas Hanni Spencer, *Weighted Matching Algorithms*, Ph.D. dissertation, Computer Science Department report STAN-CS-87-1162, Stanford University, Stanford, CA (June 1987), 120 pp. [This entire thesis was written in WEB.]

H. W. Thimbleby, *Literate Programming in C: Cweb Manual & Small Example*, Department of Computer Science report, University of York, Heslington, York YO1 5DD, England (August 1984), 33+3+1+28 pp. [The "small example" is a spelling checker.]

H. Thimbleby, "Experience of 'Literate Programming' using cweb (a variant of Knuth's WEB)," *The Computer Journal* **29**,3 (June 1986), 201–211.

Harold Thimbleby, "The design of a terminal independent package," *Software—Practice & Experience* **17**,5 (May 1987), 351–367, §6.

Edward J. Thomas and Paul W. Oman, "A bibliography of programming style," *ACM SIGPLAN Notices* **25**,2 (February 1990), 7–16.

Sho-Huan Tung, "A structured method for literate programming," *Structured Programming* **10** (1989), 113–120.

Christopher J. Van Wyk, "Literate Programming: An assessment," *Communications of the ACM* **33**,3 (March 1990), 361, 365.

Mark Weiser, "The programming culture and the reuse of code," *Computer* **20**,11 (November 1987), 72.

Jim Welsh, Brad Broom, and Derek Kiong, "A design rationale for a language-based editor," *Software—Practice & Experience* **21**,9 (September 1991), 923–948.

Y. C. Wu and T. P. Baker, "A source code documentation system for Ada," *ACM Ada Letters* **9**,5 (July/August 1989), 84–88.

Kongshi Xu, "Report on R and D at the Software Institute," *Information Processing 89*, edited by G. X. Ritter, Proceedings of the IFIP 11th World Computer Congress, San Francisco, CA (28 August–1 September 1989), 73–76. [Mentions Yunmei Dong's CDS system of literate programming, which combines C with a language called SP for typesetting Chinese and English texts.]

Index